ROCK OVER THE EDGE

DUKE UNIVERSITY PRESS ✴ DURHAM & LONDON 2002

ROCK OVER THE EDGE

Transformations in Popular Music Culture

Edited by Roger Beebe, Denise Fulbrook, and Ben Saunders

© 2002 Duke University Press   All rights reserved
Printed in the United States of America on acid-free paper ∞
Typeset in Scala by Keystone Typesetting, Inc.
Library of Congress Cataloging-in-Publication Data
appear on the last printed page of this book.

CONTENTS

ROGER BEEBE, DENISE FULBROOK, AND BEN SAUNDERS * INTRODUCTION

Rock isn't what it used to be. Or so the essays in this collection suggest. Of course, without immediate qualification, such a claim won't sound like news to anybody; the insistence that "the music must change" is a long-standing commonplace within rock's rhetorical repertoire of self-descriptive figures. To borrow Woody Allen's famous definition of a successful relation-ship, rock is a shark that must constantly move forward lest it sink and die. Indeed, because it has so successfully incorporated the possibility of its own demise into its discourse, rock might be most accurately described as a paradoxical animal that lives *by* dying, the cultural equivalent of a coral reef that atrophies in order to advance.[1] Thus, according to its own preferred logic, rock is *never* what it used to be.

For some time now, however, that very logic has itself been subject to scrutiny. For example, rock's characteristic mode of self-representation has been critiqued by Simon Frith and Andrew Goodwin as a theory of "prog-ress by attrition," one with obvious antecedents in some of our oldest and most comforting cultural narratives.[2] These narratives generally serve to contain our worst entropic nightmares—"things fall apart; the center cannot hold"—within a recursive cycle of death and resurrection. After the loosing

of the blood-dimmed tide: the glories of the Second Coming; or in specifically rock-oriented terms, after the dominance of a mass-market "monster"
like Bon Jovi: Nirvana. Rock(ist) institutions such as MTV and *Rolling Stone*
still prefer to tell this kind of story;[3] but most would challenge such historiography as a reinscription of what has elsewhere been described as "*the*
foundational myth"[4] of rock music—a myth based on a falsely hypostatized
opposition between virtuous authenticity on the one hand and crass commercialism on the other.[5]

The deconstruction of this mythic opposition has had significant consequences for both the status and the deployment of the term "rock" within
much popular music criticism. For example, questions that may have appeared purely aesthetic or generic, such as what counts as "real" rock music, have given way to a set of social and historical questions about *why*
some kinds of music are deemed worthy of the designation, and others are
not.[6] Thus, whereas "rock" was once defined as an automatic honorific
"applied . . . to the groups which . . . [take] themselves more seriously than
overtly pop groups,"[7] it is now recognized as frequently performing a central role within a rhetoric of exclusion, enabling invidious distinctions on the
bases of gender, sexuality, and race. (The "Disco Sucks" movement of the
1970s serves as one of the more memorable concrete instances of this
exclusionary power; proclaiming itself as "an expression of the counterculture's distaste for studio-produced synth music," "disco sucks" also gave
voice to motivations generally recognized today as being at least "partly
homophobic [and] partly racist."[8])

The authors gathered in this volume are all situated after this deconstruc-
tive turn within rock criticism, and the insights derived from this turn
constitute the theoretical baseline from which their analyses proceed. That
their essays should also be so diverse in content, given this common intellectual ground, is indicative of just how broad and far-ranging the theoretical critique of rock historiography has been in its consequences. Indeed,
one purpose of this volume is to assess those consequences more fully. For if
the exposure of the authenticity myth (and its attendant exclusionary sub-
texts) transforms the discursive function and status of the term "rock," it
also raises fundamental questions about the nature and enterprise of "rock
criticism" itself. Framing one such question as bluntly as possible, we might
ask whether the phrase "rock criticism" even has a useful function anymore,
if it no longer says anything descriptive about the kind of popular music

under discussion.[9] Other, equally difficult, questions follow. For example: If "rock" doesn't mean what it used to mean, then what *does* it mean now? Does it mean the same thing all the time? If not, when and where does it mean differently? What are the consequences—social, aesthetic, economic—of such contingencies? What forms and genres are now seen to fall within the "rock" rubric? What remains excluded, and why? How and why are these boundaries maintained and policed? What constitutes an appropriate *object* of "rock criticism" these days, let alone an appropriate methodology? What does the field of popular music historiography look like now that we have learned to be suspicious of "rockist" rhetoric? What, shall we say, is rock post "rock"?

The urgency of these questions is rendered all the more pointed when we consider that despite the best efforts of Frith, Goodwin, Grossberg, and others the authenticity myth has not been entirely discredited within rock historiography. Instead it returns to haunt not only MTV specials and *Rolling Stone* covers,[10] but also such book-length histories as Fred Goodman's *The Mansion on the Hill* (1997) or Martha Bayles's *Hole in Our Soul* (1994).[11] The die-hard persistence of the authenticity myth within these texts indicates just how difficult it is to discuss rock music apart from rock's rhetoric; it is as if rock would somehow cease to exist without the opposition of "real" and "fake" musics to underwrite it (and, of course, it would cease to exist to the degree that "rock" is supposed to be the name given to "authentic" music).[12]

At this point the objection might be voiced that the change in the function of "rock" thus far described is by and large a semantic one, and therefore only significant within the rarified intellectual circles of academic critics and historians; fans and musicians seem to know what they mean by the term, after all. But such an argument simply subscribes to yet another version of the authenticity myth by insisting on a false opposition between critics/academics ("fake") on the one hand, and fans/musicians ("authentic") on the other, as if it were impossible for someone to occupy all of these places at once. Such false oppositions are refuted in this volume by R. J. Warren Zanes, whose essay clearly demonstrates that his career as a guitarist with the Del Fuegos is continuous with and implicated in his roles as critic, teacher, and fan.

However, a skeptic might also point out that *Rolling Stone*, MTV, VH1, and so forth, not to mention numerous musicians, continue to use the term "rock" as if it worked as an unproblematic signifier. If "rock" *really* doesn't mean what it once did, then why hasn't anyone noticed? Here the best response is a simple refutation: we argue that the coherence of the term is only apparent, and, more important, that rock's recent semantic transformation within academic criticism mirrors numerous and more basic transformations within popular music culture at large, the implications of which have yet to be absorbed but have nevertheless been noticed within many of rock's primary sites of production and consumption. These transformations include the following: the gradual transmutation of rock into alternative and the subsequent disappearance of alternative as a meaningful category;[13] the apparent proliferation of musical genres and/or niche markets, "youth" oriented and otherwise, that no longer fit the old systems of classification (a proliferation which, according to Larry Grossberg's essay here, is matched by a similar hybridization of contemporary listening practices); and the paradoxical attempt to incorporate those "new" genres/markets within an expanded conception of "rock."[14]

Ultimately, then, this volume represents an attempt to address and to inhabit the ever more fragmentary terrain of contemporary popular music and the similarly fragmented discursive terrain of popular music studies. But before turning to the various ways in which our authors map our transformed musical and cultural space, it may be helpful to describe a little more precisely the critical consequences of the recent shifts that have taken place within what Grossberg has influentially termed "the rock formation." As we shall see, these shifts work to render problematic even Grossberg's widely circulated phrase.[15]

✶

As the foregoing discussion has implied, analyses of how the boundaries of "rock" are established, maintained, and policed have long been among the chief raisons d'etre of academic popular music criticism. Up to now, these debates have tended to highlight two pairs of binary oppositions (and their consequent exclusions) as the dominant tropes of "rockist" discourse: rock versus pop (focusing on the often gender- and race-based exclusions predicated on an understanding of pop as a less-substantial form than rock) and rock versus rap (focusing on the racial exclusions that such division effects). It is against this background that Andrew Ross, for example, declares his admiration for "attempts at genre fusion and . . . crossover." As Ross astutely comments, "the music industry's primary form of regulation is cultural,

4   Beebe, Fulbrook, and Saunders

and is evident in the strict management of taste cultures that still correspond to racial and class divisions in our society"; therefore, he continues, genre crossovers are "politically significant" because they are both "difficult to market in an apartheid-based industry, and difficult to police as a social phenomenon."[16]

However, the political significances of such crossovers—and perhaps even the critical significance of the rock/pop and rock/rap dichotomies that Ross is happy to see disrupted—are less obvious today than they were even as recently as 1994 when Ross penned his remarks. While aesthetic preferences are undoubtedly still conformable to racial, gender-based, and social divisions, the task of determining *where* the lines get drawn in contemporary popular music culture has become harder than ever. We suggest that one reason for this increased difficulty is that fact that, in the present climate of proliferating musics and markets, the dominant status of "rock" as a musical genre and a discursive label has become more open to question, without actually being displaced altogether.

To illustrate, let us turn back for a moment to MTV's 1997 wrap-up, "The Year in Rock"—that is, just three years after the publication of Ross and Rose's *Microphone Fiends,* from which the above-cited remarks are taken. Apart from its titular evocation, the only specific references to "rock" in this particular program occurred in discussions of the "shock-rock" hysteria surrounding Marilyn Manson, and in the significantly nostalgic context of summer reunion tours by Mötley Crüe, Black Sabbath, Jane's Addiction, and Fleetwood Mac. This information appeared in just one nine-minute segment of the hour-long program, and it shared even this limited airtime with substantial digressions about the Lilith Fair and the Rage Against the Machine/Wu Tang Clan tour. The rest of the program was devoted to such topics as the ascension of Sean "Puffy" Combs and the death of Notorious B.I.G.; the pop resurgence spearheaded by the Spice Girls and Hanson; the fate of electronica; controversy about sampling; and, tellingly, the musical diversity of 1997—a "year in rock" that saw the successes of Sarah McLachlan, Jamiroquai, Missy "Misdemeanor" Elliot, Erykah Badu, Fiona Apple, and the Wallflowers. Although the program ostensibly presented these diverse musics under the aegis of "rock," it is arguably only the Wallflowers that would be recognized by a traditional (that is, predominantly white male boomer) audience as a "rock" band; and indeed, MTV, perhaps shocked into self-consciousness by the content of this year-end review, subsequently decided to change the name of their weekly news program, "The Week in Rock," to "MTV 1515" (referring to their studio at 1515 Broadway) shortly after "The Year in Rock (1997)" aired. This change of title would seem a vivid illustration of the desire to be placed on less contestable (or more contemporary) ground.

Even as "rock" seems to be struggling to survive in one context, however, it proves resilient in others. Particularly revealing is the recent fate of so-called alternative music. After momentarily seeming to challenge the centrality of the term "rock" with popular music discourse, "alternative" became a historical label with astonishing rapidity. To return briefly to the MTV example, "The Year in Rock (1997)" included two declarations about the end of the alternative revolution: the first, a comment on how the Spice Girls "displaced the alterna-rockers of yore"; and the second, an outright death sentence claiming that although "alternative was over" we might look to the future in electronica. On another year-end wrap-up, Matt Pinfield, former host of the alternative-when-alternative-wasn't-cool program *120 Minutes*, declared alternative to be part of a past historical moment, asserting that "the term . . . now sounds somewhat anachronistic."[17] Indeed, the mainstreamed term "alternative" currently goes by a number of different monikers, depending on where one looks. Arbitron, the radio industry's primary source for ratings information (which consequently has a massive stake in the classification of types of music), continues to use the label "alternative," as well as the faintly comic-sounding tag "adult alternative." It distinguishes these labels from "oldies," "70s/classic rock," "active rock" (another seemingly idiosyncratic designation that has no real currency as a musical genre), "hot adult contemporary" (whose prime audience is age twenty-five to thirty-five), and a plain old "rock" classification (which is somehow not seen as redundant among the other six classifications). At the same time, in the language of radio station tags the place once held by alternative in relation to rock is now routinely evoked through an appeal to some notion of the "mix," "variety," or the "best of" formats (typically, the "best of the 80s and 90s"). These radio tags tend to claim that their format's diversity promises the greatest good for the greatest number, a claim that effectively erases alternative's origins in subcultural practice and, ultimately, its very existence as any sort of recognizable musical genre. As if to confirm this development, *Billboard* has now started using the label "modern rock" for this nebulous area of popular music, and *Rolling Stone* has followed *Billboard*'s lead.[18]

6   Beebe, Fulbrook, and Saunders

This shift in nomenclature signifies at some basic level that the opposition between alternative and rock was, of course, only another version of the authenticity myth by which rock has always sustained itself—this time with alternative playing the role of "real" to rock's "fake." In such a context the "success" of alternative could only ever mean its destruction (for such is the fate of all "successful" musics within a historiography enslaved to the authenticity myth). Paradoxically, the return of "rock" to *Billboard*'s chart in the form of "modern rock" reveals just how "successful" alternative was.

But, at another level, the resurrection of rock as modern rock only begs the question; what work is the prefix "modern" supposed to do here, after all? What, precisely, is the character of the "modern" rock and roll animal? Or, to put the question differently, how much resemblance does "modern rock" bear to "the same old rock" of exclusion and division?

Recalling the extraordinary proliferation of musics listed in "The Year in Rock (1997)," it might be tempting to respond that, while retaining a residual and specific meaning as the name given to the music made by white boys (or aging white men) with guitars, "rock" is now a dereferentialized catch-all, encompassing even those musics (dance, pop, hip hop, and so forth) that it once defined itself against. This usage would appear to be the one currently favored by *Rolling Stone*, for example, as used on the cover of their thirtieth anniversary issue, which collectively groups a grunge icon (Courtney Love), a soul diva (Tina Turner), and a pop queen (Madonna) under the label of "Women of Rock."[19] Such deployments of the term seem to suggest that "rock" as a musical category really is dying off (finally, after so many false pronouncements) while at the same time surviving as a generically nonproscriptive term encompassing many formerly excluded musics (which in turn are enjoying a triumph of heretofore unlikely popularity). In other words, if one were to adopt such a point of view, rock (post "rock") would appear only to be the nonevaluative name given to the massive proliferation of popular musical choices available for the contemporary consumer.

Of course, there remain obvious problems with such a conclusion, not least of which being that, despite the breezy invocation of rock by *Rolling Stone* and MTV, the specific and residually "rockist" uses of the term have obviously not vanished altogether. Perhaps still more problematically, however, to frame the problem as a choice between *either* happily (re)accepting *or* unequivocally rejecting the notion of "rock" as a dereferentialized signifier for youth music and culture is to commit oneself to yet another falsely hypostatized binary, this time in the form of an opposition between inclusive plurality and hegemonic domination.[20] On the one hand, to insist on the capacity of "rock" to encompass the musics it once neglected or excluded is to insist, once again, that although there may be some unpleasant and residually hegemonic valence still clinging to the term, "rock" is "really" a multigeneric cultural form that can afford to congratulate itself for its generous inclusivity. On the other hand, to refuse "rock" outright as naming nothing more than the culturally dominant noise of white boomer boys reduces that culture to a monolithic caricature while also presuming that "dominant" forms are necessarily aesthetically uninteresting or can only perform negative cultural work.[21]

Clearly there is something unsatisfactory about having to choose between a vision of "rock" as the new and friendly promoter of difference, and "rock" as the hegemonic corpse that continues to dominate popular music culture from its graveyard of "classics"—if only because such polarized binary conceptions ignore the recent transformations in the ways the term is deployed, both in academic and critical discourse and in the mainstream of popular music culture at large. What we require, then, is an understanding of the term "rock" and of its place within contemporary popular music culture (and popular music studies) that does not insist on locking the proliferating forms of modern musical expression on one side or the other of a pluralistic/hegemonic divide.

*

One obvious place to turn to for help in forging such an understanding is the music itself. Without intending to privilege any single artist or song as exemplary of the current scene, we will select one particularly resonant illustration of the ways in which "rock"—both as a generic label and as a distinctive musical idiom—has recently been deployed: Sean "Puffy" Combs's rock remix of his song "It's All about the Benjamins" and its accompanying video.

The video, directed by the "alternative" auteur Spike Jonze,[22] opens with a sequence (which returns at the end of the video as a narrative frame) in which Combs and his companions are traveling on a tour bus that gets a flat tire. The group of musicians is deposited outside a high school, where on entering to relieve themselves, they discover that they are at a prom. On the stage a cover band, "the Fuzzytones," fronted by a pompadoured crooner (one of two roles played by Combs in the video), is completing a parodically amateurish version of the R.E.M. hit "Everybody Hurts." When the Fuzzytones leave for a break, the "real" band takes over, with a supposedly improvised group of musicians made up of Puffy and his original traveling companions and some members of the audience ("Hey, my man, check it out—would you happen to know how to play the guitar?"), who then proceed raucously to shake the place up.

One of the most fascinating aspects of this video is the way it incorporates several different and competing narratives of the rock/rap dichotomy, presented here not so much as an opposition but as a dialectic. The jab at R.E.M.—a band once considered to be at the forefront of alternative music— can be imagined as appealing both to hip hop *and* rock fans through the selection of a song that is suspiciously "soft" (a ballad about the ubiquity of human suffering, quiet in arrangement and slow in tempo).[23] This implicit condemnation of the "soft" is, of course, a testament to the masculinism common to both rock and hip hop; a masculinism that here enables the crossover between the two genres and thus further complicates the "political significance" of such hybrid forms: the negative binary of race is disrupted, but that disruption is affected at least in part through a reinscription of the negative binary of gender.

However, even as one ("soft") version of alternative is repudiated by this narrative, Combs also stakes his claim to another branch of the alternative tree (that is, grunge) through the song itself, with its guitar riff written by none other than Dave Grohl, Foo Fighters frontman and former Nirvana drummer. Combs's commercial savvy as one of the chief architects of later 90s hip hop is clearly matched by a keen sense of rock historiography, for he has, at least from the dominant point of view of present rock commentators, rejected one set of white boys with guitars while maintaining a proxy musical connection to the most "legendary" white-boy guitarist of recent years: Kurt Cobain.

Having carefully indicated exactly which version of "rock" it wants to be seen appropriating, Combs's video goes on to reinvigorate some of the most familiar rock (and even "rock and roll") clichés. First, members of the audience are shown taking the stage in the spirit of democratic, DIY enthusiasm generally associated with punk rock; then the musicians trash their equipment, à la the Who or Jimi Hendrix (though not to the sound of shrieking feedback but rather the rapping of a disturbingly absent Notorious

B.I.G.); and finally the audience runs riot through the school in a classic display of youthful rock and roll rebellion. The symbolism is not terribly complicated (for example, a trash can is hurled into the school trophy cases, thereby belittling the institutionally legitimized forms of success represented by academic and sporting achievement) but no less effective for all that. Perhaps most important, the marriage of black and white musical styles conveyed by the song is also symbolically represented by the concluding moments of the video, which show the crowd of predominantly white high school kids riding off into the sunset on Puffy's now-repaired (magic?) bus, chatting amiably with the predominantly black musicians in Combs's entourage. However, as if the conflict between rock and rap that the song and video have so skillfully repressed had to return, the very last image of the clip reveals in classic psychoanalytic fashion that the white guitarist has actually been left behind, alone on an empty stage and deserted by his audience. Then again, we don't have to dig very deeply for contradictions in this little story; the general narrative of social rebellion and racial harmony that the video tells is already more than slightly at odds with one of the song's lyrics that insists, repeatedly, that "it's all about the Benjamins" (that is, $100 bills bearing the image of Benjamin Franklin)—or, in other words, that the desire for money motivates every action, and that the performers are "only here for that green paper."[24]

The "political significance" that Andrew Ross claims to find in earlier rock/rap fusions (such as, perhaps, the reggae/hardcore of Bad Brains, or the rap/metal combination of Anthrax and Public Enemy) is not immediately apparent here. Instead, Puff Daddy's melange of rock and rap is neither entirely subversive of "rock" myths nor entirely dominated by them; rather, it judiciously appropriates elements of both styles and stories. The relationship between rock and rap suggested by this crossover, while hardly hostile, is still one of distance (this, after all, is implicit in the term "crossover"). "It's All about the Benjamins" vividly displays a version of "rock" as perceived within the hip hop imaginary, doing two paradoxically incompatible jobs: on the one hand functioning as a negative standard or structuring principle ("this isn't R.E.M."), and on the other as a positive term ("this is rap that rocks").

Thus, the crucial point running through this exploration of Puff Daddy's remix of white and black styles is not that the lines drawn between "rock" and its once-repudiated others have been erased in a liberatory moment of generic miscegenation. (In fact, as long as people continue to use the term "rock" to signify something distinctive—and there doesn't seem to be any stopping them—lines will always be drawn somewhere.) Instead, for our purposes here, the chief lesson of "It's All about the Benjamins" is that although lines between aesthetic genres and social communities are always in place, they are not always in the *same* place.[25] Moreover, in recent years it seems that the lines between rock and its musical others have been drawn and redrawn with ever-increasing frequency. The resulting proliferation of musical styles and listening communities challenges any single coherence principle, as it multiplies the number of possible musical markets (and the number of musics) that can make (positive or negative) use of the myths of "rock." Therefore, one important task of the contemporary critic is to attend to the multiplicity of styles that form the complex of contemporary popular music and to find ways of engaging with that multiplicity, without being hoodwinked into thinking that a point of either absolute (and unproblematic) inclusiveness or pure (utopian) heterogeneity could ever be reached.

*

The less-than-stable boundaries of the notion of "rock" itself constitute "the edge" referred to in the title of this collection. These essays not only seek to *go over* (that is, scrutinize) that edge, to examine the various power dynamics and constraints that the notion of "rock" has imposed, but also to go "over the edge," in the more familiar idiomatic sense, by enabling new types of border crossings within the various interpretive communities of popular music culture. It is in this spirit that the authors in this volume focus on formerly neglected or overlooked musics (country, the Pet Shop Boys, rock en español, and so forth), to a new musico-aesthetic spaces capacitated by new technological and cultural forms (Star TV, lo-fi, recent MTV, postmodern punk), and to the languages and critical assumptions of the various discourses of popular music (musicology, cultural studies, rock historiography). Thus, each author considers his or her subject not as it has traditionally been analyzed—as a form or culture defined either through or against "rock"—but as a site of contestation marking the possible transformations of the musical and critical terrain.

In the opening essay of the collection, Larry Grossberg offers an overview of the shortcomings of academic rock criticism as he sees them. His contribution challenges contemporary critics to develop a discourse for writing about popular music that would both respect the specificity of musical media and articulate this specific vision within a larger cultural context. Grossberg sets the stage for the emergence of such a discourse by elaborating the nature of the transformations of popular music culture in the 1990s, many of which we have begun to indicate here. The essays that follow Grossberg can therefore be read as responses to his challenge, each of them in their own way attempting to reinflect, contest, or expand the ways we currently imagine popular music and culture.

In the first of these indirect responses to Grossberg, Robert Fink asks why there seems to have been so little interchange between critics of popular music who are influenced by the discipline of cultural studies and those who work within the older academic discipline of musicology. Fink locates his answer in a witty and polemical account of the origins of traditional formalist musicological methodology, which is at times unblinkingly critical in its conclusions. At the same time he insists that outright rejection of musicological tools and concepts by critics working in the field of cultural studies can produce equally impoverished readings that lose sight of the specifically *musical* effects (and affects) of popular music texts. His essay offers some engaging suggestions for the kinds of readings that might be produced through a disciplinary rapprochement of cultural studies and musicology— taking in recordings by Beck, Aphex Twin, and many others—before turning to Susan Sontag's notion of a critical "erotics" as suggestive for new directions in musicology itself.

In the essay that follows, Fink's fellow musicologist John J. Sheinbaum offers precisely the type of analysis that Fink seems to be calling for in his more metacritical moments. Sensitive to the fact that musical objects do not exist in a cultural vacuum, Sheinbaum combines musicological techniques of close reading with a broad knowledge of rock historiography and cultural context to reveal the complicity of recent attempts to establish a rock and roll canon with a residually racist ideology. Sheinbaum neatly exposes the ways in which popular music criticism, against its own best intentions, continues to imagine black artists such as Aretha Franklin as craftspeople and white artists such as Bob Dylan and the Beatles as geniuses.

The final essay in this section, by Michael Coyle, further complicates our understanding of the dichotomy between black and white music through his investigation into the history and concept of the "cover." Acknowledging the role played by racism in the practice of hijacking hits, Coyle refuses the facile reverse argument that would reduce all white covers to "fake" appropriations of "authentic" black originals. Instead he offers a vision of the cover as a far more subtly revealing index of cultural exchange.

The essays contained in the second section of the volume move from historical and metadiscursive discussions to concentrate on musical genres and artists traditionally neglected under the older "rock" rubric (although often also raising the same types of metadiscursive questions along the way). Trent Hill's treatment of country illustrates this kind of analysis most straightforwardly: noting that country has officially outsold rock in the United States for some time, Hill asks why country remains absent from almost all previous considerations of youth music. Hill also considers the question of what happens when country music *is* considered youth culture. Through a combination of close analysis and an in-depth knowledge of the contemporary country music scenes (the plural turns out to be important), Hill demonstrates the ways in which popular music studies might be improved by taking country into account.

In the next essay, Gayle Wald focuses on the social and political assumptions that lie behind statements of aesthetic evaluation. Her wide-ranging work explores the similarity of exclusionary and dismissive rhetorics across national and racial as well as gendered boundaries. By focusing primarily on the recent emergence of "the girl" as a discursive figure in popular music culture, Wald considers the ambivalence of that sometimes feminist, sometimes objectifying, discourse. Examining the various deployments of the notion of the "girl" as applied to such diverse figures as No Doubt's Gwen Stefani, Japanese pop band Shonen Knife, and Riot Grrrl band Bratmobile, Wald ends her piece by arguing for the validity of a disciplinary arena centered on "girl studies."

Many similar themes are explored in Lisa Parks's close reading of Asian popular music videos aired on Rupert Murdoch's Star TV. Her essay raises questions about the relation of contemporary media technology to the formation of both gendered and national identities. In an era of globalization, Parks posits that such multinational media lead to the articulation of "transnational genders," thereby creating new forms of desire that cross national borders. By exploring the various portraits of femininity offered by these videos, Parks begins to map the ways in which such international media both upset and reinforce national and international gender norms.

Tony Grajeda continues the interrogation of gender within popular music discourse by looking not at the gender construction of performers but at the gendering of an entire musical movement: the intentionally low-fidelity recordings collectively labeled "lo-fi." His essay explores in detail the various ways that lo-fi has been effectively "feminized" as a "weak" form by a number of critical camps. Grajeda suggests that it is precisely those traits that ultimately allow lo-fi to function as a critical response to the corporate hegemony of the music industry. Grajeda complicates the familiar binaries of subversion/hegemony or authentic/sellout by considering the ways that lo-fi embodies the contradictions of its time, thus allowing for a more nuanced understanding of the place of this music in the contemporary sphere.

The final essay in this section is Josh Kun's fascinating study of rock en español. As with Parks's essay, Kun's inquiry serves as a salutary reminder of the fact that popular music culture is hardly unique to the Anglo-American experience. Kun delves into this transnational musical phenomenon (or rather, phenomena, since a large part of his essay demonstrates the diversity even within this single term), and, like the other authors in this section, Kun complicates and even explodes the simple binary logics that come to dominate the discourses of popular music.

The essays grouped in the final section of the volume focus on the power of popular music to mobilize different forms of desire and to produce different kinds of affect. As a result, each of these essays focuses to a greater or lesser degree on the relationship between specific musical forms and the social organization and affective responses of specific audiences and/or identity positions. Thus R. J. Warren Zanes's article combines elements of the confessional with a rigorous scholarly framework in order to examine the psychological construction of fans and fandom. His meditation on the processes of desire and identification literalizes Robert Fink's metaphorical invocation of a critical erotics, while avoiding the common tendency of Lacanian psychoanalysis to reify heterosexuality as the dominant principle of desiring subjects.

The question of sexuality is also Ian Balfour's concern. Once again combining the techniques of subtle and persuasive close reading with larger cultural and political questions, Balfour's essay tentatively suggests that the deliberate ironies of the Pet Shop Boys constitute a deconstruction of the hetero/homo binary. Thus Balfour finds a new and hitherto unimagined political significance in the work of a band previously criticized for ducking their responsibilities by refusing to "come out."

Roger Beebe's essay shifts away from desire-driven psychoanalytic accounts to focus on the less subject-oriented notion of affect. After first exploring the apparent postmodern transformation of the "sad" affects of mourning and nostalgia, Beebe turns his attentions to the political consequences of this transformation. In so doing, he challenges the orthodoxies of postmodern politics by suggesting that popular music culture may already be offering a way around the bleakly postmodern vision of total alienation and political confusion in the paradoxical form of the commodification of the present.

Jason Middleton also takes postmodernism and affect as his themes, this time in relation to D.C. punk. Although this subculture is generally thought of as a *locus classicus* of punk authenticity, Middleton explores the increasing difficulties that arise in sustaining such an image. Taking the example of the steadfastly independent group Fugazi, Middleton investigates their increasingly belabored production of sincerity and their struggle to maintain a modernist "authentic" posture in a postmodern world.

The spaces and sounds mapped by many of these essays are unfamiliar, and even those essays that do examine the work of more well-known rock artists—such as Beck (Fink), the Beatles (Sheinbaum), or Elvis (Coyle)—approach these familiar figures in unfamiliar ways. But given the fragmentation of contemporary popular music this sense of unfamiliarity is only appropriate. If the music must change, then we must change with it; otherwise, we run the risk of being left behind on the stage of an auditorium that everyone else has abandoned.

Notes

1. As Larry Grossberg has pointed out, rumors about the death of rock are as old as the music itself, going back "almost to the emergence of rock in the 1950s" (Grossberg, "Is Anybody Listening? Does Anybody Care: On Talking about 'the State of Rock,' " in *Microphone Fiends,* ed. Andrew Ross and Tricia Rose [New York: Routledge, 1994], 42).

2. Simon Frith and Andrew Goodwin, eds., *On Record: Rock, Pop, and the Written Word* (New York: Pantheon, 1990), ix.

3. See, for example, MTV's documentary program *It Came from the 80s,* discussed in note 10. For one of the more recent of the many versions of this recursive narrative offered in *Rolling Stone,* see their cover story on the Verve from April 16, 1998,

entitled "The Return of Rock & Roll." However, the story of Nirvana obviously represents the most frequently reiterated and compelling version from the 1990s of this narrative. For example, one of the better books on the band, Michael Azerrad's *Come as You Are*, opens with the claim that Nirvana was a breath of fresh (that is, authentic) air for audiences who were "tired of having . . . artificial creations such as Paula Abdul and Milli Vanilli rammed down their throats" (Azerrad, *Come as You Are: The Story of Nirvana* [New York: Doubleday, 1993], 4–5). The inadequacy of this "explanation" for Nirvana's success is implicit in Azerrad's own text, which goes on to provide a detailed account of the band's complex attitude toward their mass audience, which is far more nuanced than this initial appeal to the authenticity myth would suggest. In fact, Azerrad's book makes clear that the band often consciously constructed their music for commercial appeal and even occasionally embraced (albeit with some degree of irony) the desire to sell out. Thus, while Kurt Cobain can at one point dismiss *Nevermind* as "closer to a Mötley Crüe record than . . . a punk rock record," he can also declare that "it was all for the best . . . because it sold eight million records and now we can do whatever we want" (180).

4. Michael Jarrett, "Concerning the Progress of Rock and Roll," in *Present Tense: Rock & Roll and Culture*, ed. Anthony DeCurtis (Durham: Duke University Press, 1992), 167.

5. Once again, Grossberg provides one of the most succinct and persuasive analyses of this rhetoric and its consequences in "Is Anybody Listening?" (41–48). Although the critique of the authenticity myths might be thought to have received its strongest articulation within the academy, it has hardly been confined to academic criticism; and increasingly, performers such as Bono of U2 and Jon Spencer of the Blues Explosion have embraced what might be called a deliberate inauthenticity in an attempt to foreground the issue. It is also important to note that the "authenticist" position is itself hardly monolithic in construction (for example, the "authenticism" of Lester Bangs is clearly not identical to that of, say, Dick Hebdige). Because "authenticity" is for many authors merely the best metaphor for a certain kind of pleasure, there may be as many authenticities as there are pleasures. At the same time, critics in search of different metaphors have always existed (for example, Richard Goldstein and the aforementioned Simon Frith). Finally, the critique of "the great authenticity myth" should not be seen as a dismissal of those writers who have subscribed to it in some form, anymore than Derrida's critique of Plato's metaphysics of presence should be regarded as claiming that there's no point in reading Plato anymore. The editors of this volume are profoundly aware that the work we have set out to do is enabled by all those of a previous generation who were committed to the principle that the "ephemeral" culture of popular music repays the closest critical attention.

6. DeCurtis's *Present Tense* and Ross and Rose's *Microphone Fiends* contain several essays that perform this kind of interrogation, and many other examples may be adduced. For a collection focusing on the exclusions and implications of "rock" in relation to gender alone, see Sheila Whiteley, *Sexing the Groove* (London: Routledge, 1997).

7. Peter Gammond, *The Oxford Companion to Popular Music* (Oxford: Oxford University Press, 1991), 495.

8. Ross, "Introduction," *Microphone Fiends*, 10.

9. Of course, in light of rock's more recognizable exclusionary tendencies, some commentators have preferred to abandon the term "rock" altogether in favor of less honorific alternatives such as "popular music," but this does not entirely solve the problem and may even create new difficulties (the question of what gets called "popular music" and what doesn't remains unanswered; what, for example, is to be done with "popular" versions of "classical" music, such as *Classics Go to the Movies?*). Thus, despite the great diversity of opinion in academic writings on the subject, almost all commentators seem to agree that all of the various available terms—rock, pop, popular music, youth music—are in some sense provisional or inadequate as descriptions of their object.

10. Consider, for example, the program *It Came from the 80s, Part II: Metal Goes Pop*, which aired repeatedly during early 1997 as well as several times since. Although primarily concerned with the sudden popularity of big-hair metal/pop bands (for example, Winger, Poison, Warrant, and Dokken) in the late 1980s, the end of the program shifts to the future of rock, after the necessary crash of "inauthentic" metal/pop, by suggesting that rock was saved by the advent of the harder-edged bands Guns n' Roses and Metallica. Interestingly, much of the program is devoted to therapeutic testimonials by the performers of that era, wherein they accept the blame for the corruption of a more authentic tradition, some even remarking that they deserved their fall for betraying their metal/rock ideals. A clearer illustration of the persistent power of the authenticity myth would be hard to come by. Moreover, from here, the narrative *again* imagines the story of rock's history as one of desecration and salvation, jumping ahead to 1991 (in America, the so-called year that punk broke) and cutting short the earlier Guns n' Roses narrative with the release of Nirvana's *Nevermind;* the explosion of "alternative"—despite the name change or perhaps because of it—signaling once again the resurrection of rock. This gesture toward the grunge/alternative rock revolution ends the program (seemingly suggesting that "the rest is history . . ." or perhaps even that "the rest is the present . . .").

11. Goodman's book, an informative account of the relationship between avowedly populist artists such as Bob Dylan or Bruce Springsteen and their more commercially minded managers and labels, is ultimately marred by its commitment to a classic version of the authenticity myth, summarized on the book jacket as the unfortunate transformation of the "personal artform of a generation in search of authenticity and values" into "a $20 billion global business" (Goodman, *The Mansion on the Hill* [New York: Random House, 1997]). Bayles's book, as its subtitle indicates, is an attempt to explain "the loss of beauty and meaning in American popular music," and has little to recommend it to any reader sympathetic to postwar popular culture (as is also noted by Robert Fink elsewhere in this volume). However, it also represents one of the most reactionary (and forceful) restatements of the authenticity myth in recent years, in this case positing traditional jazz, roots R&B, and some forms of 50s rock and roll as the "real" American music against which all subsequent developments are measured and found wanting. See, if you must, Martha Bayles, *Hole in Our Soul: The Loss of Beauty and Meaning in American Popular Music* (New York: Free Press, 1994).

12. It is again worth emphasizing that the discourse of authenticity is not *necessarily* attended by a discourse of exclusion: not all authenticists are exclusionists. Indeed, two of the authors in this collection (Grajeda and Middleton) make some productive use of the term "authenticity." Nevertheless, the (on the face of it, neutral or mild) distinction between "real" and "fake" is at least implicitly hierarchical, and the tendency toward an exclusionist, value-laden rhetoric of authenticity that springs from this implication demands great caution.

13. Should this suggestion require proof, it can be easily fleshed out by recourse to another of MTV's self-narrations; namely, the extensive list of all-time Top 10s (first aired in October 1997). The Top 10 lists cover a wide variety of subjects of both historical (e.g., Top 10 most expensive videos, Top 10 videos of the 80s) and contemporary interest (e.g., Top 10 videos with Sean "Puffy" Combs). In this context, the "all-time Top 10: rock videos" and the "all-time Top 10: alternative videos" overtly document the transmutation of rock into alternative. A quick look at these lists will help us illustrate this movement.

> MTV's all-time Top 10: rock videos
> 10. Metallica, "One"
> 9. Beastie Boys, "Sabotage"
> 8. Pearl Jam, "Jeremy"
> 7. Van Halen, "Hot for Teacher"
> 6. Red Hot Chili Peppers, "Under the Bridge"
> 5. Nine Inch Nails, "Closer"
> 4. Aerosmith, "Janie's Got a Gun"
> 3. Metallica, "Enter Sandman"
> 2. Nirvana, "Smells Like Teen Spirit"
> 1. Guns n' Roses, "Welcome to the Jungle"

MTV's all-time Top 10: alternative videos

10. Nirvana, "Come as You Are"
 9. Beck, "Loser"
 8. Red Hot Chili Peppers, "Give It Away"
 7. Pearl Jam, "Jeremy"
 6. R.E.M., "Losing My Religion"
 5. Beastie Boys, "Sabotage"
 4. Smashing Pumpkins, "Tonight, Tonight"
 3. Nine Inch Nails, "Closer"
 2. Red Hot Chili Peppers, "Under the Bridge"
 1. Nirvana, "Smells Like Teen Spirit"

Shown together, these lists starkly graph the substantial overlap between rock and alternative (with five of the videos appearing on both lists). This repetition of a small canon of songs indicates the almost direct transmission of the mantle of rock to alternative. Indeed, as the configuration of these lists also reveals, the Top 10 alternative song list even replicates the traditional exclusions forged by the category of rock; notice that aside from one singular exception—Slash, the half-black guitarist from Guns n' Roses—all of the groups represented by these lists are comprised solely of white males. Where discrepancies do appear they follow a specific temporal pattern. Of the five songs that appear on the rock list but remain absent from the alternative list, none was released after 1991, whereas, not surprisingly, the alternative list consists solely of videos dating from 1991 or later. In terms of their overall positioning within MTV's canon of all-time best videos, the alternative list fares better than the rock list; "Welcome to the Jungle," the number one rock video, only charted at number thirty-six of all time on the MTV 500 (which aired in November 1997), while "Smells Like Teen Spirit" in that same countdown finally unseated "Thriller" as the number one video of all time. MTV itself documents its own valuation of the relative import of these two categories of music by their respective placement within their programming sequence. While MTV afforded the alternative video list primacy of place by using it to wrap up the weekend-long marathon of all-time Top 10s, it sandwiched the rock list between the "Top 10 female videos" and the "Top 10 videos featuring Puffy." In the wake of these events, we might use Raymond Williams's vocabulary and say that rock (as represented by Aerosmith, Guns n' Roses, and Van Halen) appears as a residual form whose popularity hails from an older era, while alternative represented the dominant form of youth music (at least, at that moment and in MTV's estimation).

14. Importantly, we are not pretending that contemporary popular music is "really" more diverse now than it was, say, thirty years ago (indeed, it is hard to imagine how such a claim would be empirically demonstrated); hence our "and/or" construction here. An examination of the *Billboard* charts from 1968 will, after all, often reveal a wide variety of musics gathered under the rubric of the popular. The transformation we are describing here is therefore one that has taken place at least as much at the level of systems of categorization and market strategy as at the level of musical genre.

15. Grossberg first coined this phrase in *We Gotta Get Out of This Place: Popular Conservatism and Postmodern Culture* (New York: Routledge, 1992).

16. Ross, *Microphone Fiends*, 11.

17. The history of MTV's *Alternative Nation* traces this shift. First, the early successes of the alternative movement prompted the expansion of the formerly late-night-only program to two additional daytime time slots (12 P.M. and 7 P.M.), while Kennedy, the show's host, began veejaying in other time slots dedicated to regular MTV programming. Increasingly, alternative songs found more and more airplay in these nonspecified programming slots, an event culminating in the seeming redundancy of *Alternative Nation* as a distinct show. Ultimately, the program returned to its late-night-only schedule before disappearing altogether in 1996.

18. Our analysis of the collapse of alternative into mainstream is not intended to suggest that there is no literal alternative to the present-day mainstream (e.g., Britney Spears, "nice" boy bands, Eminem, and "naughty" boy hip hop/metal fusions of the Kid Rock/Limp Bizkit variety, at the present time of writing). Far from it: the *Village Voice* "Pazz and Jop" poll of critics choices for 1999 shows only the slightest overlap with *Billboard*'s Top 100 albums of the year. But the fact that the *Village Voice* poll is precisely a *critics* poll, with its problematization of generic categories foregrounded in the title, confirms our sense of an ever-more fragmentary and generically confused popular music culture in search of a single name. Under such circumstances, "Pazz and Jop" will do as well as any, and perhaps better than most, since it at least names the very confusion that the logic of the "best of" list must necessarily repress.

19. Despite good intentions, rock's repressed exclusions return on this "Women of Rock" issue in the form of three Xs that adorn the cover. Although they are clearly meant to signify the thirtieth anniversary edition, this "XXX" (printed in gold over the image of three attractive women dressed in fairly revealing outfits) ironically attest to the masculinist gaze of *Rolling Stone* as a rockist establishment. Interestingly, the Xs are placed over the women's crotches, which might also be taken as an attempt to deny (to cross out) the "difference" of these women.

20. It will probably come as no surprise to discover that this opposition between musical pluralism and musical homogeneity is reducible to yet another evaluative version of that dreaded authenticity myth, where "good" rock is now seen as diversity friendly, and "bad" rock is seen as narrowly exclusionary.

21. As Fred Pfeil has argued in *White Guys: Studies in Postmodern Domination and Dif-*

ference (London: Verso, 1995), the cultural products of white males reflect a broader range of aesthetic and political interests than standard subcultural critiques have hitherto suggested.

22. Jonze's credentials include the Beastie Boys's "Sabotage," Weezer's "Buddy Holly," Sonic Youth's "100%," and Björk's "It's Oh So Quiet." More recently he directed the feature-length movie *Being John Malkovich,* which received widespread critical acclaim.

23. Li'l Kim's transformation in the video from a hyperfeminine schoolgirl in a pink party dress to a foul-mouthed dominatrix might also be considered another symptom of this masculinism.

24. Interestingly, it is almost as if the comingling of cultural codes that constitutes the aural and visual text of "It's All about the Benjamins" works to efface (or excuse) what would normally have been cast in strictly rock terms as the "sellout" aspect of the lyrics and title.

25. Vivid confirmation of this fact can be seen in the relative decline of Combs's career since this introduction was written. It remains to be seen whether Puff Daddy will become another of the many victims of the "authenticity myth."

DISCOURSES/HISTORIES

LAWRENCE GROSSBERG * REFLECTIONS OF
A DISAPPOINTED POPULAR MUSIC SCHOLAR

Every once in a while, people invested in a particular body of scholarly work should take stock. They should stop and ask themselves what they have accomplished and what they have failed to accomplish. And they may even need to ask whether the questions that they have been asking, the questions that propelled their (collective) research project, need to be reevaluated. There are a number of different reasons why the questions might need to be reconsidered: perhaps what we have already learned has redefined and re-constituted the relevant domain; or perhaps theoretical arguments have raised different issues; or perhaps the field of practices and relations have themselves changed as a result of other forces. Of course, different individuals will end up with different conclusions, not least because they understand the project of their (collective) work differently, or care more about one aspect of the project than another, or because they have different approaches to intellectual work in general.

I think it is time to take stock of the work of the past decades in what has come to be called "popular music studies"; more particularly, that subset of the field that addresses what I have always called, using the term in the broadest possible sense, rock culture. In this brief essay I only want to offer some preliminary judgments, and I do not intend to try to cover the full range of work of which account should be taken. I intend to point to three interrelated problems or, even stronger, "failures" within the discourses of popular music studies. In taking up these three problems, I do not intend to dismiss the writing that has been done both inside and outside of the academy. I don't want to deny that this work is often full of insights or that it is often valuable, fun, and so forth.

In fact, I think it is important to accept that different kinds and sites of writing about popular music—considered as an everyday cultural practice within specific and multiple contexts, in definite relations with other practices and relations—can and should serve lots of different functions. It would be interesting to know something about these differences, differences concerning the questions they attempt to answer and their relationships to or places within the cultures of popular music. Consequently, I am not demanding that all writing about popular music be defined by a single definition or project, least of all by my own. In fact, I think that my view of the project and responsibilities of popular music studies is probably a minority view at best. But I do think that there are specific—empirically, theoretically, and politically inflected—questions that have yet to be significantly addressed in anything like a sustained or collective way. This is not only a matter of one's theoretical paradigm or empirical research practice; it is not only a matter of knowing more but of understanding better. And I do think that the project that I had in mind when I entered the field has been shared over the years by many others who have attempted to take up the challenges of popular music studies.

My own interest in the study of popular music, and therefore the shape of my current misgivings about it, derives from my commitment to and my understanding of cultural studies. In another context I twice tried to define it in the following terms:

> If there is no fixed definition of cultural studies, perhaps the terrain on which it operates can at least be identified: cultural studies is concerned with describing and intervening in the ways "texts" and "discourses" (i.e., cultural practices) are produced within, inserted into, and operate in the everyday life of human beings and social formations, so as to reproduce, struggle against and perhaps transform the existing structures of power.[1]

And again,

Cultural studies is about mapping the deployment and effects of discursive practices and alliances within the context of specific social spaces and milieus. It is about the relations or articulations between (1) discursive alliances as the configurations of practices that define where and how people live specific practices and relations; (2) the practices and configurations of daily life (as the sites of specific forms of determinations, controls, structures of power, struggles, pleasures, etc.); (3) the apparatuses of power that mobilize different practices and effects to organize the spaces of human life and the possibilities of alliances.[2]

My own researches have attempted to theorize and analyze the relations among popular music, popular culture more broadly understood, popular politics, and the systemic structures and forces of inequality and domination (or the balance in the field of forces as it were). Consequently, I have argued for over twenty years (and I have certainly not been alone in this) that rock music cannot be studied in isolation, either from other forms and practices of popular culture or from the structures and practices of everyday life. Studying rock for me was never about further carving up the field of popular culture into media and genres, or the field of cultural studies into increasingly narrow and less-relevant disciplines. But I did think that it was important to legitimate the study of popular music, not only because of its obvious social and economic power, but also because I believed it was an especially exciting and unique entrance into the world of the popular and the quotidian, that it offered (to echo Richard Hoggart) unique insights into and perspectives on the question of how people live their lives in a particular time and place. I thought it was important to recognize the specificity of musical expression and culture, especially in relation to its role in youth cultures in the second half of the twentieth century. I was convinced that popular music studies could force the most radical demands of interdisciplinarity onto the agenda because I was sure it would be impossible to study it in any serious way without a serious critique of the limits and constraints of disciplinarity. And finally—and why I went back to it again in the 1970s after my initial frustrated attempts in the late 1960s—I was certain that it was the most powerful pedagogical tool we had to try to teach new generations of students to take a critical and self-reflective look at the culture they live in and consume. I must admit that I do not think I would give the vast majority of popular music studies very high grades on any of the dimensions I cared (and still care) about. (There are probably lots of scholars who would reject these dimensions entirely, and others who, while accepting one or more of them, might come up with an entirely different set of judgments.)

Obviously, I am disappointed in popular music studies. I wonder whether the academic disciplinization (through organizations, journals, etc.) of popular music studies—by which I mean the identification of popular music as an object of study and specialization equivalent to literature, film, television, and so forth—has taken on such a force of its own that it has now become a serious stumbling block to the kind of work I wanted (and want) to do. I am no longer confident that the academic study of popular music is a particularly useful place from which to begin the sort of project—the project of cultural studies—that has always driven my work. Too often it has fulfilled Raymond Williams's worst fears, tracing out the line that distances the project from the actual work:

> There remains the problem of forgetting the real project. As you separate these disciplines out, and say "Well, it's a vague and baggy monster, Cultural Studies, but we can define it more closely—as media studies, community sociology, popular fiction or popular music," so you create defensible disciplines, and there are people in other departments who can *see* that these are defensible disciplines, that here is properly referenced and presented work. But the question of what is then happening to the project remains.[3]

So what are the failures or lacunae that concern me now? First, at the level of theory, I do not think that we have gained a significantly better understanding of how popular music works. In fact, one would be hard pressed to even describe the major theoretical paradigms (or the major debates) that have defined the academic study of pop music. This is not to say that there have not been some important and interesting contributions to a possible discourse, but they are not taken up and discussed, they are not commonly integrated into empirical work, and there is no sense of the desirability of reaching common understandings (which is not the same as consensus) of the strengths and/or weaknesses of particular positions, even to the point of asking whether some positions (in fact, positions that are often assumed within various empirical and interpretive studies) are not fatally flawed. At this level, I do not think that writing about popular music has significantly changed (to say nothing of "progressed") in forty years.[4] I realize that "progress" is a suspect concept in the contemporary world, but I think that one can at least expect that over the course of decades there would be some sense that the debates and discussions have moved, even if not in one direction.

The second issue, closely related to the first, is that I do not think we have developed (or even attempted to develop) a common vocabulary in which to argue about the differences between musics or musical cultures, and between critical interpretations and analyses. What is the difference between rock in the 1950s and 1980s? What is the difference between heavy metal in Detroit and heavy metal in rural Illinois? What is the difference between listening to the Beatles in the 1960s and in the 1990s? What is the difference between dance music in the 1960s and the 1990s? What is the difference between 70s British/N.Y. punk, 80s California punk, 90s (straight-edge) punk, and 90s alternative? What is the difference between "Born in the USA" for a thirteen and a thirty year old, an American or a Taiwanese? What is the difference between Springsteen and Mellencamp? How do we begin to answer these questions? How do we understand and make some evaluations of the different interpretations that have been offered of punk or disco, of hip hop or new country? I do not think these questions can be approached in entirely musical or sonic terms. They are complicated, multi-dimensional questions that involve us in considerations of the social significance, relations, and effects of music. But if we have no theory of the effectivity of popular music, or of its contextuality, how can we possibly distinguish between the different organizations of effects that specific musical practices, in specific contexts and for specific audiences, may produce? Too much of the unarticulated, taken-for-granted theory of popular music is really the generalization of specific formations of popular music culture, one that marks both the biography of many of the writers and the specific and intense forms of investment that many of us who write about popular music have had and continue to have in the music. The question is whether such experiences, relations, and investments can be unproblematically universalized or assumed to be somehow intrinsic to the nature of the music itself. Personally, I do not think that the normative terms of most rock writing, which depend on those relationships that were dominant in the 1960s and 1970s, are up to the task of describing what is happening to popular music cultures in the 1990s. To take only one small but crucial change, there is growing evidence that people make the sorts of investments that were reserved for postwar popular music in a wider range of media products and practices.

The third issue is that too often (but fortunately not universally) I am disappointed by how infrequently our engagement with popular music as a set of fragmented and changing "discursive apparatuses" (to use Foucault's term) has forced us to take up the new and urgent political struggles of recent decades. I am not saying that scholars of popular music are apolitical; on the contrary, they are probably as politicized as any discipline-defined body of researchers. But their politics are rarely shaped by the knowledge they gain about what is happening in the world through their ongoing research into popular music cultures. The terms and urgency of their political engagement are usually defined by their own general experience of the music, by the theoretical and political discourses that they bring to the research, and by their own generational experience, rather than what they take from the research. Consequently, the objects of their political energy are usually either relatively independent of the music or are defined entirely within the sphere of the music. Now I am sure that much of my own earlier faith that popular music offered a particularly powerful place to enter into the fields of culture and power (both as a political agent and as a scholar) was the product of a naïve (and certainly generational) belief that the music had the potential to serve as an organizing site if not force of resistance and alternative possibilities. But the terms on which youth (in the United States and the world) have to live their lives and engage with their music have changed so significantly that I doubt that it is now possible to be so naïve, or even as optimistic. In fact, youth has become *the* most devastated battleground in the war being waged against the postwar status quo (and the baby boom rearticulation of that formation) by a tense alliance between neoliberalism and neoconservatism. The "state" of youth and children has to be obvious to anyone studying popular music culture, and my question is simple: Where are the outraged and articulate voices that attempt to make sense of, give voice to, and intervene into these struggles? I cannot help but feel that popular music scholars should be the leading edge of such a politics, but the truth is, sadly, otherwise.

These problems, however, have not diminished my commitment to the need for academically defined, cultural-studies-aligned work around popular music. Such work would not attempt to offer and defend a particular set of judgments about musical texts and tastes; and it especially would not begin with such judgments.[5] The question is not whether or how one defends popular music (or some part of it), but what popular music practices are doing and what is being done with them and to them, and such questions cannot be entirely answered in terms of individuals, whether texts or audiences. Nor are they questions about intentions, experiences, and uses, although these might be relevant dimensions of the empirical puzzle. This is, it seems to me, one of the absolute distinctions between scholars and critics. I do not believe it is the function of the scholar of popular culture to attempt to substitute his or her judgment (or more often taste) for that of his or her students. I do not believe that the academic study of popular music is about making judgments, especially not in the first instance. As Proust put it: "That bad music is played, is sung more often and more passionately than good, is why it has also gradually become more infused with men's dreams and tears. Treat it therefore with respect. Its place, insignificant in the history of art, is immense in the sentimental history of social groups."[6] That doesn't mean that individuals cannot enrich or change their experiences by being made to understand the complexity of how such experiences and judgments are produced and how the music functions not only in their own lives but in the larger contexts of social relations of power. Obviously, there are important questions at stake here about an individual's relationship to everyday popular culture, and about the value of different voices or positions from which to speak—for example, the immersed participant, the ethnographer (externalized visitor), or the fascinated describer.[7] But perhaps, at least for the moment, we can circumvent the question by accepting that, in the words of John Frow, "our attention must be turned away from that mythical popular subject immediate to observation, and focused instead on the relation between two different kinds of practice: a first order practice of everyday culture and the second order practice of analysis conducted by a reader endowed with significant cultural capital."[8] It is this reference to "significant cultural capital" that I want to elaborate, although I doubt that the market for such capital is booming these days. Given the fact that the second absence described here depends on the first, and that the third depends on the second, I will devote the greatest part of this paper to fleshing out the first of these lacunae, devoting less time to the second and, unfortunately (to say nothing of ironically), even less to the last.

The academic study of popular music can be roughly and ungenerously divided into three distinguishable but related styles or bodies of work. First, some work attempts to gain "empirical" knowledge, at a variety of levels, about the music, its institutions, audiences, producers, technologies, economies, paths of distribution and dispersion, related activities, and so forth. We are certainly, if slowly, increasing our knowledge about some of the dimensions and aspects of the existence of popular music. There has been a proliferation of studies of the music and musicians, of audiences and tastes (cultures), of technologies and institutions. And yet only slowly are scholars beginning to realize that the musics and audiences that constitute popular music are much more diverse and multiple than we have been willing to admit (including, even in the United States, for example, Indian film music, Vietnamese pop music, Vegas pop, and Broadway musicals). At the same time, even as we learn more about some aspects of popular music, we seem to know less and less about other absolutely crucial dimensions of its existence—namely, its institutional and economic conditions. Moreover, scholars have too often ignored the relations among these various dimensions and aspects, to say nothing about how they are contingently linked together within specific contexts and apparatuses.[9]

Second, some scholarship attempts to "interpret"[10] the personal and/or social significance of particular musical texts, practices, and genres, presumably relative to particular audiences.[11] This often brings the work of the scholar close to that of the critic, except that the latter has a definite and explicit role in the socioeconomic circulation of popular music. No doubt this role is harder to define than that of the film critic, for example; for unlike the film critic it is not clear how much rock critics actually influence the decisions, behaviors, or tastes of fans. There are complicated relationships at stake in the different cultural positions of both music critic and film critic. Much of the academic writing on popular music, like journalistic work, operates *within* the discourses and relations of popular music culture and fandom, and often from within specific taste cultures, even though it presents itself as offering something else—namely, an analysis of such discourses, relations, and cultures.[12] Sometimes this occurs because the biography or taste of the author (or some surrogate) is taken to exemplify, if not the story of rock and roll, then at least a normative version of that story.

Some circumscribed experience of the music and its social context are taken to signify its proper meaning or social effects. The aesthetic and political stakes overwhelm everything else. In such work the line between the academic and the nonacademic disappears. At other times it occurs because popular music has become little more than an excuse for the scholar to reenact his or her own theoretical (and under its aegis, aesthetic and political) agenda. In such work it almost doesn't matter that one is talking about popular music, and the line between the academic and the nonacademic becomes overwhelming. (I suppose I must admit that my own work shows a strong tendency toward the latter.)

Moreover, whether such interpretive work presents itself as a description (the writer's position being merely a matter of access) or as an interpretation (the writer's position enabling a privileged set of aesthetic and political judgments), it often embodies and expresses a limited number of strategies. Sometimes it is obsessed with discovering the esoteric (e.g., comparing riffs from different artists or songs, demonstrating the collector's knowledge of trivia of performers and performances). Other times it is content to rediscover what we already knew; in fact, it often seems to "discover" what it has already presupposed (e.g., that music is either increasingly hybrid or that it has always been built on appropriation; that musicians make compromises or that they are caught in a rigid choice between artistic and economic pressures; that pleasure is an alibi for ideological domination or that audiences are actively involved in feeling and doing things; that record companies don't feel anything and rarely do anything). Rarely am I surprised by the interpretive work; instead, my most common experience is that I have heard it before—been there, done that.

The third body of work attempts to produce a better understanding of how popular music works (both generally and specifically), of what it is doing in the world and how it changes in relation to a changing world. (Cultural studies is, for me, a version of this third project.) Such efforts may well depend on the knowledges produced through the first and/or second projects, so that commonly, someone attempting to carry out such a contextual study of popular music will also be simultaneously involved in other kinds of research. But unlike the first style, such work is not content to describe the facticity of some isolated feature of the larger economy of music culture. And unlike the second style, it is not involved in making judgments of quality in the first instance (whether on aesthetic, political, or quotidian—

e.g., is it fun? danceable?—grounds); instead, it attempts to look at the place of the music (in its various aspects) in an articulated set of relations. That articulated place determines its specific effects (whether the audience is aware of them or not) in relation to the ongoing organization of quotidian and social power. But such work often goes one step further to look at the possibilities of changing the way the music (in its various aspects) is articulated. That is, the musical apparatus becomes a site of possible contestation and a point of articulation in its own right for other relations. It is only at the end of the research that value judgments become possible and useful.

All of these approaches eventually have to face the limitations of using communicative models to study mass phenomena. Such models isolate production and consumption, texts from audiences, institutions from relations, one context from another, and then struggle to reconstitute the relationship through notions of expression, signification, and representation. But popular music is so deeply and complexly interwoven into the everyday lives of its fans and listeners that its study, even more so than that of other cultural forms, has to recognize that the music is inseparable from the entire range of activities that fill up our lives, activities that are defined by and respond to the contrary, sometimes terrifying, and often boring demands of work (paid and unpaid, domestic and nondomestic), education, politics, taxes, illness, romance, and leisure (whether sought out or enforced). As a result, the meaning and effect of specific music always depend on its place within both the broad context of everyday life and the potentially multiple, more specific contexts or alliances of other texts, cultural practices (including fashion, dance, films), social relationships, emotional investments, and so forth. These alliances, or "apparatuses," define the material reality of so-called taste cultures. I define an apparatus as a set of practices and relations, on the one hand, and a set of logics—modes of operating or working—that produce the actual effects, on the other hand.

Consequently, the study of popular music, especially in the first two styles discussed here, poses what seem to be almost insurmountable methodological problems.[13] How does one limit the number of texts or trends to be studied? How can one locate significant exemplars? How can one isolate a particular text (or what aspects are responsible for its success) from other texts, media, and activities? How can one know the relevant relations between texts or between texts and other practices? Similar questions can be raised about the attempt to identify and isolate particular audience fractions, taste cultures, or communities. In the end, while the pool of information and knowledge about popular music is growing in important ways, it is unclear what one can conclude from such research. What do we know when we know?

These difficulties are further exacerbated by the fact that there are at least three distinct constructions of the world of popular music, three different vocabularies (although they may all use the same signifiers) that each attempt to occupy and control this world, to make it over in terms of their own values and interests. First, a productive logic constructs the music culture by segmenting it according to identifiable generic (often paradoxically both rigid and temporary) distinctions supposedly grounded in "objective" features. Actually, this logic encompasses at least two distinct variations because it characterizes both the industrial/commercial and the artistic sides of music culture. Second, fans deploy a distinct logic of consumption (of which there are multiple possibilities) through which the music is appropriated into and constructed within the terms of specific contexts and apparatuses. Finally, there are the various academics' logics of analysis, which attempt to describe the structures, modes, functions, and effects of the music's production, consumption, distribution, and so forth in the context of people's lives, in the organization of social realities, and in the structures of power of the social formation. Too often, scholars assume a logic of either production or of consumption, thereby implicitly conflating the competing constructions of popular music culture. Using phenomenological theory, we might say that such a conflation fails to distinguish between first-order (naïve, commonsensical) and second-order concepts.

Such a conflation is one of the simplest ways that scholars in popular music have ignored or erased the need for serious and rigorous theoretical work. As an intellectual, I am committed to what Marx called "the detour through theory" and to the need to develop concepts (and a logic by which they can be related) that will enable us to redescribe and transform the empirically available world into something else, what Marx called the concrete. Such theoretical concepts are, inevitably, abstractions, operating without all of the specific determinations that provide the density of everyday life.[14] At the very least, such work is a necessary (but probably not sufficient) condition for being able to understand and describe what is the same and what is different (between popular musical and other cultural apparatuses and among popular musical apparatuses themselves), and what is changing and what is not. How can you talk about what is new or different and what is the same (or what is "the changing same") unless you have a vocabulary in which both sorts of relations can be described? How can you begin to offer new insights into the concrete workings of particular musical and cultural practices if you have not yet figured out a vocabulary within which to ask and answer questions about the specificity of such practices?

There are obviously a number of dimensions to such a theoretical project.[15] First, and most abstractly, one has to have a theory of culture or discourse, of its mode of being and functioning, and of its relationship to the noncultural. Obviously, such a concern is shared with many other scholars in the field of culture studies who have not the slightest interest in *popular music*. Second, one has to have a theory of the specificity of "the popular" (as opposed to nonpopular discourses). While slightly less abstract, again this concern is, at least in principle, shared with other scholars who are not particularly concerned with popular *music*. Finally, and probably about as abstract as the concern with the popular, one has to think about the specificity of musical or sonic discourses (as opposed to other—nonmusical and nonsound—forms of material articulation/expression). In the end, this separation is too artificial and counterproductive because the real questions cannot be so neatly divorced from one another or from a dialectic with the more concrete material contexts of our research. Answers to these questions will require a constant movement across different levels of abstraction (and concretion). The answers will themselves involve empirical and historical considerations. After all, part of the very existence and nature of popular music has been historically produced—or more accurately, genealogically produced. This is true as well for all of the other related concepts, including culture, music, and even the sonic.[16] But in the end, more practically, we need to begin to pose the question of how popular music works—as culture (or discourse), as popular, as sound, and as music—along its various axes or planes of relations.

Let me offer a brief example. This example is based on the assumption, one that I hope we all share, that a large part of the power of postwar popular music depends in part on the mechanisms and systems of identification—both real and imaginary, of all different kinds (e.g., fantasy, alliance, affiliation), and between different fractions of the population (e.g., black and white, male and female, gay and straight)—that it calls into existence and deploys. Such identifications involve complex economies of perception, imagination, and desire around issues of subordination and alienation on the one hand, and response and transcendence on the other. But to go further we would need to begin to develop a better theory of identifications, and then we would need to develop a better vocabulary for making useful distinctions between apparatuses and economies of identification. Some of this work on theories of identification and of popular identifications is being done in other fields (such as film and television studies, or feminist theory) but not enough, because none of it addresses precisely those questions that have to be raised at the beginning of our researches—namely, what difference does it make that we are talking about *popular music*? Does music operate through different practices or mechanisms of identification? Does it rearticulate practices that operate in other discursive materialities? Does it produce different possibilities of identification and of their structure and articulation to other dimensions of our lives?[17]

The work I am calling for is not entirely abstract and theoretical, because it cannot be separated from the specific context in which we are working. It cannot be separated from the specific mechanisms, processes, and possibilities of concrete apparatuses. But the answers to such concrete questions also cannot be accomplished without the detour through theory, without doing some of the theoretical work—and at higher levels of abstraction as well. Thus, a better understanding of the place and effects of popular music demands that we develop theories that move between "the more abstract" and "the more specific."

Let me give another example. Consider a question that, while dating back to the 1950s, has recently become an important issue for many critics and scholars: the significance of live performance in rock culture, and its relationship to produced images. I would suggest that the relation between performance and image has to be seen as one term in a complex set of relations among the various forms of the objectification/commodification/exploitation of the performance/image couplet. First, it is commonly assumed that the live event produces certain experiences unavailable through other means. But such experiences cannot be understood simply in terms of the copresence of other people, even in an imaginary community. Nor can they be a matter of the feelings that result from people having a common object of investment. Such experiences need not depend on live performance; they could be produced through the collective viewing of videos or simply listening to recordings together. However, I think the question

itself—searching for some unique experience produced by the live experience—is mistaken, for it takes the productivity of the performance as a
necessary and universal effect. I think the argument takes the experience
and values of certain apparatuses as normative and proper and universalizes
them instead of recognizing that performances may function differently in
different apparatuses. My own sense is that, at the most abstract level, the
social investment in rock culture does not depend on the productivity of the
live moment but on the possibility of producing "the coming community."
That is, rock culture in its most abstract sense is in part about what Giorgio
Agamben would describe as a community that is not predicated on any
identity but purely on a set of identifications.[18] Moreover, at this level it isn't
only that performance and image are inseparable from one another, but that
they are and always have been inseparable from rock culture itself.

Second, has the relationship between performance and visual image
changed? Is there a new ratio, as it were, between an emphasis on the music
and on the visual image, or has the quality of the visual image changed,
presumably making it easier to overwhelm the music? And, following from
that, are there now two kinds and meanings of performance? Can one see an
opposition between live performance and "packaged" visual appearance, or
has rock performance always deployed a whole range of "marketing" strategies, whether spectacular or minimalist? Beyond the fact that image and
style have always been a crucial part of rock (which is not to say that the ratio
has always been the same), it is worth recalling that, at least since the 1960s
(if not earlier), a part of rock culture (including British pop, glitter and glam,
disco, and I would argue, even hip hop) has championed the artificiality and
ironic possibilities of style. While often presenting itself as different from
(and even opposing) the mainstream commitment to authenticity, I would
argue that such apparatuses are equally implicated in such logics.

Third, assuming that something has changed, what are the politics of this
new kind of performance? What is its relation to late capitalism? To conventional iconographies? And on the other side, what are the politics of live
performance in the face of this new visual economy? Of course, it is important to point out that there is nothing new about the form of this question. In
fact, it is part of one of the dominant logics of rock[19] (and of being a rock
fan), for it simply records the fact that rock culture always involves a distribution (actually, a number of competing distributions) of texts, audiences,
and practices along at least one of the following dimensions: economics

(majors versus independents); success (mainstream versus marginal); audience (mainstream versus subcultural); sound (commercial versus underground or alternative); and sometimes even a political/ideological (mere entertainment versus resistance). Such distributions or differentiations are precisely how certain rock apparatuses work. Often, the different dimensions of this distribution are all conflated, as if they were guaranteed to be equivalent, as if one could read from one "fact" to another. This condensation is linked to notions of authenticity and cooptation, and it is usually intimated to be tied up with claims for rock's power (as transcendence, or resistance, and so forth). I do not mean either to dismiss this logic or to buy into it entirely, although in a sense I do want to argue that from a theoretical point of view the question (asked at the beginning of this paragraph) exists only within certain apparatuses, for certain fans or critics. It is a question shaped from within the logic of a particular set of apparatuses—in fact such questions were a necessary and constitutive part of these apparatuses—that together defined the dominant popular music formation in the 1960s and 1970s, at least in terms of youth culture and popular music, if not more broadly in terms of the national popular culture of the United States. And insofar as that formation has continued to speak as the dominant (whether or not it is) through the voices of many performers, critics, and scholars, the question of authenticity has been reproduced over and over again, albeit in slightly different ways.

If we are to answer any of these questions concerning the (changing) nature and place of the performance/image couplet, we need to put the questions in the context of what has happened and is happening to rock culture. At the very least, we need to ask ourselves if we are assuming (and if so why) that such questions—the meaning or value of live performance, the politics of style—have only one referent, only one answer, that is adequate to the entirety of rock culture. In order to begin to answer these questions, we need to locate them (as well as the performance and style) in a specific context, understood both as an apparatus and as the conditions of possibility of that apparatus (a doubling that, unfortunately, many versions of popular culture studies too often ignore). But as I have tried to suggest here, this can only be accomplished if we are simultaneously developing the theoretical frameworks and tools that will enable us to understand what it is that binds the various apparatuses of popular music together and what it is that separates them.

I would like to compare the relative absence in popular music studies of any conversation aimed toward such theoretical grounding with the emergence of so-called film theory,[20] especially as it developed out of *Cahiers du Cinema* and *Screen*. It seems to me that the discipline of film studies became productive (and progressive—at least in the sense that there arises a common position to argue with, over, and against, and a common vocabulary to argue in) when it moved beyond commonsense-based discussions of texts, oeuvres, and genres (although it can and has come back to them after the moment of "*Screen* theory," but in new and I think more productive ways). So-called *Screen* theory embodied an attempt to develop a theory capable of describing the specificity of both cinematic communication in general (e.g., by arguing that the cinema was a language deeply implicated in psychoanalytic processes) and in a particular (classic Hollywood) cinematic apparatus. This is not to deny that there are problems with both the actual theory and the ways it is enacted and practiced. Too often, film analysts privilege if not universalize a particular apparatus, thus ignoring the radical contextualism of the theory, or the radical implications of such a contextualism (e.g., viewing videotapes at home cannot be explained in the terms used to analyze the classic Hollywood apparatus). They seem to forget that concepts (of the gaze, of subjectivity, and so forth) are specific to and generalized from specific apparatuses. Too often, the discourse of film theory seems to assume that it can provide answers to all the significant questions one might want to ask about film (or that the only significant questions are the ones it can answer). It is not the particularities of *Screen* theory that concerned me here, it is the model of cultural theorizing based on the complex relationship between general and specific concepts, where the latter are adequate only in response to particular contexts and apparatuses. Even more, I am attracted to its success at enabling an ongoing theoretical conversation.[21]

I can put this in a slightly different register by asking what concepts have emerged from and reentered into (thus, energizing) the study of popular music. If we consider film studies, we can point to concepts such as the gaze and the cinematic apparatus. Or we could point to television studies, and concepts such as Williams's concept of flow as a description of the televisual text, or the glance, or the domestication of media. Such concepts have provided at least a common starting point for many discussions—theoretical and empirical—of the televisual text.[22]

My claim, then, is simple: the study of popular music has not undertaken the necessary theoretical project in a serious and collective way. Let me be clear about what such work would involve. To say that music is a way of seeing or knowing (I would prefer to say "constructing") the world is not a theory but the statement of a theoretical problem. To say that music is socially constructed (I would prefer to say that sound is constructed) is not a theory but the statement of a theoretical problem. To say that music mediated or is mediated is not a theory but the statement of a theoretical problem. And to say that music is affective (one of the most commonly claimed concepts for music studies) is not a theory but the statement of a theoretical problem.

In fact, for whatever reasons, scholars of popular music seem unwilling and unable to take on this project. The fact that we have not advanced significantly toward theorizing the specificity of popular music provides, I believe, the most damning judgment of the field of popular music studies. We seem collectively unable to recognize the theoretical basis of our work, to discuss various issues and positions, and to move beyond our own individual agendas and unreflective, unacknowledged theoretical assumptions.[23]

At the same time, I must admit, the problem is not unique to popular music studies. There is, in fact, too little theoretical work on the specificity of "the popular" within popular culture studies more generally, and within its specific empirical fields of research (e.g., film studies). What little theoretical reflection and resources are explicitly exhibited and deployed in both popular music studies and popular culture studies are almost entirely drawn from general theories of culture (e.g., concepts of ideology) or theories of specific (and in the case of popular music, other) cultural domains. For example, most surveys of "theories of popular culture" are organized by paradigms of cultural theory (structuralism, poststructuralism, feminist theory, etc.) and do not seriously address the issue of the construction and specificity of the popular.[24] The discussions of the application of different cultural theories are never directly linked to different conceptions of "the popular." Similarly, much of the work in popular culture has never taken up, theoretically, the nature of the connections that constitute the contexts of popular culture practices (what I have called apparatuses). Again, such general work has to go hand in hand with the slightly less abstract attempt to develop a theory of popular music apparatuses. Paradoxically, in a lot of work, from a theoretical perspective, it seems to make little or no difference that we are talking about music, despite constant reminders in the writing that we are dealing with music and vague claims about its specificity. Such reminders are usually made through the use of a set of signifiers—the body, fun, affect, feeling, energy, pleasure, sentiment, emotion—with little recognition of the fact that these signifiers require serious theoretical elaboration.[25] I think the truth of this can be seen in recent texts that purport to introduce and survey the field of popular music studies (one even explicitly claims to do so in terms of "theory").[26] While such texts are often remarkably similar in both structure and content, they rarely include any theory beyond the most broad and banal concepts of cultural theory.

At the same time, I want to acknowledge that there are some serious attempts to at least begin to develop, usually in only the broadest of terms, a theory of popular music. For example, my own theoretical and political inclinations have drawn me into the arguments of Jacques Attali, Gilles Deleuze and Félix Guattari, and Paul Carter.[27] But there are other important traditions and bodies of work, from such diverse perspectives as semiotics/structural (for example, John Shepherd, Peter Wicke, and Mark Slobin) and phenomenology/hermeneutics (Don Ihde, David Sudnow, Susan Crafts et al., and Michel Chion).[28] Recently there have also been some interesting conceptual proposals as well as outstanding examples of empirical, interpretive, and cultural studies work that take seriously the need for undertaking and integrating rigorous theoretical reflection.[29] Such efforts could have profound implications for how we conceptualize popular music and how we do our work as popular music scholars. At the very least, we would have hoped that they might have given rise to serious and engaged conversations, but these conversations have not taken place. Instead, for the most part, the issues and conceptual proposals have been largely ignored. If anything, the field not only continues on with little serious theoretical self-reflection but also increasingly embraces a sense of hostility to such efforts in the name of a rather anachronistic empiricism.[30]

It is interesting to speculate why these theoretical problems and works have been ignored or avoided for so long, and I want to offer a few suggestions.[31] First, the struggle to legitimate popular music did not have available to it an accepted model, whereas both film and television studies had the model of the literary text with its associated celebration of the author. Thus, the latter initially appealed to (and often limited) the study of film and television as art. The struggle to legitimate popular music studies (outside of the models of art and folk culture) has been a much more difficult one.

Partly as a consequence, the field of popular music studies is a relatively small and intimately connected body of scholars and students (often with little or no power). The social relations that have contributed to its successes have perhaps also made it more difficult for individuals to seriously engage with and criticize each other's work. Moreover, the fact that popular music scholars come from a very wide range of disciplines has not made the task any easier. Finally, and perhaps most important, I believe the nature of the investment of those studying popular music have in the music is often qualitatively different from that in other areas of research. Perhaps we are too invested, but most certainly the music matters in ways that often transform the intellectual project into a defense of particular tastes.[32]

Mapping Rock at the Turn of the Century

My second claim is that the field of popular music studies has largely failed to describe and understand the significant changes occurring in popular music culture in the United States in the 1990s. There are two reasons for this failure, I think. First, as I have already argued, popular music culture has not developed a vocabulary capable of providing the framework for such a history. Second, and ironically, the frameworks it has provided are often the product of the writers' immersion with and normalization of particular and usually older popular apparatuses. Without moving to an appropriate level of abstraction, scholars too often apply categories derived from one apparatus to newer formations for which they are inappropriate. Thus, if my first claim is that popular music studies has inadequate theoretical resources, my second claim is that it is now trying to apply those inadequate resources to conditions that are seriously different from those from which the resources themselves were derived.

Let me begin to elaborate by offering the barest outline of the conclusions of my own researches on rock culture.[33] First, I have argued that the emergence of rock has to be understood in relation to a number of conditions of possibility operating in economics, politics, everyday life, youth (as a population and signifier), culture (including technologies, industries, "media economies," [comparative investments in different media]), and, I would certainly add, music[34] and the available images of alienation and rebellion.[35] Second, I have argued that what emerged—in the most general and abstract fashion—was a cultural logic or mode of productivity that can be described by the following terms: affective (rather than ideological); differentiating (us versus them without providing necessary content to the "us"), a celebration of fun (where "fun" takes on different meanings depending on what it is opposing); politicized primarily within the realm of everyday life; and operating as a mode (or practice) of survival in the face of the very conditions that called it into existence.[36]

The question of what, in my opinion, is happening to what we might broadly call rock culture in the 1990s has to begin by addressing these two issues: first, how have the conditions of possibility for rock culture changed from the 1950s, 1960s, and 1970s to the 1980s and 1990s? Second, how has its mode of productivity changed? Since there is no way here I could do justice to the first question, let me simply provide some brief and over-simplified examples of how the conditions have changed: (1) The economy has been transformed from a Keynesian (ameliorist) welfare state built on a corporate compromise to a neoliberal "free market" in which corporations but not populations are protected, and a naïve optimism about the future has been replaced by uncertainty and renewed selfishness. (2) The dominance of a distinctly American liberalism has given way to the growth of both conservatism and cynicism. (3) Regarding everyday life, both the boredom and the terror of earlier decades have given way to a more normalized sense of insecurity and fright. (4) The transformation of the media, in every aspect from economics to technology, is, I assume, relatively obvious. (5) Although earlier music was the only cultural form that "belonged" to youth (if only in the sense that it was directed at and defined by them), since the 1980s clearly this is not the case, as measured by the rise of computers and videogames and by the growing power of youth as the primary audience for both movies and television. (6) Viable images of opposition and protest have virtually disappeared, but when present they are often defined by investments in issues of identity and victimage. The result is that youth has become the only image of its own alienation. (7) This outcome is perhaps reasonable in the face of the enormity of the social, cultural, political, and economic attack on the body of youth, both in the United States and abroad. In the first decades of postwar American culture, youth was celebrated and nurtured. It was treated as a site for profitable investment and future hope. Surely I do not have to do too much work to emphasize the transformation that has occurred in the past decades; surely it is not necessary to repeat all of the statistics about youth poverty, unemployment, and homelessness, about

44　Lawrence Grossberg

the incarceration and disciplinization of youth. Hopefully, I can simply call to mind the abandonment of any real commitment to education and the transformation of schools into virtual zones of martial law, the withdrawal of medical care, the increasing criminalization of youth and the attacks on the various activities (including sex, drugs, and rock and roll) associated with youth culture. Youth has become the enemy, that which we seem to fear most and care about the least. Insofar as popular music is intimately tied to youth and youth culture, as well as to the larger culture and society, how can these changes, changes of enormous magnitude and significance, not have their effects on popular musics and the apparatuses in and into which they are articulated?

I will attempt to address the second dimension, the changing modes of productivity of rock, by offering a brief description of some of the changing apparatuses of rock. Actually, I should say invocation rather than description, since all I can do in this brief space is to point at a certain configuration, a certain set of relationships, and hope that the reader will recognize something in it. Such apparatuses describe organizations of relations, investments, and practices and not generic musical distinctions. Thus while we might almost automatically associate one apparatus with so-called classic rap, and another with rap, this is not a necessary relationship. It is just as possible that a significant fraction of rap fans live out their relation to the music through the former, while some fans of acid rock live out their relation to the music through the latter. This is not to say that the primary and most visible embodiments of an apparatus may not be strongly articulated to a specific set of musical texts, practices, and tastes. But such articulations may not exhaust the possibilities of the apparatus. Let me now offer the outlines of something like a map of rock culture in the 1990s by distinguishing four broadly defined apparatuses of popular music.[37]

First, the formation that has been central (albeit not exclusive) in my own work, which emerged in the 1960s to become the dominant U.S. cultural formation of "American" youth at least until the mid 1980s, had, by the end of the 1980s, been displaced. I believe this apparatus is "becoming-residual." Raymond Williams defines the "residual" as follows:

> The residual has been effectively formed in the past, but it is still active in the cultural process, not only and often not at all as an element of the past, but as an effective element of the present. Thus certain experiences,

meanings and values which cannot be expressed or substantially verified in terms of the dominant culture, are nevertheless lived and practiced on the basis of the residue . . . of some previous social and cultural institution or formation. It is crucial to distinguish this aspect of the residual, which may have an alternative or even oppositional relation to the dominant culture, from that active manifestation of the residual . . . which has been wholly or largely incorporated into the dominant culture.[38]

This apparatus, usually organized around generic commitments and differences, although still active and important, is slowly moving toward the edges along paths that are often erratic and sometimes even reversed. It is no longer dominant in terms of either commercial success or what might be called cultural or discursive power.[39] I do not think this apparatus speaks any longer for or as the most widely distributed or most powerful "version" of rock, although there is no doubt that it is still struggling to speak normatively as the "proper" form of rock. In so doing, it sometimes has the effect of marginalizing other apparatuses and other forms of cultural practice and social relationship. In fact, we have to acknowledge that, given the changes in the conditions of possibility of rock, it is now harder to anchor this residual formation in actual social and cultural relations than it was, say, twenty years ago.

Within this apparatus, for example, live performance is both the imagined originary event and the site for authenticating the claim of authenticity. As a result, the presence of the fan is not only the measure of his or her own commitment, but also the occasion for him or her to measure the performer's commitment. Furthermore, while the logic of this apparatus can allow for the recognition of image as part of the performance, this recognition is usually actualized in an experienced contradiction between the image and the performance, or at least as a fear that the image can and is overwhelming the performance, which is the essential moment of rock culture itself.

However rapidly this apparatus is becoming residual, it nevertheless continues to dominate much of the writing and thinking about rock, partly because it is where a majority of academics and journalists are interpellated.[40] This is no doubt largely a function of the generational identity of the writers and of the lack of an adequate theoretical vocabulary to address the incongruity of the assumption of its continued dominance. But its ability to continue claiming dominance, despite its increasingly residual existence, is helped along by the fact that one of the ways in which both rap and alternative musics are experienced appears to share some of its explicit ideology of authenticity.[41] But there is another issue here: How is this change—from dominant to residual—itself being accomplished? I believe that the residual status of this classic rock apparatus is being constructed by the growing power of three other apparatuses: a new dominant neoeclectic mainstream apparatus, and two relatively recent, closely related emergent apparatuses. I am not denying that these apparatuses may have histories of their own, but as their places and relative power to speak for rock culture have changed, their relations to each other have also been significantly restructured.

The apparatus that is "becoming dominant" is a new mainstream[42] that actually looks a lot like and is committed to much of the logic of the Top 40. Top 40 has a long history, and it is one of the most frequently ignored (and commercially successful) apparatuses of popular music itself. But before the present moment, it has never really had the authority to speak for or even as the larger rock formation. Top 40 has always been hybrid, bringing together in a statistical sample the disparate tastes of various taste cultures. The result is a collection of music the totality of which no one actually liked, but that, given the alternatives, many people listened to. Yet I believe that today the dominant apparatus embraces a similar kind of eclecticism. Rather than claiming some sort of rock purism, it celebrates rock hybridity at its most extreme and celebrates as well its own eclecticism. On one level, at least, it refuses to draw and empower generic distinctions as meaningful. It does not set classic rock, rap, country, and so forth in opposition, but rather embraces at least selected examples of each. In fact, this apparatus—and the individuals within it—embrace an extraordinarily wide and (at least by my musical sensibilities) jarring range of music. The fans within this formation may like some classic rock, some country, some punk, some disco, some rap, and so on.[43] And because these fans happily switch among these genres from song to song, spending an evening with them can be a strange experience for someone who still lives within the becoming-residual formation.

This is not to claim that this neoeclectic mainstream gives up all distinctions or judgments, since it is selective about what songs it includes in its own space of acceptability. It refuses to allow popularity or radio play entirely to define inclusion (as in Top 40), but instead relies on the judgments of specific members with investments in particular genres and sounds (although such investments can never be so strong as to result in the exclusion of other genres and sounds). In other words, rather than either success or authenticity, this apparatus operates with a logic of sampling in both senses of the term (i.e., as a production technique and a habit of listening). This apparatus willingly embraces, simultaneously, the global megastar and the local rebel, the rock star who requires an appearance of authenticity and the dance music star who couldn't care less about it. Particular embodiments of this apparatus are not built on judgments about the categorization of music but rely more on collective judgments of quality and taste. And while such judgments are sometimes rhetorically framed within a discourse of authenticity and cooptation, even the briefest analysis reveals that these categories are neither consistently deployed nor affectively charged. People dislike what they dislike (or what particular individuals in the group dislike) but they do so largely without the mediations of a logic of authenticity.

Moreover, if those located within such an apparatus are eclectic about their own musical tastes, they are also tolerant about musical tastes more generally. That is, they do not seem to use musical taste and judgment as the basis for a differentiating logic, and while they continue to judge other people's tastes, such tastes are not taken as the grounds for other larger and more significant types of judgments of other people or groups. They have largely given up the differentiating function of rock even as they attempt to hold onto its "territorializing function" in relation to a politics of fun and everyday life. They are tolerant beyond anything that the once dominant, now residual, paradigm could understand. Taste is increasingly lived as if it were merely a site for individuality and shared entertainment, nothing more and nothing less. Finally, this apparatus cannot be described in the first instance as a musical formation, because its center is defined as much by other sorts of practices, activities, and media—including film, television, videogames, and computers—as by musical ones. Often they like music because of the other activities (e.g., collective movement through line dancing) that it enables them to carry out. It is not that the music is not there all the time, but that the quality (rather than the quantity) of the investment in it has changed. Music's power is increasingly defined by its relation to other activities and functions.

Consequently, within this apparatus music's ability to organize other investments, to define what matters, has diminished considerably. I suppose one could argue that this is a nonutopian yet integrative apparatus (unlike the older apparatus, which tended to be utopian and disintegrative). Yet it is also cynical: if those within this apparatus embrace commodification without illusions, it is because they cannot imagine an outside to or a way out of commodification. If they continue to seek a way to challenge everyday life, they can only imagine such a challenge within an economy of pure entertainment as an isolatable fraction of their lives. They are no longer "dancing all over their blues" but "for their right to party," for some claim to feel and care, usually about each other rather than about the music, and to reassert some sense of their own agency, even if it is within an extraordinarily constricted space within their own lives. I think that some people have misunderstood and misjudged this apparatus because they have not understood it in relation to the context from which it emerges and to which it responds. In those terms, it is, as much as any other rock apparatus, a way for youth to survive the conditions of its subjection and subjectification, to make it through the day. Is this resistance? I see no reason to call it that (although it is a necessary condition for resistance). But I don't think resistance is what the effectivity of rock is generally about, and I doubt that the vast majority of rock apparatuses, or of logics of consumption, have ever actually functioned as resistance as such.

To be honest, I have yet to figure out the politics of style, and the relationship between image and performance, in this apparatus. It is perhaps too early to know the answer, but the question of the meaning of live performance is a different matter. In fact, I can find little or no evidence that any significance is attached to it; there is little or no commitment to the value or necessity of live performances in defining some sort of unmediated relation to the performer and the music. The performative side of rock seems to be simply another occasion, another activity, with no privilege beyond that of a night out on the town, a potentially good time. Such occasions are important opportunities for a variety of social activities (dancing, hanging out, driving, drinking, drugs) in addition to the music itself, as well as being occasions for making identity-claims that everyone knows to be somewhat artificial and temporary.

In addition, contemporary rock culture involves at least two intertwined "emergent" apparatuses, both built on a reorganization of the fan's investment in the music. This combination is the third apparatus, which is based on a spatial reorganization of the relations and investments that constitute the apparatus itself. The music and fans are organized around various networks of dispersed and differentiated local scenes. A scene is not only geographically identifiable; it also defines its own systems of differentiation that are not binary but territorializing.[44] This apparatus is already redefining the notion of authenticity, and even affecting the operation of the concept in the residual rock formation. Authenticity here is spatial rather than temporal; it is a measure of commitment to and investment in a particular place, although place itself is also being redefined within the logic of this apparatus,[45] and to particular networks of places. Part of the specificity of this apparatus is that a scene, despite the attempts of the industry to give it musical content, is usually defined less by a sound than by a social style and/or a set of social relationships and allegiances. Thus scenes can bring together dance, rap, and alternative musical communities. In fact, most of the scenes, if viewed from inside (i.e., the logic of consumption) rather than through the lens of a logic of production, are marked by a range of diverse musical styles (e.g., Minneapolis, Austin, or Chapel Hill). That is, scenes have no generic identity and hence they are not equivalent to the commercialized notion of scenes, which are actually residual and/or mainstream formations. Here the function of live performance is obvious—it involves the constitution and affirmation of the local scene through a sense of a local space of performance. On the other hand, the relation between performance and image is more difficult to analyze, precisely because the scene can be so diverse. The relation is more polyvalent and situational than in other apparatuses; rather than defining a single standard or proper relationship, such scenes are bound to celebrate the possibility of diversity on almost every dimension, even while they hold onto a rearticulated notion of authenticity.

These spatial scenes are often utopian, precisely because they are based on an integration of the audience, even while they compulsively differentiate themselves from (and from alliances with) other scenes. I am convinced that this logic operates at the center and border (simultaneously) of everyday life by constructing a series of identifications among the various populations integrated into the self-representations of the scene. One result of the system of identifications on which this apparatus is constructed involves an interesting transformation of both the rock and roll apparatus of the 1950s and the increasingly residual apparatus of the 1960s and 1970s. In these apparatuses there was an important but imaginary system of identifications across both racial and class lines. For example, in their music white kids lived out a fantasy of being black. Yet, at the same time, youth as the site of optimism, celebration, and investment contradicted the very sense of oppression and marginality that marked the assumed experience of being black. But one of the very conditions of possibility (and effects) of the apparatus of scenes is that these systems of identifications have become real. That is, within the apparatus the shared social conditions of youth are producing an actual sense of equivalence across class and race; the identifications are becoming (or lived) as increasingly real. To be young and to be black are more and more alike because they mark the shared reality of oppression and exploitation. Youth no longer contradicts race.

The fourth apparatus—"dance"—is similar to the apparatus of scenes (and much of what I have said about the latter is true of the former as well), although I am less certain about how to describe it or what its limits and parameters are. The reorganization of the relations and investments of this apparatus is defined by the body as much as by the music, and by a series of bodily activities, most centrally dancing, that become the affective alibi of the music itself. This dance apparatus has explicit ties with (and may include) hip hop culture, but it hybridizes hip hop, disco, techno, "world beat," and so forth into a vibrant, largely urban "house" culture. Here live performance is increasingly irrelevant except insofar as it is the audience (and the mediated performance of the music by the deejay and/or the technology) that is performing. The "original" is irrelevant, mediation is everything. While it began as a variant of a logic of scenes (with the distinctions between dance cultures across space being as important as what happened in the local scenes), I think that hybridization across scenes has overpowered the scenes themselves, creating a rapidly changing global apparatus. The odd thing about this apparatus is that, like certain instances of a scene, it returns to a logic of authenticity (most clearly imported through rap but no longer contained there). While the rhetoric of authenticity within such an apparatus often echoes that of the once dominant 1960s and 1970s apparatus, I think its notion of authenticity is significantly different, since it is based on very different forms of investment and judgment. It celebrates its marginality not in spatial terms as an investment in the local (as opposed to the globality of capitalism) but in terms of its social marginality and (explicit) claim to resistance. And this marginality is, at least in the United States, partially exhibited by the very fact of the failure of this apparatus to find a significant presence in the mainstream musical media.

The third aspect of my disappointment in popular music studies was, as stated above, the all-too-frequent absence, on the part of scholars working in the field, of a politics that comes out of and responds to the field on which they are working. The first dimension of that politics has to be a theoretically informed reflection on the politics of the various apparatuses themselves. I do not want to claim that any apparatus determines its own appropriate politics, but it is the case that particular apparatuses are being articulated to specific political positions and struggles, and that they at least open or close new political possibilities. Here I want to make three observations. First, I am cautiously optimistic about the possibilities of articulating the two emergent formations (and even the new mainstream) to an effective progressive politics. Certainly there is a growing sense within these apparatuses that youth is getting screwed and this opens the door to an explicitly antagonistic politics, operating on the borders of everyday life by imagining an identification between country's poor white trash, black youth, and white middle-class youth, between male and female, between gay and straight. Punk tried to get to such a politics, but in the end it failed (perhaps because it also failed, even though it tried, to escape the once dominant, now residual apparatus). Somewhere among these new apparatuses, I would like to begin to imagine new possibilities for a popular politics.

But I do not want to put such optimism forward without a necessary pessimism. The new mainstream is easily articulated to a new individualism and apathy, which taken together have become the primary response to social changes in the past decades. My greatest pessimism, however, is reserved for what has happened, increasingly, to the once dominant rock apparatus (and to those who grew up within its logics, the so-called baby boomers). For I think that a significant proportion of the baby boomers have become the biggest stumbling block to a progressive politics, especially one willing and able to take up the struggle over and on behalf of youth and childhood in U.S. society. It is precisely those generations, which themselves benefited from an enormous social and economic investment in youth, that seem to have abandoned youth (and even joined the attack) in the 1990s.

Whatever dimension of social and quotidian life one takes as a measure, the condition of youth in this country (and around the world) has declined precipitously. The struggles of the 1960s to empower youth have disappeared from visible national politics. Moreover, in many cases the undermining of whatever gains were made by these struggles in postwar America seems to have become one of the leading goals and strategies of the new and fragile alliance between neoconservatism and neoliberalism. And the hypocrisy of the baby boomers has become a key weapon in such struggles: generations that indulged in sex, drugs, and rock and roll now tolerate and even support what can only be described as wars against sexuality, drugs, and popular music. Demanding lower taxes and reduced government, these generations witness if not demand the deconstruction of all the institutions that enabled them to "succeed." Acceding to the increasingly powerful representations of youth as simultaneously helpless (in need of radical forms of protection and incapable and undeserving of any freedoms, rights, or self-expression) and dangerous (allowed to be criminalized, penalized as adults, incarcerated, and increasingly monitored in every aspect of their lives), these generations are producing a generation gap that is far worse than that which it embraced in its youth. And because this gap continues to be unrecognized, because it is deemed unworthy of being allowed into public expression and consciousness, its consequences are potentially devastating.

Whatever the problems of trying to represent others, it is clear today that youth needs both allies and representatives. Where are the advocates for youth? Where are the scholars who force the issue onto the public agenda? Where are the teachers who provide youth with the resources they need to understand how their conditions are being produced, and how they are connected through those conditions with other populations that are also being attacked and devastated, across every aspect and dimension of life, by the new politics? And where are the people who, embracing the energy of popular music, can share with them the faith they need to struggle against these conditions? I don't want to sound naïve, but is it entirely unreasonable to think that some of this has to come from those of us most intimately involved with their cultures, even if that involvement is always mediated by conceptual and research agendas. But, to return to my first argument, the possibility of such interventions depends in part on our ability to gain a better understanding of what is going on and how it is being produced. And to do that, I am firmly convinced that we need to develop theoretical resources adequate to the task. The fact that some of us, as popular music researchers, use that music (and often its relation to youth cultures) to cut into the question of what is going on would seem to accentuate our political responsibilities and the unavoidable articulations between politics and theory. But my sense is that there is little commitment to engage with such a project. In my more cynical moments I wonder whether popular music studies has not become an exemplary field for the new century: interdisciplinary and yet with no theoretical anxieties and no political pressures. And that is my ultimate disappointment.

Notes

An early version of this paper was first delivered at the Dia Foundation conference "Stars Don't Stand Still in the Sky: Music and Myth" New York, February 1997, and later published in Karen Kelly and Evelyn McDonnell, eds., *Stars Don't Stand Still in the Sky: Music and Myth* (New York: New York University Press, 1999).

I want to thank the editors of this volume, especially Roger Beebe, for their useful criticisms and suggestions.

1. Lawrence Grossberg, *Bringing It All Back Home: Essays on Cultural Studies* (Durham: Duke University Press, 1997), 237.

2. Ibid., 271.

3. Raymond Williams, *The Politics of Modernism* (London: Verso, 1989), 158.

4. I am always surprised to see how many people still use Frith as the latest statement of our understanding of rock (Simon Frith, *Sound Effects* [New York: Pantheon, 1981]).

5. Although obviously the very fact of my decision, twenty years ago, to teach and write about popular music already embodies a set of judgments. But I don't want to talk about issues of what is good or bad music in my classes. I don't want to talk about my taste, if only because I believe that taste is always determined elsewhere through a complex set of relations. The question of quality, of which music is good or bad according to whatever criterion one might use, is only interesting and important, at least within the project I am trying to describe, in the very last instance.

6. Quoted in D. A. Miller, "Place for Us (Essay on the Broadway Musical)" (Cambridge: Harvard University Press, 1998).

7. See Meaghan Morris, *Upward Mobility: Popular Genres and Cultural Change* (Bloomington: University of Indiana Press, 1998).

8. John Frow, *Cultural Studies and Cultural Value* (Oxford: Oxford University Press, 1995), 87.

9. For example, although we know little about the actual financial operations of the industry, we do have some good studies of the general business/production process; see Rob Burnet, *The Global Jukebox* (London: Routledge, 1996); and Keith Negus, *Producing Pop* (London: Edward Arnold, 1992). We also have learned about the sociology of the music in various forms; see Sarah Thornton, *Club Culture* (Cambridge,

Eng.: Polity, 1995); Sara Cohen, *Rock Culture in Liverpool* (London: Clarendon, 1991); and Ruth Finnegan, *The Hidden Musician* (Cambridge: Cambridge University Press, 1989). And we have begun to explore the functioning of race and gender relations in music culture; see Simon Jones, *Black Culture, White Youth* (London: Macmillan, 1988).

10. I do not intend the division between the empirical and the interpretive to be taken literally or too seriously. It is a shorthand way of describing different projects and styles within scholarly work on popular music.

11. For some excellent studies of genres, see Robert Walser, *Running with the Devil: Power, Gender, and Madness in Heavy Metal Music* (Hanover, N.H.: Wesleyan University Press, 1993); and David Laing, *One Chord Wonders* (Milton Keynes, Eng.: Open University Press, 1985). Also, there are interesting detailed historical studies of the interrelation of music and other cultural practices in Van Cagle, *Reconstructing Pop/Subculture* (Thousand Oaks, Calif.: Sage, 1995).

12. The criticism is also true of much of my own work. Although I attempted to take a range of possible apparatuses into account, I still assumed a set of conditions of possibility that bound those apparatuses together. Thus, I do not mean to reject this practice but just to argue that, for the field, it is insufficient if left to stand on its own. I would also argue that if the location of the discourse is defined by a single apparatus and remains unacknowledged, this does present serious problems. For examples that, to varying extents, speak from within a particular apparatus, see Deena Weinstein, *Heavy Metal* (New York: Lexington, 1991); Tricia Rose, *Black Noise* (Hanover, N.H.: Wesleyan University Press, 1994); Paul Friedlander, *Rock & Roll* (Boulder: Westview, 1996); Reebee Garofalo, *Rockin' Out* (Boston: Allyn and Bacon, 1997); Craig Werner, *A Change Is Gonna Come* (New York: Plume, 1998); Johan Fornas, Ulf Lindberg, and Ove Sernhede, *In Garageland* (London: Routledge, 1995); and John Street, *Rebel Rock* (Oxford: Blackwells, 1986). This is often a common practice of rock criticism, including most of the work of such important and insightful critics as Greil Marcus and Dave Marsh, as well as the work of many of the younger punk and post-punk critics, including Kodwo Eshun, *More Brilliant than the Sun* (London: Quartet, 1998); and Jon Savage, *Time Travel* (London: Chatto and Windus, 1996).

13. Television scholars, for example, are only now beginning to confront a comparable problem with the proliferation of channels, technologies, modes of delivery, and so forth. Yet, when dealing with popular music, not only is such diversity and quantity the norm, it has almost always been the case.

14. I do not mean to take a position on the nature of concepts here. Actually, my own understanding of concepts would probably be close to that of Walter Benjamin (concepts cut into the real) or Deleuze and Guattari (concepts have a direct material relationship to the real). See Gilles Deleuze and Félix Guattari, *A Thousand Plateaus:*

Capitalism and Schizophrenia, trans. Brian Massumi (Minneapolis: University of Minnesota Press, 1987).

15. But in no sense would I equate theories with ways of analyzing.

16. On culture, see Zygmunt Bauman, *Legislators and Interpreters* (Cambridge, Eng.: Polity, 1987); and Lawrence Grossberg, "The Victory of Culture, Part I: Against the Logic of Mediation" (*Angelaki* 3 [December 1998]: 3–30). On the genealogy of sound, see Jonathan Sterne, "The Audible Past: Modernity, Technology, and the Cultural History of Sound" (Ph.D. diss., University of Illinois at Urbana, 1999).

17. Warren Zanes's work (see his essay in this volume) is an important exception, as it tries to explore some of these issues.

18. Giorgio Agamben, *The Coming Community,* trans. Michael Hardt (Minneapolis: University of Minnesota Press, 1993).

19. Of course, such a binary question is also constitutive of certain forms of critical theory, although it is opposed by cultural studies. See Stuart Hall, "Notes on Deconstructing the Popular," in *People's History and Socialist Theory,* ed. Ralph Samuels (London: Routledge and Kegan Paul, 1981).

20. I recognize that film is a medium as well as a broad cultural form, while popular music is not in any usual sense a medium.

21. This is not to say that everyone writing about film has joined the conversation, but it seems to me that even someone who rejects the semiotic/psychoanalytic/marxist discourse of this theory has to define himself or herself against this theory. I also want to avoid celebrating the historical moment of *Screen* theory or the practices by which it was, however briefly, made hegemonic—there were a lot of negative aspects and results of the historical moment. I only mean to appropriate its model of general and specific concepts.

22. Similarly, Lynn Spigel's *Make Room for TV* (Chicago: University of Chicago Press, 1992) transformed the field of television history. See also John Ellis, *Visible Fictions: Cinema, Television, Video* (London: Routledge & Kegan Paul, 1982).

23. I do not mean to claim that there is no work in the field that attempts to bring theory into its researches in significant ways. As one might imagine, the success of the projects varies enormously, both in terms of how sophisticated and self-reflective the theory is and how well it is integrated into the argument. Previous attempts also differ significantly on the question of whether the theory they use is related in any way to the specificity of music. See, for example, Dick Bradley, *Understanding Rock 'n' Roll* (Buckingham, Eng.: Open University Press, 1992); David Laing, "Rock Anxieties and New Music Networks," in Angela McRobbie, ed., *Back to Reality? Social Experience and Cultural Studies* (Manchester: University of Manchester Press, 1997), 116–32; Andrew Goodwin, *Dancing in the Distraction Factory* (Minneapolis: University of Minnesota Press, 1992); Richard A. Peterson, *Creating Country Music: Fabricating Authen-*

ticity (Chicago: University of Chicago Press, 1997); and Alan Durant, *Conditions of Music* (London: Macmillan, 1984). Others have done interesting things with broader borrowings from cultural theory, again with varying degrees of success and interest. See Steve Redhead, *The End-of-the-Century Party* (Manchester: University of Manchester Press, 1990); Lipsitz *Time Passages, Collective Memory and American Popular Culture* (Minneapolis: University of Minnesota Press, 1990); Angela McRobbie, *Postmodernism and Popular Culture* (London: Routledge, 1994); Theodore Gracyk, *Rhythm and Noise* (Durham: Duke University Press, 1996); Tony Mitchell, *Popular Music and Local Identity* (London: Leicester University Press, 1996); Sanjay Sharma, John Hutnyk, and Ashwanu Sharma, *Disorienting Rhythms: The Politics of New Asian Dance Music* (London: Zed, 1996); and Simon Reynolds and Joy Press, *The Sex Revolts* (Cambridge: Harvard University Press, 1995). Still, I would argue that almost none of these examples has gone far enough to theorize the specificity of popular music.

24. See, for example, Dominic Strinati, *An Introduction to Theories of Popular Culture* (London: Routledge, 1995); and John Storey, ed., *Cultural Theory and Popular Culture,* 2nd ed. (Athens: University of Georgia Press, 1998).

25. Without such theoretical work, such terms are little more than mystifications.

26. See, for example, Keith Negus, *Popular Music in Theory* (Cambridge, Eng.: Polity, 1996); Roy Shuker, *Understanding Popular Music* (London: Routledge, 1994); and Brian Longhurst, *Popular Music and Society* (Cambridge, Eng.: Polity, 1995).

27. Jacques Attali, *Noise: The Political Economy of Music,* trans. Brian Massumi (Minneapolis: University of Minnesota Press, 1985); Deleuze and Guattari, *A Thousand Plateaus;* and Paul Carter, *The Sound in Between* (Kensington, Aus.: New South Wales University Press, 1992). There is also a long history of the philosophy and theory of sound and music, which has spilled over into anthropology, communication, and technology studies, as well as musicology (see works by Wilfrid Mellers) and ethnomusicology (see works by Charles Hamm and Bruno Nettl). See, for example, Malcolm Budd, *Music and the Emotions: The Philosophical Theories* (London: Routledge, 1985). There is also an extensive body of work on oral cultures of which Ong is the most frequently cited representative. Additionally, there is a large body of social theorizing on music, including writings by Theodor Adorno, Max Weber, Hans Werner Henze, Hanns Eisler, and Alphons Silberman.

28. John Shepherd and Peter Wicke, *Music and Cultural Theory* (Cambridge, Eng.: Polity, 1997); Mark Slobin, *Subcultural Sounds* (Hanover, N.H.: Wesleyan University Press, 1993); Don Ihde, *Listening and Voice* (Athens: University of Georgia Press, 1978); David Sudnow, *Ways of the Hand* (Cambridge: Harvard University Press, 1978); Susan Crafts, Daniel Cavicchi, and Charles Keil, *My Music* (Hanover, N.H.: Wesleyan University Press, 1993); and Michel Chion, *Audio-Vision,* trans. Claudia Gorbman (New York: Columbia University Press, 1990).

29. As one might imagine, the success of the projects varies enormously, both in terms of how sophisticated and self-reflective the theory is, and how well it is integrated into the empirical argument. They also differ significantly on the question of whether the theory they use is related in any way to the specificity of music and the popular. But it is worth looking at, for example, Charles Keil and Steven Feld, *Music Grooves* (Chicago: University of Chicago Press, 1994); Will Straw, "Systems of Articulation, Logics of Change," *Cultural Studies* 5 (1991): 368–88; Charles J. Stivale, "Of *Hecceitis* and *Ritournelles:* Movement and Affect in the Cajun Dance Arena," in *Articulating the Global and the Local,* ed. Ann Cvetkovich and Douglas Kellner (Boulder: Westview, 1997), 129–48; Paul Theberge, *Any Sound You Can Imagine: Making Music/Consuming Technology* (Hanover, N.H.: Wesleyan University Press, 1997); Bradley, *Understanding Rock 'n' Roll;* Laing, *One Chord Wonders;* Goodwin, *Dancing in the Distraction Factory;* Peterson, *Creating Country Music;* and Durant, *Conditions of Music.* Others have done interesting things with broader borrowings from cultural theory, again with varying degrees of success and interest; see Redhead, *End-of-the-Century Party;* Lipsitz, *Time Passages;* McRobbie, *Postmodernism and Popular Culture;* Gracyk, *Rhythm and Noise:* Mitchell, *Popular Music and Local Identity;* Sharma, Hutnyk, and Sharma, *Disorienting Rhythms;* and Reynolds and Press, *The Sex Revolts.* Still, I would argue that almost none of the work in these examples has gone far enough to theorize the specificity of popular music.

30. Simon Frith, *Performing Rites* (Cambridge: Harvard University Press, 1996).

31. Steve Jones has suggested to me that another reason may be that the study of popular music, unlike either film or television studies (and like "internet studies") does not actually define a specific medium.

32. Interestingly, such relations may be becoming more common as a generation raised on television and other forms of popular culture comes to power in the academy (see Sterne, "The Audible Past"). It is interesting to think about why the concept of "visual culture" has become so popular without a parallel construction of "sound culture." See Gilbert B. Rodman, *Elvis after Elvis* (London: Routledge, 1996).

33. See Lawrence Grossberg, *We Gotta Get Out of This Place: Popular Conservatism and Postmodern Culture* (New York: Routledge, 1992) and *Dancing in Spite of Myself: Essays on Popular Culture* (Durham: Duke University Press, 1997), for earlier but more elaborate presentations of many of the arguments presented here.

34. Laing, in "Rock Anxieties and New Music Networks," is correct to point out that I have often not stressed this last point enough. I suppose I assumed it was obvious when I should not have.

35. I think the fact that rock culture is willing to acknowledge its debt to black culture and music but always seems to underestimate its relation to country and western culture and music can be explained in part in these terms.

36. I should admit that of these terms, the only one that I would claim operates at some level of generality with respect to both the popular and the music is the first (affectivity), although I am increasingly convinced by Sterne's argument (in "The Audible Past") that even this mode of effectivity has to be taken contextually and genealogically.

37. These apparatuses do not correlate in any simple way with radio formats, partly because, as has commonly been observed, the logic of economics of radio is significantly different from that of the music industry.

38. Williams continues: "At certain points the dominant culture cannot allow too much residual experience and practice outside itself, at least without risk. It is in the incorporation of the actively residual—by reinterpretation, dilution, projection, discrimination, inclusion and exclusion—that the work of the selective tradition is especially evident" (Raymond Williams, *Marxism and Literature* [Oxford: Oxford University Press, 1977], 123).

39. After all, in commercial terms the dominant forms of popular music would be pop, Top 40, and so forth. Both of these overlapping apparatuses exist outside of any logic of distinction, the former often characteristic of preadolescent tastes. The Top 40 has become more interesting since the mid-1980s and the emergence of what can be called, following Tony Kirschner, a "hip mainstream." But these must still be recognized as changing apparatuses; for example, it would be interesting to talk about the changing temporality of pop—in the 1990s one heard statements like, "oh, that's so 1994" and even, "oh, that's so five minutes ago."

40. See for example, Friedlander, *Rock & Roll;* Garofalo, *Rockin' Out;* Werner, *A Change Is Gonna Come;* and Street, *Rebel Rock,* as well as the writings of critics such as Greil Marcus and Dave Marsh.

41. But note that "authenticity" means different things in the different logics of consumption of these apparatuses. While the logic of production of rap might be built on sampling, it still operates with an ideological and logic of authenticity.

42. Note that the mainstream is not always the dominant apparatus of rock.

43. This description is based on ethnographic research I conducted with a group of high school students during summer 1995 in Illinois. In fact, there were limits to the generic possibilities for the kids in the group—they were unwilling to listen to techno, for example, but even that might have changed when they were in college. Also, interestingly, these kids were not, despite common assumptions, into computer culture as much as video games.

44. See Straw, "Systems of Articulation," and Mark J. V. Olson, " 'Everybody Loves Our Town': Scenes, Spatiality, Migrancy," in *Mapping the Beat,* ed. Thomas Swiss, John Sloop, and Andrew Herman (Oxford: Blackwells, 1998).

45. For a discussion of the meaning of place, see Doreen Massey, *Space, Place, and Gender* (Cambridge, Eng.: Polity, 1994).

ROBERT FINK ✳ ELVIS EVERYWHERE: MUSICOLOGY AND POPULAR MUSIC STUDIES AT THE TWILIGHT OF THE CANON

This essay is an expanded version of a paper originally delivered at a 1996 conference, "Representing Rock," sponsored by the English department of an East Coast university. I was one of a small group of gate-crashing musicologists who slipped onto the program to address the very question of why (or whether) we should be there at all. The argument and tone of the present version still retain the performative tension of that rather tense interdisciplinary essay, and I beg the musicological reader's indulgence for passages of exposition—and the inevitable oversimplifications and tendentions as I work my way through an avowedly programmatic piece of disciplinary diplomacy.

In particular, I saw the task that afternoon of my lecture as interpreting the "New Musicology"—and specifically new musicological relationships with popular music—for popular music scholars outside of academic music departments. Much work on popular music within cultural studies, communications, and sociology proceeds largely unaware of the recent and intense ferment of ideological self-critique within musicology. Scholars can be cut off from valuable syncretic insights into musical culture by out-of-date dualisms marching in lockstep: musicology versus cultural studies, analysis versus interpretation, even classical music versus popular music.

That last binarism seems to underpin all the rest, and it seems especially indefensible under present cultural conditions. The driving assumption in what follows—a wide-ranging, idiosyncratic survey of cultural trends, ideological battles, and methodological issues—is that the ruling hierarchy of musical styles that supported the very idea of "classical music" in Western (particularly American) culture for the last two centuries is simply no longer operative. Musicology, long viewed as both a constituent and a beneficiary of that hierarchy, needs to be reconceptualized for what Joseph Horowitz has presciently dubbed "the post-classical" era.

And if it appears that the hierarchy of musicological style has collapsed in what follows—well, that is, for better or worse, intentional.

Introduction: The "Musicological Problem"

[Low fidelity recording:] "You can't play if you can't do Elvis. Can you do Elvis?" The twangy, impatient voice is that of an unnamed impersonator of—who else?—Elvis Presley, and as it happens, her question is a digital sample, a piece of musique concrete. It is the first of many samples of Elvis impersonation that composer Michael Daugherty (more on him later) incorporated into an encore for the Kronos Quartet that he called *Elvis Everywhere* (a perhaps unintentional homage to Mojo Nixon's infamous "Elvis Is Everywhere"?). Our sampled faux-Elvis is too busy launching into a truly unfortunate rendition of "Viva Las Vegas" to raise metatheoretical issues, but her question resonates: Can academic musicologists "do Elvis"? Can we add anything of value to the study of popular music? Are musicologists who venture out from their crumbling ivory towers of Music Appreciation doomed to be the Elvis impersonators of popular music studies—wiggling our hips as best we can, slipping a "Hey baby" or two in among the chord analyses and the surveys of historical influence, as we try to look cool?

That has certainly been the fate of many of us. Popular music scholars have been telling musicologists for the last decade that if we want to come out and play with them our unique disciplinary training is in fact a crushing liability. A key moment in almost every recent metatheoretical book on pop music studies has been a stern warning against institutionalized musicology: David Brackett tells us to steer clear of "the musicological quagmire"; Richard Middleton seeks to avoid "the musicological problem." Almost ten years ago, and from the inside, Susan McClary and Robert Walser were exhorting scholars of classical music to abandon "the hidden ideological claptrap of their musicological training."[1] One cannot fault the accuracy of the picture. If only all practitioners of "traditional" musicology could see themselves this clearly!

Musicology is not historically neutral; it has not always "been there." It arose at a specific moment, in a specific context (nineteenth-century Europe, especially Germany) and in close association with the movement in the musical practice of the period that was codifying the very repertory taken by musicology as the center of its attention. The result was an evolutionary sense of history (progress being usually defined in terms of structural complexity, "intellectual" level, and expressive capacity), intertwined with the notion of a canon of "good music." For the core of musicology, the main assumptions remain strong: works are autonomous; art has transcendent qualities; the individual, the genius, the "great man" should be the focus of historical explanation; listening should be detached and contemplative, and analysis therefore text centered.[2]

For many popular music scholars, it has been axiomatic that a discipline so ideologically compromised by its narrow focus on Western art music is not going to travel well, especially "down scale," to the kind of music that most musicologists have spent their professional lives pointedly ignoring. But the "core of musicology"—even the idea that musicology has a single ideological core—was already under internal attack when Middleton read its beads so dispassionately; and there has been a steady increase in the amount and intensity of self-criticism within academic musicology since.[3] It was only a year or two after the above paragraph was written that people began talking about a "New Musicology"—a gawky, speculative set of interdisciplinary trends that bore little resemblance to the traditional discipline whose methodological and ideological rigidity popular music scholars had feared and shunned for decades. Given the intense reevaluation of dogma roiling within the musicological quagmire, it seems appropriate to speculate on what the changes within our discipline taking place under the rubric the "New Musicology" mean for popular music studies. Has anything really changed in that swamp? And why should anybody outside of the (Classical) Music Department care?[4]

We might begin by asking, from the perspective of popular music studies, just what a "New" Musicologist might look like. A shorthand definition: a New Musicologist looks at institutionalized musicology from the *inside* the way popular music scholars have always looked at it from the *outside:* with a certain ideological suspicion. The New Musicology is one product of a decade-long general disciplinary crisis within the academic study of music. In a sense it represents a generational split; it is the collapse for many younger scholars of some of the field's ruling ideological assumptions, often as a result of acknowledging the very historical contingencies catalogued by Middleton above. (In other words, New Musicology is what you get when musicologists themselves become aware of the musicological problem.) There is a large overlap between these so-called New Musicologists and the small but growing number of "crossover" musicologists who study popular music from within traditional music departments; for many of us, it seems natural to combine new approaches to canonical classical music with interest in various repertories of popular music, especially post-1955 rock and pop.

These linked imperatives—to expand the field of study, to change the methodology and ideology of the discipline—represent more than just a hankering after something "new." As Middleton points out, the ideological and professional moorings of academic musicology are driven deep into the bedrock of the canon of classical music it grew up with, around, and for. Thus it should come as no surprise that the ideological collapse that engendered the New Musicology is in many ways the internal consequence of the most profound external shock to hit American musicology in its brief seventy-five-year history: the imminent collapse of the cultural authority of the classical music canon. Digging out from the aftermath of this tectonic shift, battered and chastened, our "mainstream" academic musicology and its once-privileged repertoire are no longer the complacent, convenient targets they once were for popular music studies.

We have our own problems now.

Beethoven Has Left the Building (Tales from the Collapse of the Canon)
Classical Music Is Dead?

The most pressing problem is that we may soon have nothing (living) left to study. As the new millennium begins, surveys of the classical music world have become astonishingly apocalyptic in tone. To judge from the pages of the *New York Times* or the reports of the American Symphony Orchestra League, we are in the End Times, and the arrival of Antichrist, in the form of either the latest popular music style or the next advance in the storage and distribution of sonic entertainment, is close at hand. "The (Unnatural) Death of Classical Music" is now a standard journalistic trope, so accepted that reporter-gadfly Norman Lebrecht has begun looking for someone to take the rap. His book-length exposé *Who Killed Classical Music?* (1997) fingers winner-take-all market capitalism and a cabal of predatory managers, impresarios, and record company executives. Lebrecht's hysterical conspiracy theories skate over abysses of systemic cultural and technological change, but his statistics, laid out in a grim "coroner's report," are impossible to ignore. As aging audiences quite literally die off, school music programs vanish, regional orchestras collapse, and U.S. classical record sales drop below 2 percent of the industry total, we must all admit it: Beethoven has finally rolled over.

Indignant partisans will point out, quite correctly, that in absolute terms classical music has never been so widespread; certain genres, most notably opera, are even enjoying a moderate growth spurt. But the problem is really one of market share: the vastly expanded realm we now recognize as "American culture" simply dwarfs the puny scale of even the healthiest classical music institutions. Sometimes the material consequences are humiliatingly obvious: Lebrecht has wicked fun pointing out that the entire budget of Sony's classical music subsidiary is less money than the conglomerate has tied up in a single notoriously unstable pop star like Michael Jackson; when one of Jacko's records tanks, dozens of arty projects at what used to be Columbia Masterworks go down with it.[5]

But even the least vulgar marxist will recognize that this shift in the music industry's base is bound to have some more general effects on the superstructure. Classical music long ago ceded economic primacy to pop; but as the shelf space devoted to it in the American cultural supermarket decreases to the vanishing point, when the majority of educated middle-class professionals have entirely lost sight of it, something new happens. For the first time in a century, classical music has lost even its symbolic or ritualistic power to define hierarchies of taste within the larger culture. Classical musicians have long complained, with voluptuous self-pity, that their position at the top of the hierarchy of musical taste was lonely, cold, and poorly paid. They will now have to get used to ceding that drafty, if prestigious, position altogether. Having long ago accepted loss of financial control (the final, bitter stages of this process are chronicled by Lebrecht), the institutions of classical music need to adjust to a much more disorienting loss of semiotic control. What they do is no longer paradigmatic; it is no longer Music-with-a-capital-M.

Classical musicians who venture out into the larger world of music will find this out the hard way; they are in for some rude shocks to their egos. David Schiff, composer, critic, and professor of music at Reed College, recently published what he intended as a blackly humorous account of his local orchestra's attempt to entice a faded pop star, the pseudonymous "Rock Bottom," into a crossover collaboration. Here is Schiff's mordant version of their first creative meeting:

> Bottom arrived ten minutes late and entered the room as if he knew he was walking into a booby trap. He looked fortyish and darkly handsome, more presentable than the Afro-haired, gold-necklaced disco idol I had found on the cover of an album from the seventies. [Oregon Symphony conductor Murray] Sidlin laid out the theme of the concert and expressed his hope that we could reach a common goal. . . . Bottom listened sullenly. "I have a few questions," he began. "First of all, I keep hearing this word 'collaboration.'" He glared across the room at me. "How is that supposed to happen?" Sidlin explained that he would like a piece demonstrating improvisation within different styles, including Baroque, Romantic, modern, and rock; I had written such a piece, he continued, which would alternate sections for the orchestra and the rock band. Bottom looked around the room with an expression of impatient disbelief and then his face lit up. "I know what you want. You want to give a concert of contemporary music. I am a contemporary musician. Let me tell you what you need to do." I had watched the term "music" become synonymous with "rock," at least in the weekly entertainment section of the Portland paper. *But this was the first time I had heard a rock musician claim the present historical moment exclusively for himself.* Bottom continued, an emerging mammal addressing dinosaurs. [emphasis mine][6]

Professor Schiff tries to be a good sport, but he clearly sees himself as the innocent victim in this spiky exchange. Who is this washed-up disco idol to dictate musical terms to a trained classical composer? The ironic truth is that Bottom is stepping into a booby trap; he has a much better right than Schiff to "claim the present historical moment exclusively for himself." The musical conception that emerges as the rock star lectures the orchestra management about the facts of contemporary concert life—each orchestra player must be individually miked, they will need a state-of-the-art amplification system to surround the audience with sound, an expanded virtuoso percussion section, and so on—sounds much more interesting and, well, contemporary than the paleozoic variations on (get this) "Hit the Road, Jack" that Schiff had planned. (It was a formulaic choice: however tired as pop music, "Hit the Road, Jack" has the descending minor tetrachord in its bass, a familiar tonal progression that has been the basis for many improvisatory forms in the history of Western art music.)

Note: The battle is not over money. (A simultaneous players' strike allows Schiff to demonstrate quite clearly that the Oregon Symphony's worst economic enemy is itself.) The fight is over something much dearer to a music professor's heart: cultural authority, specifically the authority, even in absentia, of the classical music canon. Rock Bottom is undeniably a contemporary musician; he is just not in David Schiff's musical canon. His rock-bottom music is not supposed to aspire to be canonical music (the music that needs no qualifying adjective like "rock" or "popular"), especially when Bottom is face to face with what is left of the classical institutions of what used to be canonical no-adjective-needed "Music." Unfortunately for Schiff, and all the rest of us making our living off that classical canon, its hegemony over musical culture is gone. Vignettes like this one occur all over the musical world every day.

What does it mean to say the cultural authority of the classical music canon is gone? Indulge me in a very synoptic overview. Since about 1830 or so we have lived in the West with a quite circumscribed repertoire of so-called Classical Music. Obviously not everyone listened primarily to this music—that was a large part of its class appeal—but almost everyone accepted that Beethoven was Music the way the Mona Lisa was (and still is) Art. From the late nineteenth century to about 1965, canonical European concert music occupied a secure—if hard-won—position at the top of a generally accepted hierarchy of musical culture.[7]

Lest I be misunderstood, let me point out that this relatively brief moment of classical music hegemony was hardly a "Golden Age" of natural cultural creativity and utopian relations between composers, performers, and audiences. Most of the canonical pieces that it enshrines were written well before the mummifying hierarchy of taste solidified around them. Even during the final middlebrow paroxysm of classical music canon worship (ca. 1930–1960), many commentators saw how canonic power was being deployed as much to discipline the disruptive forces of modern mass culture as to preserve and transmit a unique cultural heritage.[8]

In its heyday, this classical music canon had two secure domains: first, a performing canon of masterworks, centered in nineteenth-century Romanticism. This was art music for the masses—the repertoire of the conservatories, the big symphony orchestras, and the opera houses; "great" music hedged around with powerful social mystifications like genius, transcendence, and autonomy. Second, *an* avant-garde canon, also hedged around with powerful social mystifications like genius, transcendence, and autonomy. This was the realm of difficult and intellectually challenging "modern music," not much listened to outside of small coteries and (by the end) university music departments, but possessed of tremendous cultural authority.

Both of these domains are in the final stages of a forty-year collapse as we speak: as Rock Bottom's refusal to kowtow dramatizes, for the first time since the mid-nineteenth century, neither the performing canon (the Oregon Symphony) nor the avant-garde canon (Professor Schiff, contemporary composer) has any real authority in American culture. The cultural evidence is simply overwhelming, as the following quick survey of musical current events circa 1997 demonstrates.

The Disneyland Symphony Orchestra (Classical Music as Simulation)   First, the Masterwork Canon. One of the sad ironies of recent musicological discourse has been the amount of time we spend nerving ourselves up to challenge the awesome cultural power of the Great Works, when outside the Music Department that same music is, at best, marketing fodder and, at worst, totally ignored.[9] The Western classical music establishment today bears little resemblance to an oppressive fortress of High Art. The effort to keep the money coming in has turned it into something akin to Disneyland's Magic Kingdom: behind the papier-mâché battlements is a carnivalesque scene of frenzied and quasi-random marketing efforts. Onto the covers of classical CDs and record magazines troop phalanxes of sexpot violinists in revealing poses, diminutive virtuosi, floating monks—and at the head of the parade, the infamous Three Tenors, the single most popular classical music phenomenon of all time, hammering their way through famous opera arias, in unison and at great amplification, for soccer stadium after soccer stadium of enthralled "fans." Pallid collections of classical "greatest hits" are thematized according to time of day (Bach at Bedtime);

hawked by spurious scientific claims (Mozart Makes You Smarter); marketed like computer manuals (Beethoven for Dummies); even sorted by sexual preference (Sensual Classics, Out Classics). More and more traditional media outlets for high art music are, to paraphrase Daniel Patrick Moynihan, "defining classical music down." Turn from MTV to PBS in search of musical programming, and the only string players you can rely on seeing are those backing Yanni, Lawrence Welk, and John Tesh.

Representative of a historical moment, perhaps, was the sad saga of the *Shine* pianist, David Helfgott: a schizoid who had nothing left to offer audiences but a weird array of onstage tics and mannerisms; the remains of a fluent technique; and, crucially, the kind of gripping, if heavily fictionalized, dysfunctional life story familiar from tabloids and talk shows.[10] Yet his empty run-throughs of canonic warhorses topped the *Billboard* charts; his recording of Rachmaninoff's Third Concerto has by now probably outsold all others (including the composer's own and those of such crowd-pleasers as Horowitz and Van Cliburn) combined. I submit that this type of success could never happen with popular music, music most people actually know and care about. Brian Wilson may have been tragically poignant in the documentary *I Just Wasn't Made for These Times,* but old (or new!) Beach Boys records didn't start outselling Alanis Morrisette.

This is by no means the beginning of a neoconservative jeremiad about the corrupting effects of modern mass media on Great Art. None of the above is new; in fact, to a music historian the explosion of hype feels weirdly familiar. In its postcanonic state, the musical world is quite naturally starting to revert to the lineaments of its precanonic guise. After all, it was P. T. Barnum (of Barnum and Bailey fame) who successfully marketed the first classical music superstar back in 1850. Barnum only had one soprano to work with—not three tenors—but by the time he was done with Jenny Lind, the "Swedish Nightingale," she had become the biggest box-office draw in U.S. history. If the American classical music scene looks like a circus today, it is simply returning to its roots.

Joseph Horowitz sees Barnum as the epitome of an American tradition of "ballyhoo"—art as hype and spectacle—which has been fighting it out since the mid-nineteenth century with a Puritan marketing rubric of art as moral uplift.[11] The classical masterwork canon has always been firmly on the side of selling art as serious moral endeavor; indeed, the more strenuous the rhetoric of uplift, the more narrowly the musical canon has been interpreted. The narrow, uplifting canon of classical music, like the expensive imported wines and automobiles with which it is indelibly associated, has demanded to be marketed with discretion—a discretion often sniffily contrasted with the high-pressure tactics associated with more popular musical products. It is comforting to decry the explosive resurgence of ballyhoo in classical music marketing as an intrusion from the world of rock and roll; but it is just as much the consequence of the institutions of classical music continuing to operate—and reverting to time-honored marketing strategies—in the absence of the proprieties enforced by an authoritative canon of classical music.

Thus the attraction of Lebrecht's modernist, crypto-marxian analysis of this development: it neatly shifts blame away from the world of classical music itself. Isn't this just a textbook example of what happens when the late-capitalist "cash nexus" bulldozes through a backward, helpless sphere of cultural production, one that is in many ways still pervaded by the mentality of the guild? Lebrecht is right to point out the radically destabilizing cultural effect of folding classical music institutions into multinational conglomerates and subjecting them to unmediated market forces. It is his insistence on fixing individual blame in the face of inevitable, systemic economic transformation that makes no sense; it actually weakens the effect of his Cassandra-like pronouncements.[12]

But we are much more cautious now about questions of priority in the base-superstructure relationship; in postmodern analyses of cultural production, changes in the cultural sphere often precede and presage transformations in the material sphere.[13] Did greedy record company executives—or even impersonal market forces—really swoop down and decimate the mores and customs of a vibrant and unsullied "classical" music? Or were they just moving into the vacuum left when its historically contingent construction of a normative hierarchy of musical tastes collapsed all by itself? Boosters are right to point out the tenacity of classical music institutions and the often-heroic struggles by individual musicians and scholars to uphold their constructions of the "classical"; but no amount of material struggle can resurrect the epistemological power of a dead canon. All we have left is ballyhoo.

From this postmarxist perspective, moments of surreal marketing excess like Helfgott and the infamous Three Tenors are the symptom, not the disease. Their brand of hyped-up "Classical Music," like the shiny fakeness of Disneyland, functions as what postmodern theorist Jean Baudrillard would call a "third-order simulacrum": the obviously inauthentic simulation that disguises the fact that there is no underlying authentic reality left. David Helfgott and John Tesh have not cheapened the image of the concert pianist; their joint ascendancy proves that there is no such thing anymore as a "concert pianist." That particular cultural role has collapsed (shrunk?) into meaninglessness, and these flamboyant simulacra—almost dialectical extremes of the bizarre and the bland—help disguise the fact. As Baudrillard says, such simulacra help create "a deterrence machine set up in order to reverse the fiction of the real."[14] To paraphrase one of his most notorious quips (originally about Disneyland), David Helfgott and John Tesh are there to conceal the fact that it is the "real" pianists, all of them, who are Tesh and Helfgott.

The unanimous systematic attack on the post-*Shine* Helfgott phenomenon shows the process in action. As he toured city after American city, every major music critic felt obligated to weigh in, verifying that the shattered pianist was bad in Boston, still bad in New York, even worse in San Francisco, and so on. Underneath the frowning denunciations of a deplorable media spectacle there was a secret relief, a condescending smile that readers and recordbuyers reacted to with fury. Helfgott was obviously a fake—which meant there had to be a "real" somewhere. By painstakingly insisting on the difference, journalistic apologists for high art music could switch on the deterrence machine and pump a little reality back into the collapsed canon of "great music" and its "great interpreters." Alert readers will ask what part musical academia plays in this game of deterrence and simulation. The New Musicology asks the same question.

Radical Chic (Bring in da Noise, Leave Out da Funk) The situation of the Avant-Garde Canon is less dire than the crisis in classical music in some ways, but much more disorienting. There is as much good composing going on in academies as ever; it is just getting harder to believe that the academy is an independent source of cultural and stylistic authority. Composers are rummaging through every discard bin of popular culture searching for the hipness and cultural cachet they used to think they could create for themselves. The single biggest trend in "serious" music composition is the wholesale borrowing of the attitude of rock music to get a rise out of audiences and critics. (The days are long gone when Leonard Bernstein could ruffle feathers by confessing that he was more interested in the next Beatles record than anything his colleagues were doing. Everybody's into radical chic now.) Composers used to be photographed in front of some intimidating computer equipment or a row of scores; now the done thing is to be holding an electric guitar.

The 1970s rise of the so-called downtown minimalists (Philip Glass, Steve Reich, Terry Riley, La Monte Young), with their openness to jazzrock textures and modes of production, was a relatively tame foreshadowing. These guys were driving cabs, not going for tenure. Now Steve Mackey, Milton Babbitt's junior colleague at (once so austerely modernist) Princeton, openly pastiches alternative rock, writing electric guitar solos with titles like "Grungy." More flamboyant still is Michael Daugherty, the author of *Elvis Everywhere* and the even more wonderful *Dead Elvis*. (A bassoonist dressed as Elvis gyrates in front of a chamber ensemble playing the "Dies irae" chant as a high-volume, high-speed gallop. *Cool*.) Daugherty's music drama on the life of Jackie Onassis had its premiere at the Houston Grand Opera, but the composer is running away from "grand" opera as fast as he can. He would much rather have you think of *Jackie O* as fun, campy musical theater—what his liner essay calls a "pop opera." Daugherty downplays his impeccable pedigree as a member of the University of Michigan composition department, and plays up his pop chops: "I'm a musician who came of age during the sixties, playing in rock and jazz ensembles, performing in avant-garde improvisation groups, and paying my dues as a cocktail pianist in nightclubs."[15]

The rise of postminimalism in the late 1980s and early 1990s has almost worn out the accolade "the power and punch of a rock band with the precision of a chamber ensemble." Inspired by Dutch iconoclast Louis Andriessen and expatriate radical Frederic Rzewski, an entire generation of composers (Steve Martland, Elliot Sharp, David Lang, Julia Wolfe, Michael Gordon, Evan Ziporyn) has been attempting to repackage, and thus redeem, musical modernism by insisting on its solidarity with a particular reading of popular music as anarchic critique of society. Highly amplified ensembles feature horns, guitars, and percussion; the musical language emphasizes aggressive, explicit backbeats, virtuosic rhythmic play, and a deliberately restricted harmonic and melodic palette; the composers dress, talk, and sometimes preen like rock musicians.

The music is really very good, sometimes it even rocks hard—but the ideological imbalance is striking. Although composers talk with equal reverence of Stravinsky and Coltrane, Mondrian and Chaka Khan, Iannis Xenakis and Wile E. Coyote, they consistently put their pop foot forward. It seems that the rock references that dot their record covers and interviews are what really confer "authenticity." The situation of the 1920s, when modernism first encountered popular music, has been almost exactly reversed. Modernist composers like Eric Satie, Igor Stravinsky, Darius Milhaud, and Aaron Copland tried to provoke bourgeois audiences, dada style, by transgressive borrowings of low-status jazz and ragtime; today's postminimalism attempts to resuscitate the same modernism by appealing to the now-higher status of alternative rock and jazz. These "popular" styles have more cultural prestige than classical music for their prospective audience, that same bourgeois intelligentsia in its present boomer/gen-X American incarnation. Andriessen and his followers may be trying to reassert the cultural priority of the avant-garde canon, yet with every grungy, out-of-focus album cover they confirm only the opposite.[16]

Still it would be a grave mistake to see postminimalism's fusion of modernism and popular music as slack cultural relativism, hipster irony, or just selling out. These composers care deeply about art, believe in its ethical importance, and proclaim their strenuous idealism in the ringing tones of the *Blaue Reiter* and the Vienna *Secession*: "An entire generation of composers has been drawn to Louis Andriessen's rigorous radicalism. There is something about his personality that is like a call to battle. Are you for him or against him? Do you want to join the defenders of true originality and art? Or go to the other side where everyone is entrenched in old, superstitious ideas?" "For Steve Martland, all stages of composition—production, reproduction, and consumption—are as political as they are inextricably intertwined. His ideal: to make the world a better place."[17]

Really, postminimalism's embrace of alternative rock/jazz culture is arty composers turning not away from artiness, but toward it. It is a tacit admission by university-trained musicians that they and their institutions have lost control of what constitutes "art music." Sometimes that loss of control is material and obvious. The rules governing the eligibility of musical compositions for the Pulitzer Prize were modified in 1997 to remove their implicit bias toward classical music. The jury promptly selected Wynton Marsalis's "jazz oratorio" *Blood on the Fields,* putting an end to decades of insider trading.

But this is a trivial epiphenomenon of the deeper (and profoundly positive) phenomenon that postminimalist composers have intuitively understood: for the first time, the production and consumption of contemporary art music has broken quite free of institutionalized classical music. It is the classical avant-garde (the oxymoron is telling) that is "entrenched in old, superstitious ideas." That composers and critics within the academy are largely unaware of this development can only be charged to myopia. It may come as a surprise to those enmeshed in campus compositional politics, but the intellectually adventurous are not sitting around in coffeehouses complaining that the continued dominance of high modernist ideologies within academic music departments has alienated them from serious contemporary music. They have plenty of avant-garde music in their lives. It's just not "classical."

No, I'm not talking about people who think Kate Bush's lyrics are "deep," or the amateur musicologist who has a catalogue of every extended jam by Phish. I'm not even concerned with the graduate student who can tell you how the Talking Heads act out the dissolution of the subject in postmodern society. I'm talking about people who will buy (and listen to) a fifty-five-minute collage of radio speeches in German; who will sit in the audience while their favorite band "plays" by attaching a contact microphone to an industrial belt-sander; who regularly consume huge stretches of dissonant, often achromatic sound, pulsed or pulseless, screamingly loud, vanishingly soft—contemporary music that would have the audience for the Oregon Symphony tearing up their seats and throwing them at the stage.

It has been years since a musicologist's search for interesting contemporary art music recordings (and there are so many of them now) could responsibly stop with the classical bins. You won't find Glenn Branca's mind-bending symphonies for massed electric guitars in various temperaments there; nor will you find the dissonant high-frequency assault of John Zorn's *Kristallnacht*, built on layer after layer of sampled shattering glass, so literally excruciating that the composer warns it may cause nausea, headaches, and ringing in the ears; and don't expect to find any of John Oswald's CDs there, even though he has worked with the Kronos Quartet and his *Plexus* album purees Top 40 hits into insanely precise digital collages that make Luciano Berio's *Sinfonia* look like a child's puzzle. Today, serious art music has to be tracked down all over the cultural landscape: the grittier end of the new age; the spookiest and most ethereal corners of ambient; the most uncompromising slabs of hardcore and techno; and, sometimes, the least academic products of the university new music ensemble. As you explore this postmodernist, postclassical explosion of sonic creativity, you will be rubbing elbows with fans and fierce partisans who will not necessarily share your interest in Bach, Beethoven, Babbitt—or academic musicology.

This is the quiet, hopeful truth behind sensational announcements that "classical music is dead." Classical music institutions like symphonies and record labels will continue to function, and many people will derive pleasure and meaning from the composition, performance, and consumption of classical music. But both classical music canons, performing and avant-garde, have lost their roles as cultural validators; they have lost control over what is defined as "art" music. The ultimate result is a fundamental decentering— not just of avant-garde or institutional authority, but of music culture in general. No longer is there classical Music-with-a-capital-M and its "Others" (such as jazz, pop, folk); the canon of Western classical music is now just one among many, and not the most culturally prestigious anymore, at least in America. Other canons are forming busily, and other kinds of music are making credible plays for the top of the taste hierarchy. These days, Wynton Marsalis might persuasively nominate pre-bop jazz as the most "classical" American style; a baby boomer, following his 60s idols Eric Clapton and Jimi Hendrix, might counter with Mississippi Delta blues. Ask any street-corner goth, or an East Village performance artist, and they'll tell you that boomer nostalgia sucks; the most culturally challenging, sonically difficult styles of contemporary music are techno, ambient, and (for the really arty) industrial.

Fate hands me the perfect summary example. This article was revised in the shadow of Princess Diana's public funeral ceremony, one of the most powerful media events of the decade, seen live by over thirty million and rebroadcast to hundreds of millions more. Since the funeral contained music from the masterwork canon, the avant-garde canon, and from the world of pop, it was a vast, uncontrolled experiment on a significant fraction of the world's population: how paradigmatic did each style of music seem at this moment of high ceremony and emotional drama? How well did it function as Music-with-a-capital-M?

The representative of the masterwork canon, the "Libera me" movement of Verdi's *Requiem*, fared worst, even though it would seem to have been perfectly tailored to the pomp of a big state funeral. (Some of this was circumstantial: the orchestra part had to be replaced by organ, and the acoustics of Westminster Abbey were obviously not designed for Italian opera!) Although it became known that this was one of Diana's favorite classical pieces, there was little positive reaction to it. The representative of the avant-garde canon, John Tavener's anthem "Song for Athene," actually provoked more interest, at least among those already familiar with classical music. (Tavener's piece was chosen by Prince Charles, an acquaintance of the composer; it was originally written for another young woman who died in an auto accident.) Internet mailing lists devoted to choral music lit up with questions about the author, where the sheet music could be had, and whether a recording was available.

Meanwhile, of course, everyone in the English-speaking world ran out to buy a copy of a rewritten 1973 ballad about Marilyn Monroe called "Candle in the Wind." It became the biggest-selling single in the history of recorded music (600,000 copies were sold in Britain in one day, which along with the 1.5 million advance orders meant it went double platinum in twenty-four hours); every newspaper printed Bernie Taupin's new lyrics, and CNN camera crews captured crowds of British mourners swaying and singing it together over and over during extravagant midnight vigils. This was the music of the moment, not Verdi's *gran scena* or Tavener's hieratic chant, or even the sturdy Anglican hymns that once would have spoken most directly to the masses. The classical canon was outclassed on its home turf (Westminster Abbey is where Handel is buried). Rock Bottom, in the person of Reginald Dwight, aka Elton John, had effortlessly "claimed the present historical moment exclusively for himself."[18]

That is why it does no good to spout statistics about the sudden mass-market craze for this or that classical music phenomenon—Helfgott, Gorecki, chant, and so on. As we shall see below, the collapse of the canon does not mean the *disappearance* of classical music. Far from it. But classical music will never be paradigmatic or hegemonic again.

Don't think this is a lament or a call to arms. Calls to "revitalize" the classical music world do not seem very helpful, especially from within the academy. If "keeping it alive" is just academic musicology's code for restoring the canon's cultural hegemony, then we really do have a "musicological problem." Here is another shorthand definition of a New Musicologist: one whose entire professional training took place after the classical music era; who feels no nostalgia for its distinctions and no desire to be a mandarin of canonical high art music; who questions whether the mission of academic musicology is to reify and reinscribe the distinctions that create a canon of art music. In the second part of this essay, I want to address some ideological and methodological issues that arise from reconceiving musicology (and perhaps pop music studies as well) for the "postclassical" era. But first, why would any musicologist tell this tale to popular music scholars? What does it mean for you—beyond the occasion of a little discreet gloating over our discomfiture? Is this the beginning of a beautiful friendship?

Interlude: Baby, Let's Play House (Why You Need
a Musicologist to Listen to Beck)
Guess Who's Coming to Dinner? (The Amphibious Musicologist)

It doesn't take much imagination to picture popular music scholars awaiting the influx of postcanonic New Musicologists with decidedly mixed feelings. They have a perfect right to conceptualize their situation in terms of the classic 1950s science-fiction scenario of invasion from outer space. "We have exhausted the resources of our home world . . . so now we need yours!" And indeed, it has often seemed that, in the face of alien interlopers with superior technology ("Their ability to analyze music is centuries ahead of ours, Mr. President!"), the only honorable response from popular music studies has been guerrilla resistance—a scorched-earth antiformalism backed up with marxist accusations of cultural and class imperialism (or at the very least, a few tart reminders about the musicological problem). The rise of the "amphibious" musicologist, the scholar who glibly claims to be simultaneously researching sixteenth-century polyphonic treatises and the Mighty Mighty Bosstones, has not necessarily helped matters. Such ambidexterity might mean transcending the classical canon and its hegemony—or it might just signal overweening confidence in the canonizing power of musicological method. Do we really come in peace, for all mankind?

Let us admit that the recent path of historical musicology has been progress by annexation. Something very like a fear of limited resources—how many Mozart editions do we need?—has indeed driven musicologists toward canonic expansion. (Music theory, on the other hand, has tended to emphasize increasing depth of formal insight into a relatively restricted canon of masterworks.) As long as it is just the corners of the European concert music tradition being "rehabilitated," musicology can move in easily, with few external accusations of cultural insensitivity and incremental modifications of canonic faith. But the assimilation of rock and pop brings with it greater challenges.

Although it may seem unprecedented, this situation is unique only in degree, not in kind. Each musicological annexation of territory has involved what, from the inside, felt like wrenching ideological self-transformation. Studying Rossini and Verdi meant dispensing with lingering Germanic cultural chauvinism (the invidious "two cultures of music" argument), and reassessing long-held beliefs about organic structure, fixed musical texts, and the primacy of abstract instrumental music. Dealing with Chopin, Tchaikovsky, Ives, and Britten meant confronting entrenched homophobia and misogyny masquerading as an ideology of musical "genius." Forays into twentieth-century historiography, seeking to situate problematic antimodernists like Stravinsky and Weill, proved to be fatal to venerable beliefs in music's political autonomy, both from totalitarianism and the mass audience of capitalism.[19]

There is reason to hope that an engagement with popular music will be the catalyst for musicology's most profound self-transformation yet. That is undoubtedly a large part of its attraction on the part of those who wish to study it and still call themselves "musicologists." We will gain new tools and ideological freedoms to apply to what used to be canonical music; we may also be able to catalyze some transformations in the ideological and methodological approaches that have crystallized around pop and rock music. In the final part of this essay, I would like to take a first step, and ask what a New Musicologist, freshly scarred from fierce internecine battles over formalism and hermeneutics in the analysis of classical music, can add to the debate over formal analysis of popular music. All too often, the positions of musicologists and popular music scholars vis-à-vis "formalism" or "structural analysis" harden into a pat dialectical opposition that serves neither repertory well. Perhaps, as we explore the same music we can find some common epistemological ground.

Classical Music as . . . Whatever But first, a brief plug for the practical services of historical musicology in the postcanonic era. Allow me to unfold a paradox: the collapse of classical music's cultural hegemony makes a specialist's knowledge of classical music more necessary for pop music scholars, not less. Remember, the walls of the canon served not only to keep barbarians and their music out; they also served, very conveniently, to keep the high art music safely walled in. Now that those walls are down, the sounds of classical music are drifting out into the bloodstream of popular music like a new and disorienting virus. (This is the flip side of the rock seepage into postminimalism.) While the canon and its hegemony were strong, the cultural prestige of high art music was an effective antigen. Upon encountering the stuff, either the rock host rejected it immediately as foreign or a distinctive inflammation set in, which we used to call, perhaps unfairly, "being pretentious." The Bach trumpet in "Penny Lane," rock operas, the entire corpus of Emerson, Lake, and Palmer. You know . . . Art Rock.

Art rock's fusion of styles could be studied and understood, from both sides, within the old patterns of classical music's cultural hegemony. But now—and Baudrillard could have predicted this—now that "real" classical music is dead its ghostly simulacra have developed the ability to move freely through the mediasphere. And these decontextualized, culturally neutral shards of classical music turn up, unheralded, in the strangest places.

Who could have predicted, for instance, the fascination with classical music signifiers in mainstream rap and soul videos? Lushly lit orchestras of (almost always black, very rarely real) string players fill the set, when the only musical correlative is a synthesized "analog string" patch down in the mix. Often rappers will lead the orchestra, in one video even conducting with a white, phallic baton. The association of classical orchestras with wealth and (white) power is of long standing in black soul music;[20] yet one marvels at Coolio's "C U When U Get There" (which samples Pachelbel's famous canon for a somber meditation on death) complete with a white-robed Coolio conducting a heavenly choir also dressed in white. Sean "Puffy" Combs (aka Puff Daddy) took some heat for swallowing the Police's "Every Move You Make" whole on his massively successful *No Way Out* album; but the musicologist's ears perk up when, as an intro to the much-condemned "I'll Be Missin' You," he indulges in a maudlin Barry White-style confession of loss for the Notorious B.I.G. over (Lord!) Samuel Barber's *Adagio for Strings,* in the composer's own treacly arrangement as an "Agnus Dei" for choir.

Even more enigmatic is Combs's video for "Can't Nobody Hold Me Down," which begins with the artist-producer asleep in his luxurious digs. In the grips of a nightmare, he struggles underwater for breath—and the soundtrack starts by dropping us right into a grand opera climax, soprano and tenor caterwauling as if the whole thing were going to be a high-concept BMW ad. But as soon as Puff Daddy wakes up ("Man, I just had the illest dream," he remarks), the opera vanishes, never to return. There is nothing in the rest of the video to support a class reading of the operatic intro; it appears to be a straight shot from the cultural unconscious—an evocation of something uncanny, totally strange, like the surreal imagery of dreams.[21] (Or like the sound of Verdi to the teen audience for MTV's soft rap videos.)

Whether or not we can identify the opera in question, the grand operatic voice as "numinous intruder"—whether from the beyond, or from the Lacanian imaginary—is a phenomenon familiar to musicological discourse; there are many analogous moments in the avant-garde canon.[22] It might behoove a popular music scholar to inflect the material class and race oppositions that spring immediately to mind (rap is to opera as low is to high as black is to white as poor is to rich) with insights from musicology, where opera has been studied both as a medium for the display of wealth and power and as a direct route into the depths of the collective (and perhaps, culturally constructed) psyche.

It is probably not possible for black artists to invoke European concert music without at least some class and racial tension; but some middle-class whites these days can achieve a perfect indifference to classical music that is chilling and at the same time oddly refreshing. Consider "High 5 (Rock the Catskills)," from Beck (Hansen)'s second album (*Odelay,* 1995). As in the best Beck tracks, a thrift-shop cascade of five sampled musical styles, including 60s bossa nova lounge guitar, vocoder-inflected 80s rap, and funky orchestral hits from 70s soul, is crammed into less than two minutes. The last sample is always shocking to musicological audiences: a moment of electronic noise ushers in a brief, bleeding chunk of the year 1822, as Beck samples the first movement of Schubert's "unfinished" symphony.

What does this piece of the masterwork canon signify? As far as I can tell, it can best be translated by that all-purpose 90s interlocution: "Uh, yeah; whatever." By the time Schubert shows up, we have been so pummeled by stylistic overload that we'll accept whatever comes next. And, conversely, the sound of the symphony orchestra is so gloriously out of any possible context that it has a hallucinatory immediacy—for a minute, before recognition sets in, we hear the raw sonic impact of the classical canon without its distancing cultural halo of "significance." How foreign, how different it sounds! (Kind of like a dream; thus Puff Daddy, above.) This is what Cage was aiming for when he claimed to be interested in the Beethoven symphonies only if he could play them all at the same time. A different strategy, but the same decanonizing (or postcanonic!) overload.

Don't make the mistake of thinking that the Schubert quote stands for "high and/or serious art." We are given absolutely no sign during the rest of the song that the classical sample is to be considered special, that it is any more prized or stigmatized than the rest of the cultural detritus that blows through Beck's sound collages. Surprisingly enough, given his media status as vacant slacker icon, Beck can claim his own, quite different avant-garde pedigree: his grandfather was a minor neo-dadaist, and his mother hung out at the Factory with Andy Warhol. The closest he has ever come to identifying with a "classical" musical style was his association with the early 90s L.A. neofolk scene; it seems that Delta blues and acoustic slide guitar (remember "Loser"?) are the sound of "the classics" for Beck. Schubert is just . . . whatever.

As a final example, I would adduce the complete indifference to canonic boundaries within the ambient/techno scene. As everybody knows by now, ambient has its roots as much in the avant-garde canonical experiments of Brian Eno (and behind him the American pulsed minimalists, La Monte Young, and, ultimately, John Cage) as in the "chill-out" rooms of underground raves.[23] Sometimes the hybrids are obvious to even the low-resolution ear. Enigma's spectacularly successful packaging of a standard deejay cool-off trick, the layering of Gregorian chant over spacious mid-tempo dance tracks, epitomizes ambient for many. But quite a few ambient and techno musicians seem to know as much about American minimal music as the best-trained musicological specialists. It takes an extremely discriminating ear to spot the cross-breeding and insider references, because we are now talking about "pop" musicians quoting "classical" composers in a context where there is little or no clear-cut sonic differentiation between the styles. One has to be able to identify the sound of dance musicians quoting the marginal bits of the avant-garde canon that already sound like dance music.

Taking stock of this repertory does not require an amphibious musicologist adroit at crossing heavily defended canonic boundaries; nor is it easily decoded by a pop music and culture specialist, proudly uninterested in anything "classical." Ambient needs a music scholar willing to research as if there were no canonic boundaries, to see that for electronic musicians there is only one distinction that matters. There are people who use tape and electronics—you, me, the Chemical Brothers, 808 State, Steve Reich, μ-Ziq, Stockhausen, Public Enemy—and people who don't.

To map even the single interaction between ambient/techno and American minimalism is beyond the scope of this essay; all I can do is sketch in some relationships I have spotted. The testimonial evidence is copious and unequivocal, as Kenny Berkowitz of *Option* magazine recently proved. In a clever piece of journalistic shuttle diplomacy, he first asked cutting-edge British techno artists like the Orb, Orbital, μ-Ziq, Aphex Twin, and Underworld what they thought of Philip Glass and Steve Reich. They all obligingly claimed pulsed minimalism as a formative influence and raved about their favorite pieces. Underworld's Rick Smith cherishes Reich's *Music for Eighteen Musicians;* Richard D. James (aka the Aphex Twin) is busily remixing the same piece for a proposed album. Alex Paterson of the Orb (age thirty-seven) boasts he watched *Koyaanisqatsi* six times in one evening ("All my mates went out to play. They thought I was quite mad"); and Mike Paradinas of μ-Ziq (age twenty-four) recalls "the first time I heard Philip Glass was in 1987. I was playing in a rock band, it was over a p.a. in the hall. It was 'Music in Twelve Parts, Part One.' And I thought, what the fuck is this? It's brilliant, and it hasn't changed for 12 minutes." Berkowitz then headed off to Reich and Glass bearing fan messages from the techno avant-garde and a fistful of cds—but, ironically, the pioneers of minimalism remain underwhelmed by their electronic nephews and grandchildren. (Glass on Orbital: "It's really not very edgy, is it?")[24]

That's okay, because techno artists aren't all that interested in the acoustic orchestral work Glass and Reich are doing now, either. They prize the early abrasive recordings with their fuzzy tape loops and buzzy analog synthesizers, aurally attracted to the style roughly insofar as it sounds like "electronica." Paterson's groundbreaking double album, the Orb's *Adventures Beyond the Ultraworld,* samples, among dozens of other things, the *Allegri miserere,* Ennio Morricone's soundtrack for *Once Upon a Time in the West,* and Minnie Ripperton warbling "Loving You (Is Easy 'Cause You're Beautiful)."[25] But when the opening track, "Little Fluffy Clouds," seamlessly incorporates into its groove Pat Metheny's 1989 recording of Steve Reich's *Electric Counterpoint,* the resulting loop hardly screams "classical." Reich's original is scored for electric guitar; it is already funky, is already a loop, and is already built up out of overdubbed recordings. It fits right in. A sly vocal overdub points us toward the trans-canonic common denominator: as a plummy British voice intones over and over again, both minimalism and ambient work by "layering different sounds."

Sometimes the collaboration is more interactive. "ICCT Hedral" is a classic ambient track by Richard James, who records under the pseudonym the Aphex Twin. It was first realized using James's trademark recreations of classic analog synthesizers, and that is how you hear it on his 1995 album *I Care Because You Do*. But the *Donkey Rhubarb* EP single from the next year contains a transcription of "ICCT Hedral" for chamber orchestra and electronics, in which guise it sounds uncannily like an excerpt from an opera by Philip Glass. The original track must have sounded uncannily like Philip Glass to Philip Glass, since the composer himself is credited with the "remix." When Glass's orchestration was released as an Aphex Twin single, it did not self-consciously "cross over" into ambient, aiming for the frisson attendant on anticanonic moves like the Kronos Quartet's transcriptions of Evans, Monk, and Hendrix. What the "classical" version of "ICCT Hedral" did was give Glass at least a provisional place inside the interlocking economy of remixes that helps cement relationships within the ambient/techno culture. (Glass actually dug up this remix to play for Berkowitz, who reports Glass seemed "genuinely disappointed that he liked it so much more than anything I'd played for him.")[26]

There are even times when ambient music appears to make coded historical references to minimalism on the level of technique, as in "Time Becomes," the first track from Orbital's second album (*Orbital 2*, 1993). Most fans probably thought that putting the voice of Commander Worf through a phase loop was just a cool reference to *Star Trek: The Next Generation;* a few Orbital diehards would have recognized the gesture as a clever expansion of the vocal snippet that begins "Moebius," from their 1991 debut release. But a musicologist might identify a different precursor: the phase process is identical to that developed by Steve Reich in early repetitive tape pieces like "It's Gonna Rain" (1965) and "Come Out" (1966). It is hard to hear this as art rock. I doubt that many ambient/techno fans care enough about the status of minimalist music within the Western canon—positive or negative—for it to matter. Nor does it seem that any of these bands are trying to claim some cultural prestige that "classical music" still holds for them. It seems rather that the distinction between classical and popular is totally irrelevant. Thus Paterson of the Orb: "I am using sounds and styles that are so different to be able to obtain in the long run a music so peculiar and definitive that it would be pointless for the critics to try to label it."[27]

The ne plus ultra: I recently discovered, quite by accident, that there is a track on *Sweetback*, the eponymous 1996 debut album by Sade's backing band, which samples and distorts the opening seconds of a performance of John Cage's 1956 "Radio Music" that took place in a Milan radio studio on April 5, 1974, and was released on the impossibly obscure Cramps label later that year. How did this snippet of aleatoric sound collage find its way onto a mainstream soul album? Who was supposed to recognize it? What could it possibly mean?

Welcome to the brave new postcanonic world.

Love Me Tender (Postcanonic Notes toward an Erotics of Popular Music)
Canon and Method

QED, I hope. The collapse of the canon has left bits and pieces of classical music all over the place, and you never know when you might need a musicologist to help you sort them out. But that is hardly all that is at stake. The distinction between canonic classical music and its Others also has traditionally enforced methodological choices that separate the musicologist from the pop music scholar—especially when they engage in analysis.

Battles over analytical methodology have been some of the most bruising interdisciplinary engagements within musical academia in the last fifteen years; and yet it seems that one of the most controversial and significant paths between musicology and popular music studies cuts right through those contested relationships between musical sounds, structural abstractions, and social meanings. Of course, analysis of musical texts is only one of the things musicologists do, and it is worth pointing out that much of musicology's methodological toolchest has already been productively applied to popular music. For example, the rubric under which the journal *American Music* is published has traditionally defined an area where musicologists and their historiographic techniques could participate unproblematically in the study of both folk and commercial repertories. (The exemplary work of Charles Hamm, H. Wiley Hitchcock, and Richard Crawford is musicology, as are Gunther Schuller's magisterial studies of Early Jazz and The

Swing Era.) Similarly, the paleographic and philological skills practiced on vellum and parchment have been employed to catalog vinyl; and chronicling the day-to-day operations of a major record label poses no fundamentally different documentary problems than sifting through the musical and financial records of a minor German principality.

But (and we narrow our focus decisively here) analysis is different. It has been different within academic musicology for the last twenty-odd years, ever since the institutionalization of a burgeoning discourse of structuralist analysis within the secessionist Society for Music Theory. One of the unfortunate effects of naming a New Musicology is that it erroneously implies the existence of a self-consciously reactionary Old Musicology, against whose canonic rigidity and "positivism" the new paradigm would naturally battle.[28] Actually, the fights within historical musicology have mostly been pragmatic struggles over limited resources on program and tenure committees. The truly rancorous ideological battle is not between New and Old Musicology, but between competing definitions of the New: the 1978 New (structuralist/music-theoretical) versus the 1988 New (poststructuralist/feminist/cultural). The ground of the battle is analysis, and the most powerful ideological fireworks erupt when the New Musicology challenges Music Theory for analytic authority over canonic musical texts.

The basis of the challenge will seem quite familiar to popular music scholars:

> If the musicologists' characteristic failure is superficiality, that of the analysts is myopia. Their dogged concentration on internal relationships within the single work of art is ultimately subversive as far as any reasonably complete view of music is concerned. . . . Along with preoccupation with structure goes the neglect of other vital matters . . . everything else that makes music affective, moving, emotional, expressive. By removing the bare score from its context in order to examine it as an autonomous organism, the analyst removes that organism from the ecology that sustains it.[29]

At the end of the chapter in *Contemplating Music* from which the above is taken, the author, Joseph Kernan, calls himself a "traditionalist critic" prone to scolding "formalists."[30] Identifying analytical formalism as myopia, as the ideological buttress of an extraordinarily, even dangerously narrow musical canon, and calling for an analysis that was less formalist and more critical, older musicologists like Kerman and Leo Treitler prefigured a full-blown assault on formalist music theory and analysis by younger musicological critics (McClary, Walser, Richard Taruskin, Lawrence Kramer) who are anything but traditional.[31] (More on that below.) Ironically enough in the present context, Kerman has always been rather pointedly elitist in his musical tastes. ("For better or worse, I am not very much interested in non-Western music or in the popular music of the West.")[32] But the critique of formalist canon worship coming from within musicology has found powerful echoes from without, as popular music scholars translate arguments about how to discuss "great" Western music into wider multicultural and subcultural contexts.

Both of Kerman's central complaints about music theory's approach to the classics—that formalist analysis assumes the musical text as autonomous and transcendent, thus severing musical structure from cultural context; and that formalism obsesses over structure while neglecting how music makes us feel—immediately arise whenever popular music scholars consider "musicological" analysis of rock and pop. Middleton's musicological problem ("[musicology assumes that] works are autonomous; art has transcendent qualities; listening should be detached and contemplative, and analysis therefore text-centered") echoes quite precisely the first point of Kerman's indictment. McClary and Walser, on the other hand, saw Kerman's second charge as evidence of a full-blown analytical defense mechanism: "No wonder so many products of musicology seem so obfuscating. They aim precisely at displacing and obscuring the focus, at diffusing the music's energy."[33] (At our current level of disciplinary focus, "products of musicology" in the above should probably read "products of music theory.")

It seems that a key aspect of the "musicological problem" is actually a music-theoretical problem: how to deal with the ideological dangers of unrestrained analytical formalism. New Musicology has been wrestling with this problem as it relates to canonic repertories for some time. But popular music scholars sometimes seem blissfully unaware of this deep unease over formalist music theory. Assuming that anybody studying music formally must be a formalist, they dismiss all technical discussion of music, popular or classical, as "musicology"—and they want none of it. The following is, of course, a caricature-composite of many more nuanced views, but some variant of this dichotomy has been the basic starting point of almost all recent discussions of analytical methodology and popular music:

1. Canonic "classical" music rewards formal analysis. It is thought to have complex structures that are essentially autonomous of society and deal with abstractions that transcend culture. It thus naturally has moved musicologists, especially music theorists, to develop and refine elaborate structural methodologies. The question from this side is: Don't popular music scholars want to know how music works? Why won't they accept our powerful tools?

2. Popular (jazz, folk) music, like noncanonic classical music, rewards hermeneutic analysis. Embedded in culture, its primary significance is as a carrier and constructor of social meanings and identities. It makes no pretense to autonomy or transcendence: in fact, its value is thought to lie in the cultural specificity of its message and effect. It naturally has moved scholars to develop complex readings of musical texts as cultural signifiers, and to research the material specifics of production, dissemination, and consumption. The question from this side is: Don't musicologists and music theorists want to know how music works in culture? Why must they parade their irrelevant expertise in parsing forms?

Thus, within the academy, discrimination between high and low musics still appears to be made primarily on the grounds of form. An emphasis on form, and the analysis of formal structures, marks one as a devotee of art music; an emphasis on content, particularly as it intersects with social structure, predisposes one toward popular music.

I want to problematize this all-too-easy set of matched binarisms. (That might well be another handy definition of a New Musicologist: someone who goes around problematizing things his or her colleagues thought were just fine the way they were.) All discussion of musical form need not be formalist. Nor need the divide between formalist and hermeneutic approaches coincide with the crumbling divide between the popular and the classical. There is no longer any agreement within musicology (new or old) that formalist analysis is the best way to approach classical music, nor has there ever been unanimous consensus that cultural hermeneutics is the best way to account for popular music. Let's take a few historical turns around what will turn out to be a dialectical spiral.

[First Turn.] Against Interpretation: From Content to Form   Given the current anxiety over formal analysis of popular music, it may come as a surprise to remember that at the moment when rock burst onto the cultural landscape, the main obstacle to understanding it was thought to be an overemphasis on content in art. The key text here is Susan Sontag's 1966 collection of essays, which bore the programmatic title of its lead essay, "Against Interpretation." Sontag saw rock music—along with happenings, minimalism, and New Wave cinema—as evidence of a "new sensibility." This new sensibility, with its emphasis on new varieties of sensation, and its cool indifference to what Sontag dismissively called "the Matthew Arnold idea of culture"—art as a "species of moral journalism"—completely effaced the prevailing distinctions between high and low culture. Hence the final sentence of Sontag's book: "From the vantage point of this new sensibility, the beauty of a machine or of the solution to a mathematical problem, of a painting by Jasper Johns, of a film by Jean-Luc Godard, and of the personalities and music of the Beatles is equally accessible."[34]

The reason contemporary critics had missed this new sensibility was their retrograde obsession with content. Art-with-a-capital-A was tied to a lofty yet narrow didacticism, and the demand that all art be about something important led to a smoggy miasma of interpretations: "Like the fumes of the automobile and of heavy industry which befoul the urban atmosphere, the effusion of interpretations of art today poisons our sensibilities."[35] Sontag despised the kind of great books readings of art where every novel or play turns out to be about "man's inhumanity to man." (The recrudescence of the great books propaedeutic in the 1980s, right alongside hysterical denunciations of rock and roll—cf. Allan Bloom and William Bennett—proves that the "old sensibility" is very much alive and kicking.)

The cure for this "philistinism of interpretation"? A cool, analytical emphasis on form: "What kind of criticism, of commentary on the arts, is desirable today? . . . What is needed, first, is more attention to form in art. If excessive stress on content provokes the arrogance of interpretation, more extended and thorough descriptions of form would silence it. What is needed is a vocabulary—a descriptive, rather than a prescriptive, vocabulary—for forms."[36] Rock music, the epitome of the new sensibility, cannot be understood or canonized by interpreting it. Sontag, had she troubled to read them, would have been appalled by the irrelevance of (to take a notorious example) Wilfred Mellers's overheated hermeneutic excursions into Dylan and the Beatles.

Nothing could be stronger evidence for the truth of Sontag's position than the hash the old sensibility makes of popular music in a neoconservative diatribe like Martha Bayles's *Hole in Our Soul: The Loss of Beauty and Meaning in American Popular Music* (1994). As one might expect from the tendentious juxtaposition of abstract nouns in her subtitle, she lays waste to large tracts of American popular music by demanding that its beauty come from its meaning—in other words, that it always display affirmative content, full of "the triumph of the human spirit" and the "transcendence of suffering." Everyone has to be Louis Armstrong, all of the time. Even the most powerful formal innovators are ruthlessly dismissed if their politics are wrong, or even just muddled; if their anger and hopelessness are too corrosive; if they seem too anarchic in their embrace of hedonism; if their critique of white middle-class mores and institutions is too "perverse."

On the other hand, it is not clear that Sontag would have appreciated Hebdige-style subcultural theory either. Interesting sociology, she might murmur, but bad aesthetics. In other words, too much (subcultural) content, not enough form. As an exactly contemporary pundit of the new sensibility put it, stop looking for the message—the medium is the message. "When l.p. and hi-fi stereo arrived, a depth approach to musical experience also came in. Everybody lost his inhibitions about 'highbrow,' and the serious people lost their qualms about popular music and culture. . . . Depth means insight, and insight is a kind of mental involvement that makes the content of the item seen quite secondary."[37] According to the new sensibility, the way across the old cultural divide between high and popular music was (and is) to move away from content and toward form, away from shallow, bodiless interpretations (what Sontag saw as "the revenge of intellect upon art"), and toward the physical depth of real musical experience. We must stop asking what rock means and start asking how rock makes you feel. We need to know how rock musicians engage in the key activity of the new sensibility: "The programming of sensations" (Sontag, again). This form-to-sensation path is not the only one into popular music—it ignores a whole spectrum of sociopolitical significance—but I think we can all agree on a gut level with Sontag that it is one of the most promising.

[Second Turn.] From Form to Form-as-Content   Interestingly enough, when Sontag praises examples of this new formal criticism she mentions analyses of film, drama, painting, and literature. Writing about music, pop or classical, is conspicuously absent, and this even though Sontag accords the Beatles, Pierre Boulez, and John Cage prominent positions within the new sensibility. Ironically, if she had looked over at what academic musicology was doing, she would have seen a veritable explosion of formalism. Between 1955 and 1965, new vocabularies for describing form were springing up like weeds, and cultural hermeneutics of music was in deep disrepute. This period saw the founding of the first periodicals devoted primarily to pure musical analysis (the *Journal of Music Theory* in 1957, and *Perspectives of New Music* in 1962), and the first breakthroughs into the academic mainstream of all the seductively powerful abstract formal vocabularies that still dominate analysis of art music today—whether tonal (the voiceleading theories of Heinrich Schenker), atonal (Alan Forte's theory of set-classes), or serial (the mathematical invariance theories of George Rochberg, Milton Babbitt, and David Lewin).[38]

And so academic musicology should have rushed to embrace the analysis of rock music, since we were already asking the right—that is, the right formal—questions. Or were we? One of the effects of the collapse of the classical canon has been to leave formalist musical analysis open to intense self-critique, as well as an accelerating barrage of criticism from musicology. Let me be clear here: it is not that the continuing cultural prestige of classical music was buttressing the very idea of doing formal analysis—and vice versa. The point of bringing up Sontag and McLuhan was to show how abstract formal analysis was first seen as deeply subversive of that canon. What the prestige of the classical music canon was actually shielding from critique were some fundamental ideological assumptions about music itself; these assumptions both validated the pursuit of formalist musical analysis and forced it into a mold relatively hostile to the understanding of popular music. (And, if you are a New Musicologist, "classical" music, too. But that's another, intramural battle.)

It would not be the best use of my space here to rehearse this argument at length; there are many full-blown accounts in print.[39] A schematic outline of formalist ideology might run like this: There is a complex of deeply held beliefs about abstract instrumental music in the academy that can be traced back as far as the early Romantic period. These beliefs boil down to an assertion that music is valuable insofar as it exhibits the qualities that also define bourgeois subjectivity: autonomy, organic unity, hierarchical depth, and long-range teleological patterns of tension and release. If these formal conditions are met, as in, say, a symphonic movement by Beethoven, music can have transcendental immediacy: it is directly present to us without cultural or bodily mediation, and with the force of a profound and timeless human truth. If the conditions are not met, as in almost all popular music, the music is inferior. Most of the key qualities of music that enable immediacy are not directly perceptible during ordinary listening—in particular organic unity and hierarchy—so it is the task of formal analysis to demonstrate their presence axiomatically and thus validate the music.[40] Analysis upholds the cultural prestige of the canon and maintains a powerful hierarchy of taste, based on the ability to create and perceive complex forms.

At this point, one of the truisms that all music students imbibe in analysis classes—that in abstract music, form is content—takes on the sinister ring of the "old sensibility." (It is a very old sensibility indeed, traceable as far back as Eduard Hanslick's 1854 work *On the Musically Beautiful*.)[41] Musical form, thus constructed, has little to do with Sontag's "programming of sensations"; it is pressed into service, just like content was in the bad old days, to transmit cultural capital, cultural truths, maybe even some suitably abstracted version of "the triumph of the human spirit" (cf. Beethoven's Ninth Symphony). The kind of hard-headed and specific description of material sensations and structures that Sontag wanted has little to do with what all but the most progressive music theorists today practice as "formal analysis."

These theorists may think they are looking for objective form, but what they are finding is subjective form as content—and a particularly midcultish, affirmative content it turns out to be, time and again. In the world of the masterwork canon, every great piece is formally perfect and complete, and every perfect form is hierarchically, organically unified. Thus every formal narrative, however complex, has a simple and obligatory happy ending: it worked. All the notes are accounted for and, one more time, the triumph of the human spirit is assured. The relevance to popular music has been, for all practical purposes, nil. In general, popular music, whose forms almost never exhibit complex hierarchic depth, organic unity, or long-range patterns of tension and release, is as badly served by this cultural construction as it was by the old Matthew Arnold idea of culture as moral journalism.

[Third Turn.] Against Against Interpretation: *Letting Content Be Content*
There have been two basic reactions to this formalism from the New Musicology. One is a full-throttle return to hermeneutics. If form is being asked to do the job of content, and the form-as-content that is uncovered is, often as not, "this piece mirrors what I value about my own subjectivity back to me, and is thus great," and you don't care anymore whether it is great or not—why not go in search of a funkier, more satisfying hermeneutic? Start from Adorno rather than Hanslick; assume that cultural and political content is immanent in musical structure, and that music is a signifying cultural production that does cultural work. Music's formal abstraction—its supposed inability to represent anything outside itself—is a defense to be breached, not a Grail to be worshipped. Readings of canonical works in terms of body politics, sexuality, religion, race, and so on have lent a new fascination to the content of musical artworks. This project has allowed us, as one (old, perhaps new) musicologist said, not to "get out of analysis, but out from under."[42] The suspicion has arisen that overemphasis on the form-as-content of musical works has displaced more challenging contents. There has been a concerted effort to reenergize the history and criticism of music by recapturing their power to be the history and criticism of culture.

This puts the New Musicology directly in sync with the prevailing paradigms of popular music studies, where discussion of music in terms of politics, race, class, gender, and sexuality is refreshingly unproblematic and central. This is why I began by defining a New Musicologist as someone who looks at academic musicology from the inside the way popular music scholars look at it from the outside. If you fear that a call to master complex technical vocabularies, to concentrate on formal abstractions, and to consider music as autonomous and transcendent of culture is a call to strip it of cultural content, fill it with reified form-as-content, and to inscribe it in an already-collapsed canon—well, the New Musicology is intimately familiar with these anxieties. We're not here to "help" you by handing over our advanced technology in the blithe certainty that it will solve all your interpretive problems. We now know that those tools come with a price and an agenda. And that agenda is singularly hostile to sensation—and to popular music.

[Fourth Turn.] Dancing about Architecture, or, Toward an Erotics of Music
And yet—we are still musicologists, and we do have something to offer as musicologists. It may seem that I am working my self-abnegating way to-

Elvis Everywhere   91

ward a proposal to eliminate all the Departments of Musicology and Music Theory and replace them with programs in Music and Cultural Studies. But that would be the easy way out. Before we all gather at the cultural studies river, we have to acknowledge that popular music study, no less than classical music study, is still struggling to answer Susan Sontag's demand for a descriptive vocabulary of form that can give insight into the new sensibility—in particular, into the way popular music works materially to "program sensations." The common goal is a formal vocabulary developed free of the compulsion to produce form-as-content, and free of the crippling burden of validating the canon of great music. That formal vocabulary may be verbal, but the words may not be the ones with which classically trained musicologists are familiar. It will have to do with our complex system of Western notation, but only in places: the places where the creators and consumers of popular music avail themselves of its powers.[43] Perhaps the vocabulary will be mediated by recording and digital technology, so that a specialized training in the transcription of Western classical music is no longer the back-breaking (and mind-bending) prerequisite to any formal description of the world's music.

The experience of trying to forge the new vocabulary of sensation out of the pieces of the old vocabulary of canonic validation is what New Musicology can bring to the table. Another Susan, Susan McClary, echoed Sontag's call for formal investigation of pop music as sensation a quarter century later: "What musicologists can contribute to the study of popular music is some way of explaining how the powerful moments in music are accomplished, without discrediting the impression that they are exciting, disturbing, or pleasurable. The focus should be on constructing models that serve only as flexible backdrops, up against which the noise of the piece can reverberate."[44] Here the New Musicology and popular music studies confront each other directly. Many popular music scholars are familiar with McClary's stinging critiques of formalist analysis, and her repeated assertions that an understanding of how any music constructs bodily desire ("kicks butt") must be the goal of any analytical description. The most successful moments of the New Musicology are when analytical tools, partially reconfigured to capture some aspect of music as a construction of physical desire (the "flexible backdrop"), ground a sexual-political hermeneutic, some specific cultural content, in equally specific and perceptible features of the musical experience. Success along these lines is hardly automatic, and much of the work still feels provisional or exploratory compared with the hermetic elegance of traditional form-as-content analyses. (The criticism from within academic musicology has been withering.) But these provisional successes are probably the only ones that can be transferred into the world of popular music.

They may also provide an alternate model for popular music analysts who seem quite eager, sometimes, to generate their own kind of distancing form-as-content. There are those who argue passionately and by example that we should apply music theory's full arsenal of analytical methodologies forthrightly to rock, but Schenkerian reduction graphs will probably always be a hard sell within popular music studies.[45] Still, the kind of analysis that popular music scholars do today, even as they self-consciously step around the musicological quagmire, sometimes seems just as likely to grind the musical experience to pieces. This may be the last thing you expected to hear from the keepers of the canon, but there are moments when a little less rigor might be nice.

Philip Tagg's justifiably celebrated attempt to exhaust the semiotic field of the Kojak theme may stand as paradigmatic.[46] Here we certainly avoid the musicological problem: there is no truck with ideologies of genius and expression, no bias toward large-scale narratives, no compulsion to produce the complex, hierarchical forms that serve as content for canonic classical music. On the other hand, Tagg's rigorous structuralism generates what we might call code-as-content: again, the immediate experience of the music disappears, not behind an architectonic form, but behind a complex semiotic web that has to be built up from scratch, museme by primitive museme. The code is a significant advance over musicology's reified forms, since it incorporates and integrates both musical and cultural constructions; but in its attempt to show the whole structure within which musical meaning comes to exist, it risks spreading the musical experience so thin that we are just as effectively alienated. Musicology has been guilty of welding refractory pieces of music into falsely organic fetish objects, but popular music scholars sometimes seem overly fascinated with analytical methods that pulverize them into ever-more-fundamental structuralist primitives—often as a conscious outflanking maneuver:

The basis of syntactic structures in music lies in metamusical processes of the human mind, either innate or connected with very deep levels of psychological development. And it is in this more general area—where cognitive science, experimental music psychology, and artificial intelligence theory come together—that work is going on which may eventually not only reveal a universal framework underlying the different types of musical structure and sense, but also provide both ethnomusicology and popular music studies with the weapons that will dethrone traditional musicology from the center of the analytical stage.[47]

A fascination with cracking deeply embedded cultural codes energizes the most ambitious attempts at pop music analysis. If musicologists seem overanxious to mystify canonical music from high above, popular music scholars often seem to think that they can best surprise their pop quarry from far below. When David Brackett spends forty-one riveting pages dissecting Elvis Costello's "Pills and Soap" in *Interpreting Popular Music,* he is deliberately taking on the suspicious pop intellectual who famously dismissed all writing about music as useless, like "dancing about architecture." But Brackett is not intimidated. He has just brilliantly sidestepped the musicological problem by interpreting the complex proportional symmetries uncovered in a performance of James Brown's "Superbad" not as (reified) form, but as cultural code, signifyin(g) on both themselves and the classical canon. He now provides an exhaustive phenomenological description of "Pills and Soap" in terms of musemes and their complex signifying codes, down to the unanswerable level of adducing spectrum photos of the registral variation in the overtone patterns of Costello's voice. Coming up at Declan McManus from below, he demolishes the ambivalent artist's claim to an impossible semiotic innocence: "Without mastery of a code, creative work is impossible. But the very fact that a narrative is 'coded' means that it lends the appearance of the natural to the artificial, thereby rendering form invisible in a novel or pop song."[48]

Let me erect a flimsy binarism for which Brackett need accept no direct responsibility. It seems that art ("artificial") music is formed, while popular ("natural") music is coded. The musicological problem can then be defined as attempting to describe visible, autonomous form where there is only invisible cultural code. Ascribing formal autonomy to popular music can fatally entangle the analyst in a morass of nineteenth-century German idealism with little or no explanatory power when faced with the material reality of popular music. It can also make him look like a colonializing chump, projecting his own arty artificiality and canonic preoccupations onto cultural productions that use deeply embedded codes precisely to communicate with a carefully constructed (and fiercely defended) "effortless naturalness."

But cultural code-as-content has its own complementary pitfall, which one might call the semiological problem: the claim that deciphering rock's codes and identifying its low-level music-semiotic primitives is the same as understanding the physical message that this amazing, visceral medium is. As Costello said in 1983, putting rock music in a "frame"—attempting to exhaust its significance by modeling it completely, either as organic form or semiotic code—"only drags down its immediacy." Brackett has little patience with this "romantic notion of unmediated artistic spontaneity," and why should he—or any of us?[49] Musicology is stiff from centuries on its knees in front of the icons of genius.

But when McClary and Walser talk about "constructing models that serve only as flexible backdrops," the key word is, undoubtedly, flexible. Perhaps our common strategy should begin not with swallowing outmoded notions of artistic spontaneity, but with embracing a new-old ideal of interpretive spontaneity. This is the only real advice New Musicology (taunts of sloppiness and dilettantism from our own colleagues ringing in our ears) has to offer pop music scholars. Loosen up. We had analytical rigor, and it felt dangerously close to rigor mortis.[50] Avoid totalizing (framing) critical gestures altogether, whether in the service of autonomous form or cultural code; stop trying to put the entire piece together (musicology) or take it totally apart (popular music studies). Get in, say something that helps convey the immediacy of the musical experience, and get out. Stop marching through the music's architecture—and dance a little.

Valedictory: Doing Elvis

I deliberately withheld Susan Sontag's best line until now, because it prepares a particularly satisfying final cadence. Sontag ended her essay "Against Interpretation" with a famous and ringing assertion: "In place of a hermeneutics we need an erotics of art." Let us by all means heed the call; but recent musicological history has shown us that formal analysis, segregated from the vital cultural content acknowledged by hermeneutics, is too easily co-opted. It becomes not the erotics that Sontag wanted—the formal study of how art organizes our bodily sensory experience—but instead an ideologically driven, antierotic search for disembodied structures of transcendental form-as-content.

We really need both an erotics and a hermeneutics of music, together. There have been notable attempts to synthesize this unstable compound, to meld precise phenomenological description of musical effects with cultural interpretation: Adorno's *Philosophy of Modern Music;* Roland Barthes's famous essay "The Grain of the Voice"; Greil Marcus's *Mystery Train.* But such work can hardly be said to be a main focus of institutionalized musicology and music theory—not yet. Rather than expound the virtues of such a mix in the abstract, I want to make a small valedictory intervention in the complex discourse around a famous piece of music whose erotic and hermeneutic fields are already inextricably mixed: Elvis Presley's 1956 recording of "Hound Dog." The aim is to explore how musicological analysis can help popular music studies "do Elvis."

"Hound Dog" is the song that earned Presley the moniker "Elvis the Pelvis." The sexual consequences of his 1956 live and televised performances of the raunchy novelty number have been inflated to near-mythic proportions: "ONE OUT OF THREE AMERICANS SAW ELVIS ON 'ED SULLIVAN' IN 1956! And to paraphrase Texas songwriter Butch Hancock, Elvis wiped out four thousand years of Judeo-Christian uptightness about sex in fifteen minutes of TV. The King shook the fig leaf away and the kids of 'The Donna Reed Show' would soon find themselves high as a kite and fornicating in the mud at Woodstock."[51] If ever there were a promising subject for an erotics cum hermeneutics of music, this would be it. The search for the cultural context and hermeneutic content of "Hound Dog" has led Elvis devotees on dizzying intertextual journeys like the one chronicled in Peter Nazareth's "Elvis as Anthology," wondrous and complex stories that twist the simple binarisms of race, sound, and authenticity into unrecognizable knots.[52] Begin with two New York Jews, Jerry Lieber and Mike Stoller, who wrote an "imitation" rough blues number for legendary blues shouter Big Mama (Willie Mae) Thornton, a song that became a huge R&B hit in 1953. Elvis evidently knew that record, but only thought about covering the song during a disastrous Las Vegas engagement in April 1956 when he saw a (white) lounge act called Freddy Bell and the Bellboys do a comedy-burlesque

"Hound Dog" with show-stopping va-va-voom choreography. Elvis started working the number into his live show as comic relief, basing the lyrics and his "gyrations" (to use the famous word) on what he had seen in Vegas. The song always got a big reaction, and it became Presley's standard closer, a witty multiracial piece of signifyin' humor, troping off white overreactions to black sexual innuendo.

But nobody got the joke. Turning to Elvis's *recording* of "Hound Dog" allows the construction of another, tighter hermeneutic, one that situates the July 2, 1956, session within a short, bitter struggle over the performance of sexuality in America's mass media. On June 5, Elvis performed "Hound Dog" on the *Milton Berle Show*, gyrations and all.[53] The display was not taken as parody. "Hound Dog" confirmed mainstream America's worst fears about rock and roll, and sparked nationwide vituperation; for the first time, Presley, who in "Heartbreak Hotel" had the number one record in the country, and who still saw himself as basically a good, churchgoing boy, was attacked in the media as a sexual exhibitionist with no musical talent. On July 1, Elvis appeared on the *Steve Allen Show*. It is still not certain whether Allen (a middlebrow jazz devotee) was intentionally trying to embarrass Elvis, but the format of his appearance ensured that any dangerous sexual charisma was totally dissipated. Presley was dressed in the white tie and tails of a "high-class" musician, the clothes were intentionally made so tight he couldn't move freely, and—the crowning humiliation—he was immobilized completely during "Hound Dog," directed in a gesture of heavy-handed satire to address the tune to a real bassett hound.

By most accounts Presley was a good sport about all this, but Scotty Moore has testified that when the band went into the studio the next day to record "Hound Dog," they were all angry about their treatment the previous night. Elvis drove the band through thirty-one takes, slowly fashioning a menacing, rough-trade version of the song quite different from the one they had been performing on stage. Nazareth quite plausibly interprets this as revenge on Steve ("you ain't no friend of mine") Allen, and as a protest against being censored on national TV.[54]

The musicologist can provide the erotics to back up this hermeneutic. "Hound Dog" is notable for an unremitting level of what can only be called rock and roll dissonance: Elvis just shouts, leaving behind almost completely the rich vocal timbres ("romantic lyricism") and mannerist rhythmic play on added syllables ("boogification") that Richard Middleton identifies as the cornerstones of his art.[55] Scotty Moore's guitar is feral: playing rhythm, he stays in the lowest register, slashing away at open fifths and hammering the strong beats with bent and distorted pitches; his repetitive breaks are stinging—and even, when he begins one chorus in the wrong key, quite literally atonal. (Moore, embarrassed, would later dismiss this solo as "ancient psychedelia.")[56] And the Jordanaires, a gospel quartet who would provide wonderfully subtle rhythmic backup on the next song Elvis recorded at the session, "Don't Be Cruel," are just hanging on for the ride during this one, while drummer D. J. Fontana just goes plumb crazy. Fontana's machine-gun drumming on this record has become deservedly famous: the only part of his kit consistently audible in the mix is the snare, played so loud and insistently that the RCA engineers just gave up and let his riffs distort into splatters of clipped noise. The overall effect could not be more different from the amused, relaxed contempt of Big Mama Thornton; it is reminiscent of nothing so much as late 1970s white punk rage—the Ramones, Iggy Pop, the Sex Pistols. ("Never Mind the Bollocks Here's . . . Elvis Presley?")

Or is it? Elvis asked for acetates from the July 2 session so he could learn to duplicate the sound of the recordings in subsequent stage performances. And it was this angry, hopped-up version of "Hound Dog" that he performed on September 9 when he appeared for the first time on the *Ed Sullivan Show*. Even though sexual censorship continued during this pivotal appearance—reviewers noticed and commented on the fact that the camera cut away from Elvis when he went into his gyrations—by that point it didn't seem to make any difference, the girls still screamed and wept. The sexual tension had been transferred into the music itself.

The precedent had been set a month earlier in Jacksonville, Florida. Elvis's August 10 performances were accompanied by a carnival of sexual panic: the local representatives of the American Guild of Variety Artists (which represented exotic dancers) demanded that he join the union and post a bond, and a crusading local judge had warrants drawn up for Presley's arrest if he "acted in a fashion that put vulgarity and obscenity in front of our children." It was made quite clear in a meeting with the judge after the afternoon show that if Elvis so much as shook his hips once, he was going to jail. And so all physical movements below the waist were eliminated that evening. But, as Elvis recounted to his current girlfriend, the band found another way to get the point across: "Baby, you should have been there. Every time D. J. did his thing on the drums, I wiggled my finger, and the girls went wild. I never heard screams like that in my life. I showed them sons of bitches."[57]

*

The musicologist asks: what, exactly, *was* that thing D. J. did on the drums? Undoubtedly it was some version of the thing he does on the July 2 recording, a thing we might transcribe as:

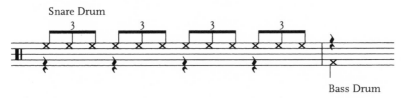

Given that the whole idea of doing "Hound Dog" came from a moment of burlesque in a Vegas lounge, and that Presley and his drummer later colluded to slip the audience a musical sign for the sexy gyrations whose absence was enforced by the Jacksonville judiciary, we can hear Fontana's "angry" machine-gun drumming on the record of "Hound Dog" in a new way. His playing now sounds like an amped-up, rockabilly-speed version of the bump-and-grind triplets familiar to every drummer from decades of striptease performances. Mentally slow down the drumming on the record to half-time, as Presley usually did in live performance for his big finish, and the resemblance is inescapable. Elvis was repeatedly compared to a stripper during 1956; after the Berle show, for instance, the *New York Times* declared that "his one specialty is an accented movement of the body that hitherto has been primarily identified with the repertoire of the blond bombshells of the burlesque runway." Yes, well, that was the joke. The Gray Lady was sensitive to the presence of quite traditional musical erotics—formal devices that cued the performer and audience to experience their bodies sexually—but not quite hep enough to accept a male performer recycling these musical signifiers of sex back to a female audience.

Thanks to media treatment like this, there was very little tease left in the striptease by the time "Hound Dog" came to be recorded. Elvis and the boys' comic travesty of sexuality had melded with something fierce, angry, and real. Fontana's drums blast out of tired burlesque convention into an elec-trifying new erotic register: sexual availability tinged with sullen, inarticulate violence. Nothing like this had ever occurred in the Sun studio sessions; it was a fusion with explosive power. Not for nothing was Presley being touted as the new James Dean.

Elvis complained bitterly in a June 27, 1956, interview about being singled out as "obscene" for his *Milton Berle Show* appearance, when there had been a bona fide burlesque queen on the same program: "This Debra Paget is on the same show. She wore a tight thing with feathers on her behind where they wiggle most. And I never saw anything like it. Sex? Man, she bumped and wiggled all over the place. I'm like Little Boy Blue. And who do they call obscene? Me!" Of course, Elvis was more than a little disingenuous; he went on in the same interview to throw the reporter what now looks like one of the biggest red herrings of popular music scholarship: "The colored folks been singing it and playing it just like I'm doin' now, for more years than I know. They played it like that in the shanties and in their juke joints, and nobody paid it no mind 'til I goosed it up. I got it from them."[58]

This is a fundamental assumption of almost all Elvis reception, the basic matrix of ideas being neatly summarized in the title of a paper delivered at the First International Conference on Elvis Presley in 1995: "A Revolution-ary Black Sexual Persona: Elvis Presley and the White Acquiescence of Black Rhythms." The African American author, Jon Michael Spencer, argues that "the syncopated leg and body movements that Elvis displayed [while singing 'Hound Dog'] on television that evening [are attributable] to the rhythms that undergird African American culture and give it its distinctiveness," and that these rhythms transmit "the attendant sexualities of the irrepressible black cultural presence in the South."[59] There is a general sociocultural truth here that no one can deny, but the specific case of "Hound Dog" subsumes itself under that rubric only with extreme difficulty. (Spencer makes no mention of Leiber and Stoller, or of Freddy Bell and the Bellboys.) According to this analysis, the consistent attacks on "Hound Dog" as (white) burlesque striptease are a racist cultural misreading; the correct reading was given by Elvis himself in the quote above.

One waits in vain for Spencer to articulate precisely the phenomenologi-cal outlines of black rhythm. In a gesture that would have Sontag weeping in frustration, he blithely turns away from the formal erotics of black music ("It is impossible to capture in notation the sexualities conveyed by the rhythms that have long brought the therapeutic black ritual places into existence") and starts analyzing the content of black blues lyrics.[60]

I would argue that it is quite easy to discuss the sexualities conveyed by the rhythms of "Hound Dog"—you don't even need notation to do it—and yet Spencer may still be right, because the distinctive rhythmic structures of that specific performance and recording of "Hound Dog" are irretrievably white. Every time Fontana lets loose that tommy-gun burlesque lick—twelve nervous snare hits leading to a heavy bass thud—he creates a massive downbeat accent. In fact, he turns one entire unit of the song (snares) into a large upbeat to the next (bass drum). This is the crucial rhythmic gesture of the song, and it creates no syncopation and no polyrhythmic play. What it does do is create a rigid hierarchy of weak and strong units, and enforce a regularly recurring structural downbeat at the end of each verse. (That's why the whole band stops playing each time he does it.)

Such absolutely square delineation of upbeats and downbeats is not at all characteristic of African American rhythm. A. M. Jones completed his first pioneering studies of African rhythm in 1956, and the patterns he transcribed bear little resemblance to those underpinning what was then the current number two single on America's pop charts. African rhythm, in general, is additive not divisive—it avoids strong hierarchies of beats, avoids strong coordinated downbeats altogether, and maintains an even fluidity through complex noncoincident polyrhythms. African American music has had to compromise with the rigid upbeat-downbeat structures that rule European forms (see Gunther Schuller's *Early Jazz*, which makes this point in a still-useful introductory discussion of Jones);[61] but, over its syncopated (and thus recognizably Afro-Caribbean) rumba bass, "Hound Dog" careens so far toward an angry, jerky, hierarchy-of-beat-dominated whiteness that it is impossible for this listener to hear the creation of any sort of "therapeutic black ritual space."

All one has to do to hear the problem is compare Presley's version of "Hound Dog" with Big Mama Thornton's 1953 original. Of course Thornton did not sing the number in the uptempo rockabilly style—but her slower, more relaxed reading, with its flexible phrasing, just makes much, much less of the inevitable downbeats. She starts out, as does Elvis, singing each line as one long upbeat ("You ain't nothin' but a *hound* dog"); but as soon as the words change, she shifts the line around so that the "downbeat" falls at the beginning, with a remnant of the original end stress still perceptible

("You *told* me you was high-class / But I can *see* through that"), and sticks to that phrasing even when the opening text comes back ("You ain't *nothin'* but a hound dog"). Each line has a focal accent somewhere (and never in the same place twice), but Thornton's elegant syncopations and microinflections of the beat keep the rest of the syllables energized, too. The overall effect of macro and micro flexibility is enticingly additive: Thornton loosens up the stress hierarchy of the text, evens it out, and lets it float sexily above the steady backbeat underneath.

Presley's reading of the song holds rigidly to end-accented phrasing ("You ain't nothin' but a *hound* dog," every time). Each line has a clear feeling of upbeat leading to final downbeat, and when Elvis rhythmically activates some of the lines through "boogification" ("You-*ain't* ah-*nuh* thin-*but* ah-*hound* dog") the link between his singing and Fontana's playing becomes clear: each of them is enforcing a strict rhythmic hierarchy by making an entire phrase of weak upbeats lead inexorably to a heavily stressed downbeat. What happens very obviously in the recording is that the two are in a sort of rhythmic canon. Fontana's arrival on the downbeat always energizes Presley's leap toward the next stressed downbeat, as if the singer is being shot out of a cannon. (When Fontana launches Scotty Moore into his second solo this way, it's with a downbeat so strong that it throws the guitarist briefly into another key!)

These macho rhythmic gestures are cadences—alternations of tension and release—and they appear nowhere in Big Mama Thornton's conception of the blues. The drive of the twelve snare hits to the bass drum, of the "You-*ain't* ah-*nuh* thin-*but* ah-" to the "*hound* dog," of the grind to the bump, is, like the drive of the dominant to the tonic, a feature of European music. And the bump-and-grind erotics of the tonic-dominant polarity are well established in the West.[62] Elvis the Pelvis is not necessarily out of Africa; he may well remind us of another sexually dangerous Western musical artist recently recognized as prone to pelvic pounding:

Roll over, Beethoven. You ain't nothin' but a hound dog.

Notes

1. David Brackett, *Interpreting Popular Music* (Cambridge: Cambridge University Press, 1995), 19; Richard Middleton, *Studying Popular Music* (Buckingham, Eng.: Open University Press, 1990), 103; Susan McClary and Robert Walser, "Start Making Sense: Musicology Wrestles with Rock," in *On Record: Rock, Pop, and the Written Word,* ed. Simon Frith and Andrew Goodwin (New York: Pantheon, 1990), 281.

2. Middleton, *Studying Popular Music,* 106–7.

3. The opening salvos came from Joseph Kerman, whose calls for a musicology oriented more toward criticism and dismissals of the quasi-scientific fact-finding he called "positivism," still rankle some today. His article "How We Got into Analysis, and How to Get Out" (*Critical Inquiry* 7, no. 2 [1980]: 311–31), was followed by a provocative book: *Contemplating Music: Challenges to Musicology* (Cambridge: Harvard University Press, 1985). Janet M. Levy raised key ideological issues in her short but much-cited article "Covert and Casual Values in Recent Writings about Music," *Journal of Musicology* 5 (1987): 3–27. Leo Treitler's collection *Music and the Historical Imagination* (Cambridge: Harvard University Press, 1989) disseminated twenty years of often idiosyncratic challenges of the status quo to a ready audience.

Much of the direct impetus for critical revaluations within musicology came from investigations of politics, gender, and sexuality—subjects notably taboo in traditional musicological discourse. Susan McClary provided propaedeutic essays for the English translations of two influential texts: Jacques Attali's *Noise: The Political Economy of Music,* trans. Brian Massumi (Minneapolis: University of Minnesota Press, 1985), and Catherine Clement's incendiary *Opera, or the Undoing of Women,* trans. Betsy Wing (Minneapolis: University of Minnesota Press, 1988). McClary's own collection, *Feminine Endings: Music, Gender, and Sexuality* (Minneapolis: University of Minnesota Press, 1991), kicked things off in America, assembling most of her pioneering critical work from the 1980s. With the roughly contemporaneous publication of Rose Rosengard Subotnik's *Developing Variations: Style and Ideology in Western Music* (Minneapolis: University of Minnesota Press, 1991) and Lawrence Kramer's *Music as Cultural Practice, 1800–1900* (Berkeley: University of California Press, 1990), the paradigm shift that Kerman had been calling for appeared to be taking place. The American musicological response is representatively, although of course not exhaustively, accessible in three important collections of essays that appeared in the early 1990s. Ruth Solie edited the first, *Musicology and Difference: Gender and Sexuality in Musical Scholarship* (Berkeley: University of California Press, 1993). Beating her to press, though conceived later, was Katherine Bergeron and Philip V. Bohlman, eds., *Disciplining Music: Musicology and Its Canons* (Chicago: University of Chicago Press, 1992). Both Bergeron and Bohlman contributed carefully worked essays that already showed the self-critical awareness of the interdependence of canon and ideology that seemed so obvious—and so obviously unexamined!—to Richard Middleton in 1990. See also Philip Brett, Elizabeth Wood, and Gary C. Thomas, eds., *Queering the Pitch: The New Gay and Lesbian Musicology* (New York: Routledge, 1994).

A more general Anglo-American perspective, including wide-ranging reconceptualizing work by both musicologists and music theorists, can be found in Nicholas Cook and Mark Everist, eds., *Rethinking Music* (Oxford: Oxford University Press, 1998). Richard Taruskin has filtered a fundamental critique of musicology through the lens of historical performance practice; see his *Text and Act* (New York: Oxford University Press, 1995) for a collection of important work. Less accessible, but symptomatic, are early issues of the journal repercussions: critical and alternative viewpoints on music and scholarship, published since 1992 by graduate students of the musicology department at the University of California, Berkeley. See especially Lawrence Kramer, "The Musicology of the Future," *repercussions* 1, no. 1 (spring 1992): 5–18, and my editorial in that inaugural issue. (Kramer went over some of the same ground again in his *Classical Music and Postmodern Knowledge* [Berkeley: University of California Press, 1995], 1–32.)

The critique has not always been received gratefully: negative reviews of McClary and Kramer, to take the two most salient voices, far outnumber the positive. Perhaps the most passionate and systematic attempt to "refute" the calls for paradigm shift has come from music theory; see Pieter C. van den Toorn, *Music, Politics, and the Academy* (Berkeley and Los Angeles: University of California Press, 1995); Kofi Agawu, "Does Music Theory Need Musicology?" *Current Musicology* 53 (1993): 89, and "Analyzing Music under the New Musicological Regime," *Music Theory Online* 2.4 (1969) (http://boethius.music.ucsb.edu/mto/issues/mto.96.2.4/mto.96.2.4.agawu.html). Coming full circle, one might check in with Joseph Kerman again; see "Musicology in Transition," *The Maynooth International Musicological Conference 1995 Selected Proceedings: Part One,* ed. Patrick F. Devine and Harry White (Dublin: Four Courts Press, 1996), 19–33.

4. Following the usage of most popular music scholarship, I will be using the term "musicology" to refer to the entire project of studying canonical classical music. When it becomes necessary to distinguish the goals and ideology of academic music theory, I will call out that discipline explicitly.

5. Norman Lebrecht, *Who Killed Classical Music? Maestros, Managers, and Corporate Politics* (Secaucus, N.J.: Birch Lane Press, 1997), 386–91, 399.

6. David Schiff, "Classical Appeal," *Atlantic Monthly* 280, no. 2 (August 1997): 7071.

7. For America, see the account in Lawrence Levine, *Highbrow/Lowbrow: The Emer-

gence of Cultural Hierarchy in America (Cambridge: Harvard University Press, 1988). For a European perspective, see William Weber, *Music and the Middle Class: The Social Structure of Concert Life in London, Paris, and Vienna* (New York: Holmes and Meier, 1975).

8. Joseph Horowitz presents a useful roundup in the context of the Toscanini cult, including Adorno's key attacks on the "culture industry" and Virgil Thomson versus the "music appreciation racket"; see his *Understanding Toscanini: How He Became an American Culture-God and Created a New Audience for Old Music* (New York: Knopf, 1987), 229–50.

9. Some of the key texts include Bergeron and Bohlman, *Disciplining Music,* especially the article by Bohlman on "Musics and Canons"; Joseph Kerman, "A Few Canonic Variations," *Critical Inquiry* 10, no. 1 (1983): 107–25; Marcia Citron, *Gender and the Musical Canon* (Cambridge: Cambridge University Press, 1993); and Susan McClary, "Terminal Prestige: The Case of Avant-Garde Musical Composition," *Cultural Critique* 12 (spring 1989): 57–81.

10. See Margaret Helfgott, *Out of Tune* (Beverly Hills, Calif.: Warner Books, 1998).

11. Horowitz, *Understanding Toscanini,* 22–42.

12. Lebrecht makes a rather coarse Jeremiah: "Inside the belly of the corporate whale, classical music nestled contagiously with its new bedfellows. The masturbating antics of Michael Jacksonish pop music, the moral decay of *Fatal Attraction* movies and the monotony of over-organized sport all left their mark on the classical slow-coach of the infotainment highway. When George Michael sneezed, classical recording seized up with pneumonia. Michael Jackson's arrest on child-sex charges precipitated emergency surgery at Sony Classical" (*Who Killed Classical Music?,* 399). Is this just journalistic bombast—or (homo)sexual panic?

13. Attali, *Noise,* 11–12.

14. Jacques Baudrillard, *Simulations,* trans. Paul Foss, Paul Patton, and Philip Beitchman (New York: Semiotext[e], 1983), 11–12, 25.

15. Michael Daugherty and Wayne Koestenbaum, liner notes for *Jackie O* (Argo, 1997).

16. In *Hole in Our Soul: The Loss of Beauty and Meaning in American Popular Music* (New York: Free Press, 1994), Martha Bayles argues at great length that the alternative aesthetic itself recycles old modernist riffs, but the point remains: modernism has to be filtered through "the alternative" before it can reenergize the postminimal.

17. "Bang on a Can" (Michael Gordon, David Lang, Julia Wolfe), liner notes for *Industry* (Sony Classical, 1995); Stevan Keane, liner note for Steve Martland, *Crossing the Border* (Factory, 1992).

18. Or did he? Alex Ross finished up a survey of Britpop for the *New Yorker* (August 29, 1997) by raving that the neo-Pink Floyd band Radiohead had "pulled off one of the great art-pop balancing acts in the history of rock." He then attempted to describe their "essentially indescribable" sound with the following amazing analogy: "I had one last idea while watching the very English spectacle of Diana's funeral: the varieties of lament heard during the service—an Elgar elegy, an Elton John ballad, an otherworldly contemporary dirge by John Tavener—could have been telescoped into a fairly typical Radiohead song." That Ross conceives of rock as having the stylistic range to encapsulate all of classical music, and not the other way round, is clear. What could be more powerful evidence that rock music has earned its new paradigmatic status? (Ross writes regularly on both classical and rock for the *New Yorker.*)

19. See Carolyn Abbate and Roger Parker, eds., *Analyzing Opera: Verdi and Wagner* (Berkeley and Los Angeles: University of California Press, 1989); Jeffrey Kallberg, *Chopin at the Boundaries: Sex, History, and Musical Genre* (Cambridge: Harvard University Press, 1996); Judith Tick, "Charles Ives and Gender Ideology," in *Musicology and Difference,* ed. Solie, 83–106; Maynard Solomon, "Charles Ives: Some Questions of Veracity," *Journal of the American Musicological Society* 40, no. 3 (fall 1987): 443–70; Philip Brett, "Benjamin Britten," "Peter Grimes," *Cambridge Opera Handbooks* (New York: Cambridge University Press, 1983); Richard Taruskin, "A Myth of the Twentieth Century: The Rite of Spring, the Tradition of the New, and 'The Music Itself,'" *Modernism/Modernity* 2 (January 1995): 1–26.

20. Mitchell Morris, "Black Masculinity and the Sound of Wealth: Barry White in the Early 70s," paper delivered at "Cross(over) Relations: Popular Music, Scholarship, and the Canon," Rochester, New York, 1996.

21. One of the most overt recent uses of this symphonic surrealism is in Oasis's 1997 video for "Don't Go Away" (*Be Here Now,* 1997), where somber instrumentalists in formal wear file onto a hyperrealistic canvas carrying black umbrellas. (A shot of multiple floating men in suits with umbrellas à la Magritte immediately follows, proving that the director is one of those who likes his avant-garde references big and obvious.) As in rap videos, the string and horn lines in the mix are hardly prominent enough to justify the elaborate staging of "classical music."

22. Carolyn Abbate, *Unsung Voices: Opera and Musical Narrative in the Nineteenth Century* (Princeton: Princeton University Press, 1991); Michel Poizat, *The Angel's Cry: Beyond the Pleasure Principle in Opera,* trans. Arthur Denner (Ithaca: Cornell University Press, 1992). For avant-garde canonical examples, listen for the heartbreaking quotes of Isolde's *Liebestod* in B. A. Zimmerman's *Requiem for a Dead Poet* (1969–71); and the oddly sweet liberties Charles Dodge's *Any Resemblance is Strictly Coincidental* (1977) takes with a 1903 recording of Enrico Caruso singing "Vesti la giubba."

23. See David Toop, *Ocean of Sound: Aether Talk, Ambient Sound, and Imaginary Worlds* (London: Serpent's Tail, 1995).

24. Kenny Berkowitz, "Minimal Impact," *Option* 77 (November/December 1997): 50–55.

25. A material correlative for the boundary-erasing position of ambient: the Orb demanded and got pressings of their *Adventures beyond the Ultraworld* on new vinyl so as to get the widest dynamic range. New vinyl is customarily reserved for audiophile classical recordings. See Vanni Neri and Giorgio Campari, *The Orb: The O.O.B.E. Adventure* (Stampa Alternativa Sonic Book SB 04, 1996 [unpaginated]).

26. Berkowitz, "Minimal Impact," 55.

27. Neri and Campari, *The Orb*, n.p.; the quote appears to be a back translation from the Italian!

28. On "positivism," a still-controversial epithet, see Kerman, *Contemplating Music*, 31–59.

29. Ibid., 73.

30. Ibid., 112.

31. See the literature survey in Robert Fink, "Arrows of Desire: Long Range Linear Structure and the Transformation of Musical Energy," Ph.D. diss., University of California, Berkeley, 1994, 1–23. The critique has been echoed vigorously from within music theory itself (yes, there is a "New Theory" also); the key recent work along these lines has been published by, among others, Fred Maus, Marion Guck, Marion Kielian-Gilbert, and Kevin Korsyn.

32. Kerman, *Contemplating Music,* 19.

33. McClary and Walser, "Start Making Sense," 287.

34. Susan Sontag, *Against Interpretation* (New York: Doubleday, 1966), 304.

35. Ibid., 7.

36. Ibid., 12.

37. Marshall McLuhan, *Understanding Media: The Extensions of Man* (New York: McGraw-Hill, 1964), 282–83.

38. Some representative references include Allan Forte, "Schenker's Conception of Musical Structure," *Journal of Music Theory* (hereafter *JMT*) 3, no. 1 (1959): 1–24; Forte, "A Theory of Set-Complexes for Music," *JMT* 8, no. 2 (1964): 136–51; Milton Babbitt, "Twelvetone Invariants as Compositional Determinants," *Musical Quarterly* 46 (1960): 246–59; Babbitt, "Set Structure as a Compositional Determinant," *JMT* 5 (1961): 72–94, no. 1; David Lewin, "A Theory of Segmental Association in Twelve-Tone Music," *Perspectives of New Music* 1 (1962): 89–116; Donald Martino, "The Source-Set and Its Aggregate Formations," *JMT* 5, no. 2 (1961): 224–73; George Rochberg, "The Harmonic Tendency of the Hexachord," *JMT* 3, no. 2 (1959): 208–30.

39. Ruth Solie, "The Living Work: Organicism and Musical Analysis," *Nineteenth-Century Music* 4, no. 2 (fall 1980): 136–54; McClary, *Feminine Endings*; Robert Fink,

"Going Flat: Post-Hierarchical Music Theory and the Musical Surface," in *Rethinking Music*, ed. Cook and Everist, 102–37.

40. This argument is made uncompromisingly in van den Toorn, *Music, Politics, and the Academy*, 11–64.

41. Eduard Hanslick, *On the Musically Beautiful*, 8th ed., trans. Geoffrey Payzant (1891; Indianapolis: Hackett, 1986), 77–84.

42. Kerman, "How We Got into Analysis, and How to Get Out," 331.

43. It happens more than you might think; see Robert Walser, *Running with the Devil: Power, Gender, and Madness in Heavy Metal Music* (Hanover, N.H.: Wesleyan University Press, 1993), 57–107.

44. McClary and Walser, "Start Making Sense," 289.

45. For a metatheoretical discussion, see John Covach, "We Won't Get Fooled Again: Rock Music and Musical Analysis," in *Keeping Score: Music, Disciplinarity, Culture*, ed. David Schwarz, Anahid Kassabian, and Lawrence Siegel (Charlottesville: University of Virginia Press, 1997), 75–89. For a programmatic use of Schenkerian techniques of reduction, see Walter Everett, "Fantastic Remembrance in John Lennon's 'Strawberry Fields Forever' and 'Julia,'" *Musical Quarterly* 72, no. 3 (1986): 360–93.

46. Philip Tagg, *KOJAK, 50 Seconds of Television Music: Toward the Analysis of Affect in Popular Music, Studies from the Department of Musicology* (Göteborg, Musikvetenskapliga Institutionen vid Göteborgs Universitet, 1979).

47. Middleton, *Studying Popular Music*, 191–92.

48. Brackett, *Interpreting Popular Music*, 157–98.

49. Ibid., 157–59.

50. This point was made by Leonard Meyer, a musicologist passionately interested in analysis and criticism, during public discussion of the formation of the Society for Music Theory in the late 1970s.

51. The speaker is Mojo Nixon, introducing *The Elvis Reader*, ed. Kevin Quain (New York: St. Martin's Press, 1992), xiv–xv.

52. Peter Nazareth, "Elvis as Anthology," in *In Search of Elvis: Music, Race, Art, Religion*, ed. Vernon Chadwick (Boulder: Westview, 1997), 56–60, 69–70.

53. "With Scotty's solo he lurches backward in what might be interpreted as an upbeat adaptation of the shrugging, stuttering, existential hopelessness of a James Dean, there is a jittery fiddling with his mouth and nose, and as the song comes to an end he is dragging the microphone down to the floor, staggering almost to his knees. [He] then goes into his patented half-time ending, gripping the mike, circling it sensuously, jackknifing his legs out as the audience half-screams, half-laughs, and he laughs, too—it is clearly all in good fun" (Peter Guralnick, *Last Train to Memphis: The Rise of Elvis Presley* [Boston: Little, Brown, 1994], 284. My brief narration of the events of summer 1956 is indebted to Guralnick's).

54. Nazareth, "Elvis as Anthology," 58.

55. Richard Middleton, "All Shook Up? Innovation and Continuity in Elvis Presley's Vocal Style," in *The Elvis Reader*, ed. Quain, 3–12.

56. Guralnick, *Last Train to Memphis*, 289.

57. Ibid., 321–22.

58. Ibid., 288–89.

59. Jon Michael Spencer, "A Revolutionary Black Sexual Persona: Elvis Presley and the White Acquiescence of Black Rhythms," in *In Search of Elvis*, ed. Chadwick, 110.

60. Ibid., 118–19.

61. Gunther Schuller, *Early Jazz* (New York: Oxford University Press, 1968), 10–22.

62. See McClary, *Feminine Endings*, 12–16, 68–69, 124–30.

Rock music was formed largely in the racially charged cultural context of the United States during the 1950s. A common trope of rock histories is to discuss the origins and development of rock music as integrationist; although the new genre was first brought to a large audience by white performers like Elvis Presley and Pat Boone, authors stress the influence of African American music and culture.[1] As Michael Bane suggests with reference to Memphis white and black gospel, "in the late 1940s and early 1950s the two gospel musics began touching again for the first time since the Civil War. Sparks flew, and from those sparks rock and roll was kindled."[2] These were surely not neutral exchanges, as white performers effectively colonized, popularized, and redefined black styles, but in Simon Jones's words, as music for white teens became coded with "blackness," the "desegregation of musical tastes [was] profoundly subversive."[3]

From this reading of rock's roots, many scholars view 1960s rock similarly, as a "universal" genre. The Beatles's early music has been interpreted as a repackaging of African American rhythm and blues that could be marketed to a white American audience who might not purchase the original recordings.[4] Bob Dylan's protest songs have been seen as a reflection of the momentum of the civil rights movement, and much late-60s rock on both sides of the Atlantic is largely blues-based.[5] On the other side of the racial divide, Aretha Franklin's soul performances could "cross over" and make an impact on the mainstream popular charts, and Motown's distinctive recordings have been called the "sound of integration."[6]

The nuances essential for understanding rock in the 1960s should compel us to problematize clear-cut notions of race. However, this has not generally been the case in much rock history literature. While historical treatments of 60s rock usually avoid overt value judgments, the conventional narrative reasserts largely segregated spheres of activity in the mid-1960s at the same time that it disproportionately values those spheres. The separate episodes on "white" and "black" 1960s rock contained in the 1995 PBS documentary series *Rock & Roll* are a case in point. The "white" episode, titled "Shakespeares in the Alley," constructs performers like Bob Dylan and the Beatles as iconoclastic "geniuses" creating "art" not fully comprehensible to the public; the "black" episode, titled "Respect," inscribes musicians such as Motown artists and Aretha Franklin as hardworking "craftspeople" eager to make themselves acceptable to a general (read: white) audience. No matter how much we may enjoy these repertories with little or no concern for such boundaries, the implicit acceptance of racial difference inevitably affects our reception of the music. Thus, as rock's admittedly "unruly history"[7] begins to give way to a conventional narrative often recapitulated with each offering in a growing bibliography, it is important to critically examine the assumptions underlying the processes of assigning value that give these histories their shape.

*

Of the myriad themes used to construct white rock musicians of the 1960s, such as the Beatles and Bob Dylan as "artists," the most important is perhaps the assertion of originality in their compositions. Joe Stuessy sets the Beatles apart from the rock norm of following convention: "Usually once pop artists establish a successful style they cling to it desperately. . . . But the creative mind strikes out into the new and uncharted territory. . . . The Beatles had that spark of creativity."[8] Robert Palmer discusses Dylan along similar lines in his companion book to the PBS documentary: "Dylan's new electric music . . . was not guitar-band pop rock; it was a wildly original, high-energy brand of electric blues, as gritty and unpolished as the rural folk music that

had inspired his earlier acoustic work. . . . He was writing lyrics of unprecedented complexity and scope that seemed to come rushing out as intensely as
the crackling, driven music that supported them."[9] This music is constructed
as more than original; rather it is seen as art that transcends the bounds of its
social functions and contexts.[10] As Palmer puts it, "the mid-sixties Beatles
and Bob Dylan created a kind of rock and roll art music, explicitly designed
for listening and thinking rather than dancing and romancing."[11]

Closely connected to these themes is the focus on iconoclastic images of
the performers themselves that correspond to popular notions of the "artist"
as above and beyond understanding. For example, through the oft-told story
of Bob Dylan introducing the Beatles to drugs, and the episode of the Beatles
getting high in the bathrooms of Buckingham Palace, rock histories assert
an explicit association of drug use with the creation of serious art, contributing to a picture of the original artist that operates beyond the limits of
conventional society.[12] The performers themselves cultivated their image as
iconoclasts, sometimes flaunting the fact that they were not expected to
follow social norms. Soon after he "went electric," for example, Bob Dylan
appeared on a 1966 radio call-in show and showed utter disdain for his
audience.[13] From patronizing to defensive to downright mean, Dylan positioned himself as above the crowd and beyond questioning. He did not wish
his audience to understand the stylistic and poetic aspects of his songs, and
he "drift[ed]" off and paid little attention to their questions. When talking to
one caller, he sarcastically quipped that he got "paid by the word," and
replied that "you shouldn't think about anything." Further, when a caller
wondered what had happened to the "sweet lovable Bob Dylan," Dylan
suggested that he would rather have no audience at all than cater to the
public.[14]

In almost all conceptions of rock history, the Beatles occupy a lone special
place, analogous to that of Beethoven in (for lack of a better term) classical
music. Indeed, without the phenomenon of serious Beatles reception, popular music studies in general might have largely remained taboo.[15] But the
tendency to construct our image of the Beatles with the same valorizing
ideological baggage as is often brought to a figure such as Beethoven is
worth comment. As a way of considering the Beatles as figures of rock
history, consider each part of the title of Walter Everett's 1995 essay "The
Beatles as Composers: The Genesis of *Abbey Road*, Side Two."[16] The Beatles
are not merely described as songwriters but "composers," supposedly of the

"great Western art music tradition," and therefore worth taking seriously.[17] The term "genesis" constructs the Beatles as creators, prime movers, and originals.[18] By focusing on *Abbey Road,* the project that occupied the final recording sessions the Beatles attempted as a group, the essay considers their careers as a teleologically coherent trajectory that ends with a culmination of what has come before.[19] And targeting the entire second side of the recording invites a perspective that considers separate songs as an organic unity, an artistically inseparable whole.[20]

In addition to the manifold strands of the "artist" image woven in discussions of the Beatles, the group's special place in rock history is further secured through the abundance of scholarship directed toward the group. The entire weight of the positivistic and analytical musicological enterprise is brought to bear on the Beatles in a way no other rock artist or group has yet to experience.[21] Many of these publications are not colorful books for the casual fan, but attempts at authoritative research to document the staggering weight of information that has been collected.[22] In the realm of actual musical documents, there are the three recent "Beatles anthologies" recordings, which compile rare tracks and alternate takes, and the 1989 "complete scores," which are transcriptions of every recorded Beatles song, including guitar and bass tablature and notated drum parts (a far cry from the usual format of piano-vocal-guitar chord diagram sheet music found for popular music).[23] Further, the Beatles's music has been treated as *the* rock music of choice for serious musical analysis.[24] The analyst's bag of tricks is often used in an unrestrained way, as if the music's value is a function of the applicability of traditional music theory methodologies.[25]

In striking contrast to these images of white performers are the pictures usually painted of their black contemporaries. The performers under contract to the Motown record company run by Berry Gordy Jr. are routinely presented as having had their creativity imposed from outside. Images abound of "assembly-line production" and a "stable" (rather than, say, a pantheon) of performers pushed to attend finishing school so as to be "acceptable."[26] Joe McEwen and Jim Miller, in *The Rolling Stone Illustrated History of Rock and Roll,* characterize Motown as "a wholly mechanical style and sound that roared and purred like a well-tuned Porsche."[27] The image is complex: Motown is likened to one of the most prestigious of sports cars, but the evocation of the automobile serves both to ground the company in its Detroit-based origins and to reinforce the notion that the music, however fine, is a machinelike commercial product. The many Motown performers who took control of their own music and careers, like Smokey Robinson, Marvin Gaye, Stevie Wonder, and Michael Jackson, are seen as exceptions to the rule of autocratic artistic control, rather than as the protagonists in a different potential narrative that could concentrate on these stars transcending the system of their record company.[28]

Soul music of the 1960s is usually characterized as more "authentic," than its white contemporaries because the performers and their material are strongly associated with the social and political issues of the time.[29] But as a result this repertory is treated more as a sociological and political phenomenon than a musical one.[30] Discussions of the music tend to suggest an intuitive, improvisational basis that runs contrary to popular notions of "art," which needs to be thoroughly studied to be understood.[31] For example, according to Russell Gersten in his *Rolling Stone Illustrated History* essay on Aretha Franklin, "there is something profound and magical about the woman that references to formal aesthetics do not catch. . . . Long after the mediocre works are forgotten, the beauties of her intuitive, improvisatory work will remain."[32] There is a clear subtext within these words of praise that the learned criteria for understanding and appreciating true art are simply not applicable to the soul performer. An additional question begged here is one of gender; Gersten is suggesting that Franklin, specifically referred to as a woman, produces "beautiful" and "magical" music through "intuitive" processes, implying that thinking and reasoning lead her to accomplish "mediocre" work.

A few direct comparisons of the treatment of white and black 1960s rock musicians reveal a subtle, but clear, differentiation of value along racial lines. This can be observed from the earliest rock histories, such as Carl Belz's *The Story of Rock,* first published in 1969.[33] Belz states that "Negro music has always been more inextricably bound up with social developments than has white music."[34] Thus, white music is somehow more autonomous than black music, and it is not as important to consider black music as *music.* Belz goes on to argue that "the Negro Rhythm and Blues scene has exhibited less . . . sophistication [than the Beatles and Bob Dylan]," and that "the meaning of the soul is more evasive, more closely related to an aesthetic experience than to the color of an individual artist."[35] As Belz would have it, black music is not so complex, and further, its essence can be successfully appropriated by anyone without regard to issues of authenticity. In a more recent text Joe Stuessy spends a good amount of time on technical descriptions of the Beatles's innovations, covering rhythm, meter, melody, harmony and tonality, timbre, form, texture, and lyrics,[36] but begins his chapter on soul music by stating that "you know when it's there, and you know when it's not. . . . Soul, as a musical genre, defies accurate definition."[37] Further, his analysis of an Aretha Franklin gospel performance concentrates solely on melody, avoiding the manifold parameters that intelligently inform his discussion of the Beatles.[38] In Michael Campbell's 1996 textbook on popular music, *And the Beat Goes On,* the Beatles and Bob Dylan are discussed under the heading "The Dominant Artists of Sixties Rock." But black artists can not exist in this context, since the next major heading announces "Soul: African American Music in the Sixties."[39] The more informal instructor's manual that accompanies the text continues along these lines. In it, the Beatles's "greatness" is indicated through their range, defined as "how an artist or group of artists can create quite different sound worlds from one composition to the next and still retain a distinctive identity." But when a similar ideal is hinted at with reference to Aretha Franklin two pages later, as "the only singer of the rock era who is equally at home in James Brown-like music and tender ballads," constructions of value like "greatness" are not to be found.[40] Furthermore, when Campbell *does* identify facets that he values in the music of black artists, he reserves these interpretive stances for the instructor's manual as well, and therefore leaves such shading to the individual professor to include in a less formal way. For example: "Indeed, you can introduce the point, implicit in the content of the last two chapters, that black music of the '60s certainly did as much to diversify the sound of contemporary popular music as the basically white rock discussed above."[41] Thus, as the content of a popular music canon solidifies, too many scholars are actively searching for value in the music of certain performers, while leaving similar observations about others as footnotes, presumably not worthy of inclusion in the main body of the text. The value of the canon becomes fallaciously confirmed as explicit assertions of value are reserved largely for the canon's limited and predetermined membership.[42]

The overwhelmingly polarized notion of white "artists" and black "craftspeople" in 1960s rock is ripe for a skeptical deconstruction. The "race issue" itself is replete with nuances that could influence more strongly our historical framework. For example, the construction of a racially determined stylistic polarity loses its force with a critical look at personnel. Memphis's

Stax Records, whose recordings appealed primarily to blacks, was largely powered by the integrated house band Booker T. and the MGs.[43] Aretha Franklin's historic first recording session for Atlantic Records in Muscle Shoals, Alabama, was backed by session musicians who were all white.[44] In Robert Palmer's words, "these are the sort of ironies that virtually *defined* the soul-music era. . . . The issue of race seems so evident and straightforward, so close to the surface in rock and roll, and particularly in soul music; but things are not always what they seem."[45]

Indeed, constructing 1960s Motown and soul as primarily assembly-line craft deliberately sets numerous factors aside for a smooth, stereotypical story. Recent work on Motown and Stax makes a convincing case that their artists *did* have a good degree of creative control and created in a diversity of styles, and that they are worthy of analytical attention in a way previously explored only with reference to white performers like the Beatles.[46] In the case of Aretha Franklin, Atlantic attempted to create an artistic persona for her, arranging performances in the late 1960s in symphony concert halls with printed programs.[47] The image of the Beatles as Artists-with-a-capital-A should also be considered in a more subtle way. George Martin, the Beatles's longtime producer, baldly states that "the Beatles themselves never pretended they were creating art with *Sgt. Pepper,* or scrabbling after some kind of musical 'integrity.' They just wanted to do something different, and *Pepper* was it."[48] A striking 1968 John Lennon quote suggests that the Beatles thought of themselves as primarily craftspeople, and questioned the notion of art in general: "It's nice when people like it, but when they start 'appreciating' it, getting great deep things out of it, making a thing of it, then it's a lot of shit. It proves what we've always thought about most sorts of so-called art. It's all a lot of shit. It is depressing to realize we were right in what we always thought, all those years ago. Beethoven is a con, just like we are now. He was just knocking out a bit of work, that was all."[49] The notion of authorship is also considerably more complex than the "Lennon-McCartney" credit given to most of the group's material. Even if the main composer of a given song can be identified, the Beatles's creative process undermines any search to locate *the* author at any discrete site. For example, the final version of "Eleanor Rigby" is the inseparable product of, at the very least, McCartney's tune and first verse, lyric ideas from other Beatles as well as their friends, a refrain designed by committee, George Martin's arrangement for string octet and suggestion of counterpoint during the final chorus, and suggestions made by the studio musicians at the recording session.[50] In addition, "Rigby" is supposedly a song "by" the rock group "the Beatles" that features no sounds, apart from voices, created by members of the band. With our current models for organizing much of rock history, these images that should complicate and texture our constructions are in danger of being lost, and it becomes more difficult to examine the music without looking for evidence to confirm our steadily calcifying framework.

*

In the next sections of this paper I analyze the Beatles's "Eleanor Rigby" and Aretha Franklin's "Think" as test cases that inform a critical view of the conventional 1960s rock narrative. In order not to suggest that a given rock song must fit any single set of stylistic criteria to be taken seriously, I will explore the pronounced coding of difference between these two songs. I will particularly note context and the ways it informs our reception of each song's arrangement, vocal style, and lyrics. In the section following, I will argue that the differences between the songs should not lead to an a priori differential valuing of the performances, for both can be read to employ sensitive and nuanced interactions with conventional rock's formal structures.

"Eleanor Rigby" is intimately connected with what is usually considered an important period in the Beatles's careers: the decision to stop touring followed by the development of the studio experimentation that would result in *Sgt. Pepper*. "Rigby" was released in August 1966, less than a month before the group's last concert, in San Francisco's Candlestick Park.[51] The cessation of public performance is read as a purposefully artistic step, for the group's material is seen as becoming too intricate and wedded to artistic exploration to be performed under mid-1960s touring conditions. As James Winn puts it, "freed from the exhausting and demeaning business of touring, they were able to sustain their growing complexity and creativity for four highly productive years, during which they produced . . . albums that expanded and apparently exhausted the possibilities of the rock song."[52] Thus, "Eleanor Rigby" is central to coding the Beatles's music as universal "art" written by "geniuses" that transcends the workaday conditions of touring and performing.

In contrast, the context of Aretha Franklin's "Think," released in May 1968, is usually constructed not to aim toward the universal, but as grounded in the particulars of Franklin's background and life.[53] It is a given that any discussion of Aretha Franklin will begin with mention of her father, the legendary Reverend C. F. Franklin, which serves to place her music in a specific gospel context.[54] As constructed by Lucy O'Brien in her 1995 history of women in popular music, "Franklin drew the strength and conviction of her sound from the church that spawned her."[55] Viv Broughton's history of gospel suggests that "Aretha is altogether more deeply embedded in the gospel mystique . . . than some of the great gospel names themselves."[56] Along these lines, positive critical reception of Franklin's work is often connected to her use of gospel influences, with her "glorious" moments often those closest to her gospel heritage.[57] In addition, "Think" is one of Franklin's compositions coauthored with her first husband, Ted White. The up-tempo but bittersweet cries for "freedom" in the song evoke her troubled marriage to White, who played a strong (if not commandeering) role in the early stages of Franklin's career, but faded quickly as both a business and life partner after she signed with Atlantic in 1966. Beyond this immediate context, the same cries have been seen as epitomizing a political stance in the racially based upheavals of the late 1960s.[58]

These assumed contextual differences, between the Beatles as "artists" attempting to transcend conditions of the everyday so as to strive for "universal" expression and Aretha Franklin as a "craftsperson" at her best when engaging with and evoking her background, can be used as a heuristic that helps to describe the two performances considered here. Discussions of "Eleanor Rigby" always include at least passing mention of the arrangement, for double string quartet. Instead of being grounded in the limitations of a rock band accompaniment, "Rigby" contains no instrumental sound produced by a normative rock instrument, nor any instrumental sounds made by any of the Beatles. The choice of instrumentation is further marked by being a collection of instruments strongly associated with the Western art music tradition, and it is often commented on in exactly this way, as evoking a "classical effect."[59] However, the effect is more properly seen as closer to a Bernard Herrmann film score than a Haydn string quartet.[60] Although strings are often associated with producing an "emotional" sound, here there is little indulging in the sensuous or sentimental; instead an "objective," austere accompaniment is used in its place.[61] For example, consider the accompaniment during the second half of the third verse. Jarringly, all forward motion seems to stop as the strings play harsh downbows of the same note on each beat.[62] The suggestion of a "classical effect" is as much wishful thinking on the critic's part as actual sonic substance. In contrast, the arrangement of "Think" employs a relatively large rock band, expanding guitar, bass, and drums to include the piano and organ combination that evokes the gospel tradition, as well as the horn section common to rhythm and blues. The gospel tradition is evident from the very beginning, with heavy use of the piano, subdominant to tonic "amen" harmonic movement, and a call-and-response interaction between Franklin and the chorus of female backup singers. Whereas the accompaniment of "Rigby" creates a distancing effect, the arrangement of "Think" is primarily concerned with "groove," constructing a multilayered rhythmic texture with many surface syncopations, a strong backbeat, and (title aside) a call for a bodily, non-intellectual response to the music.

Vocal style also contributes to this reading of contextually driven difference. McCartney's lead vocal in "Eleanor Rigby" keeps itself quite reserved, even when dealing with weighty subjects like death and redemption, and the contained surface is never broken. The vocal performance of all the verses and all the choruses is practically identical, with no changes for marked words or phrases, which contributes both to a sense of a fixed musical "text" and to the effect of emotional distancing. Franklin's vocal performance of "Think," on the other hand, is quite flexible in melody, rhythm, and timbre, such that it would be quite difficult (and perhaps beside the point) to transcribe her voice part in conventional notation. Although the melodic prototype for each line of the verse is an octave descent through a blues pentatonic scale, the specific treatment of each line can be quite different, including the blurring of boundaries between discrete pitches (on the word "doctor") and octave leaps on specific syllables (such as to illustrate a "high I.Q."). At numerous places in the song, Franklin exceeds the bounds of the lyrics and "composed" melody to vocalize between phrases. Her vocal quality is strongly emotive and serves to draw the listener inside the emotional subject of the song rather than to distance him or her from it.

A reading of the two songs' lyrics can also further the notion of difference between them. The distancing effects of the arrangement and vocal style in "Eleanor Rigby" effectively set these lyrics concerned with observing, from the outside, the isolation of the song's characters. As the song begins, we are asked to "look at all the lonely people," and the entire song is narrated in the third person. Eleanor Rigby and Father McKenzie, the song's two characters, do not meet while Rigby is alive. The first verse is devoted to Rigby

alone: she cleans up after the celebration of a wedding (but does not participate), and can only watch the outside world through a window. Her face, her
identity as seen by others, is not really a part of her, but is kept "in a jar by the
door." When she dies, as described in the third verse, "her name," another
marker of her identity, is "buried along" with her, and no one attends the
funeral. The second verse describes Father McKenzie: his sermon, expressly
written to communicate to an audience, goes unheard, and as we learn later,
"saves no one." The only meeting between the two characters comes in the
third and final verse as McKenzie buries Rigby, but there is no true lasting
connection between them, for he "wipe[s] the dirt from his hands as he
walks from [her] grave."

The lyrics of "Think," however, although also concerned with the troubled
interactions between two people, break the boundaries between song, performer, and listener. Franklin uses the first person and addresses her warning to a third party, as she sings in each chorus: "You'd better think, think
about what you're trying to do to me. / Think that your mind gonna let you
set me free." Further, she envelops the audience with her perspective. The
chorus of female back-up singers repeats the word "think" after each iteration by the lead vocal, and like our reactions to the comments of a Greek
chorus in classical drama, we identify with their point of view; the audience
is effectively placed inside the space of the song. In addition, although the
language of "Eleanor Rigby" is not extremely complex or learned, the language and imagery of "Think" is decidedly vernacular and streetwise. The
second half of the first verse is a case in point. Franklin sings, "I ain't no
psychiatrist, I ain't no doctor with degrees, / But it don't take too much high
I.Q. to see what you're doing to me." Constructions like "I ain't no doctor
with degrees" and "But it don't take too much high I.Q." do not call for
abstract contemplation but a visceral, emotional, and immediate response.
The Beatles ask us to "look at" the situation from the outside, whereas
Franklin knows that, from our position inside, we can "see."

*

The clear coding of difference between "Eleanor Rigby" and "Think" does
not directly speak to the issue of value, but rather to ideologies of value. The
above discussion makes no claims as to the relative worth between the two
songs, but it is all too likely that such observations could be used to further
the implicit differentiation of value along race-based lines as currently wit-

nessed in conventional histories of rock. However, an exploration with a different set of parameters, such as nuanced interactions with rock song conventions, might show that both songs are interesting along similar lines. I will concentrate here first on interactions with norms of phrase rhythm, based on four-measure or eight-measure groups; second, on consistency of section length over multiple statements of equivalent sections; and third, on norms of form, based on discrete verses and chorus structures that retain their identity throughout the given song.

My purpose is not to suggest that the differences between the two songs as discussed above are irrelevant, but rather to argue that it is possible to embrace the differences largely coded along racial lines while concluding that both songs are worthy of value. By focusing on structural factors, I join John Covach in arguing that we should not accept "uncritically the notion that popular music is uncomplicated in the traditional sense, or that even if it . . . engages our attention along structural lines, that is nonetheless not how the song was meant to be heard anyway."[63] Rather, these songs are only two examples of hundreds of popular compositions that are carefully constructed to engage with listeners' expectations of the ways sections of a song relate to one another and the ways a complete song can be shaped. Further, I propose no simplistic tautology that would suggest that a "complex" song is, by virtue of its complexity alone, worthy of value. Indeed, by many traditional measures, both of these songs are quite simple: for example, neither employs true chord progressions, opting instead for a largely static alternation between two chords ("Rigby" between the tonic E minor and submediant C major, and "Think" between the initial tonic B-flat and subdominant E-flat). Instead, to my ears, an essential part of what makes these songs worth exploring is the ways they evoke and use the modest conventions of the rock song while simultaneously calling into question, if not negating, the very models on which they are based.

One of the most notable features of "Eleanor Rigby" is the pair of five-measure phrases that make up each verse, which cuts against the grain of normative four-measure phrase rhythm. As early as 1968, critics such as Deryck Cooke focused on play with hypermeter as a creative hallmark of the Beatles's songs. In Cooke's words, "rhythmic originality is the most important [feature], especially as regards bar-periods, since popular song has long been confined to an appalling eight-bar monotony. . . . But Lennon and McCartney have broken completely free."[64] The melody line of each verse

Figure 1. "Eleanor Rigby" verse melody

(a) mm. 9–13 (sounds 1 octave lower)

(b) sketch of principal melodic motion

(c) Viola I, mm. 19–22 (sounds 1 octave lower)

phrase is approximated here in Figure 1a. One way to approach this phrase would be to consider the last measure an extension attached to a normative four-bar phrase; this view focuses on the model and uses the rhyme scheme of the lyrics to see the last bar as separate, setting the short second line of each couplet. A different approach might use the pauses in the melody to suggest an irregular but symmetrical structure, with a one-bar subphrase followed by a three-measure subphrase concluded with another one-bar subphrase. It is also possible that the five-measure phrase is, in certain respects, a coherent single unit. Figure 1b sketches the melody as a largely chromatic descent from the 1st scale degree, E, to the 5th scale degree, B. The possible descent suggested in the third and fourth measures of each verse phrase, from C-sharp to B and on to A, is adjusted in the fifth measure, such that the C-sharp now can be seen to proceed chromatically to C-natural and then to B. This descent can be considered the primary one, as it matches the prominent chromatic descent in the first viola part during the "Chorus B" structures (see Figure 1c). This D to D-flat/C-sharp to C-natural to B descent in both verse and chorus structures is not read as imparting an ideologically suspect "unity" to the song; rather, our sense of normally discrete verse and chorus sections is weakened.

Another convention engaged in "Eleanor Rigby" is the notion of a single chorus structure that retains its identity throughout the song (thus the label "refrain"). Instead, "Rigby" employs two separate but related sections that are both treated as choruses: the "Aah, look at all the lonely people" section

Figure 2. *"Eleanor Rigby" formal diagram.*

E minor; 4/4 time signature; quarter note = ca. 138–144

TIME	TEXT	FUNCTION (# of measures)
(0:00)	"Aah, look at. . ."	Chorus A $_{4+4}$
(0:14)	"Eleanor Rigby. . ."	Verse I $_{5+5}$
(0:31)	"All the lonely. . ."	Chorus B $_{4+4}$
(0:45)	"Father McKenzie. . ."	Verse II $_{5+5}$
(1:03)	"All the lonely. . ."	Chorus B $_{4+4}$
(1:17)	"Aah, look at. . ."	Chorus A $_{4+4}$
(1:30)	"Eleanor/Father. . ."	Verse III $_{5+5}$
(1:48)	"All the lonely (aah). . ."	Chorus A+B $_{4+4}$

can be considered "Chorus A," and the "All the lonely people, where do they all come from?" section can be considered "Chorus B." Over the course of the song, "Eleanor Rigby" employs an evolutionary process with these choruses such that they begin the song separated, are later juxtaposed, and at the conclusion are superimposed (see Figure 2). In the formal diagram, each section is labeled by function, with subscript numbers representing the length of each phrase; the time on the recording and the first phrase of the lyrics for each section are placed above. Choruses A and B are initially separated by the first verse; after the second verse they are played side by side. Following the third and final verse, the two structures are effectively sounded together, as the melody of Chorus A is sung as counterpoint to Chorus B in the lead vocal and strings. Whereas the irregular phrase rhythm of the verses commands attention during those sections, the use of conventional eight-bar structures during the choruses help focus attention on the process the two chorus sections undergo over the course of the song.

Like the interconnections between verse and chorus discussed above, "Think" also introduces ambiguity into the notion of separate and discrete sections. Although the verses and choruses have distinct melodies, the chorus melody is largely centered around the tonic note, and the verse melody begins on that note and descends to the tonic note an octave lower; thus, the melodies of both sections can be read as functioning similarly, prolonging the tonic note. In addition, although the lyrics of the chorus are easily identifiable, repeatedly using the title word of the song, the harmonic movement and rhythmic textures of the accompaniment stay largely identi-

Figure 3. "Think" formal diagram.

B-flat major to B major; 4/4 time signature; quarter note = ca. 112–116

TIME	TEXT	FUNCTION (# of measures)	KEY
(0:00)		Intro₄	B-flat
(0:08)	"You'd better. . ."	Chorus₂₊₂	
(0:18)	"Let's go back. . ."	Verse I₂₊₂₊₂₊₂	
(0:35)	"You'd better. . ."	Chorus₂₊₂	
(0:43)	"Freedom. . ."	Bridge A₄₊₄	
(1:01)		Intro₂	B
(1:06)	"There ain't. . ."	Verse II₂₊₂	
(1:14)	"You'd better. . ."	Chorus₂₊₂	
(1:23)	"People walk. . ."	Verse III₂₊₂	
(1:32)	"Think. . ."	Chorus₂₊₂	
(1:40)	"You need. . ."	Bridge B₄	
(1:49)	"Oh, think about it. . ."	"Groove" (to fade)	

cal across the two formal structures, helping to further blur the lines between these sections.

However, if for the purposes of discussion we allow verse and chorus structures in "Think" to remain heuristically discrete, the formal diagram in Figure 3 suggests a process of intensification throughout the song, one that engages a convention suggesting that the length of a formal section remains constant over repetitions of that section. In "Think," the harmonic intensification that comes from the rising modulation of a half-step, moving the tonic from B-flat to B, is reflected in a formal intensification that affects introduction, verse, chorus, and bridge structures. Each important step along the way is signaled by the same powerfully syncopated rhythm on beats 3 and 4 of the preceding measure:

After a four-measure introduction on the piano, that rhythm brings in the band and Franklin for the first chorus, which lasts (as do all the choruses) for four bars. The eight-measure first verse follows, and is followed by another chorus. After this second chorus, something new, the bridge section, with its cries for "Freedom," is sounded. The bridge is made up of a four-bar rising phrase that is repeated,[65] each time concluded with the marked rhythm. The arrival after this section is not to the original tonic B-flat, but abruptly on the new, intensified tonic of B. In effect, the song begins again, but formally, all the sections have been shortened. Compare the two cycles: the four-bar introduction becomes two bars; the introduction is followed not by a chorus but by a verse; the eight-bar verses now last for only four bars; the repeated phrase of the bridge now is sounded only once. Further, this second bridge structure, which begins with the words "You need me," does not rise harmonically but statically remains on the subdominant. Following the second bridge, after the marked rhythm sounds for the final time, the listener is left in a formal no-man's-land, in a region of pure groove that is neither chorus, nor verse, nor any other previously heard section. This continues until the song fades out, presumably with the groove sounding forever. Not only are all formal structures obliterated at this point, but whatever harmonic movement existed previously is left behind as well, as only the repeated tonic chord is sounded; we have left all strictures of formal and tonic differentiation behind.

Thus, "Eleanor Rigby" and "Think" can be interpreted in a doubly subversive way. Traditional formalist approaches, developed for a rather narrow repertory with a narrow set of values, can all too easily leave popular compositions seeming impoverished. By focusing instead on matters of context and performance, we can recapture some of the richness of the recordings. However, these sorts of readings, which lie at the heart of recent strides made by musicology as a discipline, can still contribute to the exclusionary conclusions such approaches were designed to avoid. Only by incorporating matters of structure and form in a critical and self-aware way that considers rock music more on its own terms can we discuss rock songs without recapitulating preformed constructions of value.

*

Since the late 1960s, "Eleanor Rigby," among a number of other Beatles's songs, has been treated like a standard; that is, performed in numerous cover versions by various artists as a vehicle for their own expression. Covers of "Rigby" have been done by performers as diverse as Ray Charles, jazz pianist Oscar Peterson, Joan Baez, and classical guitarist Goran Sollscher. In addition, "Rigby" has been covered by Aretha Franklin herself, on the 1970 album *This Girl's in Love with You* and the 1971 live recording *Aretha Live at Fillmore West*.[66] Franklin's version serves to make "Eleanor Rigby" cross over the boundaries of difference as outlined above: where the Beatles present a dispassionate stance, Franklin blurs the lines between song, artist, and audience. The accompanying large rock band's primary function is to "groove," drawing the audience in through their corporeal response. The Beatles's recording seems to be geared toward listening, and listening from an emotional distance, but Franklin's performance is potent and calls for a heightened energy level and physical reaction. On the live recording, Franklin even begins by addressing the audience in exactly this way, telling them, "Don't fight the feeling." Further, Franklin breaks the distancing of the third person in the lyrics by singing "*I'm* Eleanor Rigby." It is a powerful move: Rigby's story, about a woman but originally sung by a man, is now given a powerful female voice; that voice, although singing about a presumably white woman, is now strongly coded as black; and the voice no longer separates itself from the fictional Rigby but instead purposely embodies the character. Rather than being pitied by a white male external to the narrative, here the character of Rigby is empowered as, through Franklin, she now is able to sing about "herself."

Aretha Franklin's version of "Eleanor Rigby" does more than add her own layer of interpretation on to a Beatles "classic." Instead, virtually every aspect of the song is changed, including form, harmony, melody, rhythm, lyrics, key and mode, accompaniment, vocal style, and affect. The sense of two choruses is gone, as the first one does not appear. In the live version, the third verse, in which the two characters meet, is largely covered by horn section licks and is barely heard. The Beatles's chord progressions and chromatic descents are exchanged for a vamp between tonic and subdominant chords, similar to those of "Think." The string octet's accents on each downbeat have been replaced by the accompaniment's pronounced offbeat syncopations. Finally, the unconventional fifth measure of each verse phrase has been removed entirely, smoothing out the verse into four-measure phrases that do not disrupt the hypermetrical sense of "groove." About all that remains is a fair part of the lyrics and a rough outline of the melody. This performance is marked as *not* "Eleanor Rigby" at least as much as it declares itself a version *of* "Eleanor Rigby."

But how are we to assign value to such a performance? Has Franklin done violence to an inviolable "text?" Is this a "corrupt" version that destroys the integrity of the definitive statement on the Beatles's *Revolver* album? Are Franklin's modes of expression only good for dancing, while the Beatles's performance is worthy of scholarly contemplation? The analyses in this paper suggest a different view. The extent of the changes Franklin is able to make, while still preserving some intuitive sense that this is "Eleanor Rigby," casts doubt on the entire notion of the song as a conventionally defined, unified work of "art." Franklin's ability to engage with her model and produce a performance so strongly coded with her own personal stamp, as an African American, as a woman, as the persona we know as Aretha Franklin, can be seen as representing a differently constructed source of value, one that doesn't stem from a predetermined set of cultural codes but instead turns on the ways a song may evoke and interact with multiple sets of codes, whatever their perceived content. As scholars of "classical" music are uncovering and interrogating the ideological bases of valuing "serious" music, we should be wary of strategies that invoke those very same systems for the purpose of valuing certain "popular" songs. "Eleanor Rigby" and "Think" are quite different, and our reasons for enjoying one certainly may be different from our reasons for enjoying the other. But the race-based constructions of difference we may hear should not lead us, unthinkingly, to assert that these songs somehow possess different levels of value.

Notes

Earlier versions of this paper were presented at Cornell University (March 27, 1997), at the conference "Representing Rock" (Duke University, April 4–6, 1997), and at the joint meeting of the Society for Ethnomusicology, the U.S. chapter of the International Association for the Study of Popular Music, and the Popular Music Interest Group of the Sonneck Society for American Music (Pittsburgh, October 23–26, 1997). I would like to thank Martin Hatch, Brian Robison, the editors of this volume, and Becky Sheinbaum for their thoughtful comments on previous drafts.
1. See, for example, David P. Szatmary, *Rockin' in Time: A Social History of Rock-and-Roll*, 3rd ed. (Upper Saddle River, N.J.: Prentice Hall, 1996), xi.
2. Michael Bane, *White Boy Singin' the Blues: The Black Roots of White Rock* (New York: Da Capo Press, 1992), 42.
3. Simon Jones, "Crossover Culture: Popular Music and the Politics of 'Race,'" *Stanford Humanities Review* 3 (1993): 103–17.
4. Bane, *White Boy Singin' the Blues,* 150.
5. Szatmary, *Rockin' in Time,* xi; Jones, "Crossover Culture," 106–7.
6. See Szatmary, *Rockin' in Time,* 170, 133.
7. I take this from the subtitle of Robert Palmer's *Rock & Roll: An Unruly History* (New

York: Harmony Books, 1995); this book is the companion to the WGBH/PBS documentary series *Rock & Roll* (1995).

8. Joe Stuessy, *Rock and Roll: Its History and Stylistic Development*, 2nd ed. (Englewood Cliffs, N.J.: Prentice Hall, 1994), 119.

9. Palmer, *Rock & Roll*, 103–4.

10. For an early discussion along these lines, see Terence J. O'Grady, "*Rubber Soul* and the Social Dance Tradition," *Ethnomusicology* 23 (1979): 87–94.

11. Palmer, *Rock & Roll*, 110.

12. See Paul Friedlander, *Rock and Roll: A Social History* (Boulder: Westview Press, 1996), 89. See also Palmer, *Rock & Roll*, 99, for his opening anecdote of the 60s rock chapter; and the *Rock & Roll* documentary episode "Shakespeares in the Alley."

13. Representative excerpts are included in the PBS *Rock & Roll* documentary episode "Shakespeares in the Alley."

14. Ibid.

15. See Dave Laing, "Editor's Introduction," *Popular Music* 6, no. 3 (1987): iii.

16. Walter Everett, "The Beatles as Composers: The Genesis of Abbey Road, Side Two," in *Concert Music, Rock, and Jazz Since 1945: Essays and Analytical Studies*, ed. Elizabeth West Marvin and Richard Hermann (Rochester: University of Rochester Press, 1995), 172–228.

17. Tony Palmer's 1968 review of the *White Album* in *The Observer*, which considered John Lennon and Paul McCartney "the greatest songwriters since Schubert," was extremely influential along these lines (cited in Philip Norman, *Shout! The Beatles in Their Generation* [New York: Fireside Books, 1981], 348). For example, Allan Kozinn's *The Beatles* (London: Phaidon Press, 1995) is part of Phaidon Press's "20th-Century Composers" series; in being thus represented, not only are the Beatles in quite distinguished company, but they stand as the only non-art music figures to receive their own volume. Similarly, Allan F. Moore's 1997 *Cambridge Music Handbook* on *Sgt. Pepper's Lonely Hearts Club Band* is the first monograph in that series devoted to a piece of music from outside the Western art music tradition (Moore, *The Beatles: Sgt. Pepper's Lonely Hearts Club Band* [Cambridge: Cambridge University Press, 1997]).

18. Tim Riley, for example, writes that the Beatles "challenged what anyone imagined pop could become. . . . Nothing equals the Beatles' catalogue: it integrates the best of what came before, and signals the array of styles that would soon follow" (Riley, "For the Beatles: Notes on Their Achievement," *Popular Music* 6 [1987]: 258–59).

19. Both Stuessy and Charles T. Brown organize their Beatles chapters so as to imply that the group's output represents a three-stage teleological process very similar to the ones conventionally associated with Beethoven, with "early" music before the group has found its "true musical style"; a "middle" period that is more creative, complicated, and "universal"; and a transcendant "late" period where their albums are masterpieces (Stuessy, *Rock and Roll*, 106, 119, 125; and Charles T. Brown, *The Art of Rock and Roll*, 3rd ed. [Englewood Cliffs, N.J.: Prentice Hall, 1992], 131, 133, 135). A different but equally pervasive three-stage narrative is related to an organic metaphor of growth and decay, with stylistic disunity and eclecticism dooming the group after the centrally located masterpiece of *Sgt. Pepper* (see Friedlander, *Rock and Roll*, 95). For an overview of periodization schemas as applied to Beethoven, see James Webster, "The Concept of Beethoven's 'Early' Period in the Context of Periodizations in General," *Beethoven Forum* 3 (1994): 1–27.

20. This sort of thinking leads numerous authors to consider the American releases through *Revolver*, on which there are some differences in which tracks were included in what order, as corrupt versions that inherently destroy an inner coherence and unity that the British versions possess. For example, see Friedlander, *Rock and Roll*, 86; and Mark Hertsgaard, *A Day in the Life: The Music and Artistry of the Beatles* (New York: Delacorte Press, 1995), ix–x.

21. I use the phrase "positivistic and analytical musicological enterprise" to encompass both sides of traditional music scholarship that are applied to the Beatles: the unearthing and reporting of "facts," and the analysis of the musical object itself. In musicological discourse, these perspectives have been strongly criticized in recent years for their unselfconscious search for "truth." However, their pronounced use in Beatles research is a clear sign that scholars still often construct an implicit sense of value by utilizing methodologies originally developed for the Western art music tradition.

22. Andy Linehan, "Reviews," *Popular Music* 6 (1987): 343–46. Studies such as these range from discographies and lyrics concordances to descriptions of the band's activities literally on a day-by-day basis. See, for example, the "Rock & Roll Reference Series" (published by Popular Culture, Ink., Tom Schultheiss, series editor), almost half of whose volumes are dedicated to Beatles subjects; Ian MacDonald, *Revolution in the Head: The Beatles' Records and the Sixties* (New York: Henry Holt and Company, 1994); Tom Schultheiss, *A Day in the Life: The Beatles Day-By-Day* (Ann Arbor: Pierian Press, 1980); Mark Lewisohn, *The Complete Beatles Chronicle* (New York: Harmony Books, 1992); and Lewisohn, *The Beatles Recording Sessions* (New York: Harmony Books, 1988).

23. *The Beatles Complete Scores* (Milwaukee: Hal Leonard Publishing Corporation, 1993; originally published by Shinko Music Publishing Co., 1989). The transcriptions are by Tetsuya Fujita, Yuji Hagino, Hajime Kubo, and Goro Sato; their work is only credited in very small type on the inside information page, and almost no information is included about the critical apparatus or how the transcriptions were accomplished.

24. As early as 1968 Deryck Cooke published an article on Lennon-McCartney songs, and the essay is reprinted in a posthumous collection side-by-side with writings on Beethoven, Wagner, and Mahler. See Deryck Cooke, *Vindications: Essays on Romantic Music* (Cambridge: Cambridge University Press, 1982), 196–200. Another early analytical study is Wilfrid Mellers, *Twilight of the Gods: The Beatles in Retrospect* (London: Faber and Faber, 1973).

25. For example, Schenkerian techniques normally reserved for canonic works of the eighteenth and nineteenth centuries are used in Robert Gauldin, "Beethoven, *Tristan*, and the Beatles," *College Music Symposium* 30 (1990): 142–52; Walter Everett, "Voice Leading and Harmony as Expressive Devices in the Early Music of the Beatles: 'She Loves You,'" *College Music Symposium* 32 (1992): 19–37; and Everett, "The Beatles as Composers." As David Brackett argues in his review of the volume from which Everett's "The Beatles as Composers" essay is a part: "Everett treats the Beatles as if he were dealing with Schubert: he makes no allowance for different contexts of production and consumption, radically different aesthetics employed by musicians and listeners, and different senses of musical tradition and authorship" (Brackett, review of Charles Hamm's *Putting Popular Music in Its Place*," in *Concert Music, Rock, and Jazz Since 1945*, ed. Marvin and Hermann). *Journal of the American Musicological Society* 50 (1997): 507–519.

26. For example, see Szatmary, *Rockin' in Time*, 134–37; Friedlander, *Rock and Roll*, 177–79; Palmer, *Rock & Roll*, 86–87; and Brown, *The Art of Rock and Roll*, 114.

27. Joe McEwen and Jim Miller, "Motown," in *The Rolling Stone Illustrated History of Rock and Roll*, ed. Jim Miller (New York: Rolling Stone Press, 1976), 230.

28. See Friedlander, *Rock and Roll*, 185.

29. Ibid., 172.

30. See Portia K. Maultsby, "Soul Music: Its Sociological and Political Significance in American Popular Culture," in *American Popular Music: Readings from the Popular Press, Volume II: The Age of Rock*, ed. Timothy E. Scheurer (Bowling Green, Ohio: Bowling Green State University Popular Press, 1989), 168–78.

31. Indeed, even today it is difficult to imagine a black performer with any "authentic" credentials as a "black" performer about whom one cannot also claim some direct interest in "political" or "street" issues. A provocative counterexample may be Prince, but his subsequent name changes, first to an unpronounceable glyph and then to The Artist, are telling. I thank the editors for this observation.

32. Russell Gersten, "Aretha Franklin," in *The Rolling Stone Illustrated History of Rock and Roll*, ed. Jim Miller (New York: Rolling Stone Press, 1976), 234, 237.

33. Carl Belz, *The Story of Rock*, 2nd ed. (New York: Oxford University Press, 1972).

34. Ibid., 177.

35. Ibid., 183, 186.

36. Stuessy, *Rock and Roll,* 141–53.

37. Ibid., 207.

38. Ibid., 232–35.

39. See Michael Campbell, *And the Beat Goes On: An Introduction to Popular Music in America, 1840 to Today* (New York: Schirmer Books, 1996), 224, 231. A notable exception to this division is Jimi Hendrix, who is presented as "rock's first virtuoso"; but the fact that Hendrix had to begin his career in Europe due to the U.S. racial climate of the time goes without mention.

40. See Campbell, *And the Beat Goes On* (instructors' manual) (New York: Schirmer Books, 1996), 65, 67.

41. Ibid., 66.

42. See Allan Moore, *Rock: The Primary Text—Developing a Musicology of Rock* (Buckingham, Eng.: Open University Press, 1993), 7, for the connections between the formation of canons for rock and classical musics.

43. Palmer, *Rock & Roll,* 90–91. See also Reebee Garofalo, *Rockin' Out: Popular Music in the USA* (Boston: Allyn and Bacon, 1997), 214.

44. Peter Guralnick, *Sweet Soul Music: Rhythm and Blues and the Southern Dream of Freedom* (New York: Harper and Row, 1986), 342.

45. Palmer, *Rock & Roll,* 81.

46. See Fitzgerald, "Motown Crossover Hits 1963–1966 and the Creative Process," *Popular Music* 14 (1995): 2–5; and Rob Bowman, "The Stax Sound: A Musicological Analysis," *Popular Music* 14 (1995): 289.

47. See Guralnick, *Sweet Soul Music,* 346.

48. George Martin, with William Pearson, *With a Little Help from My Friends: The Making of Sgt. Pepper* (Boston: Little, Brown, 1994), 2.

49. James A. Winn, "The Beatles as Artists: A Meditation for December Ninth," *Michigan Quarterly Review* 23 (1984): 2–3.

50. See Hertsgaard, *The Music and Artistry of the Beatles,* 116–17, 182–83; MacDonald, *Revolution in the Head,* 162; Steve Turner, *A Hard Day's Write: The Stories Behind Every Beatles' Song* (New York: HarperCollins, 1994), 104; Martin, *With a Little Help,* 136; and Lewisohn, *The Beatles Recording Sessions,* 77.

51. See Schultheiss, *The Beatles Day-By-Day,* 157; and Friedlander, *Rock and Roll,* 87.

52. Winn, "The Beatles as Artists," 2. See also Lewisohn, *The Beatles Recording Sessions,* 84.

53. See Mark Bego, *Aretha Franklin: The Queen of Soul* (New York: St. Martin's Press, 1989), 112, 309.

54. See Szatmary, *Rockin' in Time,* 167; and Lucy O'Brien, *She Bop: The Definitive History of Women in Rock, Pop, and Soul* (New York: Penguin Books, 1995), 86.

55. O'Brien, *She Bop,* 86.

56. Viv Broughton, *Black Gospel: An Illustrated History of the Gospel Sound* (Poole, Eng.: Blandford Press, 1985), 97.

57. See Gersten, "Aretha Franklin," 239.

58. See Szatmary, *Rockin' in Time*, 171.

59. Terence J. O'Grady, *The Beatles: A Musical Evolution* (Boston: Twayne Publishers, 1983), 98.

60. According to MacDonald (*Revolution in the Head*, 163), McCartney suggested a Vivaldi-like arrangement to George Martin, who instead produced a score strongly influenced by Herrmann's music for the Truffaut film *Fahrenheit 451*. Indeed, there was a visible reaction when, during a presentation of this paper at Duke University, I played the accompaniment of the third verse of "Eleanor Rigby" without the vocals. As Greil Marcus mentioned in his "Real Life Rock" column (*Artforum* 35, no. 10 [summer 1997]: 38), "the lights were on, but suddenly everyone in the room was watching *Psycho*."

61. See Mellers, *Twilight of the Gods*, 71; and O'Grady, *The Beatles*, 98.

62. The first cello is an exception; at this spot it doubles the voice.

63. See John Covach, "We Won't Get Fooled Again: Rock Music and Musical Analysis," *In Theory Only* 13 (1997): 117–41, and reprinted in *Keeping Score: Music, Disciplinarity, Culture*, ed. David Schwarz, Anahid Kassabian, and Lawrence Siegel (Charlottesville: University Press of Virginia, 1997), 80. Here Covach is taking issue with Susan McClary's discussion of the Earth, Wind, and Fire song "System of Survival" in her article "Terminal Prestige: The Case of Avant-Garde Music Composition," *Cultural Critique* 12 (1989): 57–81. Covach argues that by concentrating on nonstructural factors, McClary is implicitly (and incorrectly) suggesting that this song, and popular music in general, "isn't very interesting structurally" (80).

64. Cooke, *Vindications*, 198.

65. Although the melody in this section rises from scale degree 1 to flat-3 to 4 to 5, no harmonic dominant is achieved. The rhythm section clearly plays another tonic chord supporting scale degree 5, making the expected arrival that follows melodically and hypermetrically, but not harmonically, based.

66. See Bego, *Aretha Franklin*, 311–12.

MICHAEL COYLE ✻ HIJACKED HITS AND ANTIC AUTHENTICITY: COVER SONGS, RACE, AND POSTWAR MARKETING

In a 1997 release entitled *Under the Covers,* country singer Dwight Yoakam aims to demonstrate that western prairies are not the only kind of range he knows. The album invites us to admire Yoakam's boldness of choice, mixing versions of country chestnuts by Glenn Campbell, Jimmie Rogers, and Buck Owens with oldies by the Beatles, the Rolling Stones, and the Kinks, and even the Clash's "Train in Vain"—itself now an oldie for certain audiences. Proposing relations wherein the unlikely can seem "natural," the album highlights Yoakam's crossover appeal for pop audiences. Packaging visuals amplify the same semiotic process. Both inlay and program notes offer images of Yoakam in bed, "under the covers," with a comely model. Neither wears anything but a strategically draped sheet and their lavishly tooled and prominently displayed cowboy boots; Yoakam also sports his cowboy hat. As a site for intimacy, the bedroom suggests a delivery of the "real" Yoakam: half in jest, all in earnest. He can't help but be true to himself—those boots, like the identity they help perform, apparently stick out no matter what he plays. That promise is doubtless genuine, given the mainstream market for country music since the early 1990s, and is here more interesting in itself than the product for which it is a guarantee.

Despite Yoakam's showy defiance of musical genres, there's nothing particularly iconoclastic about such border crossings.[1] In an age where singers become "artists" as much by their songwriting ability as their delivery, numerous performers from the early Beatles and the Rolling Stones to Bryan Ferry or Madeleine Peroux have nevertheless made their reputations by reinventing familiar songs: they project their identity precisely *by* singing songs associated with another voice or style. Since the consolidation of rock and roll, the "cover song" has established itself as a way for performers to signify difference, much as the presentation of "standards" serves jazz musicians. But whereas standards have long provided jazz audiences with familiar points of departure, cover songs—or recordings, we should say—have a more troubled history. The practice of "covering" the recording of another artist arises at a very particular moment in cultural history, and derives not from the play of standards in jazz but from postwar forms of music industry competition. My purpose here is to clarify what is meant by a "cover record," and explore why that clarity matters.

That purpose is unfortunately complicated by the survival of this single term through various historical changes, so that it now indiscriminately designates any occasion of rerecording.[2] Disentangling the various senses of the term teaches much about the changing relations of pop music both to its audience and to the discourses that plot its significance. What we now so ubiquitously refer to as cover records developed from a practice as old as the recording industry itself. Like everything else in the United States, that practice was informed by racial segregation, and acknowledged the existence of distinctly black and white musical markets. The cover record per se developed only when "race" records began to have mass appeal on "white" pop charts, and the key figure in that process was none other than Elvis Presley: the "King" came to his throne largely on the strength of the first cover records the world had ever known.

I say this wholly aware that the identification of the first cover record has become something of a parlor game. Different critics identify different records, but they do so in large part because they understand the term in different ways. Four recent examples suffice quickly to make the point. First, Richard Aquila's 1992 essay "The Homogenization of Early Rock and Roll," exemplifies how the conflation of different historical practices can hinder even self-consciously revisionist history. In the course of an admirably balanced critique of the myth that rock and roll was virtually homogenized to death between 1958 and 1964, Aquila claims that "the first imitative cover record came in [July] 1954, when Mercury Records signed a white pop group, the Crew Cuts, to record a pop version of the Chords's R&B hit, 'Sh-Boom.' "[3] Certainly Aquila is right to sense that the Crew Cuts's cutting in on the Chords's profits exploited the market in a newly insidious way. The Crew Cuts's very name signified their whiteness; hailing from Toronto, before signing with Mercury they had called themselves the Canadaires. Nevertheless, these were earlier instances of a white "cover" record halting the crossover success of an R&B record. Charles Wolfe (my second example), in his program notes to *Your Hit Parade: The Mid-50s,* describes an instance of a few months earlier that, while accidental, first caught the industry's attention. The McGuire Sisters recorded "Goodnight, Sweetheart, Goodnight" after hearing a demo of the Moonglows doing it; but, "in the meantime, a Chicago doo-wop group called the Spaniels issued their version of the song on the Vee-Jay label and watched it climb the rhythm and blues charts. When the McGuires got their version out, they unknowingly became the first group to have a major pop hit with a cover version of an R&B song."[4]

In getting that hit the McGuire Sisters thus inadvertently knocked the Spaniels out of the game; it is the result in this instance and not the intention that exemplifies the general practice Aquila so rightly deplores. Mercury Records shrewdly seized on the accident of "Goodnight, Sweetheart, Goodnight" and over the next few years regularly used American apartheid to exploit black artists. As Reebee Garofalo (example three) observes, only the Decca label approached Mercury's level of success in this regard. But even still, Mercury's expropriation of the Chords's profits was not in any simple way unprecedented. Garofalo submits that "the practice of making cover records began in earnest in 1953 when June Valli recorded 'Crying in the Chapel' for RCA. At the time it was released, there were three other versions of the song out, two country and one R&B. The R&B release by Sonny Til and the Orioles [August 1953] had crossed over to the pop market and was enjoying considerable success until it was eclipsed by the Valli cover, which became one of the best-selling records of the year."[5] Garofalo's book is in general immensely valuable, but his account here unfortunately suggests a primarily racial basis for Valli's success. As Philip Ennis (example four) has explained, "Crying in the Chapel" was originally a "country 'sacred' song" written by "the father of a young country artist, Darell Glen, who moved it onto both the pop and the country charts."[6] The Orioles had actually begun taking chart action away from Glen when the pop recording by June Valli buried everyone.

Ennis suggests an earlier and, for our purposes, more useful instance. In late September 1951, feisty little Atlantic Records debuted a recording that charted for twenty-two weeks, including six weeks as R&B and jukebox bestseller: the Clovers's "Fool Fool Fool" (written by Atlantic president Ahmet Ertegun). As it began to cross over to the pop charts, "Fool Fool Fool" was "covered soon after by Capitol's Kay Starr," a white pop singer. "Her version of the song in August 1952 was a moderate hit and reopened the door to the practice of pop performers covering R&B hits."[7] Ennis takes interest in Starr's cover because he sees it as a formative moment in the consolidation of rock and roll, but what I find striking here is that there were but two competing versions of the song, and *that* is the harbinger of things to come. Instead of a successful song inciting several competing recordings released on several competing labels, as we see even with "Crying in the Chapel," "Fool Fool Fool" was a contest with one contender black and one contender white. In this sense, it enacts a kind of exploitation that qualitatively differed from mere market opportunism. By contrast, when Mercury recut "Sh-Boom" it did not, in today's sense of the word, create a cover record but simply engaged in the time-honored practice of *hijacking a hit*.

This is not to say that the A&R people at Mercury wouldn't have described what they were making as a cover; the term was already a familiar synonym for hijacking a hit. The point is that no one in 1954 would have used the word "cover" to mean what we mean by it today. This is the confusion in Aquila's account, although it certainly is not one of his making. The confusion here arises from the continuity of a single descriptive term across discontinuous marketing practices. The notion of covering a song has changed radically in meaning because the structure of the industry—the relation of writers to performers to audiences—itself has changed radically. Since mid-century it has become virtually impossible to hijack a hit because audiences today tend to identify songs with singers. In commenting on one of the earlier occasions of this kind of identification, Stuart Nicholson makes the point concisely. Discussing Billie Holiday's 1939 recording of "Strange Fruit," Nicholson remarks:

> "Strange Fruit" was a landmark recording of a very different kind than was perceived at the time. It was one of the very first popular songs that

became impossible to disentangle from a single, specific recording. This would later become commonplace in pop and rock music: songs such as "Heartbreak Hotel" or "What's Going On?" or "Bohemian Rhapsody" are impossible to separate from their respective performances by Elvis Presley, Marvin Gaye and Queen. Singer and song are bonded in a way that exhausts the meaning of the material, achieving an autonomy that transcends simplistic chord progressions and mediocre lyrics by embracing both musical and non-musical factors, among them style, fashion and sex appeal.[8]

That "Strange Fruit" was one of the first records to bond singer and song does not, of course, mean that the music industry marketing changed as of its release. The changes to which Nicholson refers were not perceived at the time, but required another twenty years before the industry began to recognize the changes at hand. It is nonetheless significant that this change made its historic appearance in one of the first recordings overtly to cry out against racism. "Strange Fruit" was not a record that could be hijacked by even the most sympathetic of white singers. When "cover" records later diverged from "hijacked hits," it would be precisely over this issue of racial credibility.

Despite the term's origin within the music industry itself, "the hijacking of hits" is a misleading phrase. It's misleading because it suggests that there was something illegal in the practice of producing new versions of money-making songs. In fact, there wasn't—although by the late 1950s there were lawsuits over the copying of specific arrangements. The practice had its origin in an earlier stage of the music industry, the long period unfolding across the nineteenth century and through the 1930s when the industry's principal source of revenue was the sale of sheet music: under those conditions it was good business to have as many performers plugging your song as possible. By the end of World War II, the formation of R&B was already changing all of that; but, while some recognized that the future of the music industry lay in recordings, the release of competing versions of the same song remained standard operating procedure.

Consider two postwar examples, both involving multiple parties and big sales. The first example is the song that was number one on the *Billboard* "Honor Roll of Hits" as of March 1, 1947: "Open the Door, Richard." As Arnold Shaw tells the story, the song emerged from an old routine by black vaudevillian Dusty Fletcher (who himself took the routine from comedian

James Mason). Shortly after the war, former Lionel Hampton saxist Jack McVea joined that routine to a musical riff:

> The musical riff for these words ("Open the Door, Richard . . . Open the Door, Richard") became so familiar to radio listeners in 1947 that NY Station WOR banned all airings of the tune and requested comedians to lay off "Richard" gags. By then there were as many as fourteen different versions. Among the majors, Capitol offered a disk by the Pied Pipers; Decca, by Louis Jordan; Victor, by Count Basie; Mercury, by Bill Samuels & the Cats'n'Jammer Three; and Columbia, a disk by the Three Flames and another by the Charioteers. Eight "indies" sought to mine a bit of silver out of what seemed an endless vein. Apollo was on the market with a Hot Lips Page recording; King, with Hank Penny; Manor, with Big Sid Catlett's Ork; Majestic, with The Merry Macs; Empey with Tosh "One-String" Weller & His Jivesters; [Black & White, with Jack McVea;] and National, with Dusty Fletcher himself.[9]

The crowd of competing versions of "Richard" is remembered by Shaw and other historians because it occasioned serious litigation over copyright. The "song" was really more of a routine that developed over several years with contributions from numerous performers; after industry lawyers added *their* two bits "songsheets and records carried four names: words by Dusty Fletcher and James Mason, music by Jack McVea and Dan Howell."[10] I mention "Open the Door, Richard" here, however, to illustrate what was then a common situation: it was not only that different record companies competed to win the biggest share of consumer interest in a particular song, but individual companies themselves regularly released competing recordings. In the case of the multiple versions of "Richard," some were black and some were white; some were R&B, some were pop, and some were country. None of these versions—not even Dusty Fletcher's—claimed special status as the "original." In an era when crossover was unlikely, and when the popularity of a song could still be regional, competition between different recordings of the same song helped sell sheet music, helped carry a song into new markets, and could even stimulate the sales of all the versions.

The second example involves the novelty song "Rag Mop." Originally written for Bob Wills's Texas Playboys, it was brought to the R&B charts in 1946 by trumpeter Henry "Red" Allen, and then again—in a slyly naughty remake—by Louis Jordan. In 1950 a new recording by Lionel Hampton returned the song to the charts, but Hampton's hit was immediately hijacked by three new pop versions, two additional R&B versions, and even another country and western version. None of the musicians involved was alarmed by the situation: after all, musicians tended to regard the primary purpose of records as boosting the price of personal appearances, rather than performances serving—as they have in the intervening decades—to promote the sale of records.[11]

As of 1950, consumers, particularly consumers of pop, still generally bought the songs and not the singers. Apart from the practice of having competing versions of any one song, the prevalence of this valorization of song over singer can be measured by the long-running success, from 1935 to 1959, of a radio show that eventually moved to television: *Your Hit Parade*. This program presented the top seven to fifteen tunes of the week, "served up by maestro Lennie Hayton, the Hit Paraders and the Lucky Strike Orchestra."[12] Although it featured and sometimes created nationally celebrated singers on its staff, including Frank Sinatra, Dinah Shore, and (as we'll note momentarily) Georgia Gibbs, the show's staff presented all songs. It was this feature that initially helped consolidate a national audience for *Your Hit Parade*, and it was just this feature that finally killed the show a couple of years after Elvis Presley's emergence changed the rules of pop success. However, before that change, the primary concern for any record company was not the exclusive identification of a song with one artist, but the timely release of *its* version so as to catch the wave of public interest before interest subsided. Producers recorded songs "on" singers, rather than made recordings "of" an artist.

The business of hijacking hits remained standard operating procedure as long as the market for popular music was driven more by the consumption of songs than by any particular recordings of them. Although the formation of rock and roll would eventually reverse that relation, it appeared at first only to compound it. Thus it was that the hijacking of hits outlived its original context and, by enduring into new contexts, came to function and signify in ethically disturbing ways. As pop historians have often noted, in the first fifteen years after World War II, the hijacking of hits became one of the favored means for white capital to exploit black talent. Many stars of 50s R&B lost money to pale yet promotionally powerful remakes of their most successful songs, but probably none lost more than LaVern Baker. Despite the fact that she came of age steeped in blues tradition, Atlantic Records had

The March, 1952 "teaser" from Decca Records. As *Billboard* explained, Decca here "claimed a new record of sorts by announcing it will issue four separate versions of the Fred Rose oldie." But the only thing that was new here was that four separate "versions" were being issued simultaneously by the same label. It was normal for competing versions to be out by different labels. Notice, too, that the operative word is "versions," not "covers." See Galen Gart, ed., *First Pressings: The History of Rhythm & Blues Volume 2: 1952* (Milford, NH: Big Nickel, 1992), 24–25.

decided to market her as a pop and novelty singer; this orientation, ironically enough aimed at crossover, was to make her especially susceptible to hijacking. For example, as soon as her 1955 recording of "Tweedle Dee" hit the charts, Mercury Records rushed out a copy by pop-warbler Georgia Gibbs. Even though Mercury Records was only five years older than Atlantic, it exercised at the time considerably more market muscle; the Gibbs hijack thus entered the lists with a significant advantage over Baker's small-label original. In a sense, the hijacking of hits just beginning to climb the charts had always been Gibbs's trademark; given her early national exposure as a staff member of *Your Hit Parade* (1937), hijacking was how she first had made her name. During her mid-1950s tenure at Mercury, she rarely recorded a song that was not already a confirmed money maker; besides Baker, she also made money on hits by Alan Dale, Hank Ballard, Lillian Briggs, even—her producers no doubt emboldened by earlier success—Tony Bennett.[13] In fairness, it has to be said that Gibbs had no more control over her material than did Baker; for most performers of the time—including Elvis Presley—it was producers and managers who determined the vehicles for singers. Still, the point is that the roster of Gibbs's hijackees suggests that there was no vision involved here, either heavenly or infernal; that Hank Ballard and Tony Bennett both enjoyed her attention suggests that she and her producers did not even target a particular market niche.

None of these hijackings displays any concern about artistic integrity, or about what critics today regard as "authenticity." In the 1990s, the discourse of "authenticity" informs virtually all musical idioms, from jazz to hip hop to alternative (it might be a sign of techno/electronica's claim to the pop future that it alone thus far remains outside the discourse). But as of the mid-1950s that discourse had yet to cross over from gospel (where it originated), or from the so-called folk stream (as Ennis has dubbed it), or from modern jazz.[14] For the gospel community, it was of paramount importance to distinguish between those performers genuinely committed to spreading the word and those who sought the rewards of mammon.

Of the earliest gospel performers to carry the music outside of the church (and consequently to be censured by the faithful), the case of Sister Rosetta Tharpe proves the most instructive. What distinguishes Tharpe from other performers like Wynona Carr or Ray Charles is that she never forsook her musical ministry—never wholly abandoned the narrow way for Broadway—and it was precisely her enduring commitment to God's work that made her sensitive to criticism. She was still young when that commitment was first tested. As singer-evangelist in the Sanctified Church, her growing reputation caught the attention of John Hammond, who invited her to perform in his 1938 "Spirituals to Swing" concert at Carnegie Hall. Her success there led to performances with Cab Calloway, and then in 1941 she signed with Lucky Millinder's Orchestra, where she was—with "Mr. Blues" Wynonie Harris—one of the orchestra's two featured vocalists. Although Tharpe continued to sing adapted versions of gospel tunes (re-presenting "Hide Me in Thy Bosom," for instance, as "Rock Me") church people judged her by the company she kept. Despite her protests that it was her mission to carry the word to more than just the already converted, objections to her profaning of sacred music grew increasingly intolerant. Consequently, in 1944 she recorded "Strange Things Happen Every Day." The song, perhaps because it charged "church people" with hypocrisy, became one of the very first gospel recordings to cross over to secular audiences. In spring 1945 it held the number two spot for two weeks on *Billboard*'s national "Race" charts, and charted for a total of eleven weeks. The opening lines of the song make her position clear: "Oh we hear Church people say they are in the 'Holy Way,'/There are strange things happening everyday." For Tharpe, the "strange thing" is that any believer should be so sure of their own sanctity as to declare it to the world. For us, however, the strange thing is not that her song about the church should have met with popular success, but that the insistence on "authenticity" that Tharpe endured and from which she struggled to escape should itself eventually have crossed over along with her song.

The long and complex story of how the discourse of authenticity made that crossing is beyond my concerns here.[15] The effect of this discourse on the consumption of pop music, however, is very much to the point: the consumers of popular records expect that their purchase involves more than just a recording—they are buying a "whole" product that somehow involves the ideological commitments of the artists. Pop musicians today characteristically must prove their right to trade in/on a particular musical idiom; like the gospel performers of Rosetta Tharpe's day, they are expected to live the life they represent in song. There are no formal rules on how such demonstrations should be made, but (to pick a couple of infamous examples from the 1980s) the noisy failures of performers like Vanilla Ice, M.C. Hammer, or Milli Vanilli leave no doubt as to the pressure of informal rules. Moreover, although issues of authenticity become more significant when race is involved, such issues are by no means limited to black music. As our example of Dwight Yoakam exemplifies, they also play in the construction of various models of whiteness. In such constructions of identity, the making of cover records has become a time-honored way of asserting credentials.

Nevertheless, to return to Georgia Gibbs's service in Mercury Records's exploitation of LaVern Baker, the hijacking of black hits by white artists has not always involved questions of identity. In her hijackings of Baker, Gibbs was like any other pop musician of the era—including Baker. The only issue apparently motivating Gibbs and her handlers at Mercury was commercial success. Gibbs's cover of "Tweedle Dee" certainly found that. Baker herself estimates that she lost at least $15,000 in royalties (big money in 1955) to Gibbs's enterprise.[16] Unfortunately for Baker, however, "Tweedle Dee" was only the first time that Gibbs stole the fire from one of her hits. The next year Gibbs hijacked Baker's "Tra La La," taking her version to number 24 on the pop disc-jockey charts; Baker's original didn't make the pop disc-jockey charts at all, and reached no higher than 94 in the pop Top 100. These various chart distinctions are important, because they tell us that although consumers were happy enough to put money down for Baker's records both in record shops and in jukeboxes, white disc jockeys were still refusing to play black records for white audiences.

That all of this would change, and already was changing, is old news. Even in 1955 Alan Freed was already satisfying all doubts that the color of money is green no matter what color the hands that spend it. Still, the hijacking by white companies of black records just climbing the charts was the phenomena of a particular historical moment. This is not to say that it didn't happen before or after, but that when it did it happened in different ways. Before World War II, before the development of R&B helped set the stage for Freed, Presley, and white youth culture, few "race" records could have appealed to white pop audiences. Again, as Philip Ennis and others have demonstrated, jazz presents somewhat different issues.[17] For the most part, when 30s black vocal groups like the Ink Spots or the Mills Brothers sold records to white audiences, they did so because they successfully adopted and adapted white vocal styles. But within a decade *after* Freed, white groups were striving to sound black. Rock bands of the 1960s didn't compete with contemporaneous black groups but hearkened back to material that black audiences had already largely abandoned. This tendency was as true of late-60s groups like Ten Years After or Rare Earth (the first white act signed

Hijacked Hits and Antic Authenticity   143

to Motown Records) as it was of the "invasion" bands of 1964 and 1965. Nevertheless, despite the fact that the 50s-era hijacking of hits was a practice that lingered from an earlier era, it often fed off apartheid. The targets of white copies were sometimes white, and the targets of black artists sometimes black, but we would be hard-pressed to find any evidence of a black performer proving able to hijack the success of a white original. Black performers might *revive* white standards—though even such revivals could often be knocked out of the ring—but they could not compete with them.

The larger point here, and the aspect of all of this that anticipates our conclusion, is that hijacking exploited racist inequality but did not arise because of it. So much is evident from LaVern Baker's witty response to her situation—a response that in itself reopens a virtually lost vista on the tumultuous era. Needless to say, Baker was not happy about what she called Gibbs's stealing all the gravy. She was particularly bitter because Gibbs's versions of "Tweedle Dee" and "Tra La La" didn't simply remake the songs, they reproduced almost exactly the very arrangement she and her band had so painstakingly created. In fact, when making these copies Mercury hired the same musicians used by Atlantic, and even tried to retain the same producer. Nevertheless, Baker retained her sense of humor. In an anecdote recounted by Chip Deffaa, when Baker "boarded one airplane in 1957, she named Gibbs as the beneficiary on her flight insurance, explaining that if she were to die in a plane crash, leaving Gibbs with no one to copy, [Gibbs] would still have a source of income thanks to Baker. Baker let Gibbs know what she'd done; Gibbs was not amused."[18] While the story testifies to Baker's spirit, it also clarifies the nature of her resentment. The crime was less artistic than economic—the Mercury hijackings cost Baker money. Gibbs had no more thought of signifying her street credentials as a blues shouter than she did of paying tribute to Baker's delivery or style. In view of how cover recordings came to signify in the next decade, such innocence— and such unabashed greed—is hard to imagine.

It's hard to imagine this innocence precisely because the ways in which pop music signifies have so profoundly altered. Or, to put it another way, and to borrow from the postmarxist sociology of Pierre Bourdieu, pop music today comprises a different kind of cultural capital than it did forty and fifty years ago. Contemporary pop music is created and consumed inside a wholly different symbolic field than it was two generations ago, playing a significant (and still undertheorized) role in identity formation. Less likely than their grandparents to regard pop musicians as entertainers, young people in America discern in pop recordings "a 'space of symbolic stances' which is independent of, yet homologous to, 'the space of social positions.' "[19] One of the more profound changes wrought by Elvis Presley on the semiotics of both pop and R&B markets was perhaps the consequence of his dependence on other songwriters. For all the debate over Presley's musical integrity, only once in his career did he hijack someone else's current hit. That occasion came early, just after his move to RCA, when producer Steve Scholes was desperate to recoup RCA's investment. After weeks of inconclusive sessions, Scholes called Elvis into the studio to remake Carl Perkins's "Blue Suede Shoes," which had just hit the charts. Ordinarily, however, Presley depended either on songs written expressly for him, or, when first making his name at Sun Records, on material he had known since his school days. Again, Presley's career took off on the basis of what we might call the first covers in musical history.

The songs Presley recorded for Sun Records had all long since disappeared from the charts, so long that most of Presley's young fans wouldn't have recognized his records as remakes. Those fans would, however, have recognized much of the material as black: Arthur Crudup's "That's All Right," Wynonie Harris's "Good Rockin' Tonight," Junior Parker's "Mystery Train," Ray Charles's "I Got a Woman," or Willie Mae Thornton's "Hound Dog."[20] Presley remade all of these records before the end of 1956. Moreover, unlike Georgia Gibbs's hijackings of Baker, these Presley covers were all of material whose brief moment in the limelight was over, without the songs having become standards. And unlike Gibbs's hijackings, which sought to supplant the black originals, Presley's remakes in a certain way depended on those songs first being identified as race records. This is not merely to repeat the oft-told tale of Presley's interview with Memphis deejay Dewey Phillips, on the release of his first single, "That's All Right," when Phillips went out of his way to establish Presley's racial identity.[21] The dynamics of the situation are more complicated than that. It was not that Presley needed continually to be mistaken for a black artist but, on the contrary, that he be recognized as a white artist performing black music in a miscegenated style. To argue that this music is *essentially* white or black is wholly to mistake its charge: the very formation of rock and roll testifies against essentialist identity of any kind, and its enduring popularity derives precisely from its hybridity.

In the most revealing interview of his career, in June 1956, Elvis told a reporter from the *Charlotte Observer* that "the colored folks been singing it and playing it just like I'm doin' now, man, for more years than I know. They played it like that in the shanties and in their juke joints, and nobody paid it no mind 'til I goosed it up. I got it from them. Down in Tupelo, Mississippi, I used to hear old Arthur Crudup bang his box the way I do now, and I said if I ever got to the place where I could feel all old Arthur felt, I'd be a music man like nobody ever saw."[22] Now, one way of understanding this quotation is to take it, like LaVern Baker did, as proof that "music has no color." Baker thought that Presley was "fantastic"; late in life she recalled an interview where he had said "I give it all to LaVern Baker," and she noted with pleasure that Elvis eventually sang not only "Saved" and "C. C. Rider" but also "Tomorrow Night" and even "Tweedle Dee."[23] All the same, it's no challenge to Presley's openness about his debt to African American tradition to approach an almost antithetical understanding of the same quotation. Presley's love of black music was doubtless sincere, but his covers of older blues, R&B, and gospel material are in large part meaningful precisely *because* they are "colored." His countrified take on "That's All Right," for example, is persuasive because white America felt its racial/cultural transgression. Presley defined his "whiteness" against the "blackness" of his material, and made that identity exciting. What he seems intuitively to have sensed is that, as Toni Morrison or Fred Pfiel have more recently submitted, "blackness" and "whiteness" are essentially arbitrary discursive values; as values in a discourse, neither means anything except in reference to or against the other.[24] The relative position of these terms is constantly shifting, and Presley's miscegenative recordings shifted them big time. Had he merely performed the role assumed by so many earnest rockers of subsequent decades, and feigned "authenticity" as a blues singer, he would have left the relations between "blackness" and "whiteness" exactly where he found them. Presley, by contrast, generated energy precisely because he *wasn't* authentic—he made no pretense of being anything other than "white."

In view of what happened with many of the "British invasion" bands of ten years later, Presley's insouciance is all the more remarkable. Bands like the Animals, the Rolling Stones, the Yardbirds, or even the Who (*Maximum R&B* is the title of their 1994 box set) worked overtime to create what today often looks like incongruous posturing—a merely antic authenticity. The issue isn't whether the records those bands made were really any good but to understand something of the semiotics at work in their covers of R&B material. Those covers of R&B did not try to hijack capital from current hits; rather—and here is their debt to Presley—they tended to cover older material and pay it homage as part of a tradition. These covers made money not by banking on what already was popular, but by treating R&B material as an investment—as "cultural capital." Invasion band covers valorized "blackness" by positing it as the embodiment of difference from or resistance to the mainstream. The familiar claims about the supposed affinities between Anglo-American youth culture and African American culture generally mistake the implicit "othering" that such homage no doubt inadvertently effected. But, as Nelson George has observed, the R&B musicians whose work was being covered by the invasion bands could not have missed these effects;[25] by late 1965 R&B artists like Chuck Berry could barely find work, and it is hard to resist the simple conclusion that white America in 1964 and 1965 still wasn't ready to take its black music straight. The British bands, however, were simply enlarging on the pattern of Elvis's success. Only infrequently covering recordings made by Elvis himself, they followed his example rather than his playlists: they covered records that would retain signs of their "blackness," particularly blues records.

For American audiences, the British identity of these bands heightened that sense of transgression that had so marked Presley's earliest recordings. By comparison with his English progeny, Elvis's class and regional backgrounds could make him seem a part of the African American heritage in which he participated. For British bands, however, that "Americanness" was almost as important as that "*African* Americanness." Although stateside audiences might have heard the "yeah, yeah, yeah" of the Beatles's "She Loves You" as an exuberant affirmation, for English audiences it signified a brazen cultural promiscuity. "Yeah" is, or at least was, an American colloquialism; it was bad English that the Beatles didn't just roll off their tongues but shouted repeatedly. We might say, in today's parlance, that their performance was an "in your face" violation of English usage. As invasions go, this one might more properly be seen, from an American perspective at least, as chickens coming home to roost. The point is that the British bands had upped the ante with regard to cultural transgression. Wrapping themselves (both proudly and ironically) in the Union Jack, they embodied what Umberto Eco calls, in *Travels in Hyperreality*, "the genuine fake."[26]

The Beatles's 1963 cover of "That's All Right" exemplifies this point.

Their recording of it at the BBC studios makes it clear that they were not covering Arthur "Big Boy" Crudup but Elvis—whose revival of the song invested it with a new cultural capital. For the Beatles, "Elvis" was not a mediation or a watering down of authentic tradition, but a conversion point. The excitement of the Beatles playing "That's All Right" owes to the fact that they were *not* "the real thing" rather than from their having assimilated themselves into the American blues tradition. This is why the Beatles's music—not to mention their success—fundamentally challenges the kinds of connections between music and a way of life discussed with such conviction by modernist critics like LeRoi Jones (now Amiri Baraka) or Greil Marcus.[27] For all the difference of their perspectives, and their disagreement over the nature of rock's debt to African American tradition, both Jones and Marcus affirm that musical forms grow out of forms of cultural life. This was not, however, a challenge the Beatles themselves sought to deliver. When the Beatles were making their first flight across the Atlantic in February 1964, George Harrison anxiously wondered aloud: "They've got everything over there; what do they want *us* for?"[28] Certainly the work permits they had been required to obtain were not promising; the permits allowed the Beatles "to play, within a strict two-week period, 'so long as unemployed American citizens capable of performing this work cannot be found.' "[29]

However unlikely the possibility of finding such unemployed citizens might have been, the songs being covered by the Beatles and by subsequent invasion bands were not in any case hits currently on the charts but rather were often eight or nine years old. Even covers of newer material, like the Swinging Blues Jeans's embarrassing 1964 imitation of Little Richard's apocalyptic "Good Golly Miss Molly" (1958) or the Rolling Stones's last blues single, a 1964 remake of Willie Dixon's "Little Red Rooster" (1961), still did not challenge the originals for chart action. A typical example might be the Beatles's 1963 recording of Ray Charles's "I Got a Woman": Charles cut his original in 1955; Elvis's cover was included on his first U.K. album, *Rock'N'Roll No. 1*. Again, as with "That's All Right" (recorded the same month) the Beatles's version covered Elvis. We might think further about how such covers signify by turning to the Beatles's first album for Capitol Records, *Please Please Me*. The album opens with two originals, "I Saw Her Standing There" and "Misery," and then follows with three covers: "Anna," written and first recorded by Arthur Alexander in 1962; "Chains" (by King and Goffin), which the Cookies took to the charts late in 1962; and then

"Boys" (by Dixon and Farrell), a 1960 recording by the Shirelles. Side B of the album includes three more covers: another Shirelles song, "Baby It's You" (1961, by David, Williams, and Bacharach); Lenny Welch's "A Taste of Honey" (1962, by Scott and Marlow); and the Isley Brothers's "Twist and Shout" (1962, by Medley and Russell), which closes the album. In all of these covers, allowing for changes in gender, the Beatles strove to duplicate the originals. Their purpose was not, then, to make an artistic statement, any more than it was to cut in on hot chart-action. The key to their purpose is color; although the writers for the Cookies and Shirelles material were white, all of the covers on *Please Please Me* were originally *recorded* by black artists. Like other invasion bands unfamiliar with American racial tensions, the Beatles imagined their R&B covers would help them find stateside acceptance—help make them more popular. And so their covers worked not to reinvent the individual songs but to alter the relation of their originals to their audience: the covers on *Please Please Me* are there to recontextualize the music of a provincial British pop group—to propose not an origin for their sound so much as a destination.

This distinction also would change, and would change quickly as subsequent bands revisited earlier material as an inscription of origin. Sometimes, as in LaVern Baker's 1958 album of songs sung by Bessie Smith, or in the Byrds's electric treatment of Dylans's "Mr. Tambourine Man" (1965), these covers aimed to associate the latecomer with a particular inspiration or scene. But most often covers became a way for white artists to lay claim to an artistic origin outside of the pop-consumer mainstream. In Jim Crow's America, such claims sometimes depended on the popular failure of the black original; or at least of the popular memory of them having grown dim enough that they could be reimagined as a part of folk legend. Consider the story of R&B star Chuck Willis, the turban-wearing "King of the Stroll." The stroll was a bump-and-grind, sax-driven sound, but for all the success it brought him, Willis aspired to something more. His career had begun in 1951 with the Okeh label—the old race division of Columbia Records. Once signed, Willis became the label's biggest money maker. But, by 1956, the rapid formation of the white rock and roll market was already making a diminished thing of 50s R&B. As Presley and others were richly demonstrating, the future (or at least near future) of pop music belonged to those who could cross over between the pop and R&B charts. A smart and driven man, Willis was quick to learn the lesson. He already had logged crossover success as a writer: his song "Oh What a Dream" was a hit for Ruth Brown and later was successfully hijacked by pop chanteuse Patti Page. So, in April 1956, two months after leaving Okeh and signing with Atlantic Records, Willis made his first deliberate play for the mainstream. He wrote a new ballad with a recycled title—"It's Too Late"—and used the occasion to play with recorded effects that sounded a long way from R&B.[30]

After its release, "It's Too Late" stiffed on the pop charts. But, in a surprising sign of the times, it made the R&B Top 3; a sign of the times because R&B audiences increasingly hungered for pop smoothness, while pop audiences craved R&B grit—the kind of grit that "It's Too Late" pointedly avoids. The crossover gestures of "It's Too Late" are readily apparent. First, Willis and producers Ahmet Ertegun and Herb Abramson used a marimba and a set of music-box chimes to fill out the sound of his record, instead of relying on the honking saxes and other sounds more usual with R&B. Second, they deliberately imported a white and very white-sounding choral group. In other words, at about the same time that Sam Phillips at Sun Records was trying to find a white man who could sing black, this black musician was surrounding his lead vocal with overtly white harmony, rather than the kind of gospel-derived harmonies characteristic of R&B. These studio innovations are probably what blocked the record's crossover success. Willis's sense of the pop market was in large part (although, as we'll see, not completely) dated. Missing the effect on the mainstream of music like his own, his studio work exaggerated the politeness that an R&B musician might understandably associate with pop music.

As a song, however, "It's Too Late" proved to be stronger than its first recording. It was almost immediately subject to attempted hijackings: Sun Records, in a good example of its programmatic search for material with crossover appeal, quickly released recordings by both Charlie Rich and Roy Orbison. That so fine a songwriter as Buddy Holly should soon thereafter record Willis's ballad (1957) is not only its own special tribute but also a sign that Willis did not wholly misread the pop market. "It's Too Late" was next recorded (though not released) a few years later by guitarist Link Wray, whom one imagines was attracted by very different features than the pop-oriented Holly had been. That kind of difference was a harbinger of things to come. Conway Twitty, who at the time already had one eye to the country market and was somewhat desultorily making the last of his rock and roll records, also released, in 1963, the last of the first-wave responses to Willis's composition. Coming out seven years after Willis's own recording, Twitty's record was neither a hijack nor in any significant sense a cover. Twitty didn't so much remake the tune as affirm his solidarity with the figures through whose mediation he received it: Rich, Orbison, and Holly. Twitty's recording nods to them, and not to Willis. After Twitty's record, two years went by before anyone else recorded "It's Too Late"; two years that might as well have been twenty. In those two years came the British invasion, and a renewed widening of the gap between black and white popular musics.

In something approaching the near reversal of Willis's intention, it was a younger African American artist, Otis Redding, who brought new significance to "It's Too Late," and in so doing marked the changing nature of black to white crossover dreams. Redding's passionate recording of "It's Too Late" (1965) was the first that might usefully be considered a *cover*. His record was less polite than Willis's, and by unapologetically taking the song "down home" he invested it with an unmistakably black identity.[31] Redding's work was the mediation between Willis's recording and all those that followed. In separating the ballad from its original crossover ambitions he made it available first to blues musicians, and through them (because of the late-60s "blues revival" among white audiences) to various rockers, including Ted Taylor (1970), Merl Saunders (with Jerry Garcia, in 1973), and arena rockers Foghat (1973) and—of most importance to our purposes here, and the band who doubtless inspired the Foghat cover—Derek and the Dominos (1970). In other words, it was Redding who probably inadvertently articulated the terms of crossover success for "It's Too Late." The longevity of Redding's transformation—the continued career of the trajectory he plotted—might be observed in the recirculation of "It's Too Late" in the 1990s among zydeco musicians: accordionist Lynn August recorded it in 1993 and vocalist Lil Alfred in 1996. It was then Willis's recording more than his composition that reveals a dated sense of pop balladry. Indeed, he managed in the next two years after he wrote "It's Too Late" to score four more Top 40 hits, one of which went Top 10 but all of which bore more obvious traces of their R&B roots.

It was precisely those "roots" that attracted the attention of Derek and the Dominos, who as most everyone knows were Duane Allman, Eric Clapton, and what had been the rhythm section for blue-eyed soulsters Delaney & Bonnie. Derek and the Dominos's recording of "It's Too Late" is from the famous album of October 1970, *Layla and Other Assorted Love Songs*. In view of Willis's ambitions, the Derek and the Dominos cover can't help but seem ironic. Everything about what Allman, Clapton, and company did reverses Willis's crossover gesture. The impulse is, of course, evident in their very name. When Billy Ward called his early-50s group "the Dominoes" the name played on their racial identity. When Clapton, twenty years later, called his group "the Dominos" the name gestured (even in its misspelling) toward "roots" authenticity, attempting to summon associations of a music indifferent to merely pop sensibilities. By 1970 there was a blues revival well under way, and while the black audiences for 50s-style R&B had long since moved on to other styles, there was an audience of "serious" white fans who hungered for rock that offered more than psychedelic noodling or teen anthems.

In the Dominos's cover, the pace of Willis's ballad gets something of a booster shot. The music-box chimes disappear, though not altogether—in the final verse Duane Allman's slide guitar alludes to them. Willis's embowering of his vocal line in allusions to polite, mainstream conventions is replaced by gritty slide and rhythm guitars, all of which energetically and enthusiastically invoke blues tradition. More important still, Willis's politely white chorus is replaced by the call-and-response shouting of hard gospel, with Bobby Whitlock's whiskey voice answering Eric Clapton's tensely sung lead vocal. In other words, true to their name, these Dominos work to create a distinctively R&B feel, or at least simulate that feel while rocking the blues. If Otis Redding's cover of the ballad had been "ironic" in that Redding reversed Willis's crossover gesture, then we need a different word to describe what happens in Derek and the Dominos's recording. In taking "It's Too Late" down home, Redding effectually brought it up to date and renewed its appeal for black audiences. Clapton and company follow Redding's lead "down home," but for them "down home" meant the pursuit of roots rather than modernity. As we said of the Beatles and their early covers, the purpose of such a journey was not so much to propose an origin for their sound as it was a destination.

In such a world, or such a market, with black seeking white both to make money and to legitimize a musical idiom, and white seeking black in order to establish a performative if not essential legitimacy—and so make money—it becomes increasingly difficult to affix stable values or even identities to competing musical idioms. What we have generally understood as a single practice, the covering of one recording by another, is in fact a more complex business. Generally, before the rise of Elvis Presley the old industry practice of remaking a popular record is best understood in terms of hijacking a hit. At the same time, however, we need to acknowledge that during the 1950s the practice of hijacking facilitated new forms of racist exploitation—forms that arose precisely *because* the popular music industry was opening up to black performers and African American musical idioms. Without the market dynamics of crossover, white remakes of R&B hits would not have affected the sales of recordings by black artists. I have suggested that, in our modern sense of the term, Elvis Presley was the first cover artist. In recovering nearly forgotten recordings by black artists Presley was doing much more than reviving potentially money-making properties; he was using recordings by black artists to perform for himself and for America a new identity. In this way, Presley opened a field for the British invasion of a decade later, a field defined by the transgression of "authentic" boundaries. For us, Presley's innovation serves to underscore the performative nature of racial or cultural identities.

Distinguishing between hijacking and covering can help us get beyond essentializing categorizations of black and white. Considerations of "market" have often been regarded by rock critics as the source of all evil, but paradoxically that very consideration can help us understand black and white as signifiers rather than as essential categories. In the 1980s and 1990s, newer processes in pop music increasingly contributed to the deconstruction of those categories, and electronic "sampling" is changing not just the function but the very nature of musical covers (think, for instance, of The Fugees's 1996 crossover smash-hit recording of Charles Fox and Norman Gimbel's "Killing Me Softly with His Song," which was first brought to the charts by Roberta Flack in 1973).[32] In the meantime, the notion of the cover song has become so ubiquitous as to detach from racial questions altogether. Not one of the "covers" that Dwight Yoakam gets under crosses the traditional frontiers between black and white musical vernaculars. While it might still be open to question whether Yoakam's lack of hijacking is a sign of progress in race relations, or a sign of Nashville's enduring conservatism, it's still an unmistakable sign of the times. For over half a century rock-based musics have comprised the most lucrative area of music industry activity, but that hegemony is now more generically fractured than ever before. In the 1990s, country artists "crossed over" with a regularity not unlike the crossings into pop of R&B (or country) artists in the 1950s. As always, hijackings and covers alike are attracted to the sound of money.

Notes

1. See Yoakam's interview with Associated Press writer Jim Patterson, July 17, 1997, which can be found on the Web's "Dwight site": http://www.dwightyoakam.com. Patterson has lots to say about Yoakam's "unusual combination of songs," and Yoakam himself asserts his consistent refusal to be "a prisoner to any specific genre of music." Yoakam's use of covers to construct a modern, hybrid, and unmistakably crossover "country" identity might be contrasted with Townes Van Zandt's *Road Songs* (Sugar Hill, 1994), another country album of covers released just three years earlier.

2. The term "cover" seems initially to have entered record industry parlance from the studios of Jack Kapp's Decca Records. Between 1943 and 1949, Decca routinely made sixteen-inch lacquer safety discs of all the wax masters from which it made metal parts. These lacquer safety discs were known as "covers." See Andy McKaie and Steven Lasker's note on sound sources to the MCA box set *Bing: His Legendary Years, 1931–1957* (MCA, 1993, 67).

3. Richard Aquila, "The Homogenization of Early Rock and Roll," in *America's Musical Pulse: Popular Music in Twentieth-Century Society,* ed. Kenneth J. Bindas (Westport, Conn.: Greenwood Press, 1992), 272. Reebee Garofalo points out that, under the guidance of Mercury's management, the Crew Cuts thereafter "systematically pillaged the R&B charts." In addition to "Sh-Boom," the Crew Cuts covered Gene and Eunice's "Ko Ko Mo," the Penguins's "Earth Angel," Nappy Brown's "Don't Be Angry," and the Charms's "Gum Drop" (Garofalo, *Rockin' Out: Popular Music in the USA* [Boston: Allyn and Bacon, 1997], 155). For a brief insider's view of the marketing of "Sh-Boom," see Arnold Shaw's *Let's Dance: Popular Music in the 1930s,* ed. Bill Willard (New York: Oxford University Press, 1998), 4.

4. Charles Wolfe, liner notes to *Your Hit Parage: The Mid-50s* (Time-Life, n.d.).

5. Garofalo, *Rockin' Out,* 155.

6. Philip Ennis, *The Seventh Stream: The Emergence of Rocknroll in American Popular Music* (Hanover, N.H.: Wesleyan University Press, 1992), 216. The spelling "rocknroll" is Ennis's attempt to rationalize and regularize the name for that youth music that developed in the early and mid-1950s.

7. Ibid., 216. All chart information here and throughout the essays is from Joel Whitburn's *Top R&B Singles 1942–1988* (Menomenee Falls, Wisc.: Record Research Inc., 1988); and *The Billboard Book of Top 40 Hits* (New York: Billboard Publications, 1996).

8. Stuart Nicholson, liner notes to *The Complete Commodore Recordings of Billie Holiday* (MCA/Commodore, 1996), 21–22. Readers interested in the historical context of this song should see David Margolick's *Strange Fruit: Billie Holiday, Cafe Society, and an Early Cry for Civil Rights* (Philadelphia: Running Press, 2000). Margolick has much to say about the extent to which Holiday made Abel Meeropol's (aka Lewis Allan) song her own, but he observes nevertheless that Holiday was neither the first singer to perform "Strange Fruit" not the last to lay claim to it. Blues singer Josh White began making the song a featured and regular part of *his* repertoire in 1944, only five years after Holiday's recording.

9. Arnold Shaw, *Honkers and Shouters: The Golden Years of Rhythm & Blues* (New York: Collier/Macmillan, 1978), 226.

10. Ibid, 226. As Shaw explains, there remains even still some mystery as to the identity of "Dan Howell": "Some said Dan Howell stood for Lou Levy, owner of Leeds-Duchess; others said it was Dave Kapp of Decca; and still others said that it stood for nobody, but was just a way of retaining a portion of royalties in the firm's treasury" (227). The litigation surrounding this massive hit demonstrates the extent to which the division of music industry profit depends on material being created in routinized ways. Whereas historians and critics often discuss how the making of a film involves many people, we still often overlook the number of steps required to make and market a recording. In fact, technological or commercial change comes more quickly and more often to the music industry than it does to the film industry. Any time money comes to be made in ways that confuse established divisions between writers, performers, producers, and vendors, legal trouble quickly follows—as it did, for example, with the rise of radio in the 1920s, or with the emergence of "sampling" in the 1980s.

11. "Rag Mop" recordings include, in 1946, Bob Wills (C&W), Henry "Red" Allen (R&B), Louis Jordan ("Get the Mop" [R&B]); in 1950, Ames Brothers (pop), Lionel Hampton (pop and R&B), Doc Sausage (R&B), Ralph Flanagan (pop), Johnny Lee Wills (one of the original writers of the song [C&W]), Joe Liggins (marketed as "the first dance version of universal appeal" [R&B]). See Ennis, *The Seventh Stream*, 207–8; see also Galen Gart, *The History of Rhythm & Blues: Special 1950 Volume* (Milford, N.H.: Big Nickel Publications, 1993), 21.

For a contemporaneous A&R executive's account of the relations between recordings and live performance, see John Chilton's *Let the Good Times Roll: The Story of Louis Jordan and His Music* (Ann Arbor: University of Michigan Press, 1994). Chilton quotes Berle Adams about his days working for the General Amusement Corporation. Remembering his early negotiations with Decca Records on Louis Jordan's behalf, Berle explains: "I saw records as a means of exploitation: to build audiences for personal appearances and to help us increase our fees, rather than as a money-maker" (86).

12. Quoted from John Dunning, *Tune in Yesterday: The Ultimate Encyclopedia of Old-Time Radio, 1925–1976* (Englewood Cliffs, N.J.: Prentice-Hall, 1976), 663–65. The format of the show varied greatly over the years, and in its television format it usually featured five vocalists who would perform all the songs. Lennie Hayton was followed by more than a dozen band leaders before the sociocultural changes wrought by rock and roll transformed the hit show into an anachronism. See also Arnold Shaw, *Let's Dance,* 47–51.

13. Alan Dale, "Sweet and Gentle," 1955; Hank Ballard, "Work with Me Annie," 1954; Gibbs, "Dance with Me Henry," 1955; Lillian Briggs, "I Want You to Be My Baby," 1955; Tony Bennett, "Happiness Street," 1956. Bennett, by the way, later obliquely returned the favor by remaking a 1965 Baker single called "Fly Me to the Moon" (see Chip Deffaa, *Blue Rhythms: Six Lives in Rhythm and Blues* [Urbana: University of Illinois Press, 1996], 193). "Fly Me to the Moon" was originally recorded in 1962 as a bossa nova instrumental by Joe Harnell and His Orchestra. Baker's version made the charts for five weeks beginning in February 1965 (reaching number 84 on the pop charts); Bennett's version came out a few months later. It's important to note that by 1965 this practice of multiple recordings of the same song was becoming increasingly uncommon; younger artists were already, when not recording original material, covering earlier recordings chosen for their association with some other artist or scene. The changing nature of pop success also meant that Gibbs's career did not outlast the life of the show that made her: *Your Hit Parade* was canceled in 1958 (though it was revived for a few months the next year). Gibbs's last hit, "The Hula Hoop Song" (1958), was an attempt to exploit the national toy fad.

14. See Ennis, *The Seventh Stream,* 71–98.

15. I have, however, addressed it in an essay written with *City Pages* music editor Jon Dolan. That essay appears in *Reading Rock'n'Roll: Authenticity, Appropriation, Aesthetics,* ed. Kevin J. H. Dettmar and William Richie (New York: Columbia University Press, 1999). See also Lawrence Grossberg's "Rock, Postmodernity, and Authenticity," in *We Gotta Get Out of This Place: Popular Conservatism and Postmodern Culture* (New York: Routledge, 1992), 201–39.

16. Deffaa, *Blue Rhythms,* 183.

17. See Ennis, *The Seventh Stream,* particularly 79–88, 320–22.

18. Deffaa, *Blue Rhythms,* 185.

19. I'm drawing on Edward LiPuma's "Culture in a Theory of Practice," in *Bourdieu: Critical Perspectives,* ed. Craig Calhoun, Edward LiPuma, and Moishe Postone (Chicago: University of Chicago Press, 1993), 14–34, esp. 18.

20. Arthur "Big Boy" Crudup recorded "That's All Right" in September 1946, Presley cut his version in July 1954; Wynonie Harris recorded Roy Brown's "Good Rockin' Tonight" in December 1947, Presley cut his version in September 1954; Junior

Parker & His Little Blue Flames recorded "Mystery Train" in June 1953, Presley cut his version in July 1955; Ray Charles recorded his "I Got a Woman" in November 1954, Presley remade it in January 1956; Willie Mae "Big Mama" Thornton's recording of "Hound Dog"—a song that Jerry Lieber and Mike Stoller wrote especially for her—hit the charts in March 1953, Presley's recording charted in August 1956.

21. The most complete telling of the story is in Peter Guralnick's *Last Train to Memphis: The Rise of Elvis Presley* (New York: Little, Brown, 1994), 97–101. The interview happened on the very first night that Phillips played "That's All Right." As Phillips later remembered, "I asked him [Presley] where he went to high school, and he said, 'Humes.' I wanted to get that out, because a lot of people listening had thought he was colored."

22. Quoted in ibid., 289.

23. Baker reflected on music and race, and on Elvis, in an interview with Mai Cramer and Yolanda Parks. She told them that "music is music: it has no color on it. When you put the note up for music, there's no color on it. There's no Black, there's no White. It's what you feel" (Mai Cramer, "Interview of the Month, February 1996, [with] LaVern Baker," available on the Web at http://www.realblues.com/interv4.html.

24. See Toni Morrison, "Black Matters," in *Playing in the Dark: Whiteness and the Literary Imagination* (New York: Random House, 1992); see also Fred Pfiel, *White Guys: Studies in Postmodern Domination and Difference* (New York: Verso, 1995).

25. See Nelson George, *The Death of Rhythm and Blues* (New York: E. P. Dutton, 1989), esp. 92–93.

26. Umberto Eco, *Travels in Hyperreality*, trans. William Weaver (New York: Harcourt Brace Jovanovich, 1986), 3–58.

27. See LeRoi Jones, *Blues People* (New York: Quill, 1963); Greil Marcus, *Mystery Train: Images of America in Rock'n'Roll Music*, 4th ed. (New York: Plume/Penguin, 1997).

28. George Harrison, quoted in Phillip Norman, *Shout! The Beatles in Their Generation* (New York: Simon & Schuster, 1981), 220.

29. Ibid., 220.

30. Willis recorded the jumping "It's Too Late Baby" for Okeh Records on June 27, 1951. He recycled that title (but not the music) when he recorded "It's Too Late" for Atlantic Records on April 13, 1956. It debuted on July 7, 1956, and reached number 3 on the Disc Jockey charts, number 5 on the R&B Best Seller charts, and number 8 on the Juke Box charts.

31. I do not, of course, mean to imply any inherently "black" or "white" qualities, but refer only to the semiotic and ideological charges that attend the circulation and reception of these recordings.

32. The Fugees's cover was released on their 1996 album *The Score*; Roberta Flack's version is from her 1973 album *Killing Me Softly*.

NEW SPACES/NEW MAPS

I became interested in the question posed by the title of this essay when using Andrew Ross and Tricia Rose's anthology *Microphone Fiends: Youth Music and Youth Culture* as a course text. After I had used it for a few weeks, I was struck (suddenly and with a little embarrassment, since many of my students were country fans) by the fact that out of its eighteen essays, representing many of the most important figures in the cultural studies of popular music, none mentioned country music or culture.[1] This omission seemed strange for several reasons. None of the contributors—who include the editors as well as Susan McClary, George Lipsitz, Greg Tate, and Larry Grossberg, among others—are interested in maintaining the high/low, "art culture"/"mass culture" hierarchy with its attendant distrust of the market. All the contributors seem to be at peace with commercial pop culture (albeit not always excited about the possibilities of market-driven cultural populism). Given country music's commercial importance and the significance of commercial mechanisms in the evolution of its style, the omission seemed very peculiar.[2] And this omission cuts both ways: studies of country music rarely mention or discuss "youth" or "youth culture," and insofar as they do, "youth culture" equates with rock and roll. In the standard history of country music, Bill Malone's *Country Music, U.S.A.,* rock and roll and its attendant youth culture threatens the cultural obsolescence and economic ruin of the music and the industry. Moreover, the industry's response to it—the development of the "countrypolitan" sound associated with Chet Atkins, Eddie Arnold, and Jim Reeves—works to sap the music of its aesthetic integrity even as it preserves its commercial viability.[3]

There are a variety of reasons for this pattern of mutual oversight.[4] For starters, the majority of critical accounts of popular music are driven by the critic's investment in the music as a fan, and it has been rare to find a scholar/critic equally at home in country as well as rock, rap, and related genres. Malone, for instance, confesses that when he saw the young Elvis opening for Hank Snow in 1955, he disliked him (and still does) and did not think he was "country." Furthermore, he resented that Elvis and his screaming fans cut into Snow's performance time.[5] Elsewhere, though, the ignorance and hostility is more troubling and critically problematic; Simon Frith, in his landmark 1981 work *Sound Effects,* states that

> country music, for all its realism or populism, is a conservative force carrying a conservative message. The emphasis of its lyrics is on people knowing their place, and the tensions which result, for women, for example, are treated as unfortunate, even tragic, but not soluble. . . . The message of country populism remains, "We're a loser!" . . . The obviously limiting factor of country music [for early rockers] was its very countryness, its conservatism. It provided no obvious space for rebellion or hedonism, no symbols for the social concerns and restlessness of the young; it described the problems of life as poor white trash but not the new, postwar possibilities.[6]

Frith's condescension aside, there are a number of points we can question here. It is not the case, for instance, that country music and its performers are uniformly conservative: Steve Earle, Iris Dement, and Johnny Cash spring to mind, and if we include such political folkies as Bob Dylan, Woody Guthrie, and Ramblin' Jack Eliot in the country tradition (as does Malone), the list grows even longer. (Not to mention, conversely, that the 1980s and 1990s brought their share of rockin' Reaganites and Thatcherites.) And Frith's claim that country music offered no obvious space for rebellion or hedonism is, even during the 1950s, deeply debatable, as a casual listen to Webb Pierce, Faron Young, Wanda Jackson, Carl Perkins, as well as Elvis will reveal.[7]

Frith's assessment of country music is, as George Lipsitz has pointed out, deeply colored by his assumption that the "references to the past" that punctuate country music both lyrically and musically are either innately conservative or irrelevant.[8] Yet Lipsitz—and arguably Frith himself—miss the complex performative and political irony immanent in Frith's characterization of country's mode of self-identification: "We're a loser!" Country's cultural "mirror stage," I would argue, *is* intensely fatalistic and skeptical about the possibilities of solving the tensions articulated in country songs by individual action or fiat. In this essay, I would like to develop a critical but basically sympathetic understanding of that fatalism, which will, I hope, tell us much about the structure and limitations of "youth culture" as a critical and cultural formation.[9]

*

As many sociologists and historians have pointed out, "youth" is not a "natural," ahistorical category. The concept, and the patterns of experience it articulates, emerged in the West following World War II, when young people came to enjoy hitherto unimagined degrees of economic and ideological freedom from the constraints of the nuclear family, coupled with a relative lack of individual financial responsibility.[10] While this new freedom was only enjoyed to the fullest within the (expanding) middle class, the elimination of child labor in most of the West meant that young people of all classes have enjoyed—or at least experienced—"youth" in some form or another.

In the evolution of cultural studies, "youth" has had various meanings. In the early- to mid-1970s work of the Birmingham School (I am thinking here of Paul Willis's and Angela McRobbie's studies of working-class boys and girls, respectively) "youth" tended to work as a descriptive or functional category, marking a specific biographical transition from being a ward of the nuclear family unit to being a more-or-less autonomous economic and legal agent and worker.[11] In much subsequent work—and particularly in those works that focus on music and youth culture—"youth" is defined less in terms of chronology than as an ideological, ethical, and political zone of free play, which is defined in turn by the various contradictory logics of identity (ethnic, religious, sexual, class, etc.) and the marketplace of signifiers and commodities.

If the first set of theorists define "youth" in terms of its functional position in the overall system of capitalist and patriarchal reproduction, for the

Why Isn't Country Music Youth Culture?   163

latter group "youth" is defined more normatively or ethically, partly as a mode of consumer behavior (Frith and McClary) and partly as a mode of political affiliation, conscious or otherwise; Hence, for Lipsitz, "today's youth culture proceeds from a different premise [from older models of revolutionary politics and oppositional art]. Instead of standing outside society, it tries to work through it, exploiting and exacerbating its contradictions to create unpredictable possibilities for the future."[12] Consumerism and activism, for the editors (and perhaps for most of the contributors) of *Microphone Fiends* are intimately linked; as Ross argues in his introduction to the volume, "youth culture" is implicitly a political and expressly a "consumer category," situated in a matrix with "commercial dictates" and a politics of style.[13]

Not all of the critics writing in *Microphone Fiends* agree on the future prospects of the marriage of subversion and the marketplace; Lipsitz is quite skeptical, in fact, while Larry Grossberg seems agnostic on the issue. Regardless of their position, however, all agree on one basic assumption: "youth" and "youth culture" are understandable as particular, and at times particularly individualistic, negotiations between the members of that culture and the complex of ideologies and institutions that (con)form them. These negotiations serve to grant individuals spaces outside the ideologies and institutions in question, at least for a moment (but perhaps for longer). In *Microphone Fiends,* and particularly in his book on rock, *We Gotta Get Out of This Place,* Grossberg advocates seeing "youth" as an open-ended category defined neither by age nor social position, but by protopolitical will: "[Rock transforms] youth itself . . . from a matter of age into an ambiguous matter of attitude, defined by its rejection of boredom and its celebration of movement, change, energy, that is, fun [which is not the same thing as pleasure]. . . . [Rock] creates temporary and local places and spaces of mobility and deterritorialization."[14]

In *We Gotta Get Out of This Place,* Grossberg amplifies and expands the consequences of this view; age and social position are no more important in defining youth than is "style" (albeit here "style" is "determined by cultural and institutional contexts"), and youth and its culture have the potential to transcend the limitations of individual biography and history: "Youth involves an excessiveness, an impulsiveness, a maniacal irresponsibility which escape time and potentially go on forever"; "Youth is a cultural rather than a biological category," one which promises and is premised on cultural, economic, and geographical mobility.[15]

Grossberg's passion and lyricism, here as elsewhere, signal a tension in his work. On the one hand, he neither accepts nor valorizes this vision of youth at face value: he argues that historically it was most relevant to members of the baby boom, more readily available even there to the middle and upper classes than to the lower; more to whites than blacks, to men than women, to the educated and college students than hardhats and Vietnam casualties. And he might have added that, at any rate, this experience of youth entails a whole host of voluntary commitments. On the other hand, while he acknowledges these limitations in passing, by his exclusion of other experiences of being young he threatens to transform this vision—of speed, flight, mobility, play, fun—into one that is ethically normative, historically transcendent, and culturally universalistic.

As Richard Leppert and George Lipsitz argue in reference to the career and life of Hank Williams Sr., this construction of "youth," even after World War II, did not have universal validity: "In the early post-war years (especially among the rural poor), the concept [of "youth"] had little bearing on life as it was lived."[16] As I hope to show in the remainder of this essay, country music does not map out a "youth culture"—at least not as that concept has been defined—precisely because it is deeply skeptical, as a cultural formation, of the whole body of political, historical, and class-specific assumptions invested in "youth." It is especially skeptical of the valorization of individual flight, escape, and mobility characteristic of much youth culture theory. While it recognizes tension, conflict, and contradiction at a variety of levels,[17] it does not see these oppositions as offering any possibilities of flight or deterritorialization; once they are pried apart, they don't open up "new spaces for freedom" or possibilities for the articulation of new identities, unlike the contradictions Grossberg analyzes in the rock formation. After all, within the logic of country culture, identities are organic, rooted in the specificities of region, class, and family, as well as in a very specific concept and practice of "tradition" and history, to which I will turn momentarily.[18] Hence, for example, while Johnny Cash makes clear in the first few pages of *Cash: The Autobiography* that he goes by several names ("Johnny," for example, is a stage name given him early on by Sam Phillips), these names map out modes of being that are linked to particular communities and contexts: he is "Johnny" to business associates and fans, "John" to his wife June Carter Cash and other close associates, and "J.R." to his brothers and sisters (and Marty Stuart).[19] While one of the book's sections is titled "Road," the other sections are named after Cash's various homes, and as "Road" reveals, the road (a recurring figure in rock culture's longing for deterritorialization) is, for Cash, itself a home, a known entity, complete with an extended family and an exhaustively mapped-out sense of space.[20] Radical mobility, then, is tenuous within the logic of country culture: I want to demonstrate that further by examining one of the more problematic terms in that culture, "tradition."

*

In order to understand the importance of "tradition" to country music, we should begin by noting that the concept has radically different resonances there than in most modern literary and cultural criticism. Arguably, most critics assume, following T. S. Eliot's "Tradition and the Individual Talent," that traditions are intellectual constructs informed by the demands of contemporary culture;[21] in this reading, they are interpretive "ideal orders" that link together authors—or, more precisely, texts—in disregard of patterns of spatial and historical continuity into an eternal hermeneutic present. Thus, for Eliot, Homer and Virgil can be tied together into a critical lineage with poets from Renaissance England, nineteenth-century France, and twentieth-century America. This "tradition" serves to legitimate contemporary writers; more radically, though, in Eliot's reading contemporary writers—or at least the best among them—legitimate "the tradition" through their work. Indeed, "the tradition" is called into being by the imperative of understanding contemporary writing, and the tradition's specific composition depends on that writing.

This paradigmatically modernist interpretation of tradition is sharply at odds with the historical (we might say "realist") concept of tradition. As Raymond Williams points out in *Keywords*, "tradition" has traditionally referred both to a given entity and to a process; some thing is handed down in an act or process that "entails respect and duty."[22] By using the word "tradition," Eliot attaches to his concept (and calls for it in his argument) some of this sense of obligation. But the "thing" here handed down is at least in part the artist's own creation, not handed down so much as "obtain[ed] . . . by great labor."[23]

Eliot's analysis in his essay marks the point at which the diachronic, temporal concept of "tradition" is translated into the essentially synchronic and atemporal language of "canon"; in practice, these two terms, "tradition"

166   Trent Hill

and "canon," become two different aspects of the same thing. This modernistic equation is, as Will Straw suggests, definitive of alternative rock culture, which has tended to construct (on his account implicitly, but frequently explicitly as well) "a relatively stable canon of earlier musical forms" that supplies musicians with a set of stylistic codes and musical languages, which they can then combine and recombine.[24] As a result, in Straw's lapidary formulation, "the terrain of alternative rock is one in which a variety of different temporalities have come to coexist within a bounded cultural space."[25] This space is *cultural* not physical because, as he points out, alternative rock's logic of canonicity renders problematic the relevance and definition of "the local," due to the fact that "a particularly stable set of musical languages and relationships between them has been reproduced within a variety of local circumstances."[26]

In Straw's analysis this canonical (re)formulation of tradition is chiefly characteristic of alternative rock and its "scenes"; we can, however, witness a similar tendency in mainstream rock criticism and historiography. For Robert Palmer,

> that's what rock and roll is about: not so much a distinctive style as a culture in which musicians have access to an unprecedented heritage of live and recorded music, and *the creative freedom to take what they want from it*. . . . Far more than musical hybrids, these sounds proceed from what amounts to a different tradition from the old mainstream pop and different right on down to the most basic musical values. Generation after generation, musicians have made stylistic *choices*. . . . Rock and roll has always been a recombinant art form; each of its major exponents has had to investigate the music's rich and varied heritage, constructing a "new" style and sense of identity from a distinctive, carefully chosen, highly personal array of influences.[27]

This sort of critically self-conscious reflection on "tradition" and its processes mark rock's criticism and historiography, tending in many accounts to suggest a more general "plasticity of popular music," which explains rock's potentially radical effects;[28] for Lipsitz, "when similar record collections enable Steve Berlin, a white musician influenced by black rhythm and blues, to join a Chicano rock band [Los Lobos] on the basis of a mutual affinity for country and western singers Hank Williams and George Jones, we have gone a long way toward a world in which 'all that is solid melts into air.' "[29]

Why Isn't Country Music Youth Culture?   167

I'm not here trying to question whether this sort of stylistic and cultural jump-cutting is "truly" revolutionary or subversive; in earlier cultural moments it certainly has been and in fact can still be.[30] What I would like to do is examine some of the peculiarities of this modernist concept of tradition as an "ideal order" as has been worked out in rock (and youth-culture oriented) criticism. The characteristics of this tradition are as follows:

1. *Discontinuous in time:* Rock traditions do not develop sequentially from a real or mythic origin; they "jump around" in time, bypassing entire periods (in rock historiography, particularly, the early 1960s).

2. *Noncontiguous in space:* Rock music has, since the 1950s, been defined by its ability to yoke together musical discourses drawn from places ranging from the urban north to the rural south. For example, Alan Freed, commenting on the music's popularity in 1956, says that rock and roll "began on the levees and plantations [in the Deep South], took in folk songs [from the Appalachians], and features rhythms and blues [from big cities]."[31] Rock, as a musical genre, is not "rooted" in a particular geographical space (except in a very general way in "the city") so much as it is in a particular kind and experience of rootlessness.

3. *Nonconsensual socially:* Rock "tradition" is not predicated or dependent on preexistent forms of social consensus; nor do these forms necessarily produce it. Rock traditions, again like Eliot's "tradition," are not based on or preserved by means of person-to-person transmission; rather, they are based on what Straw calls "specific forms of connoisseurship":[32] tracking down records, analyzing their musical materials either formally or informally, drawing relationships or resemblances and differences, valuing or rejecting different bands based on these analyses, and recombining these now again raw materials into new, or at least different, configurations. For example, British rock bands like the Beatles, the Rolling Stones, Eric Clapton, and Dave Edmunds learned American blues, country, and rock and roll music not through travel, informal mechanisms of personal apprenticeship, or life within a specific community, but through records. And they learned the music so thoroughly, in fact, that Carl Perkins once remarked that Dave Edmunds and Eric Clapton could play his songs truer to his old recordings than he does or can.[33] These operations of connoisseurship are by and large individual; they do not depend on membership within a specific geographical or imagined community in

which differences must be negotiated or, for that matter, even acknowledged. Insofar as they function within the logic of group identification, they serve less as markers for a preexistent, constative identity than as cause and catalyst for an identity that is created in such moments of shared connoisseurship, as with Lipsitz's story of Steve Berlin and Los Lobos.[34]

The complexities of country tradition as well as its differences with the modernist, "rockist" version of tradition can perhaps best be introduced in reference to Waylon Jennings's 1974 recording of "Bob Wills Is Still the King." Recorded live in Austin, Texas, the song is ostensibly a straightforward celebration of Bob Wills's contribution to country music—after all, as Jennings says in his stage banter before the song begins, Wills "did as much for our kind of music as anybody." The song contains a variety of country tropes: a nostalgic celebration of old times, hard as they might have been; an acknowledgment of Nashville as the center of country music culture; and, at the same time, an assertion of regional country identity and the authority of local traditions. As Jennings sings,

> You can hear the Grand Ole Opry in Nashville, Tennessee,
> It's the home of country music, on that we all agree.
> But when you cross that old Red River, hoss, it just don't mean a thing,
> 'Cause when you're down in Austin, Bob Wills is still the king.[35]

As straightforward as the song seems to be, however, we can use it to begin to understand the complex mechanisms of country tradition, not to mention those of country irony. First, we need to recognize that Jennings wrote the song as an ironic, perhaps sarcastic, jibe at his friend, collaborator, and fellow country outlaw, Willie Nelson, for booking him (Jennings) into oversized halls and auditoriums set up for Wills's western swing big bands. Moreover, as Jennings says in the liner notes to the RCA box set, "I was never a big Bob Wills fan."[36] Even lacking the liner notes, fans familiar with the dynamics of Jennings's stormy musical and commercial relationship with the Nashville country establishment would be suspicious of his endorsement of the Grand Ole Opry as the metonymical center of country music.[37] Furthermore, a listener attuned to the specificities of country style might recognize a musical irony: Jennings's song, dedicated to the continuing influence of Bob Wills, contains absolutely no stylistic reference to western swing or to Wills's music at all. The song emerges as a complicated joke—complicated because, as with so many country jokes, we cannot be sure who the joke is on: on Austin, for being mired in nostalgia; on the live audience (and, through them, us), for not realizing the song's ironic implications; or on Jennings himself, for being stuck hymning the praises of Bob Wills on a stage designed for the great man's band, a stage that dwarfs Jennings's four-piece band and that makes him look, as he says in the liner notes, "like an idiot".[38]

Or is it even, for that matter, something so simple as a "joke" at all? As Barbara Ching has astutely pointed out, much country music works by means of camp, a complicated process in which both a situation and a subjectivity are simultaneously ironized and embraced—indeed, only ironized because they are and must be embraced, and embraced through the very process of being subjected to and by irony.[39] However, while Ching believes that the camp stance is adopted toward country personae as a matter of choice, I would argue that country camp, if it is in the end camp at all, is further complicated by the fact that the element of choice, of self-formation and self-creation, is bracketed or lacking entirely. In Jennings's song, the situation in all its fullness—the space with its history, the music with *its* history, the audience with their immersion in both (and in Austin as a specific site in the mythography of country and of Texas)—defines his capacities for action. Or, in other words, Jennings, like country performers in general, is defined as a country singer insofar as he is inserted into a very real and very material tradition—there is no "ideal order" here.

In general, country constructions of tradition emphasize three features. The first of these is continuity in time. If Robert Palmer can call his book on rock an "unruly history" in part because of the way rock's narrative is punctuated by breaks and stylistic revolutions, country's history is typically written as a teleological progression from an origin. The opening paragraphs of Malone's standard text, *Country Music, U.S.A.*, assert that country music "has preserved, to a remarkable degree, the marks of [its] origin" as a musical form, in spite of the technological, economic, cultural, and aesthetic transformations it (and its cultural matrix) have undergone.[40] This history links together Anglo-Celtic precommercial and precapitalist folk musics, African American influences, and elements from early commercial pop in what Bill Sacks (writing in a special country section of *Billboard* in 1963) calls "a truly indigenous, or native, musical form."[41] In this standard narrative, such old-time fiddlers as Eck Robertson (the first commercially recorded country or "hillbilly" musician) and Uncle Jimmy Thompson (the first performer to appear on WSM's *Grand Old Opry*) are linked in an unbroken circle with Garth Brooks and Shania Twain; the music's validity is grounded, in the words of then governor of Tennessee Frank Clement (writing in that same 1963 *Billboard*), in "songs that have crossed the continent in covered wagons and rocked five generations of babies to sleep."[42]

The second feature is contiguity in space. There is a general tendency in American culture to identify country music with the southern and western United States, and historically this area—particularly the region descending from West Virginia through Tennessee and the Deep South and reaching into Texas—forms what most scholars agree is "the fertile crescent of country music."[43] More specifically, country music has long been associated with the economically and socially marginal rural areas of the Southeast and West, with the southern "white, rural, working-class"[44] or "Southern plain folk."[45] In addition to its broad regional, rural, racial, and class affiliations, country is also associated with very specific cities—Branson, Missouri; Austin, Texas; Nashville, Tennessee—and with specific places or sites in these cities, like the Grand Ole Opry.

The third feature is cultural consensus. Country's construction of tradition differs most dramatically from rock's in the ways in which it views "tradition" as a collective and real social form; it is, most definitely, something that is "handed down" through musical and institutional lineages and negotiated in a variety of discursive and social processes.[46] Several generations of prominent bluegrass musicians, for example, sharpened their abilities performing for one of the major "first generation" bluegrass band leaders, including Bill Monroe, Ralph Stanley, and Flatt and Scruggs.[47] Moreover, many contemporary country stars search out opportunities to perform and record with their predecessors and inspirations: Mark Chesnutt with Waylon Jennings; Dwight Yoakam with Buck Owens; k. d. lang with Owen Bradley (the legendary producer of Patsy Cline). At times, this mode of validating authenticity threatens to collapse under its own weight: Marty Stuart—who has backed, performed, or recorded with Johnny Cash, Tom Petty, Bob Dylan, Lester Flatt, and Bill Monroe—says, "I wear country's past simply as a purple heart on my Nudie suit."[48] When country evokes traditions they are always figured as tangible and physical; when the ghost of Hank Williams hails and recognizes Alan Jackson in Jackson's "Midnight in

Montgomery," Williams is as real as the whippoorwill, the night sky, or the evening's "lonesome chill."[49] And, to return to Jennings, the "tradition" he must encounter, engage, and enter is embodied in the hall and the stage, the musical and social discourses in which he and his audience move; ultimately, it extends to Austin itself.

Country's construction of tradition is important to the centrality in country culture of Nashville, particularly its performance spaces. It is in these sites—the Grand Ole Opry, certainly, but also longstanding clubs, bars, and informal performance spaces like Tootsie's Orchid Lounge, the Bluebird Café, and Ernest Tubbs's Record Shop—where younger country musicians can meet and perform with and for older generations of artists and fans, symbolically passing along the tradition from one generation to the next, thereby invoking the continuity of country as a musical community both in the everyday and in Straw's sense of the term.[50] As Curtis Ellison has remarked, "[the Grand Ole Opry's] induction ceremony vividly exemplifies the confirmation ritual reserved for popular stars who have also demonstrated sincerity, worthiness, and fidelity to country music culture. Foremost among those conventions is paying active homage . . . to the presence of the past." And homage is paid (and induction marked) palpably, by "the touching of hands," public embrace of new inductees, formal presentations, and collective performance.[51] The importance to country of physical, institutional demonstrations of musical and generational continuity is highlighted both by the anxiety that surrounded the move in 1974 of the Grand Ole Opry from the Ryman Auditorium (the "mother church of country music") to Opryland on the outskirts of Nashville, and by the architectural decision to transplant the Ryman's old stage to the new building.[52]

The cultural positions that produce mainstream country culture's anticanonical investment in tradition—its preoccupation with narratives of continuity, cohesion, and knowability—are also part of country's fascination with rural life, one that continues even though much of country's expansion has taken place outside of rural areas. In a series of articles published throughout 1996 in *Country America* (one of the most successful and rapidly growing country publications), several writers for the magazine articulated what constitutes a "real" small town in response to the assertion, made by "a writer from Chicago . . . in a book published in New York," that Essex, Connecticut, is "America's best small town."[53] While Essex's village charms no doubt would appeal to a harried urbanite, its geographical, cultural, and class markers are all wrong: its houses are elaborate, forbidding, "picture-perfect Colonial" affairs constructed and landscaped so as to symbolically shield their occupants from the life of the town while still signifying an abstract civic duty. Which is only to be expected since, the article points out, the great majority of Essex's residents do not live there year-round, aren't from there, and don't know the other people there. The shops (or "shoppes") don't sell items of everyday use like hairspray, suggesting that "most folks in Essex pay somebody else to fix their hair," and the local "diner" sells biscotti and cappuccino (hardly the foundation for a hard day's work) instead of meatloaf.[54]

What "America's Best Small Town . . . Or Is It?" and the rest of the articles in the series make clear is that a good small town—a real small town—is a stable, knowable community held together by collective narratives, economic structures dominated by patterns of small-business entrepreneurialism and farming, and a culture that is essentially working class. It is this sort of community organization, *Country America* suggests, that is most capable of promoting generational and cultural continuity. Essex cannot produce such continuity: "The one Essex native we found was a young waitress working on the local excursion train. 'There is a lot of old money in Essex,' she said, 'and not much for young people to do. I can't wait to get out.'"[55] And although there is some sense of tension in contemporary country's embrace of the rural—such as John Anderson's "Small Town," which paints a vision of rural stasis and outmigration—other songs, like Tim McGraw's "Everywhere," suggest that while you can leave your hometown, the matrix of rural desire is inescapable. Indeed, Alan Jackson's remarkable hit "Little Bitty" goes so far as to imply that the quotidian desires and trajectories of the everyday life of the middle class (but not necessarily the professional-managerial middle class)—including marriage, children, and "A little bitty house and a little bitty yard, / A little bitty dog and a little bitty car"—are what define the essential aspects of small-town life, regardless of whether or not it is lived in "a little hometown or a big old city," and that this form of life is finally underwritten by and incorporated in divine sanction, which is, after all, only "part of a little bitty scheme."

Country's ongoing invocation of "tradition" and its links to everyday, rural, working- and middle-class life is, and has been, a key aspect of its construction of meaning and authenticity. Yet, as Richard Peterson reminds us in his compelling renarrativization of country history, "authenticity" has always been an elusive, slippery, contested, and "fabricated" term in country discourse.[56] While historically there has been a remarkable degree of consensus as to what constitutes authentic country at any given moment, this consensus has been set in institutional and formal terms generated "from above" by the various economic agencies that produce country music: the trade associations (chief among them the Country Music Association), the Grand Ole Opry and country media like TNN, and radio programming consultants.[57]

Hence, the ineluctable contradiction in country music culture, both historical and contemporary, is as a commercial system operating in late monopoly capitalism the media conglomerates largely responsible for the production of country have a vested interest in expanding the country market, in merchandising it as effectively as it can, and in ceaselessly producing new dances, styles, and artists. Unlike rock culture, this commercial angle is not a dirty little secret in country culture; fan magazines openly discuss the process of manufacturing and merchandising country in a way that is quite jarring to a critic and music fan coming from the auteurial realm of rock and pop production.[58] Fans and fan-oriented magazines knowingly discuss the "direction" of country music as an effect of industrial and commercial decision making in a way that would seem to belie any possibility of claiming country to be anything resembling an "authentic," "organic," "indigenous," or "traditional" art form.[59]

Although the promise of country tradition has been that it is a totality in which its earlier moments live on in a musical dialogue or dialectic with the present, the practice of country tradition-making in commercial processes means that while country music culture possesses a strong sense of change, movement, and linear temporality within an organic community, this sense has been purchased by relegating a succession of styles—and more importantly for country fans, performers—to the stylistic dustbin of country history (which currently resides in Branson, Missouri). Although country culture values its connection to its "roots," it has had to constantly redefine these roots. For example, even on the early *Grand Ole Opry* show the old-time, semiprofessional fiddlers and minstrels were shunted aside in the 1930s for the first generation of pop-inflected country stars.[60] As a result, country periodically goes through crises of self-definition, crises including the rise of rock and the "countrypolitan" response in the late 1950s and early 1960s; the emergence of the "outlaw movement" and the success of country-pop crossovers (like John Denver and Olivia Newton-John) in the

1970s; the wake of the "urban cowboy" debacle in the 1980s; and, more recently, the debate swirling around "hot new country."

At this writing, "Hot New Country" (HNC) is the primary country radio format on country FM stations and TV programming throughout the United States. Some of the commercial and stylistic trendsetters for HNC are artists like Garth Brooks, Shania Twain, and (a few years back) Billy Ray Cyrus. In terms of production values and sound, HNC is at times hard to distinguish from contemporary Top 40 rock radio; there are similar mixes of up-tempo rockers and power ballads on each, with similar guitar, bass, and drum-oriented arrangements. At times the producers for the two formats are the same; for example, Shania Twain producer (her husband "Mutt" Lange) produced Def Leppard's biggest albums. Their live performances and videos often employ the mannerisms characteristic of arena rock performances; Garth Brooks, for instance, is noted for using stage mechanics to swing out over his concert audiences. And in terms of programming and marketing strategies, the formats are the same: both HNC and modern rock stations employ radio consultants and use demographic research tools like focus groups and polling, and both make use of carefully coordinated advertising campaigns to promote records and artists.[61] The differences between modern rock and HNC lie in some of the details that have, since the 1950s, served as country's idiomatic markers, including the use of fiddles and pedal steel guitars (though occasionally, as with Twain's "Don't Be Stupid," they are buried so deeply in the mix or used so sparingly that they serve only as the most formal and perfunctory of idiomatic markers); a somewhat "twangier" guitar sound that emphasizes pick attack and treble rather than heavy distortion; the prevalence of (at times affected) southern accents on the vocals; an emphasis on lyrical "realism" and particularity as opposed to "abstraction"; and, sartorially, a modified western "cowboy look" that has served as the main signifier of country authenticity since the early 1950s.[62]

The crossover potential and media-friendliness of HNC performers helped country albums obtain a 25 percent share of the market by 1993.[63] Doubtlessly, HNC has helped to make country more accessible to a younger, urban, middle-class audience, as the success of Garth Brooks's 1997 concert in Central Park testifies. The carefully orchestrated promotional campaigns of HNC artists have helped too: Billy Ray Cyrus's "Achy Breaky Heart" had earlier been covered by the Marcy Brothers with no real impact, but Cyrus's management company, sensing a possible hit, shipped a professionally choreographed set of line-dance steps to dance clubs and prereleased its video to music video outlets, all of which helped to "break" the song massively on country radio.[64] Yet many country fans feel uneasy with the implications of this sort of commercial success, a situation addressed strikingly by *Country America*'s May 1996 cover story "Where Do We Draw the Line Between Country and Rock?"[65] The cover features a picture of a fiddle grafted onto—or morphing into—a bright yellow heavy-metal-style guitar, and its accompanying caption, "Brooks and Dunn, Dwight [Yoakam], Randy Travis, Reba [McEntire], and Others *Have Their Say*," suggests a narrative of industry coercion. This is reinforced by a caption on the contents page, which asks an apparently rhetorical question: "Is the influence of rock music a blessing in disguise, the cutting edge of country, or a curse upon our traditional turf?" The implication seems transparent: of course it's a curse. Yet the article itself narrates a picture of collaboration, freedom if not liberation, and consensus; it points out that many young country stars grew up listening to rock (particularly regional and country-friendly bands like the Eagles and Lynyrd Skynyrd), that rock artists from Chuck Berry and Buddy Holly on have borrowed from country (Waylon Jennings, for instance, played bass for Holly's band), and that many contemporary stars like Brooks and Dunn feel a great sense of relief that they no longer need be "scared to say we ever listened to anyone outside of [George] Jones and [Merle] Haggard."[66]

In spite of this facile consensualism, many in the country community are convinced that country has lost its roots in the poor, white rural matrix of class experience and musical style.[67] On this account, contemporary country has less to do with tradition and community than lifestyle choice. In the words of Johnny Cash (one of popular music's most remarkable organic intellectuals),

> when music people today, performers and fans alike, talk about being "country," they don't mean that they know or even care about the land and the life it sustains and regulates. They're talking about choices—a way to look, a group to belong to, a kind of music to call their own. Which begs a question: Is there anything behind the symbols of modern "country," or are the symbols themselves the whole story.[68]

As an older star in a "tradition" that has always at least nominally valued and rewarded performers faithful to the music and the industry, and who continue to produce solid work late into their careers, Cash's own predicament is illustrative; in spite of garnering good reviews for his 1997 album *Unchained*, he received little airplay on country radio and practically no support from the Nashville country establishment, even though his fan support remains strong and the record eventually won a Grammy for best country album of 1997.[69] As a 1997 *Country Weekly* cover story points out, Cash's entire generation of country performers currently in their fifties and sixties—who include figures like Willie Nelson, Waylon Jennings, Loretta Lynn, Dolly Parton, George Jones, and Merle Haggard—have been shut off from HNC-dominated country radio, in spite of the fact that each one has released critically acclaimed material in recent years.[70] In an informal write-in poll conducted by *Country Weekly*, "thousands" of readers complained about this neglect; only twenty or so readers, according to a subsequent article, "want radio to stay the way it is."[71] While such voluntary polls always tend to be skewed toward those who are dissatisfied with the status quo, the fact remains that Branson, Missouri—with its dozens of theaters owned by and featuring the music of older country stars—has surpassed Nashville and the Opry in popularity as a country music tourist spot, with Pigeon Forge, Tennessee (featuring Dolly Parton's Dollywood theme park) steadily gaining ground.

*

One of the most compelling responses to the dominance of HNC has been the emergence of an "alternative country" aesthetic and movement. Known by a variety of names, such as "alt-country," "y'allternative," "twangcore," and "insurgent country," this movement raises some interesting questions about the survival of country traditions in a postmodern environment and the possibilities of a country-identified youth culture. As the name suggests, some of the roots of alternative country lie in the stylistic and cultural milieu of alternative rock. In the history of American alternative rock, country-inspired bands have been around at least since the heyday of the Los Angeles punk scene in the late 1970s and early 1980s, with bands like X, the Blasters, Jason and the Scorchers, Gun Club, and Tex and the Horseheads. Alternative country emerged in the early 1990s as a distinctive formation in reaction both to the dominance of the Nashville establishment and the perceived collapse and commodification of alternative rock culture; it coalesced around the commercial and artistic success of St. Louis-based Uncle Tupelo and its spinoff bands, Son Volt and Wilco.

Uncle Tupelo's discussion space on the Internet gave birth to the movement's flagship magazine *No Depression*, named after the Uncle Tupelo album and song of that name, itself a cover of an old Carter Family tune. *No Depression*'s coverage of the country scene is thoroughly eclectic; its articles and reviews insist on the continuing significance of past and contemporary figures ignored by the Nashville establishment: folk-inflected troubadours like Townes Van Zandt, Gram Parsons, and Emmylou Harris; honky-tonk traditionalists like Webb Pierce, Faron Young, and Dwight Yoakam; and older but still-active, though marginalized, stars like Merle Haggard and Johnny Cash. These artists all get some space in some mainstream country magazines, particularly *New Country*, but *No Depression* is also deeply invested in bands that explore the cusp between avant-noise indie rock and country, such as Chicago's Handsome Family and Austin's Old 97s, as well as experimental bluegrassers the Bad Livers. *No Depression* has aggressively sought to reclaim marginalized country subgenres, like "countrypolitan" and (especially) bluegrass for a new country formation. Significantly, many of the artists it features prominently are, or have been, signed to a major Nashville label (as with Steve Earle and Iris DeMent), while others, like the Bad Livers and Alejandro Escovedo, come from a postpunk alternative rock milieu. And the magazine also covers musical genres, like Cajun, folk, and reggae, that are at the margins of mainstream country.

Such eclecticism is remarkable, given the degree to which the realities if not the strategies of niche marketing have come to define the American pop marketplace in recent years. What unifies *No Depression*'s coverage and sets it apart is the implicit and explicit political affiliations it seeks to bring to the critical table. *No Depression* has from its very first issues sought to reintroduce the discourse of class politics into the practice and understanding of country music. For example, Merle Haggard's "blue-collar" identification is foregrounded in an early live review,[72] and in another piece one of the magazine's editors, Grant Alden, makes much of Haggard's limited experience (or "modest credentials") as a truck driver in his review of *Rig Rock Deluxe* "because we now live amid the fashion of trailer-park chic, where young men wear used gas station jackets and drive vintage cars they're obliged to pay others to keep running."[73] *No Depression*'s interviews and articles frequently stress this sort of class identification and experience. For Iris DeMent, "most of the people who wrote [older gospel] songs came from poorer settings where they were really struggling with life, and you hear that in the songs."[74] Further, according to longtime roadhouse veteran Johnny Bush,

> one thing I've noticed about the audience today, is when we first started we had shipyard workers, painters and pipefitters and oilfield workers. It was blue-collar music, that's what country was. Today, we're playing to judges and politicians and doctors. The music hasn't changed, but the audience has. It's gotten worse.[75]

Bush is not here complaining that his original roomful of pipefitters somehow "made good." The embourgeoisement of the country audience is a product of shifts in the class demographics of Nashville-based radio programming and promotion, away from what Mark Fenster has called "the wrong kind of demographics": working-class, rural or expatriated rural, and therefore a "less 'attractive' [type] of audience to sell to advertisers."[76]

No Depression's engagement with the symbolic dynamics of class politics is not, however, a frequent, explicit focus of the magazine; in practice, it is usually imbricated into its running critique of the Nashville establishment, of its oligopolistic control of record production and promotion, sound and style.[77] Few articles in the magazine fail to deliver some sort of critique. As an alternative, *No Depression* has from the beginning sought to foster the "DIY [do-it-yourself] spirit"[78] characteristic of 80s American indie rock culture. One of the lead articles in the first issue of *No Depression* set the tone for the magazine. Although it covered the work of Kieran Kane, songwriter and country performer who enjoyed considerable success as a member of the O'Kanes in the 1980s before falling out of favor with Nashville, the article is primarily about Kane's record label, Dead Reckoning, and the joys of operating outside the control of the industry.[79] As a result of *No Depression*'s DIY focus, the magazine has worked to promote an explosion of independent country and "roots"-oriented labels and the emergence of an alternative country network of local scenes, thereby serving to reinvent, in a postmodern moment, the distinctly regional shape of precommercial country culture.[80]

In its retrieval of lost traditions, its recovery of the local, its reassertion of the prerogatives of class conflict in country discourse, and its reinforcement of musical and commercial small-business entrepreneurialism one might think, surely, that the work of *No Depression* and alternative country signals a powerful impetus toward renewal in country culture. Yet relatively little attention has been paid to the movement in the mainstream country press, and much of that attention has been negative or, at best, cautious. Writing in the *Journal of Country Music,* Jim Ridley argues that, while alternative country artists are "keeping [the music] alive through the sheer joy of discovery," this joy is based too frequently on ignorance, naïvité, or, at worst, an ironic posturing that ridicules "real" country fans and their form of life.[81] Speaking of a song by one of alternative country's best-known acts, Whiskeytown, Ridley claims that "The sour observation [the band] makes about 'Matrimony' would be unforgivably smug and nasty if sung over a quiet neo-folk melody—but when [Caitlin Cary] sings them over a dinky little country waltz, it's impossible to tell if she's serious or joking. In this manner, the band can have its cake and beat it too."[82]

Ridley here tends to equate "consequence" and "commitment" with acceptance of and insertion into the economic and commercial prerogatives of the Nashville establishment.[83] Yet his sour observations suggest some of the important limitations of alternative country, which pertain to the problems of canon, tradition, and commitment, and ultimately to its investment in the ideologies and practices of postpunk youth culture. The eclecticism celebrated in *No Depression* has always been a part of country music, but this eclecticism has in turn always been contingent on the particularities of local tradition and individual circumstance. For example, Hank Williams Sr. fused African American blues, Cajun dancehall music, contemporary country and gospel styles, and pop into a new form that became paradigmatic for country in the 1950s (as we can see on his first major single, "Long Gone Lonesome Blues"). This fusion is a result of the circumstances of Williams's life: born of poor, working-class, Pentecostalist parents in Montgomery, Alabama, he would have been exposed to a wide variety of musical forms as a child and had the opportunity to informally apprentice himself to musicians working in these forms. (He learned his blues style, on his account, from an itinerant African American musician named Tee Tot.) Williams's articulation of a new musical language is grounded in his body and experience; it represents not so much a set of style codes freely adopted as it does a set of existential possibilities and logics of consequence.[84] It represents, in short, what it means to live in history as a member of the postwar white working class, to experience history simultaneously as "what hurts" and what enables.

Conversely, to use another of Ridley's examples, when Whiskeytown's Ryan Adams sings, "I'm a fast-talkin', hell-raisin' son-of-a-bitch," as he does in "Hard Luck Story" (from *Faithless Street,* the band's first album), the problem isn't, contra Ridley, Adams's "lack of authority"[85]; Adams is without a doubt more of a hell-raisin' son-of-a-bitch than Johnny Cash is a cold-blooded murderer (as Cash suggests he is in "Folsom Prison Blues" and "Delia's Gone"). Nor is the problem necessarily Adams's "ironic distance." Rather, the problem is one of community and consequence; if a singer in a roadhouse honky-tonk band lays claim to that sort of identity, he might have to back it up in a way that Adams, situated in the alternative/bohemian nexus of independent radio and college-town music clubs, probably won't have to do.[86]

No Depression suggests at time that, culturally speaking, "alternative country" is much closer to the "alternative" than the "country" end of the spectrum as the latest permutation of postpunk musical culture. Its preoccupation with local and "scene"-based reportage mirrors that of other postpunk publications like *Maximumrocknroll.* And that culture is predominantly canonical and archivalist in orientation; *No Depression* has always set about to articulate a canon that is a tradition and a tradition that is a canon. As the editors state in the first issue:

> We declare, first, that there is such a thing as alternative country music. There has to be when new country radio . . . declines even to notice Willie Nelson, George Jones, and other still living, still vibrant legends of the genre. We claim them as our spiritual ancestors, and Gram Parsons as our holy ghost, minister to the shotgun wedding of country and rock 'n' roll, long before the Eagles crashed the reception.[87]

Elsewhere in this manifesto-*cum*-advertisement, and throughout the magazine's run, its writers articulate canons of artists, not infrequently yoking together bodies of work historically at odds with one another. Witness, for instance, their endorsement of Mike Ireland and Holler's countrypolitan sound, even though "countrypolitanism" drove the final nail into the coffin of the honky-tonk sound of the "boom period" (and was the dominant, middle-class-oriented style that Willie Nelson, Waylon Jennings, and Merle Haggard reacted against in their early careers). The sum of *No Depression*'s archivalist inclinations is that, ironically, while much of its reportage is scene-based, there is little to distinguish between one scene and another; the same boxed-set reissues are as available in Chapel Hill, N.C., as in St. Louis, and Wilco sounds much of a piece with Whiskeytown.

It is true, as Richard Peterson has pointed out, that "hardcore" commitment is not a universal attribute of country performance; there is an entire tradition, stretching from Buell Kazee and Bradley Kincaid in the 1920s through Vince Gill and Shania Twain, of performers who adopted the "country" or "hillbilly" role deliberately for commercial or performance purposes.[88] Yet, for comparison's sake, it is worth noting that these roles in country culture take on a materiality and "personality" of their own, independently of the wishes of the performers who enact them. Buell Kazee, college-educated and a trained operatic singer, was expected by record companies and fans to sound like and sing the songs of uneducated hillbillies, quite against his artistic desires.[89] One gets the sense in reading *No Depression* that for many alternative country performers, the country role, be it hardcore or softshell, is cost-free and strictly voluntary. Menconi quotes Ryan Adams as saying, "people in punk bands around here [Chapel Hill] are starting to do other things because punk rock just gets old after awhile." Similarly, Neko Case, a Canadian singer whose debut album, *The Virginian*, did quite well on alternative country and "Americana" charts, and who moonlights as the drummer for the punk band Maow, states that to her, "country music is definitely punk rock right now, for me."[90]

Reading that quote, and looking at the accompanying photo of Case posed and dressed in vintage-shop elegance, one might be excused for thinking that alternative country might well serve as the vehicle for making country music safe for consumption by college-town bohemians. Yet, as Case also reminds us, "punk" was itself a movement committed to critiquing the commercial prerogatives of the music industry, a point made eloquently by Steve Earle: "I think Hank Williams records have a lot more to do with the Sex Pistols than they have to do with Brooks & Dunn. . . . It's really just about any kind of music that's *real*. . . . That was what my argument with Nashville was all along. It's not about country or rock. It's about *real*."[91] The "real" that is effaced and repressed in contemporary Nashville—which, Case suggests, is recovered in alternative country's moment of institutional critique—is the complex set of affiliations and articulations that made country music central to the culture of southern "plain folk." Case states:

> Have you seen those commercials where they have some young yuppie-lookin' guy going, "This isn't my grandfather's country . . . this is *real* music"? It makes me so fuckin' mad. . . . Or those ads that just say "all

country, no bumpkin"? Who the fuck do these people think they are? Obviously, these people don't care about the music; they just think of their audience as a demographic, which is also insulting to the people that listen to country music.[92]

Case and Earle's comments and music suggest much about the differences between alternative country and earlier "roots"-oriented movements. For all its affinities with the archivalist culture of alternative rock, alternative country is not particularly nostalgic and certainly not revivalist; its musicians are not, unlike the urban, college-graduate hillbillies of the folk revival, interested in recovering an authentic past so much as articulating a set of connections and alliances within a marginalized present. And these connections cut across several of the binarisms that have structured oppositional culture (and youth-cultural theory and practice) since the 1960s: blue-collar/ white-collar, urban/rural, youth/adult, popular/elite, men/women.[93] The cultural politics of alternative country are premised less on the possibilities of flight, freedom, and mobility than on immobility or downward mobility. It offers, in short, the possibility of imagining an alternative culture—at times an oppositional culture—that is not limited to and by the historical and ideological terrain of youth culture, one that might allow new affective and political alliances to understand the experience of "working man's blues," regardless of whether that working man is a truck driver or office temp, a college-town bohemian or army vet, Latino or Anglo, or, for that matter, a man or a woman.

Notes

I would like to thank Ronnie Pugh at the Country Music Foundation for his invaluable help in locating magazines and archival resources for this paper; Roger Beebe and Ben Saunders for their encouragement and patience; Bill Koon, for his collegial feedback and expertise as a reader and scholar of country music; and Melinda Morrow for being research assistant, confidant, sounding board, master gardener, editor, and beloved.
1. See Andrew Ross and Tricia Rose, eds., *Microphone Fiends: Youth Music and Youth Culture* (New York: Routledge, 1994).
2. In spite of country culture's claims to spontaneous, uncommercial "authenticity," it has historically been, in Curtis Ellison's words, "an entrepreneurial and increasingly complex entertainment business" whose breakthroughs, Richard Peterson re-

minds us, have frequently been predicated on revolutions in marketing and image formation (Ellison, "Keeping Faith: Evangelical Performance in Country Music," *South Atlantic Quarterly* 94 [1995]: 140; Peterson, *Creating Country Music: Fabricating Authenticity* [Chicago: University of Chicago Press, 1997] or, for a shorter account, his "The Production of Cultural Change: The Case of Contemporary Country Music," *Social Research* 45 [1978]: 292–314).

3. See Bill Malone, *Country Music, U.S.A.*, rev. ed. (Austin: University of Texas Press, 1985): 245–67. The "countrypolitan" sound, as crafted by producers and A&R agents such as Owen Bradley and Chet Atkins, featured lush, orchestral arrangements, background vocals, and gentle piano and guitar accompaniment that eschewed the harsher and more idiomatic sounds of the pedal steel guitar and fiddle. Not all artists submitted readily to countrypolitanism; Patsy Cline, for instance, resisted changing her style and delivery (forged as a hard-country singer in honky-tonks and road-houses) to accommodate her producer, Owen Bradley, and she did so only after she was persuaded by her commercial success that it sounded and worked better for her. See Joli Jensen, "Patsy Cline, Musical Negotiation, and the Nashville Sound," in *All That Glitters: Country Music in America*, ed. George H. Lewis (Bowling Green, Ohio: Bowling Green State University Popular Press, 1993), 38–50.

4. My argument here has some affinities with Barbara Ching's "Acting Naturally: Cultural Distinction and Critiques of Pure Country," *Arizona Quarterly* 49, no. 3 (1993): 107–25. There, Ching calls into question cultural theory's (and in particular postmodern theory's) general disregard for and denigration of country culture. She argues, persuasively but not finally conclusively, that this neglect stems from the tendency of intellectuals to assume that "authenticity" is the defining characteristic of country music and culture, thereby overlooking the play of personae, irony, and camp that she holds to be constitutive of country culture. As a consequence, she rejects the relevance of notions of authenticity for understanding country culture, a move that to my mind is too hasty given the centrality of it and related concepts in country culture itself. Yet she is one of the rare commentators to grasp the importance of irony in country—not to mention the complexities of its deployment.

5. See Bill Malone, "Elvis, Country Music, and the South," in *All That Glitters*, ed. Lewis, 51.

6. Simon Frith, *Sound Effects: Youth, Leisure, and the Politics of Rock and Roll* (New York: Pantheon, 1981).

7. Some might argue whether Jackson, Perkins, or Elvis are, in fact, "country." I would counter, though, that their records were charted as country (Perkins's "Blue Suede Shoes" in fact hit the top of the country, pop, and R&B charts) and that the distinctions between and within pop genres and pop audiences in the early to mid-1950s are terrifically fluid, not becoming articulated as rigid and distinct until later. For a fuller version of this argument, see Trent Hill, "A Distinctive Country Voice: The Nashville Sound and Country's Genre Crisis in the 1950s," *Journal of Popular Music Studies* 11–12 (1999–2000): 3–17.

8. See George Lipsitz, "Against the Wind: Dialogic Aspects of Rock and Roll," in *Time Passages: Collective Memory and American Popular Culture* (Minneapolis: University of Minnesota Press, 1990): 104–5.

9. Country music is not incompatible per se with the culture of young people; some do listen to country, and there are some country-specific youth subcultures (such as "kickers"). Frith (*Sound Effects,* 26) recognizes them, but he does not discuss them in any detail. An analysis of actually existing country subcultures would be a valuable addition to this paper; limitations of space and time prevent me from doing the ethnographical work that would be required, but there are a few essays in Lewis's fine collection, *All That Glitters,* that suggest where such an analysis might begin. See particularly the essays by Aaron Fox, "Split Subjectivity in Country Music and Honky-Tonk Discourse," 131–39; and Karl Neuenfeldt, "Alienation and Single Musicians on the Honky-Tonk Circuit," 140–48.

10. See Frith, *Sound Effects,* 181–86, as well as Richard Leppert and George Lipsitz, "Age, the Body, and Experience in the Music of Hank Williams," *Popular Music* 1 (1990): 259–74, reprinted in *All That Glitters,* ed. Lewis, 22–37.

11. See Angela McRobbie, *Feminism and Youth Culture: From Jackie to Just Seventeen* (Boston: Unwin Hyman, 1991); and Paul Willis, *Learning to Labor: How Working-Class Kids Get Working-Class Jobs* (New York: Columbia University Press, 1981). See also Jim McGuigan's critique of the Birmingham School's work on youth culture in his *Cultural Populism* (New York: Routledge, 1992), 89–123.

12. George Lipsitz, "We Know What Time It Is: Race, Class, and Youth Culture in the Nineties," in *Microphone Fiends,* ed. Ross and Rose, 25.

13. Andrew Ross, "Introduction" in *Microphone Fiends,* ed. Ross and Rose, 2–3. Dick Hebdige's *Subculture: The Meaning of Style* (New York: Methuen, 1979) marks the most significant transition between these two tendencies. What is important about the groups he analyzes in his germinal work—mods, teds, rude boys and punks—is less the specific historical and economic determinants each one faces than their work in "clearing out" some sort of semiotic and practical free space within those limitations.

14. Lawrence Grossberg, "Is Anybody Listening? Does Anybody Care? On Talking about 'the State of Rock,'" in *Microphone Fiends,* ed. Ross and Rose, 51.

15. Lawrence Grossberg, *We Gotta Get Out of this Place: Popular Conservativism and Postmodern Culture* (New York: Routledge, 1992), 176–77.

16. See Leppert and Lipsitz, "Age, the Body, and Experience," 23.

17. See George Lewis, "Tension, Conflict, and Contradiction in Country Music," in *Journal of Popular Culture* 24, no. 4 (1991): 103–17, reprinted in *All That Glitters,* ed. Lewis.

18. Cf. the Louvin Brothers's "Stuck Up Blues" (written by Roy Acuff), which mocks the social and linguistic pretensions of people who have achieved some form of upward mobility.

19. Johnny Cash, *Cash: The Autobiography*, with Patrick Carr (San Francisco: Harper, 1997), 7. In contrast, note Tricia Rose's observation that the "prolific self-naming" in hip hop culture "is a form of reinvention and self-definition" (Rose, *Black Noise: Rap Music and Black Culture in Contemporary America* [Hanover, N.H.: Wesleyan University Press, 1994], 36).

20. See for example Cash, *Cash*, 47–49. Cecelia Tichi, in *High Lonesome: The American Culture of Country Music* (Chapel Hill: University of North Carolina Press, 1994), 19–78, argues that one of the central tensions in country music (as well as in American culture in general) is between "home" and mobility as figured by "the road." My argument is rather at cross-purposes with hers—it seems to me that most country engagements with "the road" read it as an extension of, obstacle to, or surrogate for "home." In any event, the sense of "mobility" I wish to examine here has more to do with youth culture's issues of culture, class, and identity than space and geographical movement.

21. T. S. Eliot, "Tradition and the Individual Talent," in *Selected Prose of T. S. Eliot*, ed. Frank Kermode (New York: Harcourt Brace Jovanovich, 1975), 38.

22. Raymond Williams, *Keywords: A Vocabulary of Culture and Society* (New York: Oxford University Press, 1985), 319.

23. Eliot, "Tradition," 38. For a fuller discussion of the theoretical and historical implications of Eliot's argument, see Frank Lentricchia, *Modernist Quartet* (New York: Cambridge University Press, 1994), 239–86.

24. Will Straw, "Systems of Articulation, Logics of Change: Communities and Scenes in Popular Music," *Cultural Studies* 5 (1990): 378.

25. Ibid., 380.

26. Ibid., 379.

27. Robert Palmer, *Rock & Roll: An Unruly History* (New York: Harmony Books, 1995): 8–9, 289; first emphasis is mine.

28. George Lipsitz, "Cruising around the Historical Bloc: Postmodernism and Popular Culture in East Los Angeles," in *Time Passages: Collective Memory and American Popular Culture* (Minneapolis: University of Minnesota Press, 1990), 158.

29. Lipsitz, "Cruising around the Historical Bloc," 151.

30. For a more extended analysis of how this has worked out in rock music and culture, see Grossberg, *We Gotta Get Out of This Place*, esp. 137–70; and Trent Hill, "The Enemy Within: Censorship in Rock Music in the 1950s," *South Atlantic Quarterly* 90 (1991): 675–708.

31. Quoted in Hill, "The Enemy Within," 682.

32. Straw, "Systems of Articulation," 379.

33. See Art Fein, liner notes to *Carl Perkins: Original Sun Greatest Hits* (Rhino, 1986).

34. By way of further example: Malcolm McLaren asked John Lydon (aka Johnny Rotten) to join the Sex Pistols when he saw Lydon wearing a Pink Floyd t-shirt that had been modified to read "I Hate Pink Floyd" (Palmer, *Rock & Roll*, 273). By way of contrast: Steve Earle, a gifted country songwriter and performer, is an outcast in Nashville in part because of his willingness to criticize other performers (he once called Shania Twain "the highest-paid lap dancer in Nashville") (Peter Blackstock, "Steve Earle: Can't Keep a Good Man Down," *No Depression*, spring 1996, 32.

35. Waylon Jennings, "Bob Wills Is Still the King," *Only Daddy That'll Walk the Line: The RCA Years* (RCA, 1993).

36. Jimmy Guterman, liner notes to Waylon Jennings, *Only Daddy That'll Walk the Line: The RCA Years* (RCA, 1993).

37. For the full account of these troubles, see Waylon Jennings and Lenny Kaye, *Waylon: An Autobiography* (New York: Warner Books, 1996).

38. Guterman, "Waylon Jennings," 17.

39. Ching, "Acting Naturally," 113–17.

40. Malone, *Country Music, U.S.A.*, 1.

41. Bill Sacks, "The History of Country Western Music," *Billboard: The World of Country Music* supplement, November 2, 1963, 19.

42. Frank G. Clement, "Country Music: A Tennessee Heritage," *Billboard: The World of Country Music* supplement, November 2, 1963, 22.

43. Richard Peterson, *Creating Country Music*, 12.

44. Conrad Floeter, "Like the Wings of a Dove," review of Byrds's *Sweetheart of the Rodeo*, *No Depression*, March–April 1997, 83.

45. Bill Malone, "Honky Tonk: The Music of the Southern Working Class," in *Folk Music and Modern Sound*, ed. William Ferris and Mary L. Hart (Jackson: University Press of Mississippi, 1982), 127.

46. In this aspect, country music resembles both the classical and jazz traditions in their emphasis on formal and informal systems of pedagogy and apprenticeship to master performers and teachers. Classical violinists, for example, can frequently trace their pedagogical genealogy going back to Italian and German virtuosi and teachers of the seventeenth through nineteenth centuries; in jazz, many performers master their techniques in quasi-conservatory settings or by working with acknowledged master band leaders like Miles Davis or Duke Ellington.

47. For a fully account of the workings of the bluegrass tradition, see Mark Fenster, "Commercial (and/or?) Folk: The Bluegrass Industry and Bluegrass Traditions," *South Atlantic Quarterly* 94 (1995): 81–108.

48. Holly Gleason, "Marty Stuart Walks the Line with His Heart and Soul," *New*

Country Music, April 1994, 33. Stuart, Gleason informs us, also "owns some of Hank Williams' suits, Jimmie Rodgers' autograph, and Bob Wills' bus" (30).

49. Alan Jackson, "Midnight in Montgomery," *The Greatest Hits Collection* (Arista, 1995).

50. In Straw's account, "musical community" is an older notion than that of the "scene," one that "presumes a population group whose composition is relatively stable" and whose collective exploration of musical forms is "said to be rooted within a geographically specific historical heritage" ("Systems of Articulation," 373). Within musical communities, styles change with a definite sense of closure. Intriguingly, Straw argues that contemporary techno/electronica/dance culture operates as a sort of extended, postmodern musical community.

51. Ellison, "Keeping Faith," 138–39.

52. Malone, *Country Music, U.S.A.,* 369.

53. Roberta Peterson, "America's Best Small Town . . . Or Is It?" *Country America,* March 1996, 80.

54. Ibid., 82.

55. Ibid., 82. See also Robbie Peterson, "America's Smallest Towns," *Country America,* June 1996, 64–69; Robbie Peterson, "Our Kind of Town: Bodacious Bandera," *Country America,* April 1996, 54–61; Roberta Peterson, "Small Town: The Finer Points of Mineral Point, Wisconsin," *Country America,* October–November 1996, 52–59; Peg Brinkhoff, "Living Their Dream in God's Country," *Country America,* July 1996, 40–43; and Elizabeth McBride, "Country Woman," *Country America,* October–November 1996, 60–64.

56. Peterson, *Creating Country Music.*

57. See Don Cusic, "Country Green: The Money in Country Music" *South Atlantic Quarterly* 94 (1995): 231–41; Don Cusic, "QWERTY, Nashville, and Country Music," *Popular Music and Society* (1994): 41–55; and Richard Peterson, "The Production of Cultural Change" and *Creating Country Music,* 230–33.

58. The sheer number of articles in trade and fan publications is such that giving examples seems to me to be an exercise in pointlessness. For a few good ones, though, see Rick Mitchell, "Country at the Crossroads," *New Country,* September 1994, 46–52; Clark Parsons, "Chasin' That Neon Rainbow," *Journal of Country Music* 16, no. 2 (n.d.): 11–15; Tex Ritter, "Tex Ritter Speaks Out on Keeping Country Music Country," *Country Music Who's Who 1965:* 32; and Ronnie Pugh's liner notes to *Webb Pierce: King of the Honky-Tonk* (Country Music Foundation, 1994), which attends equally to Pierce's acumen as both a musical and institutional player.

59. See Tichi, *High Lonesome.*

60. Peterson, *Creating Country Music,* 69–80.

61. For an account of how marketing strategies helped make Garth Brooks's career, see Curtis Ellison, *Country Music Culture: From Hard Times to Heaven* (Jackson: University Press of Mississippi, 1995).

62. Peterson, *Creating Country Music*, 185–201.

63. Ellison, *Country Music Culture*, 230.

64. Ibid., 217–19.

65. *Country America*, June 1996, 2.

66. Neil Pond, "Where Do We Draw the Line Between Country and Rock?" *Country America*, June 1996, 38.

67. See Tony Scherman, "Country: Its Story Is Over," *American Heritage*, November 1994, 54–57; Cash, *Cash*, 12–13.

68. Cash, *Cash*, 12.

69. Consequent to winning the Grammy, Cash and his label, American Records, took out a full-page ad in the March 14, 1998 *Billboard* "acknowledging" the country industry for their support—the ad shows an enraged younger Cash flipping off the photographer. The ad can be viewed at the official Johnny Cash Web site (http://www.johnnycash.com/billboard.htm).

70. Rick Haydan and Catharine S. Rambeaux, "Legends Turned Off by Radio—But They Won't Be Silenced," *Country Weekly*, October 28, 1997, 18–25.

71. Rick Haydan, "Radio Revolution," *Country Weekly*, December 2, 1997, 23.

72. Andy McLenon, review of Merle Haggard's performance at Ryman Auditorium in Nashville, *No Depression*, fall 1995, 3–4.

73. Grant Alden, "Absolute Truckin' Twang," review of *Rig Rock Deluxe: A Musical Salute to the American Truck Driver*, *No Depression*, September–October 1996, 78.

74. David Cantwell, "Homespun of the Brave: The Courage of Iris DeMent's Convictions Goes to the Heart of Her Country," *No Depression*, November–December 1996, 45.

75. Johnny Bush and Don Walser, "Horse Opera," (interview with Don McLeese), *No Depression*, May–June 1998, 62.

76. Fenster, "Commercial (and/or?) Folk," 88; see also Roy Kasten, "Out in the West Texas Town of El Paso . . . ," *No Depression*, May–June 1997, 34.

77. It's not unusual to find criticisms of the Nashville establishment even in Nashville-oriented magazines including the *Journal of Country Music*, which is published in Nashville by the Country Music Foundation.

78. "No Depression" advertisement, *No Depression*, fall 1995, 11.

79. Grant Alden, "Dead Reckoning: How to Succeed in the Record Business (without Really Trying)," *No Depression*, fall 1995.

80. For an extended discussion of country's regionalism, see Bill Malone, *Singing Cowboys and Musical Mountaineers: Southern Culture and the Roots of Country Music* (Athens: University of Georgia Press, 1993), 6–42. It's worth noting here, however, that *No Depression* is not marked by the sort of indie-centric sectarianism that characterizes much of alternative rock culture. Because country, much like rap and R&B culture, sees no shame in making money on music if it can be done without too much compromise, *No Depression* covers major-label artists and records that fall under its aesthetic purview.

81. Jim Ridley, "No Depression, Any Country?" *Journal of Country Music,* 18, no. 2 (n.d.): 40.

82. Ibid., 41.

83. See also Daniel Cooper, "The Enigmatic Cowboy," *Journal of Country Music* 18, no. 1 (n.d.): 15–26.

84. For a more extended discussion, see Leppert and Lipsitz, "Age, the Body, and Experience."

85. Ridley, "No Depression," 41.

86. It is my impression, judging by the concert reviews in *No Depression,* that most alternative country bands play in venues normally found on the indie rock circuit (such as Chapel Hill's Cats Cradle; Columbia's Blue Note; and Athens's 40 Watt). For an interesting study in contrasts, see Ted Olson, "Steve Young: A Conversation with Country Music's Original Outlaw," *Journal of Country Music* 17, no. 2 (n.d.): 29–40 (esp. 34–35).

87. *No Depression* advertisement.

88. See Richard Peterson, "The Dialectic of Hard-Core and Soft-Shell Country Music," *South Atlantic Quarterly* 94 (1995): 273–300, and *Creating Country Music,* 150–55; see also Richard Peterson and Roger Kern, "Hard-Core and Soft-Shell Country Fans," *Journal of Country Music* 17, no. 3 (n.d.): 3–6.

89. Malone, *Country Music, U.S.A.,* 56–57.

90. Chris Vautour and Naomi Shapiro, "Neko Case: Canadian Virginian," *No Depression* November–December 1997: 27.

91. Blackstock, "Steve Earle," 34.

92. Vautour and Shapiro, "Neko Case," 27.

93. It would seem, from looking at *No Depression,* that a plurality of alternative country bands feature women members, and many of the Nashville-oriented artists that the magazine covers (like Lucinda Williams, Emmylou Harris, Nanci Griffith, and Roseanne Cash) are women. This reflects, in part, the strength of feminist politics in postpunk culture in general.

Cause I'm just a girl, little ol' me
Don't let me out of your sight
I'm just a girl, all pretty and petite
So don't let me have any rights.
Oh, I've had it up to here!
—No Doubt, "Just a Girl"

Gwen is someone that girls
can look up to and feel like they
know. She is very Everygirl.
—Tony Kanal, No Doubt bassist[1]

GAYLE WALD ✳ JUST A GIRL? ROCK MUSIC, FEMINISM, AND THE CULTURAL CONSTRUCTION OF FEMALE YOUTH

It would have been difficult to tune in to a U.S. Top 40 radio station for very long during summer and fall 1996 without hearing at least one iteration of "Just a Girl," the catchy breakthrough single that propelled the neo-ska band No Doubt to a position as one of the year's top-selling rock acts. "Just a Girl" not only earned No Doubt commercial visibility, it also established twenty-seven-year-old Gwen Stefani, the band's charismatic lead singer, as the latest in a series of female rock musicians to have attracted widespread commercial visibility as well as a loyal following of young female fans. Sporting a bared midriff, retro platinum hair, and a conspicuously made-up face (which often includes an Indian *bindi* ornamenting her forehead), Stefani quickly established a reputation as a skillful and dynamic live performer who put on energetic, no-holds-barred shows. Stefani's performance of "Just a Girl" at a 1996 Seattle concert—one variation of an act she was still performing in summer 1997—provides a memorable illustration. At first prostrating herself on the stage and repeating the phrase "I'm just a girl" in an infantile, whimpering voice, she then abruptly shifts gears, jumping up, railing "Fuck you, I'm a girl!" at the delighted audience (at least half of whom were young women), and exuberantly launching into the remainder of the song.[2]

Stefani's dramatic staging of disparate modes of femininity exemplifies her adept manipulation of rock spectacle in the tradition of female rockers such as Siouxsie Sioux, Grace Jones, Poly Styrene (of X-Ray Spex), Annie Lennox, Courtney Love, and Madonna. More significantly, her performance of "Just a Girl" exemplifies a trend that since the early 1990s has gained increasing prominence within rock music cultures: female musicians' strategic performance of "girlhood" and their deliberate cultivation of various "girlish" identities in their music, style, and stage acts. The performance of girlhood by contemporary female rockers encompasses a wide range of musical and artistic practices by women within, outside of, and on the margins of the corporate mainstream: from singer-songwriter Lisa Loeb's championing of female nerdiness and cultivation of childlike vocals; to the independent Canadian band Cub's repertoire of songs about childhood, played in an offbeat, deliberately lo-fi manner; to Courtney Love's infamous "kinderwhore" costume of a torn and ill-fitting baby-doll dress and smudged red lipstick; to the phenomenal and global popularity of the Spice Girls, the seemingly omnipresent all-female Britpop studio group that updates the manufactured glitziness of the "girl groups" of the 1960s while promoting a playful, if equivocally feminist, notion of "girl power."[3] Such calculated and, in Love's case, deliberately sexually provocative performances of girlish femininity draw on the mid-1980s precedents set by Madonna (especially around the time of her work in Susan Seidelman's 1985 film *Desperately Seeking Susan*) and Cindy Lauper, whose 1984 hit "Girls Just Want to Have Fun" is revised and updated in No Doubt's "Just a Girl." These earlier pop-rock icons—significantly, the first women in rock to attract the kind of devoted following of young female fans usually associated with male rock stars[4]—set the stage for performers like Stefani, who has attracted her own following of fourteen-year-old "Gwennabes" who clamor backstage at No Doubt shows hoping to get a glimpse of their idol. Following in the footsteps of their progenitors Lauper and Madonna, performers such as Stefani and Alanis Morissette have discovered in acting "like a girl" new ways of promoting the cultural visibility of women within rock music. At the same time, the music industry has discovered in these female stars (each with her own carefully cultivated star persona) new ways to sell its products to young female consumers (i.e., "real" girls).

This essay examines contemporary female rock musicians' representations of girls, girlhood, and "girl culture"—popular cultural practices that have a corollary in the emergence of what I call "girl studies"—a subgenre of recent academic feminist scholarship that constructs girlhood as a separate, exceptional, and/or pivotal phase in female identity formation.[5] As evidenced by "Just a Girl," the song that, not incidentally, propelled Gwen Stefani to her position as female rock icon, the performance of girlhood, although by no means a homogeneous or universal enterprise, can now be said to constitute a new cultural dominant within the musical practice of women in rock. This is particularly the case among white women "alternative" rockers, who draw on practices pioneered in the early 1990s in independent music. In this realm, female artists have ventured to celebrate girlhood as a means of fostering female youth subculture and of constructing narratives that subvert patriarchal discourse within traditionally male rock subcultures.[6] The "girlishness" so conspicuously on display among these contemporary women rockers demands attention, not only because it signals the emergence of new, "alternative" female rock subjectivities (revising earlier genre-specific models such as the rock chick, the singer-songwriter, or the diva), but because in so doing, it conveys various assumptions about (white) women's visibility within popular youth/music culture, signposting the incorporation—indeed, the commercial preeminence—of ironic, postmodern modes of gender performance. My interest in this essay is neither to celebrate nor to denigrate the girl as a new modality of female rock performance, but rather to argue that the emergence of the "girl" signals an important moment of contradiction within contemporary youth/music cultures. In the example offered by Stefani, the strategy of appropriating girlhood, like the word "girl" itself, signifies ambiguously: as a mode of culturally voiced resistance to patriarchal femininity; as a token of a sort of "gestural feminism" that is complicit with the trivialization, marginalization, and eroticization of women within rock music cultures; and as an expression of postmodern "gender trouble" that potentially recuperates girlhood in universalizing, ethnocentric terms. For one, even as the song's lyrics redefine girl in a rhetorical or sarcastic manner, Stefani's girlishly feminine persona—and her very commercial popularity, tied as it is to her performance of gender—potentially furthers the notion that within patriarchal society women acquire attention, approval, and authority to the degree that they are willing to act like children. Moreover, just as "Just a Girl" plays cleverly with the codes of good girl/bad girl femininity, so Stefani's performance is carefully calibrated to display elements of "transgressive" femininity (without abandoning the principle that a female rock musician's "pretty face" is the ultimate source of her commercial popularity and, therefore, cultural authority). Indeed, Stefani's performance evinces the possibility that the recuperation of girlhood may not, in and of itself, be incompatible with the relentless eroticization of women's bodies within corporate rock (a contradiction embodied in Stefani's look as a kind of punk Marilyn Monroe); in other words, that female rockers can play at being girls, and even mock the conventions of patriarchal girlhood, while remaining sexy and/or retaining "the charm of passivity."[7] The point here is not merely that "girlish innocence" sells records, but that Stefani's sarcastic discourse of helpless, innocent girlhood simultaneously functions as a strategy of feminism and a strategy of commerce (where feminism and commerce exist in a complex and shifting, rather than a simple and binary, relation to one another). Staged within the very corporate institutions that are agents of dominant discourses that divest women of cultural power, Stefani's performance of infantile, girlish femininity may be symbolically, if not actually, redundant.

As the foregoing analysis of "Just a Girl" is meant to suggest, seemingly transgressive gender play within contemporary rock music cultures often "fronts" for far less transgressive codings and recodings of racialized and nationalized identities. At its worst, such recuperation of girlhood has been staged in terms that equate girlness with whiteness.[8] For Stefani, in particular, playing with the signifiers of girlhood is tacitly a strategy of bolstering white racial authority—indeed, of bracing precisely that cultural power that authorizes her to engage in the parodic mimicry of gender norms without social penalty. In such a way, "Just a Girl" accentuates Stefani's gender transgression—her position as a girl lead singer—while minimizing the visibility of another, more salient aspect of her performance—her negotiation of ska, Jamaica's first urban pop style and No Doubt's primary musical influence (by way of English "rude boys" and 2-toners). Indeed, Stefani's pogo-inspired dance style and her display of raw, raucous energy are themselves hallmarks of ska performance reframed within the context of outrageous, uninhibited, and confident white female alternative rock performance. In this scenario, Stefani's self-conscious "innocence," "helplessness," and "charm" are not only crucial to her critical disarticulation of girlhood from its meaning within patriarchal discourse; they also enable her to naturalize national, and racial, identity. In focusing attention on

gender performance as a privileged site and source of political oppositionality, in other words, critical questions of national, cultural, and racial
appropriation can be made to disappear under the sign of transgressive
gender performance.

This instance of how a contemporary female rock icon's appropriation of
girlhood can mask other, related kinds of appropriation recalls Madonna's
appropriation of styles associated with black gay drag performance in her hit
song and video "Vogue," a song calculated to display Madonna's own transgressive gender/sexual identity. More recently, the emergence of the "girl"
as a newly privileged mode of white femininity within alternative rock coin-
cides with the appearance of the white male "loser" (e.g., Beck, Billy Corgan
of Smashing Pumpkins, and Kurt Cobain of Nirvana), whose performances
of abject or disempowered masculinity work to recuperate white racial authority even as they circulate within an ostensibly self-critical performative
economy of "whiteness."[9] Such observations necessitate a rethinking of
what Coco Fusco calls "the postmodernist celebration of appropriation";[10] at
the very least, that is, an acknowledgment of the need to draw critical distinctions between the feminist refusal of patriarchal discourse and performances that circulate the signs of refusal while actually expressing com-
plicitly with patriarchal discourse. As Fusco writes, it is imperative that we
"cease fetishizing the gesture of crossing as inherently transgressive, so that
we can develop a language that accounts for who is crossing, and that can
analyze the significance of each act."[11]

Fusco's insight is crucial for specifying and localizing the political efficacy
of what Ernesto Laclau terms "disarticulation-rearticulation," or the process
of symbolic struggle through which social groups reformulate dominant
codes as a means of negotiating political-cultural agency.[12] Such a practice of
critical reappropriation is frequently invoked in discussions of how various
subaltern populations discover a means of actively confronting and resisting
marginalization in the ironic repossession of signs otherwise meant to enforce marginality. Feminist-marxist critic Laura Kipnis, following Laclau,
explains this process as one in which "raw materials can be appropriated
and transformed by oppositional forces in order to express antagonisms and
resistance to dominant discourses."[13] And yet it is clear in the case of Stefani's sarcastic send-up of "girl," a word that in the context of rock music
cultures often signifies not female youthfulness, but female disempowerment, (i.e., patriarchal condescension toward and trivialization of women),

that such disarticulation-rearticulation does little to uncouple hegemonic girlhood from something more akin to the brasher and insubordinate "Fuck you, I'm a girl!"

Fusco's argument additionally insists on an interrogation of the links between the cultural practices of contemporary female rockers and various racially and culturally specific assumptions about girlhood. Acquiring its meaning, like the signifier woman, within the context of specific discursive regimes, girlhood is not a universal component of female experience; rather, the term implies very specific practices and discourses about female sexuality, women's cultural-political agency, and women's social location. Likewise, the various contemporary narratives of girlhood produced and disseminated within U.S. rock music cultures are formed within the terms of very particular struggles for social and cultural agency. Moreover, and as revealed by the contrast between the actual maturity and/or musical expertise of the performers in question and the youthfulness of their primary audiences, these struggles to specify and potentially even radicalize girlhood are inseparable from late capitalism's desire for new, youthful markets.

What, then, is the relation between feminism and strategies of representing girlhood within U.S. rock music cultures? Especially in the last decade of the twentieth century, notable for the advent of an artistically self-assured and cannily enterprising generation of highly visible women rock artists, can the strategic "reversion" to girlhood work as a strategy for feminism, or for producing feminist girls? Given the contradictions embodied in Stefani's "Just a Girl," to what degree is the appropriation of girlhood, as a strategy particularly associated with white women's rock performance, also a strategy of performing race—of racializing girlhood itself? How might female rock performers who occupy a different relation to hegemonic girlhood construct different narratives of girlhood?

In the following pages I investigate these questions in more detail and as they pertain to two specific groups of performers: first, the young women in independent rock known as Riot Grrrls, who in the early 1990s initiated their own ongoing "girl-style revolution," and, second, Shonen Knife and Cibo Matto, two Japanese all-female bands that have attracted small but significant U.S. followings, particularly among indie rock aficionados.[14] In so doing, I rely primarily on a critical analysis of the acts, images, music, and lyrics that these women produce, as well as on the public, mediated narratives that circulate (in the print media, on the Internet, in fanzines, on MTV, or in hearsay) around the music and the performers. As my opening story about Gwen Stefani suggests, the contradictions that characterize the use of the girl as a mode of cultural resistance within female rock performance are not necessarily experienced as such by the consumers of this music, who may be more or less receptive, depending on the context and the particularities of their own social locations, to the limitations (political, ideological, and even aesthetic) that such contradiction imposes on a straightforwardly celebratory narrative of such performance. From the standpoint of a certain girl consumer forbidden from using the F-word at school or at home, for example, Stefani's profane mockery of/revelry in girlness may have an air of transgression, danger, or defiance (against parental and school authority, against gendered bourgeois standards and expectations) that is far less salient to another girl consumer (potentially of the same class, national, regional, and ethnic/racial background) more inclined to see Stefani's performance as *merely* playful, without the substance that would mark it as authentically transgressive. The instability of the strategic reappropriation of girlhood is mirrored and reproduced, in other words, in the very instability of the "meanings" that consumers construe from performers who play the "girl" or who attempt to signify "girlness" in an ironic or parodic fashion.

On the other hand, and as the following discussion is meant to illustrate, the ethnocentrism that characterizes certain appropriations of girlhood *is* played out at the level of production, where female musicians operate within very differently racialized spheres of girlhood. While the example of Riot Grrrl raises specific questions about the relation between ideology and independent modes of cultural production, as well as about the potential instrumentality of girlhood to a feminist critique of the corporate music industry, the case of Japanese women bands illustrates how women who are marginalized by dominant narratives of race and gender (understood as mutually constitutive discourses) negotiate their own parodic or complicit counternarratives. Insofar as media representations of Japanese women rockers recapitulate familiar stereotypes of Asian femininity, giving rise to images of Japanese female artists as *ideally* "girlish" and "innocent" (a portrayal that is not necessarily at odds with representations of "exotic" Asian female sexualities), these artists produce distinct narratives that deny girlhood the status of universality and that instead engage the cultural and racial specificity of hegemonic girlhood. These observations have relevance, moreover, to the ways that girlhood is recuperated—or not—within the varied musical and performance practices of African American women, including popular young female performers such as Da Brat, Lil' Kim, Foxy Brown, and Brandy (as well as, perhaps, an earlier incarnation of the group TLC), some of whom (e.g., Brandy) have worked to project an air of girlish "innocence" in their music, videos, lyrics, and performance, and others of whom (e.g., Foxy Brown) have aggressively marketed their "youthful" sexuality, sometimes by pretending to be younger than they really are.[15]

My argument about the ambiguous political effects of "acting like a girl"— either as a strategy for progressive, antiracist feminism or a means of fostering the careers and the creativity of young female popular musicians—is informed by my own fan/consumer practices, as well as by my status as a relatively young white female academic. The issues I discuss here are particularly germane to my own discovery, around 1992, of the loud, fast, and unapologetically "angry" music associated with the predominantly white middle-class women in and around the Riot Grrrl movement. This musical subculture not only provided me new aural and kinesthetic pleasures, but it also encouraged me to begin writing about contemporary music culture as part of my professional practice. It is therefore with an investment simultaneously political, professional, and personal that I approach the question of how girlhood has been appropriated and coded—not, that is, to trash some of the very music and musical practices that have afforded me pleasure, but to strike a cautious and critical tone about them. Although they often are constructed as mutually exclusive in cultural studies analysis, aesthetic pleasures are indissolubly linked to ethico-political critique and hence to the practices inspired and mediated through such critique. This essay is thus not an exercise in critiquing pleasure, but is rather a critique of the production of pleasure through gendered and racialized narratives that signify as "new," transgressive, or otherwise exemplary.

*

Six years before Gwen Stefani and No Doubt burst onto Top 40 radio and MTV, a small group of young women musicians active in and around the punk music scenes in Washington, D.C., and Olympia, Washington, produced a two-page manifesto calling for a feminist revolution within independent rock—what they touted under the slogan "Revolution Girl-Style Now." At the time, members of the bands Bratmobile and Bikini Kill, the independent women rockers at the forefront of this movement, coined the term Riot Grrrl as a means of signposting their snarling defiance of punk's long-standing (although hardly monolithic) traditions of misogyny and homophobia, as well as the racism and sexism within the corporate music industry.[16] Together with other women active in various punk scenes (such as the related, albeit separate, movement of lesbians in "homocore" music, including the all-female band Tribe 8), they have not only consistently advocated the creation of all-female or predominantly female bands, but they have also emphasized women's ownership of record labels and their control over cultural representation. This last goal has been fostered by myriad Riot Grrrl-affiliated or girl-positive fanzines (such as *Girl Germs* and *Riot Grrrl*), inexpensively produced publications that circulate through feminist bookstores, independent music retailers, networks of friends, and word-of-mouth subscriptions and that explicitly envision women's fan activity as a legitimate and authentic form of cultural production.

For the young, predominantly middle-class white women who have participated in Riot Grrrl subculture, reveling in "girliness" constitutes an aesthetic and political response to dominant representations of female sexuality produced by the corporate music industry, as well as a strategy of realizing women's agency as cultural producers within independent rock. By highlighting girl themes in their music, lyrics, dress, iconography, 'zines, and the like, performers such as Cub, Tiger Trap, Heavens to Betsy, and Bikini Kill have attempted to produce a representational space for female rock performers that is, in effect, off-limits to patriarchal authority, in a manner akin to the way that girls' clubs are off-limits to boys. Such an emphasis on girliness has enabled these women performers to preempt the sexually objectifying gaze of corporate rock culture, which tends to market women's sexual desirability at the expense of promoting their music or their legitimacy as artists. Riot Grrrls's emphasis on forms of girl solidarity has important practical implications as well. For example, Riot Grrrl advocacy of all-women or predominantly women bands originates not in a belief in the aesthetic superiority or in the "authentic" oppositionality of such groups, but in the practical recognition that rock ideology (e.g., the equation of rock guitar-playing with phallic mastery) has dissuaded many young women from learning to play "male" instruments. Similarly, although it was widely derided by male punk rock aficionados as "separatist," the Riot Grrrl practice of reserving the mosh pit (the area directly in front of the stage) for girls stemmed from a desire to rethink the social organization of space within rock clubs and other music venues.

A look at one aspect of Riot Grrrl artistic practice—the carefully designed sleeves of seven-inch records—reveals that for these women in indie rock, resistance to patriarchal discourse takes the form of a rearticulation of girlhood that emphasizes play, fun, innocence, and girl solidarity. The silkscreened sleeve of a 1993 Bratmobile/Tiger Trap split seven-inch (i.e., a seven-inch record that includes one track from one band on each side) on the San Francisco-based label Four-Letter Words features a rudimentarily drawn image of a smiling girl doing a handstand (taken from Kotex tampon advertisements circa 1968), while a Bratmobile/Heavens to Betsy seven-inch released at about the same time features a photograph of the bared midriffs of two young women wearing hip-hugger jeans and tank tops, each sporting the name of a band on her stomach. Many of the images on Riot Grrrl fanzines and record sleeves use childhood photographs of band members to similar effect, as on the sleeve of the "Babies and Bunnies" seven-inch record by the Frumpies, a Riot Grrrl group combining members of Bikini Kill and Bratmobile recording on the Olympia, Washington-based Kill Rock Stars label. The cover of a 1993 Cub seven-inch titled "Hot Dog Day" (Mint Records) intimates themes of girl solidarity and budding queer sexuality by picturing a silver necklace dangling a charm that depicts two smiling girl figures holding hands.

The relentless cuteness of these representations, which might be merely sentimentalizing or idealizing under other circumstances, signifies ironically within the context of punk youth music subcultures, where "youth" is more likely to be associated with aggression, violence, and crisis, and where youth and youthfulness are frequently conflated with boyhood. Similarly, while nostalgia for an imagined past might be merely reactionary in another context (e.g., in debates over multiculturalism and in the much-touted claim that Americans have forsaken a previous commitment to civic virtue), in the context of Riot Grrrl performance these images of playful and happy girlhood are attempts at self-consciously idealizing representation. Such a recuperative iconography of girlhood contrasts—markedly, in some cases—with the music itself, which regularly explores themes of incest, the violence of heteronormative beauty culture, and the patriarchal infantilization and sexualization of girls: in short, themes that conjure not a *lost* innocence, a fall from childhood grace, but an innocence that was not owned or enjoyed, a grace that was denied.[17] The performance of nostalgia complicates and extends the Riot Grrrl performance of righteous outrage at patriarchal abuse; in other words, invoking a yearned-for innocence and lighthearted-ness that retroactively rewrite the script of childhood.

Yet such idealized representations of girlhood, while undeniably plea-surable and therapeutic, are of uncertain practical or strategic value as a feminist realpolitik, particularly outside the context of popular youth / music culture. At the very least, the nostalgia that characterizes many of these representations lends itself to the production of problematically dystopian, or postlapsarian, narratives of adult female sexualities. Indeed, one of the paradoxes of this nostalgic appropriation of (imagined) girlhood is that it primarily responds to the music industry's infantilizing representation of *adult* female sexuality, as well as to rock music's particular legacy of imagin-ing women's contributions in sexual terms (e.g., women as groupies, sexual sideshows, rock chicks, or boy toys).[18] It is telling, for example, that media coverage of Riot Grrrl—which reached its peak virtually simultaneously with the music, around 1992 or 1993—focused primarily on the display of anger, "fallenness," or aggressivity rather than cuteness, innocence, or girlish pas-sivity, not only because the Riot Grrrl name itself emphasized girlhood "with an angry 'grrrowl,' " as the *New York Times* put it, but also because these were already familiar tropes from an earlier incarnation of punk music in the 1970s.[19] The strategic reversion to girlhood not only rests on an ability to imagine girlhood outside of patriarchal representation, it also presumes cultural entitlement to "womanly" subjectivity.

*

The self-conscious performance of nostalgia by Riot Grrrls underscores the culturally constructed nature of women's and girls' access to the public sphere. Such an observation, as I have already suggested, has important implications for the transportability, across socially determined lines of dif-ference, of the Riot Grrrl strategy of reappropriating girlhood to construct alternative (i.e., nonpatriarchal) modes of visibility for women in indepen-dent rock. In short, such a deliberate performance assumes a subject for whom girlishness precludes, or is in conflict with, cultural agency. But what of women whose modes of access to, and mobility within, the public sphere depend on their supposed embodiment of a girlish ideal?

The examples of the Osaka-based trio Shonen Knife and the New York-based duo Cibo Matto, Japanese female bands that have attracted small but significant followings among U.S. indie rock audiences, provide telling illustrations of the manner in which Asian women, whose visibility within U.S. culture is often predicated on their acquiescence to orientalist stereotypes, have had to negotiate the terrain of U.S. youth and music cultures differently than have their (primarily white) Riot Grrrl counterparts. In the United States, where Japanese rock musicians (whose music has become increasingly visible since the mid-1980s) are often regarded with a mixture of "sincere" musical interest and objectifying, ethnocentric curiosity, the recurring portrayal of Japanese women bands as interesting novelty acts, cartoonish amateurs, and/or embodiments of western patriarchal fantasies of "cute" Asian femininity presents particular challenges for understanding how evocations of girlhood overlap with discourses of race, gender, and nation in U.S. popular music culture. In contrast to Riot Grrrl bands, whose reappropriations of girlhood are part of a broader effort to harness rock's oppositional energy for feminist critique, Japanese women rockers have negotiated (i.e., resisted, appropriated, or otherwise engaged) a feminist cultural politics from within the context of Western patriarchal discourses that insist on positioning them as the exotic representatives of an idealized girlish femininity.

A look at the portrayal of Shonen Knife in the independent and corporate music media illustrates this point. Formed by two sisters, Naoko and Atsuko Yamano, and their friend and schoolmate Michie Nakatani, Shonen Knife was unknown in the United States until 1985, when the Olympia, Washington-based K Records (also known for promoting Riot Grrrl work) released *Burning Farm,* previously a Japanese recording, on cassette.[20] Two independent releases, *Pretty Little Baka Guy/Live in Japan* (Gasatanka/Rockville 1990) and *Shonen Knife* (Gasatanka/Giant 1990) followed, but it wasn't until the band's 1992 major-label debut, *Let's Knife* (Virgin), featuring the remakes of earlier songs, some recorded for the first time in English, that Shonen Knife won significant airplay on college radio and a coveted opportunity to accompany Nirvana on tour. The immediate, enthusiastic embrace of Shonen Knife in the mid-1980s by indie rock luminaries such as Kim Gordon and Thurston Moore of Sonic Youth is often explained in terms of the band's kitschy punk/pop sound and its trademark parodic "twisting" of icons of American and Japanese commodity culture. Named for a brand of pocket knives (perhaps as a way of encapsulating a succinct critique of patriarchal masculinity?), Shonen Knife readily appealed to U.S. indie rockers, who admired the band's pomo way of blurring the boundaries between advertising jingles and "serious" punk/pop (a practice evident in songs such as "Tortoise Brand Pot Cleaner's Theme").

Despite such affinities, the women in Shonen Knife have repeatedly been portrayed in exoticizing and infantilizing terms, as demonstrated by the liner notes to a late 1980s indie-rock tribute album of Shonen Knife covers, titled *Every Band Has a Shonen Knife Who Loves Them* (in ironic reference to an album of Yoko Ono covers, despite the fact that Shonen Knife had no apparent connection to the most famous of all Japanese women rock artists in the United States). Here, band members are described in frankly patronizing language: "They are happy people and love what they are doing. . . . They are humble, kind people who do not realize that they are the most important band of our time."[21] Variations on this basic theme abound in later representations, where the band is often cited for sporting "cute" accents—a "lite" version of the more overt and aggressive racism of an infamous *Esquire* magazine article about Ono titled "John Rennon's Excrusive Groupie."[22] "Mostly [Shonen Knife] sing in their native tongue," writes *Rolling Stone*, "but what needs no translation is how their awkward humility mixes with their irrepressible vivacity."[23] The band fares no better in *Melody Maker*, where they are described as the "orient's answer to the Shangri-la's," a phrase that tellingly conjures nostalgia for the manufactured sexual innocence of Phil Spector-managed 1960-era girl groups.[24] One music journalist, in a description that conflates infantilizing images of Asian women's sexuality with stereotypes of female musical incompetence, has asserted that the band's fans like Shonen Knife because "they're little, lots of fun and can't really play."[25] Most tellingly, perhaps, in publicity materials for their 1993 album *Rock Animals*, Virgin Records (which in 1996 released, with very little fanfare, an album of "rarities, curiosities and live tracks" titled *The Birds and the B-Sides*) explicitly distinguishes Shonen Knife's "simplicity," "charismatic innocence," and musical charm from the restive, confrontational femininity of their U.S. indie rock counterparts. These "Ronettes-meets-the-Ramones," gushes the press release, "are definitely not cut from the same battered cloth as their Riot Grrrl and flannel shirted colleagues."

Such a binary opposition pitting Shonen Knife, a charming and adorable Japanese novelty act with musical roots in the classic 1960s girl groups, against unfeminine, unkempt Riot Grrrls provides insight into the work performed by racialized representations of Asian femininity, as well as the specificity of the Riot Grrrl reappropriation of girlhood. For example, because she was widely perceived as having "stolen" John Lennon from his first wife, Cynthia Lennon, and perhaps because of her affiliation with the highly cerebral New York-based avant-garde and noise-rock scenes, Yoko Ono was subjected to a very different set of images: masculinized and desexualized, cast (along with her music) as impenetrable and inscrutable, intimidating and unpredictable, she was portrayed in a manner that recalls earlier, World War II-era stereotypes. By contrast, the major-label marketing of Japanese women bands such as Shonen Knife and Cibo Matto emphasizes girlishness as a way of establishing that these performers will be "fun"—that is, amusing, clever, and entertaining—for U.S. consumers.[26]

While Riot Grrrls have been able to reappropriate girlhood as a part of their political and musical practice, Japanese women bands have had to negotiate an unreconstructed, unironic version of the term "girl" that circulates within U.S. discourses of Asian femininity. As the above examples make plain, the media representations of Shonen Knife (and, more recently, of Cibo Matto) have tended to reinscribe their lack of cultural agency rather than explore their artistic practices as a potential source of such agency. In fact, however, both Shonen Knife and Cibo Matto have produced feminist work that counters dominant notions of a priori girlish Asian femininity, revealing how these notions are shot through with racialized sexism. For example, Shonen Knife's "Twist Barbie," an upbeat pop/rock song that is probably their best-known work among U.S. audiences, articulates an ambiguous relation to European ideals of femininity through the image of a Barbie doll: "Blue eyes, blond hair / Tight body, long legs / She's very smart / She can dance well. . . . O, sexy girl!" This initially humorous parody of Barbie as a miniature and synthetic "embodiment" of ideal European womanhood (a parody that imputes stereotypes of girlish femininity to U.S. white women) is punctuated, later in the song, by the phrase "I wanna be Twist Barbie"—words that potentially express a more ambiguous relation to Western beauty culture and that cleverly play off of the notion of the "wannabe," a means by which young women articulate their subjectivity through their consumption of popular culture. "Twist Barbie" is noteworthy, too, insofar as it expresses U.S.-Japanese trade relations through the figure of a doll marketed to girls. The trope of a toy is perhaps not incidental, since Shonen Knife themselves are imaginatively "toying" with Barbie as a twisted and impossible ideal of (Western) femininity—the word twist here referring both to a popular dance and to the band's own cultural practice, which twists the signs of Western commodity culture. "Twist Barbie" conjures a specific mode of girls' leisure within U.S. commodity culture (the activity of playing with Barbie dolls) to critique a culturally specific expression of patriarchal femininity. The song suggests that women can toy with ideals of femininity themselves as artificial (i.e., as unnatural or nonessential) as the Barbie doll.

This is not to say that a song such as "Twist Barbie" cannot also abet U.S. stereotypes of "cute" or "innocent" Asian femininity: indeed, the deadpan enthusiasm with which Shonen Knife plays and sings "Twist Barbie," on record and in live performance, suggests that they are less critical of a European, Barbie-type ideal than an analysis of their lyrics might imply. The balance of *Shonen Knife* (the 1990 U.S. release that features the first of several English-language versions of "Twist Barbie") is taken up with songs that, in English translation at least, seem to toe the line between parody and complicity. The album's cover art contributes photographs that support this reading of a fundamental ambivalence in Shonen Knife's self-representation: one features what looks like a snapshot of the band members taken when they were schoolgirls, and a second depicts the trio primping for the camera, wearing white dresses festooned with small multicolored bows. (The only element that distinguishes this second photograph is its backdrop: a graffiti-filled wall hints that the photograph may have been taken backstage at a show.)

*

The title and the cover art of *Viva! La Woman,* Cibo Matto's critically acclaimed 1996 debut album on the Warner Brothers label, illustrate how musicians Yuka Honda and Miho Hatori (who first met in Manhattan) frame their cultural-political agency quite differently. Musically, there is little that connects Shonen Knife's straightforward pop/rock with Cibo Matto's intricate sound, which relies heavily on sampling technologies to produce what one critic describes as "an enticing cross-cultural fusion that mixes bossa nova, hip hop, jazz, African drumming and disco . . . over which Hatori gleefully chants, screams, wails and raps in English, French and Japanese."[27] As their name (Italian for "crazy food") suggests, hybridity is a central theme of Cibo Matto's artistic practice: not only the hybridity that originates in the global circulation of popular youth/music culture, but the hybridity that marks Honda's and Hatori's own "hybrid" locations as Japanese-born New Yorkers whose music draws inspiration from white artists' interpretations of African American hip hop. The duo fosters an image of cosmopolitan sophistication that is distinct from Shonen Knife's (calculated?) image of playful, good girl simplicity. Such a notion is reinforced by the dada quality of the duo's lyrics and the cool, technologically hip image they project in live performance, during which Honda nonchalantly inserts floppy disks into a computer-synthesizer while Hatori sings.

A band photograph from *Viva! La Woman* depicts the musicians as denizens of a high-tech playground: dressed in sequins, Honda (posed on a bicycle) and Hatori appear surrounded by turntables, tape recorders, synthesizers, musical instruments, and, most conspicuously, skateboards, while various other figures (producers? engineers?) busy themselves in the background. As such an image implies, sampling and dubbing technologies, as well as synthesizers that filter and/or distort Hatori's "natural" vocals, afford Cibo Matto a variegated and intricate musical "voice." Cultural agency for these women performers is not staged primarily within the terms of the paradigm offered by U.S. Riot Grrrls, or even within the ambiguously complicit/parodic economy of signification modeled by Shonen Knife. Rather, they demonstrate how the appropriation of girlhood may at times conflict with women's cultural agency.

*

In their 1995 book *The Sex Revolts*, Simon Reynolds and Joy Press claim that U.S. alternative rock, increasingly focused on "gender tourism" as a source of its rebellion and therefore its identity formation, has witnessed a corresponding decline in the significance of race to its musical and cultural practice.[28] (Although I am appropriating Reynolds and Press's language here, I want to distance myself from their use of the phrase "rock rebellion," a term that is not only potentially condescending but also explicitly masculinist.) According to *The Sex Revolts*, the emergence of "alternative" music (actually a fully corporatized *style* that is, by and large, an object of derision for indie rockers) in the early 1980s is pivotal, marking the end of an era during which black sources served as the primary inspiration for white cultural innovation, and heralding a new era in which the performance of gender, not race, is paramount. If rock cultures were once conceived as, alternatively, a meeting place and a battleground between black and white identities—a cultural sphere where white and black youths violated social taboos against "race mixing" and where white youths fashioned dissident identities according to the models offered by black musicians and black musical culture—these cultures are nowadays more concerned, as Reynolds and Press argue, with the production of new gendered subjectivities that are less apparently marked by dominant discourses of race.

My own analysis of the representation of Shonen Knife and Cibo Matto belies this relatively simplistic thesis, which in turn belies the inevitable interarticulation of racism and sexism. Here, too, I want to register the disturbing resonance of the phrase "gender tourism" in Reynolds and Press's text with "sex tourism," and to note that while it implies the fluidity of gender identifications in rock performance, the term "gender tourism" in this context actually reinscribes the stability of gender in explicitly neo-colonialism terms, where (white) men are the explorers and (Japanese) women the colony to be explored. The analogy is not too farfetched, given the argument I have been developing about the cultural construction of girlhood and girl culture within rock music. Indeed, one of the points of my analysis of contemporary rock cultures has been to show that "girlhood," far from signifying a universal, biologically grounded condition of female experience, instead implies a relation to agency, visibility, and history that emerges within a particular discursive context. The different counternarratives of girlhood produced by a Riot Grrl band like Bikini Kill and a Japanese band like Shonen Knife occupy different antagonistic relations to hegemonic girlhood, whose meaning is itself unstable. The fact that these different narratives take root in very different cultural contexts suggests that we cannot assume the portability of contemporary white U.S. women rockers' critical discourse of girlhood and their advocacy of girl culture.

By way of concluding, then, I want to explore some implications of these themes outside of the specific context of rock music. An anecdote about my own relation to work on girl culture provides a starting point. This essay was inadvertently inspired by a presentation about Riot Grrrls that I gave as part of an academic job talk at New York University several years ago. At the end of my talk, one audience member asked me whether such work on female youth/music culture—and perhaps here he was also implicitly referencing my advocacy of Riot Grrrl as a noteworthy development within punk and postpunk musics—tacitly shifted the emphasis of, or even supplanted, women's studies (and the various critiques integral to its practical interventions within the academy) with something he provocatively termed "girl studies." My answer at the time was something like, "What's wrong with girl studies?"; a response that was calculated (inasmuch as I had time to calculate) to legitimize girls and their specific cultural formations (something integral to the Riot Grrrl project) as well as to authorize my own work on girls/grrrls. I admit, too, that as a candidate performing in front of various tenured faculty and curious graduate students, I felt at that moment like something of a girl. I argued then, as I would now, that research into the discourses of girlhood is crucial if we want to understand how contemporary female performers and their audiences have attempted to create avenues of feminist agency within traditionally masculinist popular forms.

I couldn't then anticipate how resonant this brief and admittedly superficial exchange about the status of "girl studies" would later seem in light of the emergence both of a popular psychological literature of girlhood (which depicts girlhood as a period of crisis in female subjectivity), and of a burgeoning academic subfield of the cultural studies of girls. My own reading of Shonen Knife's playful mimicry of a Barbie-esque ideal of femininity is in tacit dialogue with recent feminist studies that use Barbie as an important cultural text. In such work, Barbie bears the inscription of various overlapping and sometimes contradictory ideologies of race, gender, class, and nation.[29] The "new Barbie studies," particularly when undertaken from queer feminist perspectives, uses this most ubiquitous and notorious symbol of ideal femininity to explore and critique girls' appropriations of patriarchal commodity culture, suggesting that such appropriations may be important to their identity formation. This essay represents my own analogous reading of young women rock musicians' feminist appropriations of hegemonic girlhood, based on the related notion that youth music provides an important cultural venue for the articulation and rearticulation of youthful subjectivities.

And yet some of the limitations of this intellectual project, if not of the very notion that girlhood can be unproblematically reclaimed for feminism or for feminist cultural practices, are also implicit in this reading of the cultural construction of girlhood within rock music. It is noteworthy that "Just a Girl" peaked in popularity at about the same time that Madonna and Courtney Love, two of the female rock performers most associated with the cultural subversion of girlhood, chose to "grow up," at least in terms of their public performance of gender: Madonna through her very public staging of mother-hood and her role as Evita in the film version of the famous Andrew Lloyd Webber musical; Love through her starring role in the movie *The People vs. Larry Flynt* and her highly publicized beauty/fashion makeover. There is something predictably depressing, too, about the global popularity of the Spice Girls, who have appropriated the spunky defiance associated with English Riot Grrrls in a patently opportunistic fashion. Particularly within the context of the global struggle for women's rights, it is clear that girlhood cannot yet be spoken of as a universal right or property of women. Moreover, even work that eschews girlhood as the universalizing complement of very particular constructions of human biological development can end up essentializing girlhood as a necessary phase within the life cycle imagined by global capitalism. Rock music cultures, especially the cultures of independent rock, provide crucial sites within which young women can negotiate their own representations of girlhood in varying degrees of opposition to, or collaboration with, hegemonic narratives. As the foregoing analysis of various contemporary female rockers suggests, however, women—especially those who benefit from their privileged national, racial, or economic status—will need to stay alert to the necessity of interrogating, in an ongoing and self-critical fashion, the conditions that govern their access to social and cultural agency. If I am sounding a note of particular urgency, it is because I believe that youth music cultures continue to offer girls important sources of emotional sanctuary and acts as vital outlets for the expression of rage and pleasure, frustration and hope.

Coda

Looking back, 1997 appears to have ranked as *both* the Year of the Girl or the Year of the Woman—or at least this is the "split" conclusion readers of the two leading rock magazines, *Rolling Stone* and *Spin,* might have drawn after consulting each magazine's November special issue devoted to coverage of female rock musicians. Set to coincide with the thirtieth anniversary of the magazine's founding, the *Rolling Stone* special issue features a memorable cover photograph of Courtney Love, Tina Turner, and Madonna collectively hamming it up for the camera, behind a headline that announces "Women of Rock." Unusually heavy with advertisements, even by *Rolling Stone* standards, the issue features a thirty-thousand-word "anecdotal history of women and rock" by veteran rock critic Gerri Hershey, as well as brief interviews (all conducted by female journalists) with twenty-eight women musicians, from Ruth Brown and Yoko Ono to Joan Jett, Me'Shell Ndegeocello, Liz Phair, and Ani DiFranco. Although it was the commercial power of contemporary women musicians such as Mariah Carey, Jewel, and Fiona Apple that apparently first inspired *Rolling Stone*'s editorial board to devote its thirtieth anniversary issue to women of/and rock, the issue highlights many of the current generation's forebears (Hershey's long piece, for example, begins by tracing the influence of female blues singers such as Ma Rainey on rock's first acknowledged female superstar, Janis Joplin). Consistent with *Rolling Stone*'s credo of rock music as "legitimate news and history" (as founding editor Jann Wenner puts it), "Women of Rock" has the feel and heft of a women's literature anthology or a "greatest hits" boxed set: there, together with the "backstage history" of the music, are careful profiles of the genre's canonical figures.

If *Rolling Stone*'s "Women of Rock" issue is shaped by self-consciousness about its status as the "granddaddy" of contemporary popular music magazines, *Spin*'s "The Girl Issue" seems to reflect its own industry position as a youthful upstart seeking to upstage its established, if graying, competitor. "The Girl Issue" not only eschews encyclopedic leanings of "Women of Rock," but its coverage weighs it heavily in favor of the new, the young, . . . and the "girl." If *Rolling Stone*'s cover suggests three "generations" of women rock musicians, *Spin*'s cover contrastingly features a close-up of the slightly pouty face of twenty-year-old singer-songwriter Fiona Apple, who only two months earlier had received MTV's award for best new artist. Inside the magazine there are articles about "girl power," women fashion designers, and women's/wymyn's music festivals, as well as a compendium of icons to "girl culture" that heavily favors a "riot grrrl" sensibility.

As I've tried to allude to in these brief descriptions, *Rolling Stone*'s and *Spin*'s disparate presentations of women/girls in/and/of rock depends, in large part, on the relative positioning of the magazines within the corporate music press and with respect to the different market demographics that each targets.[30] Yet it nevertheless may be possible to draw tentative conclusions based on each magazine's representation of female performers within the context of rock's history as well as its "futures." While "Women of Rock" highlights the "coming of age" of female rock performers, as well as of rock music itself (as underscored by its choice of cover models: a postmakeover

Love, a postpregnancy Madonna, and Turner, a woman notable for having been dubbed rock's "godmother"), "The Girl Issue" is most notable for its "postmodern" refusal to historicize ("girls," as the cover copy implies, are known by first names only: "Alanis, Ani, Gwen, Xena, Chloe, Chelsea, Daria . . ."). Whereas "Women of Rock" emphasizes the contributions of African American women, including blues singers, R&B artists, disco divas, and contemporary rappers, "The Girl Issue" is noticeably silent on the subject of girls who are not also white, with the exception of athletes in the WNBA.

In the coincidence of "Women of Rock" and "The Girl Issue" one might infer a certain gendered generational struggle within rock music journalism, in which *Spin*, in order to differentiate itself from an aging, patriarchal forebear, deploys the "girl" not only to win over a young female readership, but to signify its rejection of the very musical and cultural values that seemingly render it necessary, even at this late date, once again to showcase the "contributions" of female musicians to rock music cultures. While the celebration of the "girl" in such an instance might signify a rejection of a certain patriarchal discourse that trivializes women's participation within rock music even as it extols it, there is also the danger—as evidenced by *Spin*'s own contents—that such a critique recuperates gender in terms that quite literally invisiblize the very issues of race and ethnicity which, as *Rolling Stone* demonstrates, are crucial to an understanding (or at the very least to an accurate recounting) of rock as a musical/cultural practice. There is little doubt that the cultural apparatus of rock music (here including both the recording industry and professional rock journalism) has proven notoriously unfriendly, even hostile, to women performers. On the other hand, and as the *Spin* special issue suggests, playing "the girl" may not always be as "innocent" as it sometimes looks.

Notes

A version of this essay previously appeared under the title "Just a Girl? Rock Music, Feminism, and the Cultural Construction of Female Youth" in *Signs: Journal of Women in Culture and Society* 23, no. 3 (spring 1998): 585–610.
1. Kanal refers here to No Doubt's lead singer Gwen Stefani (quoted in Alona Wartofsky, "Girl without a Doubt," *Washington Post*, June 15, 1997, G1.)
2. This description is based on an account by Jonathan Bernstein ("Get Happy," *Spin*,

November 1996, 52). In a performance in Worcester, Massachusetts, Stefani got the boys in the audience to sing, "I'm Just a Girl" and then instructed the girls to chant, "Fuck you! I'm a girl!" (Wartofsky, "Girl without a Doubt," G1.)

3. Barry Walters, "Alreadybe," *Village Voice* 42, no. 7 (1997): 69. I can add little to what already has been said and written about the Spice Girls's decidedly cynical appropriation and recirculation of "girl power" (the "girls" here including the late Princess of Wales and even Margaret Thatcher) as a record industry commodity. As a friend of mine succinctly and appropriately put it, "the Spice Girls are a text that already has been written." Two aspects of the Spice Girls's success story remain interesting, however: first, the fact that the Spice Girls phenomenon, from the start, has been accompanied by the anti-Spice Girls backlash (interested browsers of the Web, for example, can find sites with titles such as "Spice Girls Suck Club" and "Spice Shack of Blasphemy"); and, second, that for all that the Spice Girls represent an obviously "cosmetic" feminism evacuated of commitment to combating patriarchy, the anti-Spice Girls movement seems to have given license to people to use the group's commercial success to voice antifeminist, even misogynist, sentiments. Many of the anti-Spice Girls Web sites exemplify this tendency to conflate disdain for the group's musical production (i.e., disdain for musical commodities) with disdain for women, generally speaking. This latter aspect of the anti-Spice Girls backlash seems particularly insidious given the tendency to elide female subjectivity not only with consumption, but with the commodity form itself.

4. Lisa Lewis, *Gender Politics and MTV* (Philadelphia: Temple University Press, 1990), 10.

5. "Girl studies" emerges not only from fields such as psychology, with its longstanding interest in human social and psychic development, but also from newer fields such as cultural studies, which has its own traditions (by way of Birmingham and the Centre for Contemporary Cultural Studies) of analyzing "youth" and the politics of youth subcultures (particularly working-class, predominantly male youth subcultures). The popularity and visibility of the "girl" within popular youth/music cultures, combined with renewed interest in forms of violence/trauma that primarily affect girls (e.g., incest, eating disorders, self-mutilation or "cutting") may have had the effect of spurring academic interest in studying the specific cultural formations and cultural practices of girls. At the time when I began thinking about this essay, for example, a number of other calls for papers and/or book chapters on this topic were circulating. This essay might be said to constitute my own ambivalent and critical venture into girl studies, a subject I return to later.

6. "Alternative" rock is often defined in terms of an aesthetic that disavows, or evinces critical mistrust of, earlier rock subjectivities as well as the music industry itself (see Eric Weisbard and Craig Marks, eds. *Spin: Alternative Record Guide* (NY: Vintage

Books, 1995, vii). And yet "alternative" is also, for my purposes, a corporate demographic and a new set of industry practices spurred by the discovery that independent labels could effectively serve as major-label A&R departments, according to the logic of outsourcing.

7. Simone de Beauvoir, *The Second Sex,* trans. H. M. Parshley (New York: Vintage, 1989), 337.

8. The conclusions of this paper were brought home by the commercially successful Lilith Fair concert tour in 1998, which, although touted by organizer Sarah McLachlan as a "celebration of women in music," in fact primarily functioned as a celebration of white female singer-songwriters, despite the participation of performers such as Missy Elliot and Erykah Badu. The corporate and independent press made much of the Lilith Fair's demonstration that a music festival organized around "women's voices" could draw ticket sales and support a roster of appearances at medium-sized arenas throughout the United States, although very few writers ever noticed that this "Galapalooza," as *Time* put it, was also a universalizing recuperation of white women's music/performance as *women's* music/performance.

9. Of late there has been a great deal written about the "loser." For two good accounts, see Fred Pfeil, *White Guys: Studies in Postmodern Domination and Difference* (New York: Verso, 1995); and Cyndi Fuchs, "Losers: Postpunks and Resistance Effects," paper presented at the annual meeting of the Modern Language Association, Washington, D.C., 1996.

10. Coco Fusco, *English is Broken Here: Notes on Cultural Fusion in the Americas* (New York: New Press, 1995), 70.

11. Fusco, 76. There is, of course, an impressive body of scholarship that probes the notion of "appropriation" specifically within the context of U.S. popular music cultures. See, in addition to Fusco, LeRoi Jones, *Blues People: Negro Music in White America* (New York: Quill/William Morrow, 1963); Nelson George, *The Death of Rhythm and Blues* (New York: Pantheon, 1988); Michael Rogin, "Blackface, White Noise: The Jewish Jazz Singer Finds His Voice," *Critical Inquiry* 18 (1992): 417–53; and George Lipsitz, *Dangerous Crossroads* (New York: Verso, 1994). For more recent discussions in the context of specific genres/performers, see Jeffrey Melnick, " 'Story Untold': The Black Men and White Sounds of Doo-Wop" in *Whiteness: A Critical Reader,* ed. Mike Hill (New York: New York University Press 1997). As I argue in "One of the Boys? Whiteness, Gender, and Popular Music Studies" (in *Whiteness: A Critical Reader,* ed. Hill), to date most of the work on appropriation within popular music cultures focuses on relations between men, a fact that calls for a gendered critique of the notion of appropriation itself.

12. Ernesto Laclau, "Metaphor and Social Antagonisms," in *Marxism and the Interpretation of Culture,* ed. Cary Nelson and Lawrence Grossberg (Urbana: University of

Illinois Press, 1998); and Laura Kipnis, *Ecstasy Unlimited* (Minneapolis: University of Minnesota Press, 1993), 17.

13. Kipnis, *Ecstasy*, 16.

14. "Independent rock" (or "indie rock") is a common term that refers not to a musical aesthetic but to the means of production of the music under discussion. Independent rock is music that is produced and marketed through independent institutions; that is, institutions (record labels, distributors, concert venues) that are independent from the megacorporations that dominate the global rock music industry. Recent years have seen many "indie/major" mergers reflecting a variety of corporate arrangements; in most cases, formerly independent labels exchange some part of ownership of the label in exchange for the financing, promotion, and distribution resources of a major label.

15. These women's performances underscore the way that girlhood is both denied to, and reinterpreted within the context of, African American women, whose use of the term "girl" as a mode of address suggests a vernacular tradition of such reinterpretation/reappropriation as well.

16. For an account of the emergence of Riot Grrrl as a movement of young women within U.S. independent rock music, and for a more detailed description of the musical practices associated with Riot Grrrl, see Joanne Gottlieb and Gayle Wald, "Smells Like Teen Spirit: Riot Grrrls, Revolution, and Women in Independent Rock," in *Microphone Fiends*, ed. Andrew Ross and Tricia Rose (New York: Routledge, 1994).

17. For specific examples, see Gottlieb and Wald, "Smells Like Teen Spirit," 250–74.

18. Angela McRobbie, *Feminism and Youth Culture* (Boston: Unwin Hyman, 1991), 25.

19. See Ann Japenga, "Punk's Girl Groups Are Putting the Self Back in Self-Esteem," *New York Times*, November 15, 1992, 30.

20. According to indie rock lore, the band was first "discovered" by Calvin Johnson, a member of the lo-fi, punk minimalist band Beat Happening, cofounder of the Olympia, Washington-based K record label, and promoter of the idea of an "international pop underground."

21. Weisbard and Marks, Spin Alternative Record Guide 355).

22. Gillian Gaar, *She's a Rebel: The History of Women in Rock & Roll* (Seattle: Seal Press, 1992), 231.

23. Chuck Eddy, "Shonen Knife," *Rolling Stone* 586 (1990): 91.

24. Everett True, "Shonen Knife: Blade in Japan," *Melody Maker* 67, no. 49 (1992): 38–39.

25. Stud Brother, "Ninja Wobble," *Melody Maker* 68, no. 47 (1994): 6–7.

26. Such infantilizing images of Japanese women rockers are, of course, merely the benign complement to a more overtly and aggressively racist neocolonial portraiture of Asian femininity. The most flagrant example of this sort of representation comes from an "All-Japan" issue of the punk 'zine *Maximumrocknroll*—an issue ostensibly devoted to defining a shared political-cultural sensibility among U.S. and Japanese indie rockers. In this issue, a regular contributor muses about "nubile Nipponese lovelies" and "all these hot-looking Japanese girl bands" (Shonen Knife gets specific mention), while speculating that as a "species," "Oriental girls" (and here he includes Asian American women) have "Mongolian eyelids" that resemble vulvae, and that this explains "the source of their attractiveness" ("Making New Friends with Rev. Norb," *Maximumrocknroll*, 1994, n.p.

27. Kathy Silberger, "Eats Meets West: Cibo Matto's Cross-Cultural Cuisine-Art," *Option* 68 (1996): 61.

28. Simon Reynolds and Joy Press, *The Sex Revolts: Gender Rebellion and Rock'n'Roll* (Cambridge: Harvard University Press, 1995).

29. See, for example, Lucinda Ebersole and Richard Peabody, eds., *Mondo Barbie* (New York: St. Martin's Press, 1993); M. G. Lord, *Forever Barbie: The Unauthorized Biography of a Real Doll* (New York: Morrow, 1994); and Erica Rand, *Barbie's Queer Accessories* (Durham: Duke University Press, 1995).

30. Founded by Jann Wenner in 1967, *Rolling Stone* is generally credited with having pioneered as well as legitimated the genre of rock music journalism. *Spin* was founded in 1984 by Bob Guccione Jr., son of the founder of *Penthouse*, and was recently sold to the same group that owns *Vibe*, the pioneering journal of hip hop music and culture.

LISA PARKS ✳ SATELLITE RHYTHMS: CHANNEL V, ASIAN MUSIC VIDEOS, AND TRANSNATIONAL GENDER

In the mid-1990s a promotion for a show called *Very China* ran repeatedly on Star TV's Channel V. The fifteen-second promo intercut postcard flashes of urban Chinese life with performances by traditional acrobats, jugglers, and dancers set to a soundtrack of rumbling rock, techno, and Chinese folk music. Played out on the semiotically rich landscape of Tiananmen Square, the segment brought together Chinese nationalism with a vibrant youth music culture. It closed with a striking image of a young female acrobat standing on her hands and spreading her legs to form the letter "V." When the word "Channel" is superimposed above her toes, her inverted body not only became part of the satellite channel's logo, but also signaled global satellite media's refiguring of normative national conceptions of femininity more generally. The acrobat's open legs further alluded to Western media conglomerates' penetration of China at the same time that they marked the feminine as an increasingly significant site of national cultural struggle.

During the 1990s, satellite television services expanded dramatically throughout the Asia/Pacific region. Star TV, the first pan-Asian satellite television network, was introduced in 1991, providing millions of viewers access to five channels of American, English, and Chinese programming.

Although Star TV's channels emanate from Hong Kong—the former British colony that has become China's economic and cultural gateway to the West—both their content and audiences have becoming increasingly global in scope. In order to appeal to the disparate tastes of viewers situated across different national and local cultures, Star TV satellite services must offer a global product that incorporates local and national cultural distinctions. Motivated by the economic imperatives of Rupert Murdoch's media empire, the marketing strategy known as "glocalization" has not only made a bundle for Murdoch, but also—and most significantly for my purposes here—has made Star TV programs a burgeoning site for the elaboration of contradictory national identities.

It was precisely this strategy of glocalization that in 1993 led Star TV to replace MTV Asia—Star's initial music video feed—with the more Asian-focused Channel V. Channel V now relays an eclectic mix of Hindi and Cantonese (Canto)pop music video packages as well as Western rock, hip hop, and techno into the homes of millions of spectators from the remote regions of northern China to the Indonesian archipelago. On Channel V, a Cantonese music video by Luo Dayou might follow a lace-covered Madonna; native Taiwanese rap artist Jutoupi can be juxtaposed with the African American trio Eternal; or Japanese pop diva Seiko might follow the Irish group the Cranberries.

This radical eclecticism[1] within global music video forges a transnational space for cultural exchange. Music video, with its reliance on visual and musical systems of signification, is less dependent on strictly linguistic literacy. Among the most exportable of cultural forms, music videos are relatively open texts, accessible and adaptable to a wide range of cultural contexts. Even if the viewer does not understand the lyrics, he or she can respond to the flow of images and music and appreciate the spectacle of performance. It is critically important, however, to question the assumptions underlying the apparent "universal appeal" of the music video form.[2] It would be a mistake to assume that these open texts speak a universal language or impart universal meanings. Indeed, music videos are so popular precisely because they can be put to widely divergent localized uses. As a Western writer, my cultural competency with respect to the interpretation of Asian music videos—or the interpretation of Western music videos in Asia—is limited by my lack of familiarity with the languages and local cultures of Asia. Particularly when examining textual forms with a seemingly univocal appeal in terms of both their circulation and cultural intelligibility, it is imperative for white Westerners to trace and analyze the migrancy of Western culture while taking into account the specific locales in which it is read and the critical prejudices of the scholar. Some Western critics of international media shy away from cultural interpretation and focus on economic issues alone because it is politically dangerous to comment on a culture in which one lacks competency. But purely economic or industrial analyses invite their own risks as well. The economic infrastructure undergirding the global circulation of music videos is at its core exploitative and imperialistic, but a solely economic critique of that system does little to explain the complicated processes of identity formation engaged in by localized readers of global satellite television. And economic critiques can run the risk of perpetuating structures of cultural domination by defending highly restrictive nationalistic media systems simply because they oppose the imperializing strategies of global Western media conglomerates.

Because I am concerned with the negotiation of gendered identities that permeate and complicate the distinctions between Western and Asian media cultures, I engage here in a critique that is necessarily partial and highly interpretive. I have worked with several translators (both linguistic and cultural) in my effort to analyze the transnational gender discourses constituted through the music videos of Channel V, and each translator has inflected these texts differently. My many hours of viewing these videos both alone and with translators has reminded me that these widely circulated texts are far from univocal in their meanings. Indeed, their eclecticism gives them a polysemy that opens them to a range of culturally specific meanings. By looking at these music videos from an admittedly Western vantage point, I hope to begin to explore the multiplicity of ways different Asian cultures are negotiating Western cultural forces in the late twentieth century.

In this essay I analyze Chinese and Japanese music videos that appeared on Channel V in Taiwan in 1996, and I suggest that in the global discursive arena of satellite music culture the feminine has been positioned as the visible register of Western cultural influence—a kind of paper-doll barometer that indexes the extent to which a national culture has been transformed by the forces of Westernization. In an age when cultural, political, and economic boundaries are made ever more permeable by new information technologies and practices of globalization, nation-states have developed new ways to inscribe their control over the bodies of citizens. In some global media texts, the female body is mobilized as a defense against Westernization, and preservation of normative femininity is crucial to a nostalgic formulation of national identity. But in the music videos I discuss here, performers have appropriated Western markers of femininity in ways that complicate nationalistic constraints on gender norms. One of the by-products of Westernization is that, in specific national contexts, signs of Westernness can be mobilized to critique state control of gender. Thus, the transnational gender and sexual affiliations facilitated by global satellite television may open the floodgates to Western cultural imperialism, but they may at the same time challenge the state's power to circumscribe gender identities.

In mainland China, for example, gender and sexuality have been directly related to state efforts to control national culture. Satellite spillovers and anxieties about transnational cultural consumption have prompted Chinese political officials to turn a scrutinizing eye on media representations of Chinese femininity. New state media infrastructures have been designed to mitigate Western influences, and recent programs aired on state-run Chinese Central Television, such as *Foreign Babes in Beijing* and *Beijinger in New York,* have portrayed hypersexual American women as the vulgar antithesis of Chinese femininity.[3] The Chinese state's inability to determine national identity—a crisis brought on by such strange bedfellows as global capitalism and postcolonial transnationalism—has sparked a reactionary impulse to (re)assert an idealized, pure national culture by constraining representations of femininity.

But why has control over the feminine become so important to national cultural preservation? And why has the transnational circulation of gender representations in particular posed such a threat to normative conceptions of the nation? In part, this is because the feminine has historically been conflated with the maternal, and the female body has been positioned as bearing the nation's biological future. As Geraldine Heng and Janadas Devan suggest in their critique of state efforts to control reproduction in Singapore, the nation's "narrative of crisis" hinges on a "wishful fantasy of exact self-replication" and "posits, as the essential condition of national survival, the regeneration of the country's population."[4] Indeed, the myth of nationhood and the notion of an "imagined community"[5] are predicated on the harnessing of the female body for procreation so that the nation can continue to constitute itself as racially and ethnically homogenous.[6] The globalization of media culture, however, has reconfigured the strategies and sites through which state power is articulated. Although the state works to harness citizens into a tightly regulated economy of sexual difference, global satellite television has precipitated contestations over national identity that ultimately play out at the site of the female body.

Hong Kong Signals

Channel V's satellite relays pose an interesting challenge to a discussion of nationalism and gender, for they emanate from the contradictory cultural space of Hong Kong—a space that Ackbar Abbas characterizes as a "culture of disappearance," a culture marked by misrecognition, substitution, and fleeting visuality.[7] Hong Kong's architecture and cinema, for example, are formed by aesthetic styles that reflect the colony's uncertain relationship to its own complicated colonial past. This culture of disappearance, Abbas suggests, is a by-product of Hong Kong's colonial past. Indeed, the city's only history is that of a colony, for it came into existence as an urban center under British colonial rule. From its inception, Hong Kong has been a liminal space, tenuously positioned between China and Britain, East and West. As the cultural collisions between Asia and the West are increasingly mediatized, this port city, which has always been in search of its own distinct identity, has become an important zone of cultural exchange and transformation. As in Hong Kong architecture and cinema, Channel V's music videos sometimes elide the distinctions between West and East, so that iconic signifiers of the British colonial past might also be recognized as part of Hong Kong's Chinese cultural heritage. Because the Chinese and Japanese music videos relayed through Star TV headquarters in Hong Kong are outside specific national jurisdictions, their representations map a staging ground for the dismantling of normative national genders. The music videos of performers such as Luo Dayou and Seiko are significant because they are successful Asian music videos in a global market historically dominated by Western musicians. But perhaps more important is that they also produce transnational gender discourses within a culture of ongoing transformation, potentially challenging the power of the nation-state to delimit citizens' identities.

Channel V identifies itself as a global electronic space with international advertisements, multilingual programming, and eye-catching logos. Commercials for Calvin Klein underwear, Tummy Toner exercise equipment, and hip hop-inspired Wu-Wear run nonstop on Channel V. Coca-Cola sponsors the Asian Top 20, and Panasonic sponsors a program called *International Flight*, which features a melange of Western and Asian music videos. While station identification, advertising, and sponsorship designate Channel V as a site of global capitalism, they also constitute a specific discursive space in which the cultures of Asia and the West collide. Such cultural negotiation is evident in programs like *Go West*, which offers brief English lessons teaching Mandarin-speaking viewers how to identify stereo components or ingredients of American fast food sandwiches; or *Fashion Police*, a show hosted by a Mandarin-speaking veejay who wears Bermuda shorts and, between videos, informs viewers which Western fashion trends are "cool."[8]

Music videos have circulated Western sexual discourses via Star TV since 1991. Madonna's sexuality, for instance—which is perhaps most at home in the perpetual elsewhere of satellite media, where it can violate multiple national gender norms at once—has been globalized and downlinked to various locales where it has been negotiated by television viewers and musicians alike. Some Asian female musicians have appropriated tropes of Western femininity, donning blonde wigs or striking makeup and haute couture, refashioning American gender norms with local flair and then reglobalizing these interpretations via the Star TV satellite.[9]

Channel V's music videos provide a global window onto the gendered performance of national identity. By "performance" I am referring to the continual reiteration of regulatory gender norms at the site of the body—which, according to Judith Butler, is an ongoing practice that makes gender both visible and culturally intelligible.[10] I want to combine Butler's notion of gender performativity with Homi Bhabha's claim that the narration of nation as an "apparatus of symbolic power" inevitably "produces a continual slippage of categories, like sexuality, class affiliation, territorial paranoia, or 'cultural difference' in the act of writing the nation."[11] I want to consider what happens when the reiteration of gender norms and the narration of nation—two regulatory forces that work to constitute the body as materially and culturally recognizable—converge on bodies situated in transnational discursive spaces.[12] Particularly in the liminal space of global satellite television, the convergence of tropes of gender and nation produces slippages and incongruities that may enable the formation of transnational genders.

In order to put these theories of gender and nation into context, I would like now to examine representations in Chinese and Japanese music videos that have aired on Channel V. Luo Dayou is a Chinese pop music star whose work challenges the singularity of national identity. After a period of living and performing in Taiwan, Luo moved to New York where he had greater contact with Chinese people from Hong Kong and the Mainland. As a result of these cultural exchanges, which took place far from Chinese national territory, his most recent songs attempt to address all Chinese people rather than only those in Taiwan. Luo's work exemplifies what Chinese cultural critic Jianying Zha has called the "Whopper effect": "An impure, junky, hybrid quality in nearly all spheres of the present Chinese life—culture, politics, attitudes, ideology." Zha continues, "This is not romantic, not a picturesque scene for the camera. It's too blurry, too slippery, often shame-lessly vulgar."[13]

These moments of blurry, slippery impurity are crucial to a transforma-tive gender politics. Luo's videos infuse representations of Chinese history with references to Western popular culture. The incorporation of Western culture within Asian media is not in itself progressive or liberatory. But within a climate of nationalistic cultural containment, discourses of West-ernization can be used by performers and audiences alike to articulate iden-tities that tactically, if temporarily, evade and challenge state control. As Abbas has argued with respect to a progressive postcolonial politics: "There is one essential condition . . . that must be there if the postcolonial subject is not to be reabsorbed and assimilated: it must not be another stable ap-pearance, another stable identity."[14] For, he continues, "the very process of negotiating the mutations and permutations of colonialism, nationalism and capitalism . . . require[s] the development of new cultural strategies."[15] Indeed, Luo's videos demonstrate the impossibility of stable identities, and they implicitly critique discourses of national purity.

In the video for the Luo Dayou song "Pearl of the East," the port city of Hong Kong is figured as the epicenter of Chinese cultural change.[16] While the song's lyrics emphasize the physical beauty of Hong Kong, drawing attention to some of the iconic elements of the city,[17] singer Jiang Shuna's costume changes and movements foreground the interplay of Chinese and Western cultures. In this video, as Jiang navigates a series of diorama-like

5. Singer Jiang Shuna appears as a platinum blonde Marilyn Monroe in the music video "Pearl of the East."

sets representing the different periods of modern Chinese history, a number of symbolic Western masculine figures—including a gun-toting Chinese cowboy, a pack of naval officers, and a flexing Greek god—move through the port. Throughout the video Jiang appears in various guises: an eighteenth century aristocrat in a powdered wig; an impoverished street dweller; a Westernized woman of pre-Maoist China; a platinum blonde (à la Marilyn Monroe) in a tight black suit; and a Chinese opera singer in traditional dress. While the male characters in this video are also influenced by the West, their individual bodies are not constantly reinvented like the figure of Jiang. In this way, the video suggests that while Chinese masculinity can readily adapt to shifting sociocultural conditions, when similar transformations are wrought on the feminine they provoke considerable anxieties over the possibility of losing national historical continuity.

This complex narration of nation is structured by the look of a girl—a curious spectator of a new generation whose gaze frames the narrative. Literally holding the "Pearl of the East" before her eyes, the girl witnesses this series of performances as it plays out in a glass globe she holds in her hand. This glass globe—a *mise-en-abime* for Hong Kong itself—reveals the norms of both Western and Chinese femininity as they commingle at the site of the body, positioning the feminine as a transnational contingency rather than a set of national restrictions. Read one way, the continual metamorphosis of Jiang's body is figured as a kind of nostalgia over the loss of national culture, but the video's interplay between historical images of both Western and Chinese figures suggests that processes of cultural transformation are always already ongoing. The "Pearl of the East" video, then, suggests an alternative relationship between the feminine and the national; that the infusion of external influences into national gender distinctions may enable the feminine to be visually constructed in a multiplicity of ways. Although the enactment of Western feminine norms through the Chinese body can be read as a colonization, such an interpretation reproduces the kind of nationalistic discourse that has historically contained the feminine. Instead, the reiteration of both Western and Chinese gender norms in global music videos produces the possibility of transnational gender, and thereby loosens the state's hold on the processes of gendered identity formation. "Pearl of the East" invokes the feminine as a nostalgic longing for a univocal past. But in this video, Jiang Shuna becomes a visual register not of monolithic nationalism but of a history of gendered reinvention.

Where "Pearl of the East" reflects Luo Dayou's softer, nostalgic style, his Cantonese music video "Capital" represents his more contemporary, rock-influenced work. This video also posits the feminine as the staging ground for national cultural change, but it does so by evoking two distinct periods in modern mainland Chinese history—the Cultural Revolution and the post-Tiananmen 1990s. The flock of female characters in "Capital" wear high heels and short, tight, sleeveless red dresses (evoking the Western style of a Robert Palmer video), but they are also topped with Peoples' Liberation Army caps that place them under national control. The women sneakily drop cash into their bras, but they also revere "Big Character" posters like those that were used to denounce dissidents during the Cultural Revolution. They chat idly on their cellular phones, a marker of ascending class status, but they also ride bikes while running errands for the Communist Party. This tension within the feminine is narrated by Luo who sarcastically offers himself as a Maoist figure of the 1990s. He appears on a wall-size video screen, invoking the official state iconography of the past to inscribe China's presence within a technologized global present.

This video depends on an unstable and contradictory exchange of Westernization, Maoist nationalism, and female sexuality. The awkward incompatibility of these discourses is itself a powerful challenge to state control, particularly when articulated through the global domain of satellite media. As Rey Chow has suggested, Chinese popular music, "which often blends lurid, commodified feelings such as 'love' with a cliched mockery of both capitalism and communism, is about the inability or the refusal to articulate and to talk."[18] This is an important political intervention, she argues, "because inarticulateness is a way of combating the talking function of the state, the most *articulate* organ that speaks for everyone."[19] Particularly when

6. Luo Dayou plays a Chinese political official inspecting his female citizens in the music video "Capital."

set against nationalist efforts to contain the feminine, these moments of inarticulateness are a crucial tactic of feminist contestation. Luo Dayou's music videos introduce the possibility of transnational gender precisely because they refuse to articulate the feminine in the same way as the Chinese nation-state.

Where Luo Dayou's music videos posit the feminine as a visible register of national cultural change, those of Seiko Matsuda—known as Japan's Madonna—construct the feminine as a locus of transnational desire and as a potential contaminant to Japanese national identity. Seiko emerged as a pop star during the 1980s, and since then the pages of Japanese tabloids have been filled with details of her alleged affairs with foreign men and her recent divorce. Her sexual style is so provocative that it prompted a Japanese psychologist to write a book about adolescent femininity entitled *Seiko Matsuda Syndrome*.[20]

Seiko's sexual promiscuity challenges state-sanctioned models of feminine behavior expressed in such policies as the Eugenics Protection Law (1940) and the Mother and Child Health Protection Law (1965). As Japanese feminist Nakanishi Toyoko explains, the aim of such laws is to "reinforce the concepts of motherhood and childbirth and to nurture a population that is wholesome and superior in both body and mind."[21] While some Japanese feminists embrace the maternal role as the primary means of social power for women in Japan, others such as Ueno Chizuko have critiqued the *mazakon* ("mother complex") and suggest that "the dynamic future of Japanese feminism rests, at least in part, on its ability to network internationally in the new age of global communication and information flow."[22] Indeed, Seiko's music videos present a popular feminist discourse predicated on transnational connections, and their exploration of interracial sexuality challenges the ethnic and racial protectionism of state efforts toward eugenic purity.

Seiko's video "Missing You" beams interracial and transnational heterosexual desire into the global space of Channel V. As Seiko sings from a
rooftop about a recently lost love, pouring her passion into the open sky, a
barrage of flashbacks show her and a white American man embracing and
kissing on a sunlit rooftop and cuddling in a cozy apartment. But after
American agents surveil the two lovers walking hand-in-hand on the street
one night, we learn that Seiko's lover is an American secret agent working
for the FBM—the Federal Bureau of Medicine. Frustrated with his job he
tries to return to Seiko, but is captured by the agents and beaten, presumably
for violating national security.

In Japanese national space, interracial sexuality must be hidden on the
rooftop out of public view, but it is nonetheless scrutinized by an American
surveillance apparatus working to pull its masculine body back into service.
In the global space of the satellite-relayed music video, however, spectators
witness the transnational affections of a Japanese woman and a white American man. But within the video's narrative, the couple's miscegenation troubles the national security of both American and Japanese gender norms and
provokes a violent response from American secret agents.

In another Seiko music video, "Let's Talk about It," the seductive singer
performs a virtual-reality peep show for a "foreign" white man who is locked
into a VR machine in his apartment. The sweaty, shirtless man gazes at
Seiko through electronic goggles and a computer monitor as she glides
around a white room singing in sexy Madonna-esque outfits, writhing on a
chair, touching herself, and staring back at him. Seiko repeats the lyrics
"Baby let's talk about it . . ." over and over again, demanding that her lover
admit his desire. Finally, after a vigorous climax, Seiko's relieved cyberlover
peers into the camera and softly utters the words, "I love you."

Where Seiko's relationship with a white man in "Missing You" was hidden from public view, in "Let's Talk about It" the singer and her foreign lover
must make their sexual connection electronically. That is, they can only "talk
about it" while isolated in separate chambers. The social and spatial distance
of the couple is visually reinforced by the superimposition of VR graphics
over Seiko's image. This electronic sexual liaison between the Japanese
woman and foreign white man is not only symptomatic of historical constraints placed on interracial coupling in Japan, but also signals a challenge
to a more normative Japanese femininity. Global electronic space, then,

7. (*left*) Seiko, known as the "Japanese Madonna," performs a virtual striptease for her cyberlover in "Let's Talk About It." 8. (*right*) Seiko's cyberlover is perched at the interface watching her every move.

facilitates interracial and transnational sexual activity that would otherwise be taboo.

"Let's Talk about It" is fairly conventional in its positioning of the Japanese woman as object of a Western masculine gaze. The video does, however, emphasize the mutual pleasure of Seiko and her foreign lover. Tight facial close-ups reveal their closed-eye ecstasy and, at the same time, spotlight the couple's racial difference. And while the white man's look may reproduce an orientalist discourse on the feminine Other, Seiko constantly returns the gaze, donning goggles that enable her to view her lover's flexing washboard stomach and gyrating body. Seiko's volatile sexuality transgresses national feminine norms because it is directed across state borders and it is patently nonmaternal. The satellite relay of Seiko's music videos reinforces and intensifies this violation by projecting her autoerotic and nonreproductive sexuality into global view.

Seiko's music videos closely resonate with what Karen Kelsky has called the "yellow cab phenomenon." Since the late 1980s a wealthy class of young Japanese women has become the subject of "intense controversy" in Japan for their aggressive sexual pursuit of foreign (or *gaijin*) men.[23] "Yellow cab" is a slur derived by Japanese men that implies that Japanese women, like a New York taxi, can be "ridden any time." The term has been applied to Japanese women, explains Kelsky, as a "rhetorical weapon used by Japanese men to discredit a form of female behavior that they find threatening and disturbing."[24] The "yellow cab" is constructed within patriarchal Japan as the epitome of "female treachery, unbound sexuality, and cultural inauthenticity."[25] Seiko's sexual tastes—both in the narratives of sexual desire in her music videos and in her private life where she apparently dates a white French man—invoke tension similar to the "yellow cab phenomenon," and indicates how the feminine might become the last bastion of "nationhood"; for transnational female sexuality boldly compromises the nation's fantasy of future homogeneity and ruptures the economies of sexual and racial difference used to regulate the desires of citizens. As Dorinne Kondo insists, "How we dress, how we move, the music that accompanies our daily activities and that we create and refashion, our engagement with—and not simply the passive consumption of—media or commodities, do matter and can be included in a repertoire of oppositional strategies."[26]

Texts of transnational sexuality, such as the music videos of Channel V, are part of an important postcolonial tactic, according to Inderpal Grewal. In *Home and Harem* Grewal calls for increased attention to texts that reveal transnational movements of sexuality. "Particularly in the area of sexuality," she advises, "more texts that attempt to decolonize cultural and national forms are necessary, creating narratives of the travel of sexualities that would, once again, fracture disciplinary practices that were part of European modernity and colonial modernities."[27] By circulating genders and sexualities across national borders, these music videos of Channel V, these satellite rhythms, produce the potential to unsettle the power of the state to delimit and regulate gendered identities. This unsettling has significant cultural and political effects because it mandates the formation of an altogether new subjectivity—one that Abbas insists is "constructed not narcissistically but in the very process of negotiating the mutations and permutations of colonialism, nationalism, and capitalism."[28] Such subjectivities are based not on the strictures of nation, nor on the structures of colonialism, but in the interstices between them.

The music videos of Luo Dayou and Seiko demonstrate two strategies of nationalism at play at the site of the body. Luo Dayou's videos narrate national cultural transformation as a continual metamorphosis within the feminine. They juxtapose a nostalgic longing for coherent national culture with globalist cultural reinvention. In Seiko's music videos, on the other hand, interracial desire and cultural miscegenation position the feminine as a source of opposition to national culture. Both of these representational strategies are symptomatic of national anxieties brought on, in part, by the proliferation of new satellite and computer technologies as well as a history of Western cultural imperialism.

In the transnational discursive spaces of satellite television, nationalism is deeply involved in the reiteration of gender norms. Historically, the state has articulated and enforced gender distinctions as a necessary precondition of its continued existence. Since the nation plays such an integral role in determining and delimiting gender, race, and class distinctions, it is vital that we devise strategies to dislocate its hold on the feminine. Doing so might extend the terrain on which gendered identities are formed. I do not advocate a universal feminist strategy that would place women's bodies beyond national control to form some kind of utopian global feminine. Rather, I want to suggest that the nation, as an imagined construct in a world of fragile geography, technologized culture, and transnational desire, must increasingly be made visible at the site of the body, as a set of laws and limits imposed by and through the norms of gender, race, and class. This is how the state continues to assert its authority over the body within spaces of transnational hybridization. Therefore, it might be worthwhile to monitor and expose the discursive strategies that are applied to maintain state control over the feminine. Finally, we might well also look to the transient moments when women like Seiko or Jiang Shuna slip from the nation's grasp, for these moments of transnationalism invest the feminine with one tactic to disrupt and contest the nation's hold on women's identities.

Notes

I would like to thank Michael Kackman, Yufen Ko, John Fiske, Lance Halverson, Chia-Chin Lee and Yu-ling Lin for their generous assistance, and the editors of this book for their helpful comments. An earlier version of this paper was presented at the Console-ing Passions conference, Montreal, 1997.
1. For a discussion of radical eclecticism, see Jim Collins, "Television and Postmodernism," in *Channels of Discourse Reassembled*, ed. Robert Allen (Chapel Hill: University of North Carolina Press, 1993), 336–38.
2. As Andrew Goodwin has pointed out, MTV attempted to universalize itself in the early 1990s with such mottos as "One World, One Image, One Channel"; see Goodwin, "Fatal Distractions: MTV Meets Postmodern Theory," in *Sound and Vision: The Music Video Reader*, ed. Simon Frith, Andrew Goodwin, and Lawrence Grossberg (London: Routledge, 1993), 62. Andrew Sutton complicates this notion of music

video as a fundamentally globalizing discourse in his discussion of Indonesian music videos, which he demonstrates are simultaneously global, national, and local cultural productions. See his chapter "Local, Global, or National? Popular Music on Indonesian Television," in *Planet TV: A Global Television Studies Reader,* ed. Lisa Parks and Shanti Kumar (New York: New York University Press, 2001).

3. *Foreign Babes in Beijing* is a dramatic series about the lives of American and European girls who attend high school in Beijing. The twenty-part soap opera was so popular when it was first shown in 1996, that it has been rerun five times on Central Chinese Television. According to one review, the show attracted "huge audiences nation-wide by playing to the most negative Chinese views of foreign women—that they are spoiled rich kids who cheer loudly and inappropriately at Chinese opera performances, make frozen dumplings instead of the real thing and run around the capital in heavy-lust mode in pursuit of Chinese men" (Keith B. Richburg, "Not a Pretty Picture: 'Foreign Babes in Beijing,'" *International Herald Tribune,* July 25, 1996). *Beijinger in New York* is a Chinese television series that focused on the struggles of a male Chinese immigrant living in New York City who was seduced by American women. Programs like *Foreign Babes in Beijing* and *Beijinger in New York* position forces of Americanization as a threat to the sexual economy of Chinese society. These shows emerged as a direct response to the migrancy of Western television, and they attempt both to appease TV viewers' curiosity about the West and to defuse the threat of Westernization by incorporating it into nationalist Chinese television narratives.

4. Geraldine Heng and Janadas Devan, "State Fatherhood: The Politics of Nationalism, Sexuality, and Race in Singapore," in *Nationalisms and Sexualities,* ed. Andrew Parker et al. (New York: Routledge, 1992), 344.

5. Benedict Anderson, *Imagined Communities: Reflections on the Origin and Spread of Nationalism* (London: Verso, 1991).

6. The positioning of the female body as a reproductive agent for the nation has historically been articulated as part of different political agendas, ranging from German fascist eugenics programs to African American struggles for national power and political autonomy.

7. Ackbar Abbas, *Hong Kong: Culture and the Politics of Disappearance* (Minneapolis: University of Minnesota Press, 1997), 8.

8. MTV Asia tried to use local yet Westernized personalities to make popular American and European music comprehensible and appealing to the diverse audiences in the region. Schutze, for instance, one of the most popular hosts of MTV Asia, was described as "a funky combination of Greenwich Village and a Chinese village." A poet, artist, and musician, Schutze has lived in both New York and Nanjing and, according to one review, this dual habitation makes him "very MTV." The Chinese characters of his name ironically mean "rock village" (Maggie Farley, "MTV Hopes Chinese Will Be Staring," *The Los Angeles Times*, June 20, 1995, D1).

9. For a portrait of the *"bodi-con"* (body conscious) culture that has recently emerged among Japanese youth, see Karl Taro Greenfield, *Speed Tribes: Days and Nights with Japan's Next Generation* (New York: Harperperennial Library, 1995).

10. Judith Butler, *Bodies That Matter* (New York: Routledge, 1993).

11. Homi K. Bhabha, *The Location of Culture* (London: Routledge, 1994), 140.

12. Here I mean to suggest that the discourses that converge on the body actually constitute the sexed body. For Judith Butler, the materiality of the body does not precede the action of discourse on it. Instead, the body is materialized by discourse, which is "productive, constitutive, one might even argue performative, inasmuch as this signifying act delimits and contours the body that it then claims to find prior to any and all signification" (*Bodies That Matter*, 30). This process of materialization, I want to suggest, roughly parallels Homi Bhabha's characterization of the nation. Like the sexed and gendered body, the nation is narrated as a historically continuous, even a priori, totality. The paradox underlying both gender and nation is that both require continual discursive labor to maintain their uncontestable, "timeless" quality.

13. Jianying Zha, *China Pop: How Soap Operas, Tabloids, and Bestsellers are Transforming a Culture* (New York: The New Press, 1995), 11.

14. Abbas, *Hong Kong*, 14–15.

15. Ibid., 15.

16. My analysis of music videos in this paper privileges the visual and lyrical signification systems of this form over the musical because it is primarily concerned with how gender is made visible and intelligible within the global space of satellite television. For an interesting discussion of contemporary Chinese popular music, see J. Lawrence Witzleben, "Cantopop and Mandapop in Pre-Postcolonial Hong Kong: Identity Negotiation in the Performances of Anita Mui Yim-Fong," *Popular Music* 18, no. 2 (1999): 241–58.

17. "Pearl of the East" makes reference to the dark green ocean, mulberry trees, "unchanging yellow faces" and the twinkling lights of Hong Kong. Mulberry leaves are significant because they feed the silkworms that produce silk thread—a symbol of things Chinese and elegant.

18. Rey Chow, *Writing Diaspora: Tactics of Intervention in Contemporary Cultural Studies* (Bloomington: University of Indiana Press, 1993), 147.

19. Ibid., 147.

20. This book is mentioned in Yuko Ishikawa's online article, "Love! Love! Love! Part 13: This Is What 'GROWING UP' Means," *Friendship Japan Newsletter* 6 (1995–1996), available at http://plato.phy.ohiou.edu/~rhode/jp_letter.html, accessed November 1, 1998. This reaction to Seiko Matsuda in Japan is similar to parental responses to

Madonna during the 1980s. For a discussion of the social significance of young girls' embrace of Madonna's performative styles during the 1980s, see John Fiske, *Reading the Popular* (London: Unwin Hyman, 1989).

21. Nakanishi Toyoko, "Excerpts from *Our Bodies, Ourselves* (Japanese edition)," in *Broken Silence: Voices of Japanese Feminism,* ed. Sandra Buckley (Berkeley: University of California Press, 1997), 220.

22. "Interview with Ueno Chizuko," in *Broken Silence: Voices of Japanese Feminism,* ed. Buckley, 274. Chizuko identifies Takamure and Hiratsuka Raicho as maternalist feminists in Japan who were committed to a "maternal self [that] sees humankind as one family," and who emphasized motherhood as a way to differentiate Japanese feminism from Western feminism based on individualism.

23. Karen Kelsky, "Flirting with the Foreign: Interracial Sex in Japan's 'International' Age," in *Global/Local: Cultural Production and the Transnational Imaginary,* ed. Rob Wilson and Wimal Dissanayake (Durham: Duke University Press, 1996), 174.

24. Ibid., 175.

25. Ibid., 186.

26. Dorinne Kondo, *About Face: Performing Race in Fashion and Theater* (New York: Routledge, 1997), 13.

27. Inderpal Grewal, *Home and Harem: Nation, Gender, Empire, and the Cultures of Travel* (Durham: Duke University Press, 1996), 232.

28. Abbas, *Hong Kong,* 11.

So what are we to make of that rather curious moment in 90s pop that came to be known as "lo-fi"? By mid-decade the term had been taken up to earmark the sound associated with a range of mostly "alternative" music: Beat Happening, Guided by Voices, Sebadoh, the Jon Spencer Blues Explosion, Smog, the Grifters, Royal Trux, Tall Dwarfs, Daniel Johnston. Not exactly household names. But the label also served to entertain a wider array of pop activity, bandied about in the company of everyone from Beck, Liz Phair, and the Flaming Lips to Neil Young, Sheryl Crow, and John Mellencamp, as well as the 1995 Lollapaloozers, Pavement.

Referring as much to production values as to style, lo-fi by most accounts signaled a kind of technical shorthand for "home recordings," those small-scale efforts made on such (relatively) inexpensive equipment as four-track tape machines. Unlike state-of-the-art recording techniques, low-fidelity equipment produces an utterly coarse sound, often failing to mask hum, static, tape hiss, and other noises endemic to the very process of recording. Not simply a case of technology but also of technique, lo-fi has been used further to describe those musical performances marked by amateurish playing (often on minimal instrumentation), off-key singing, and a certain casualness in delivery. This dual aspect of amateurism (in terms of performance) and primitivism or minimalism (in terms of equipment and recording processes) initially set the tone for what constitutes lo-fi, leading discussion in the music press to something of a binary between art and commerce: to what extent has lo-fi been a question of either aesthetics or economics, a matter of choice or of necessity?

But such questions of cultural production are symptomatic of the larger debate over what is meant by the term "alternative music" (even as that particular designation itself can be isolated now as a historical artifact). That is to say, what is often at stake in the ethos of (putatively anticorporate) independent music—whether punk, rap, Riot Grrrl, techno, folk, you name it—is precisely what it means to *sound* alternative, to signify sonically an adversarial or oppositional sensibility, regardless of one's position in relation to the music industry. But then we must ask, oppositional to what? To capital, to aestheticism, to technology? At the intersection perhaps of all three, the noise stirred up by lo-fi—already implied by its name—is primarily over the question of production values. What interests me here is how those values become coded as either corporate or anticorporate, and the degree to which those production values as formal properties are said to carry social significance.[1]

While exploring both the formal traits determined as lo-fi and the range of issues interpellated by the term, I will consider the sound of lo-fi—with its altogether rough and ragged recordings seemingly indifferent to the aesthetic and technological demands of audio production and aural reception in the digital age—as one that quite deliberately plays on widespread perception of the demonstration tape. As an "unfinished" product, the demo tape had always existed in the music world as a precommodity form, something not yet for sale (at least legally) but nevertheless functioning as a necessary step in gaining the vital attention of record company A&R types.[2] With lo-fi the demo apparently has entered circulation, thereby rattling the usual order of things in the culture industry's standard grooming procedure for professionalization. So why, we might ask, were bands releasing *what sound like* demo tapes at this particular time in history? Has this been a challenge, however faint, to the conventional way things are done in the music industry? What does this mean for listeners, and how do we make sense of it?

What follows is a sketch of lo-fi as discursive formation and cultural practice. Taking issue with lo-fi's common depiction in the pop music press as a simple return to musical authenticity, as a naturalistic form of *audio verite*, I examine some media trackings that have aimed to secure it within rock culture's deep-seated tradition of Romanticism. Against this I suggest how lo-fi—given the degree to which such recordings foreground their material production—is more akin, however improbably, to the historical avant-garde: those cultural practices that attempted to challenge the aesthetics of classical idealism, itself alive and well through the digital aesthetic of "perfect sound forever." Finally, I consider one account of lo-fi that denigrates it as a form of mass culture, a characterization that, I argue, is gendered feminine and thereby provides a cue into the gender politics of lo-fi. Along the way I will offer some speculation on the demo tape as an aesthetic, perhaps even political, response to current conditions shaping sound, technology, and reception, conditions shaped by little more but nothing less than well-nigh total corporate hegemony over the field of cultural production at the turn of the century.

The Discourse of Lo-Fi

According to *Musician* magazine, "1994 was the year lo-fi arrived." But no sooner did it emerge from obscurity, quite suddenly appearing on a more indie-friendly cultural map, than it was declared already over and done, yet another "stylistic and cultural dead end."[3] Given the propensity for dramatic pronouncements in pop music writing, both assertions could be read as equal parts prediction, bluff, and wish-fulfillment. What one could say with some certainty is that, by 1995, lo-fi had arrived—arrived indeed as a discursive formation.[4]

Although the term itself had been tossed around for years in the music press, it was none other than the paper of record, the *New York Times*, that gave lo-fi headline status as far back as April 1993. In a profile on the otherwise obscure duo Ween, *Times* music critic Jon Pareles set the stage for "low-fi rockers"; the "suburban slackers," who had just released *Pure Guava* on Elektra following several independent label recordings, are found to be utilizing "primitive two-track and four-track cassette recorders." According to Pareles, the group's music "sounds casual and unadorned; instruments tend toward low-fidelity, and voices pop up at various speeds, exaggeratedly low or chirpy."[5] The last of these qualities was the result, apparently, of a malfunctioning tape recorder, the kind of propitious accident affecting artistic control that repeatedly crops up (as we will see) in stories on lo-fi.

A greater sense of authorial intentionality underwrites a Chicago *Tribune* feature on Beck a year later. Beck's song "Loser," which had made the Top 15 on the *Billboard* pop charts, is said to be "the apotheosis of a rock underground subculture built around crude, four-track home taping instead of polished studio recordings." Along with Daniel Johnston, Pavement, Sebadoh, Guided by Voices, Ween, and Beat Happening—reviewed under the banner "low-fi is the latest trend in the music biz"—Beck and "these other cassette-mongers," the *Tribune* argued, "have been releasing records with a living-room ambience, celebrations of spontaneity and humor that meld noise, melodies and good old-fashioned goofing around into music that is the antithesis of Bon Jovi."[6]

This "latest trend" is further elaborated in another *New York Times* Sunday feature, "Lo-Fi Rockers Opt for Raw Over Slick." Familiar traits of rock mythology pulse through the article: lo-fi's do-it-yourself methodology is "rooted in rock-and-roll history," from 60s garage rock to 70s punk, while "the combination of available technology and impromptu techniques democratizes pop music, putting creative power into the hands of anyone with a will." Here we might notice how artistic agency has returned to the musician from temperamental technology operative in the earlier account, a contradiction at work over who or what authors the sound (about which more later). The political implications of such populist sentiment notwithstanding, the discourse of lo-fi has begun to take on the trappings of rock ideology: "In a world of sterile, digitally recorded Top 40, lo-fi elucidates the raw seams of the artistic process."[7]

Finally, yet another *Times* piece, a mere half year later ("Fleeing Sterile Perfection for Lovable Lo-Fi Sound"), secures the terms of debate. Set against a world of "advanced technology" that makes "recordings as pristine and clear as possible," where production values are felt to be "too slick" and "sterile," lo-fi appears as the perfect response to "a very processed, perfect sound." Where aesthetics, economics, and method meet, lo-fi is posited as the "genuine" article, offering "an intimate sound with a raw edge." And where sound can be read as ideological, the discourse of lo-fi preserves a perception of authentic realism: "Instead of trying to eliminate all incidental room sounds, a lo-fi artist embraces incidental noise and incorporates it into the mix to achieve a heightened sense of reality."[8]

What can be heard here as a persistent beat throughout these accounts is a steady investment in notions of authenticity, one of the more inveterate elements to conventional rock discourse. And no less customary to such discourse is the function of technology. As Simon Frith has noted, where "the authenticity or truth of music" is at issue, "the implication is that technology is somehow false or falsifying," adding that the "continuing core of rock ideology is that raw sounds are more authentic than cooked sounds."[9] Although our experiences with music, whether live or recorded, are always to some degree technological, what often takes place at the discursive level is a stock rehearsal of these same debates, a tape loop, if you will, played out at every stage of technological development.[10] Likewise, the case of lo-fi reveals the latest cultural form to embody an enduring contradiction in pop music mythos, one that elicits a certain anxiety over the insoluble interdependence of the technological and the human, an interdependence in place since at least the late nineteenth century with the advent of the mechanical reproduction of sound. That is to say, the widespread fiction in pop of an opposition between music and technology—as if music somehow *precedes* technology, as if the latter distorts rather than enables the former—blithely ignores the extent to which technology has long been and remains a constitutive element of music.

Yet the pop press isn't alone in its near disavowal of technology and the concomitant investment in authenticity; musicians, too, are fully capable of clinging to this notion: "I prefer the lo-fi thing over a more slick sound," states Scott Taylor of the Grifters, "because we get more of a live, organic feel that way—the snaps, the pops, the accidents that always happen make it more human." On the flip side, some musicians recognize that we have passed beyond a long century of developments in sound technologies that amply demonstrate how thoroughly constructed musical recordings have become. Pavement, for example, clearly aware of the blatant artifice of pop, is quoted as saying (in response to the alleged spontaneity of lo-fi): "The Beatles managed to do it in the most expensive studios, like on *The White Album*. At least they simulated spontaneity, anyway."[11] Or consider this from Guided by Voices, which has been depicted by the music press as the nostalgic bearer of the bygone era when rock was believed to be "innocent": "About half our last album was recorded on twenty-four-track, then re-mixed to seem like four-track stuff—it sounds like messed-up arena rock!"[12] Recordings that play on this relation between technological expectations and audible trust—hovering amid artistic intentionality, aural perceptions, and the vicissitudes of what the medium itself produces—sunder the accus-

The "Feminization" of Rock   237

tomed codes for distinguishing the raw from the cooked, and thereby in effect confounding the treatment of lo-fi as a dissident demo-tape revolt against the stale regime of pop machinations.

The Gender of Lo-Fi

Most discussion on lo-fi emphasizes *home* recording, whether as an effect of low-rent studio work or as an actual site of production. One hears of Liz Phair's bedroom or Beck's kitchen, basement tapes and garage tapes; in short, spaces that function ideologically to signify intimacy, immediacy, and authenticity. In contradistinction to the outside world, with its impersonal high-tech studios and alienated corporate mass culture, home is regarded in the discourse of lo-fi as a "safe space," one presumably free of most social constraints. Here one's "true" self is allowed to emerge unimpeded by technology, at home in a presentation said to offer quite unproblematically direct access to the artist's naked soul. As one journalist asserts: "Low tech arrives as an attempt to strip away artifice. It strives to separate identity from technology, to remind us of who we are."[13] Rather than mediate the experience between listener and performer, the technology of home recording—at least in the mythology of lo-fi—actually enacts the unconcealing of the artist.

Axiomatic of the persistence of romanticism in the pop music world, this fantasy of direct, unmediated communication in the discourse on lo-fi is either celebrated as a form of personal self-expression or ridiculed as a form of excessive self-indulgence. To move beyond this particular reading of lo-fi, however, requires us to consider the extent to which such a reading is gendered. I want to suggest that not only is the kitchen or bedroom recording characterized as a "feminine" site of production but, moreover, lo-fi itself has been gendered feminine within the overall masculinist discourse of rock, a characterization that serves to devalue it on those very same grounds.

Our first hint into the gender politics of lo-fi can be heard as an undertone to a Pavement story, in which the group's Steve Malkmus, recalling an early encounter opening for the hardcore band Black Flag, describes a telling moment: "I was backstage before the show and all those guys, they looked so scary, I was afraid of them. . . . And before they played, Henry Rollins was back there with this pool ball, this white cue ball, just squeezing it to get pumped up for the show. I mean, squeezing a cue ball! . . . It's like smashing your head against a brick wall. That's what I thought punk was, you know.

That's when I knew that maybe I'm just not punk enough."[14] But wimpy lo-fi, perhaps deliberately positioning itself against a masculine principle often shoring up punk and hardcore, has something of a history. Indeed, the gendering of lo-fi as rock's feminine Other actually precedes the arrival of rock itself, a marking already in evidence from an earlier era of sound and technology.

In an exhaustive study of a decade of audiophile publications, Keir Keightley examines the pervasive gender politics of aural culture in postwar America, demonstrating how "the high-fidelity phenomenon" of this period involved "the masculinisation of home audio technology and the reclaiming of masculine domestic space." In the 1950s discourse of audio fidelity, distinctions were sharply drawn between hi-fi and lo-fi; as one 1954 article on the expanding high-fidelity market stated, "either a set was hi or it was lo." The degraded latter term, unlike the more "discriminating" realm of the former, was beset by crass commercialization and mediocre mass entertainment (often projected onto the emerging medium of television), a form of "passive" consumption, as Keightley notes, gendered feminine: where "high fidelity is cast as high, masculine, individualistic art," it stands "as a means of male liberation from feminizing mass conformity."[15]

This desire for escaping "low" mass culture and its perceived threat to male identity, already structured through fictions of gender, was overdetermined by class relations as well—all of which was played out across audio technology. As a 1959 editorial in a leading audiophile magazine viewed it, the "serious high fidelity public, who bought $400 corner-horn loudspeakers and spent a budgeted $30 per month of LPS of Haydn and Wagner [remember, this is 1950s dollars]," felt "affronted" by "low-fi Pat Boone fans [who] were going stereo."[16] This resentful depiction of so many "low-fi Pat Boone fans" bothering the "serious" connoisseurs of a besieged high culture, perhaps not unrelated to the "tin-eared ladies" supposedly responsible for Liberace's fame, reveals not only a class conflict over taste and technology but, moreover, it expresses a wider anxiety over the gender relations of aural culture, an anxiety still adhering to many discussions of music and culture to this day.

In 1995, for example, the *Village Voice* ran a major feature on the state of pop music. In his article "The Rock Beyond" critic Simon Reynolds mulls over what happened to alternative music in the wake of its corporate "mainstreaming": "Lo-fi, the mess-thetic of record collector bands like Guided by

Voices, was the U.S. underground's first response, and a weak one, since lo-fi is just grunge with even grungier production values. As the ersatz folk culture of fanzine editors and used-vinyl store clerks, lo-fi was always gonna prove a stylistic and cultural dead end (which won't stop Pavement, the genre's R.E.M., from taking the sensibility into the mainstream, four albums from now)." The article goes on to explore what Reynolds calls "post-rock," "a new breed of guitar-based experimentalists struggling to escape lo-fi's retro-eclectic cul-de-sac."[17] Setting aside for the moment Reynolds's inscription of lo-fi as "weak," I want to examine briefly his implicit model of culture, one which, relying on a surprisingly traditional notion of mass culture, is highly reminiscent of what Keightley found obtaining in the 1950s.

The first principle of Reynolds's argument holds that the "mainstream" is seemingly free of contradiction and that whatever has been assimilated or incorporated into the mainstream—or mass culture—is utterly compromised artistically. In valorizing the experimental risk-takers over the mainstream, one that stands in for a fairly undifferentiated mass culture, Reynolds posits a decidedly modernist cultural model premised on a stark binary operation, with an avant-garde uniquely outside or, literally, in front of a corrupted or degraded mass culture. This opposition between high and low entails a model of culture that many have argued is irredeemably gendered. In particular, Andreas Huyssen's landmark essay "Mass Culture as Woman: Modernism's Other," examines a range of discourses that "consistently and obsessively gender[s] mass culture and the masses as feminine, while high culture, whether traditional or modern, clearly remains the privileged realm of male activities." The cultural work such documents perform, he maintains, is to "ascribe feminine characteristics to mass culture," texts that signify "the persistent gendering as feminine of that which is devalued."[18]

Apart from reinforcing the modernist assumption of mass culture and its Other (let alone echoing the rhetorical reliance on metaphors of gender prevailing in the postwar audiophile world), what is curious about the configuration delineated by Reynolds's text is the way in which lo-fi is denigrated; not merely "retro" or "ersatz folk culture," it is the stuff of "record collector bands," "fanzine editors," and, perhaps worst of all, "store clerks." In other words, lo-fi appears as a past-oriented dalliance based in consumption, a hopelessly consumerist culture of collectors, fans, and clerks.[19] Even the depiction of fandom here—the active "guitar-based experimentalists" set over and against the passive "record collector bands"—fails to avoid trite fictions of gender, a depiction aligning with the still-protracted social hierarchy structuring fandom, reproducing a world in which, as Mavis Bayton puts it, "male fans buy a guitar; female fans buy a poster."[20]

This feminization of lo-fi—as a form of (degraded) mass culture, as a form of (banal) consumption—is exacerbated, then, by its principal distinction as home recording.[21] Although we are a long way from the nineteenth-century Victorian home, one said to have offered refuge from the cruel world outside, lo-fi arrives precisely at a time when the home has never been more suffused with technology, coinciding with the increasingly rationalized household of a postindustrial society where work and play and production and consumption are merely a keystroke and modem away. But this emergent culture of home recording also consists of a residual culture. An archaeology of the arrival of the mechanical reproduction of sound in the late nineteenth century reveals that the first casualties of the phonograph's entry into the domestic sphere were amateur musicians, many of whom were women.[22] So in many ways this more recent activity of lo-fi home recording could also be read as staging a series of reversals: inverting the conventional treatment of domestic space as a private, feminine sphere. The bedroom—our trusted guarantee for reproduction—has become instead (or perhaps once again) a site of cultural production, inverting as well the gendered coding of consumption and mass culture as "merely" feminine.

This notion of the feminization of rock, taken now in less reactionary terms, is further suggested by facets of the lo-fi aesthetic. What is often noted by critics is the rather fragmentary nature of lo-fi songs, many of which simply end "prematurely" as abbreviated and provisional pop numbers—as shards instead of songs that come and go without resolution. Instructive here is a review of Pavement's *Wowee Zowee* from 1995: "Good, complete songs" are in short supply, insists the reviewer, with "the album as a whole feeling scattered and sloppy." By producing merely "song fragments, [one of] which sounds like an unfinished rehearsal," the group is faulted for having "turned in a handful of half-baked performances."[23] Or, as another critic complained about Guided by Voices's *Bee Thousand* (1994): "Badly recorded, Beatlesque song fragments may make for an interesting aesthetic statement. But great rock? Get serious."[24]

Marked as somehow inadequate or objectionable, this particular constellation of traits—fragmented incompleteness, indefinite structure, lack of resolution—corresponds to what has been called, in the gendered terminology of traditional music theory, "feminine endings." Evidently lacking a "strong tonic" that fails to comply "with the law of the downbeat," these "incorrigibly feminine" features, as musicologist Susan McClary argues, have been castigated in the discourse of classical music criticism as "abnormal," passive, and "weak."[25] Such weakness, I would suggest, also characterizes lo-fi both formally (as fragmentation) and technologically (as disruption). This latter notation of instability, the apparent breakdown of technology and its attendant loss of mastery, control, and order, throws into question the status of the authoring agent of lo-fi sound. All those happy accidents in the recording process we kept hearing about, after all, function as minor ruptures in our cherished sense of authorship. With the artist no longer fully in charge, such proceedings recast, as in the Reynolds piece, the dismissal of lo-fi as "weak," a weakness due in part no doubt to a lack of artistic agency and technical virtuosity.

As with our earlier Pavement story, Henry Rollins comes up again, this time in an article on Lou Barlow's group Sebadoh. Barlow is reminded of reports in the music press that Rollins has thrashed Pavement for "slacking," deriding them and other bands believed to be playing "losercore." (Another Barlow project, Sentridoh, released in 1991 a single titled "Losercore.") Acknowledging the significance of Rollins to postpunk culture, as well as the influence of Rollins on his own work, Barlow good-naturedly impersonates the hardcore icon: "I fuckin' hate that Sebadoh losercore shit! They're weak! Why celebrate weakness?! You need to have strength in the world today!"[26] Of course, the insinuation here is that the musical traits of hardcore as aggressive, angry rock are bound up with the corporeal dimensions of an almost histrionic masculinity; getting "pumped up" (with or without a cue ball) is presumably the hardcore virtue of a hard (male) body, "impenetrable, invulnerable, invincible,"[27] one it is hoped that is entirely under control. Moreover, these performances—exaggerated, ironic, self-reflexive—point to a degree of differentiation within rock's production of masculinity, a less than monolithic subjectivity shaped historically, a larger context in which lo-fi can be placed.

While the histories of pop music typically have been organized around the development of genres and styles, or occasionally rendered as a dialectic of black and white social relations, far fewer efforts have been made to articulate the sexual politics of pop, to treat the culture as contested terrain across which gendered identities are constituted. In their 1978 essay "Rock and

Sexuality," Simon Frith and Angela McRobbie attempt to examine "the conventions of sexuality embodied in rock," contending that the standard history of rock posits an initial eruption in the mid-1950s, followed by a process of containment coded "feminine" (i.e., rock and roll domesticated through the overt commercialization of teen idols and girl groups). Critical of this familiar narrative, the article consequently pursues the vexed relationship of form and content in pop music, taking aim at the rather easy targets of "cock rock" and "teenybop" for the ways in which they construct ideologies of gender. Although somewhat dated in their more specific claims, the larger shape of Frith and McRobbie's argument remains suggestive, insofar as they approach the equally difficult relationship between social subjects and aesthetic strategies, between a cultural history of sexed performers and listeners and a more formal history of musical styles and conventions.[28]

A similar challenge appears in the 1990s, when one of the more insurgent moments in all pop arrives under the rubric "women in rock."[29] As the face of rock has irrefutably changed, altering among other things its accustomed forms of transgression, the question of "men in rock" could no longer presuppose its "natural" invisibility. With "queercore," Riot Grrrl, and unruly women differentiating the field, in effect shattering the regulatory aspects of a confining identity politics, rock of the straight white boy variety has become more properly situated and specified, its claim as the exclusive vox populi more thoroughly qualified and rendered conditional. Take, for example, the litter of grunge (Stone Temple Pilots, Bush, Creed), which essentially produced a sound that in the 1970s would have been called hard rock.[30] For all its earnest angst and righteous anger, the sensibility loudly declared here is chiefly that of the "angry young man" dispensation— the sentiment of male subjectivity suffused with discontent—a recurrent (and evidently still pressing and coveted) sound resonating across the length of rock history. Heard in this way, the affect of late grunge shares what Raymond Williams called a "structure of feeling" with the middle-of-the-road mode of midtempo ballad rock and sensitive, pained-guy earnestness of Hootie and the Blowfish, the Wallflowers, and Counting Crows. The tone and temper, then, of these two otherwise dissimilar styles, together functioning as the hegemony of 90s pop, provides part of the context for considering the gender politics of "losercore" and lo-fi's feminization of rock.

As for losercore and Malkmus's story that shamelessly admits to a failure of masculinity—speaking to the dread of and amusement in someone getting "pumped up" by squeezing a cue ball—in this could be heard a latent quarrel with rock as a masculine form, one still dominated by the loud, hard, and fast school of rebellion. How else is one to articulate dissatisfaction with the way things are? And what if the way things are included this very same masculinist ethos? What, in fact, would that dissatisfaction sound like?

"When You Fuck with the Form"

Consider for a moment the Silver Jews (which once included members of Pavement) and their 1993 EP *The Arizona Record*. In typical lo-fi fashion, the entire recording sounds as if it were made on a cheap portable cassette recorder—all muffled and murky and not a little bit difficult to actually hear. As is fairly predictable for lo-fi aesthetics, one of the songs suddenly drops out, followed by silence, then just as suddenly resumes—as if someone had accidently erased a segment. Another track just ends in mid-song—as if the recorder had shut off, as if the tape had run out—and clearly before the song is "resolved!" Listening to the recording is an altogether jarring experience, with songs abruptly ending or interrupted by other songs. What is further unsettling is that such seemingly experimental tactics have been employed in the recording process of fairly "traditional" pop songs. In this gorgeous mess of a recording, you can never *not* know that your listening experience is mediated, never not hear the sound of the recording in the very act of revealing its own means of production.

Usually reserved for work produced by the historical avant-garde (in Peter Burger's configuration),[31] this process of "exposing the instrumentation" might seem out of place on a pop record. But the collision of formal experimentation and mass cultural production is exactly the strategy of a politicized avant-garde, one that casts doubt on the reified dichotomy between high and low culture; between, in this case, an aesthetics of "making strange" and the breach of expectations by lo-fi pop music. "What is elided in the construction of standard music history," John Corbett argues, "is precisely the materiality of the apparatus,"[32] a legacy of disavowal shoring up the ideological notion of autonomous art—an art free from social constraints, free from economics, politics, history.

Music has always been conceptualized as the most idealized of art forms, the one least beholden to the grubby world below. Even pop music, the first to be soiled in the strict hierarchy of musical idioms, is not immune from this faith in some pure outside. In part this attests to the staying power of nineteenth-century Romanticism and its belief, as Caryl Flinn reminds us, "that music's immaterial nature lends it a transcendent, mystical quality, a point that then makes it quite difficult for music to speak to concrete realities."[33] This unfading aesthetic of autonomy, inflecting both high and mass culture alike, seems to have found, then, its proper and rightful delivery system with the most recent technological sublime of digitalization. While earlier technologies foregrounded their material production (tape hiss, radio static, turntable hum), digital technology, heralded by the commonly heard mantra of "perfect sound forever," has been designed precisely to erase any trace of its mediation, paradoxically bringing into being its own absence.[34] And yet into this context of pure, untarnished sound, defamiliarizing our experiences of sound in the age of what the Melvins jokingly referred to as "Pure Digital Silence," can be heard the less than perfect demo tape noise of lo-fi. Echoing Bertolt Brecht's call for showing "the machinery, the ropes and the flies," John Darnielle of the Mountain Goats, for one, has stated, "I don't like production that makes the fact that it's a made thing disappear." Or as David Berman of the Silver Jews (with regard to the aforementioned recording) put it, "I think people can take anything content-wise, but when you fuck with the form, you're fucking with the actual product, and that pisses people off."[35]

Although the Mountain Goats, Daniel Johnston, and the Folk Implosion have produced some of the noisiest recordings around, most of the groups heretofore mentioned as lo-fi have already moved on (if not to major labels, then certainly to "cleaner" sound productions), implying that, as an aesthetic device, lo-fi is the stuff of home recordings prior to a group's seemingly inevitable professionalization. But such movement isn't always perceivable; and so insinuates the example cited earlier of simulation staged by Guided by Voices, providing as well something of an object lesson in rock's supposedly irrevocable order of things.[36] Still, such reversals are rare, and are usually reinscribed (if our reading of the pop press on lo-fi is any indication) as a more genuine form of authentic realism—in spite of an entire history of sound technologies speaking volumes to the fact that recorded music exists as a fundamentally constructed object, one sufficiently given over to the realm of simulacra.[37]

However, here too the discourse of lo-fi can be said to reveal not so much an unerring statement on the realism of sound as one expressing the ambiguous desire for realism itself. For if the status of sound in the digital age is that of indeterminacy—the demo tape, for example, and its simulation as one and the same, at least for listeners—then lo-fi, I would argue, appears to acutely represent this very experience (entailing what Frith calls "imitative realism"),[38] which is, finally, in all its irreducible mediation, precisely the reality of sound for us these days. All of which is to say that lo-fi, perhaps more so but certainly no less than other recent cultural practices, fully embodies the contradictions of its time.

With the success of so-called alternative music in the 90s largely defined in market terms, what it means to *sound* alternative has been circumscribed by a certain level in production values. This sound threshold, below which (commercial) radio and TV will not tolerate—and where lo-fi seems destined to reside—offers us another way of reading the formal properties of pop as a means to calibrate its always contingent cultural politics. But by resisting industry incorporation and testing the limits of acceptability, lo-fi remains at the margins of social and cultural production, effecting, if nothing else, the verve of the unassimilable.[39] What I've also tried to suggest, however, is that in attempting to circumvent the somewhat deathless opposition of authenticity and artifice underwriting much of our rock mythology, primarily by instantiating how technology has been a constitutive element to all of pop, lo-fi references another, no doubt unlikely, tradition of cultural practice.

Either by refusing or by failing (both produce the same effect) to repress the signifier, lo-fi recordings (as with dub and certain tendencies in hip hop) deliberately incorporate rather than mask noises of the medium, thereby calling attention to their own constructedness.[40] But while this reading against the grain stresses how lo-fi's "realism" (or "reality effects") conveys less an authentic baring of the soul than an explicit baring of the apparatus, this very strategy indebted to the historical avant-garde has long become a function, as Thomas Crow insists, of the culture industry itself.[41] Yet, to return to the feminization of rock, in terms of cultural theory the gendered inscription of lo-fi as a feminized form of commodified culture would, perhaps dialectically, appear to complicate that treatment of the historical avant-garde itself, one that traditionally has been figured as a masculinized form of rebellion against bourgeois society.[42] Not only does lo-fi offer, then, a specific instance of interdependence between high and mass culture, which of course has long been underway (in theory if not always in practice),[43] it also suggests a kind of redistribution of methods and sentiment related to issues of gender, technology, and culture. Here we need only recall the question of artistic agency in the sound effects of lo-fi "accidents," events that serve to dispel the shroud of authenticity and intentionality enveloping creative autonomy while transmitting an implicit critique of the gendered will to mastery through technology. Hence, lo-fi's appropriation of avant-gardist procedures from *within* rather than against mass culture reminds us of the permeability of both traditional cultural boundaries and conventional cultural theory.

The pop soundscape of the 1990s appears to have been riven with nothing less than uncertainty, as perception of the reality and truth value of sound in the digital age seems very much in doubt. How else are we to take those responses at odds with the aesthetic of "perfect sound forever"? Indeed, digital's privileging of classical idealism, it could be argued, has been met with a kind of cultural disaffection through the unexpected persistence of vinyl and the ongoing craze for vintage equipment, accompanied by such sounds as retro futurism and what Tricia Rose calls "black noise." Enter also lo-fi, which, by emitting once more those elements like tape hiss that digital technology sought to expel, neither allows nor disallows such noises to become part of its sound, thereby troubling the distinction between music and noise. Less a fetishized authenticity than a critique of the dominant mode of technology, this noise, then, upsets the cliched depiction of slacker indifference underscoring lo-fi amateurism, just as what sounds to us like the demo tape upsets one of the more obstinate metanarratives of pop—the tragic loss of innocence to the rock and roll machinery of corruption. And, finally, to the extent that it has been rendered feminine, lo-fi might be said to at least gesture toward a politics of "popular" music, however attenuated, a gesture that also involves a politics of gender and sexuality that hit home, so to speak, in daily life.

Notes

I would like to thank the editors of this collection for the thoughtful suggestions that contributed to this essay. An earlier, extended version of this paper appears in Henry Jenkins, Tara McPherson, and Jane Shattuc, eds., *Hop on Pop: The Pleasures and Politics of Popular Culture* (Duke University Press, 2002).
1. The noisy garage aesthetic of 70s punk provides an obvious example of encoded production values, a direct assault on what was taken to be the creeping professional-

ization of rock, an incursion extending to "subcorporate" distribution, circulation, and reception (crack labels, 'zines, and clubs). An initial hearing of lo-fi suggests that, in its attempt to reclaim recording processes from high-tech professional studios, it has inherited from punk the aim of demystifying rock's means of production.

2. See Dave Mandl, "The Death of the Demo Tape (at Last)," in *Cassette Mythos*, ed. Robin James (New York: Autonomedia, 1992), 48–50.

3. Nathan Brackett, "Lo-Fi Hits Big Time," *Musician* 195 (January/February 1995): 44; and Simon Reynolds, "The Rock Beyond: To Go Where No Band Has Gone Before," *Village Voice*, August 29, 1995, 26–32.

4. I should note here that Canadian composer and sound theorist R. Murray Schafer, in his 1977 book *The Tuning of the World*, proposed a distinction between a hi-fi soundscape and a lo-fi one. Unlike the former, which is said to be found in the rural countryside, the latter soundscape, such as that of the modern city, is marred by "too much acoustic information," a chaotic soundfield where for the listener clarity and perspective is lost: "In the ultimate lo-fi soundscape the signal-to-noise ratio is one-to-one and it is no longer possible to know what, if anything, is to be listened to." Applying Schafer's distinction to contemporary recording and mixing techniques, we can infer that a hi-fi mix aims for clear separation of instrumentation and sound sources (i.e., aural perspective) while a lo-fi one muddies the sound, blurring foreground and background perspective so that "everything is present at once" (Schafer, *The Tuning of the World* [New York: Knopf, 1977], 71).

5. Jon Pareles, "Low-Fi Rockers," *New York Times*, April 11, 1993, sec. 9, p. 6.

6. Greg Kot, "Taking Up the Slack for a Whole Generation," *Chicago Tribune*, April 3, 1994, sec. 13, pp. 7, 21–22.

7. Matt Diehl, "Lo-Fi Rockers Opt for Raw Over Slick," *New York Times*, August 28, 1994, sec. 2, p. 26. As standard procedure, the article also makes reference to the murky recordings of the Velvet Underground, forerunners, it would seem, to anything perceived as "non-commercial."

8. Rene Chun, "Fleeing Sterile Perfection for Lovable Lo-Fi Sound," *New York Times*, January 10, 1995, B1, 4.

9. Simon Frith, "Art versus Technology: The Strange Case of Popular Music," *Media, Culture and Society* 8 (1986): 265, 266. This essay, crucial to my own argument, goes on to sketch the degree to which technological developments (recording processes, the microphone, magnetic tape) "have made the rock concept of authenticity possible" (269). Elsewhere, Frith insists that the "most misleading term in cultural theory is, indeed, 'authenticity'. What we should be examining is not how true a piece of music is to something else, but how it sets up the idea of 'truth' in the first place—successful pop music is music which defines its own aesthetic standard" (Firth, "Towards an Aesthetic of Popular Music," in *Music and Society: The Politics of Composi-*

tion, Performance, and Reception, ed. Richard Leppert and Susan McClary (Cambridge: Cambridge University Press, 1987), 137. See also Firth's "The Industrialization of Music," in *Music for Pleasure: Essays in the Sociology of Pop* (New York: Routledge, 1988), 12.

10. In our own digital age, for example, the familiar refrain of the natural and the artificial has been mapped onto debates over analog and digital technologies. As Andrew Goodwin states, "Playing analogue synthesizers is now a mark of authenticity, where it was once a sign of alienation" (Goodwin, "Sample and Hold: Pop Music in the Digital Age of Reproduction," in *On Record: Rock, Pop, and the Written Word,* ed. Simon Frith and Andrew Goodwin (New York: Pantheon, 1990), 269.

11. Pavement quoted in Diehl, "Lo-Fi Rockers," sec. 2, p. 26.

12. Indeed, as this quote attests, Guided by Voices's "authenticity" is entangled with dissimulation: "We used to do pretend interviews, pretend photo spreads, pretend liner notes, pretend lyric sheets" (Robert Pollard of Guided by Voices quoted in John Chandler, "I Heard You Call My Name," *Puncture,* no. 28 [fall 1993]: 61). Scott Taylor of the Grifters quoted in Brad Lips, "We'll Take the Lo Road: On the 4-Track Trail," *Option* 59 (November/December 1994): 78. In spite of the terminology of naturalism called on by the Grifters, I'd swear that's a blown speaker front and center of the mix on "Bummer" from *One Sock Missing* (1993), perhaps yet another recording "accident."

13. John Leland, "Sound and the Fury: The Revenge of Low Tech," *Newsweek,* February 27, 1995, 75.

14. Quoted in Jason Fine, "Catching Up with Pavement: Lo-Fi Leaders of the Stockton Scene," *Option,* no. 59 (November/December 1994): 92. Rock machismo is also spoofed by the title of Sebadoh's 1992 recording, *Smash Your Head on the Punk Rock.*

15. Keir Keightley, "'Turn It Down!' She Shrieked: Gender, Domestic Space, and High Fidelity, 1948–59," *Popular Music* 15, no. 2 (1996): 172, 156–58.

16. John M. Conly, "A Scolding," *High Fidelity Magazine* 9, no. 10 (October 1959): 47. In a cheeky piece from 1957 (written under a pseudonym "compounded from the names of two famous misogynists"), S. Strindberg Schopenhauer asks: "What shall we do with the tin-eared ladies?" Addressing a self-satisfied audience of "hi-fi husbands," the author, cracking insults passed off as the *bonhomie* of middlebrow teasing, insists that "very few women really like music" and "that far more women than men have no better than mediocre taste in music." After all, he adds, "Who put Liberace where he is today—men?" (Schopenhauer, "The Infidelical Spouse," *High Fidelity Magazine* 7, no. 3 (March 1957): 50.

17. Reynolds, "The Rock Beyond," 26–27.

18. Andreas Huyssen, "Mass Culture as Woman: Modernism's Other," in *After the Great Divide: Modernism, Mass Culture, Postmodernism* (Bloomington: University of Indiana Press, 1986), 47, 49, 53.

19. As Patrice Petro argues: "It is remarkable how theoretical discussions of art and mass culture are almost always accompanied by gendered metaphors which link 'masculine' values of production, activity, and attention with art, and 'feminine' values of consumption, passivity, and distraction with mass culture" (Petro, "Mass Culture and the Feminine: The 'Place' of Television in Film Studies," *Cinema Journal* 25, no. 3 [spring 1986]: 5–21). What's also curious about the cultural model ineluctably inhering to the *Village Voice* piece is that Reynolds himself coauthored the most ambitious attempt yet to apply 70s French feminism and psychoanalytic concepts to rock (Reynolds, with Joy Press, *The Sex Revolts: Gender, Rebellion, and Rock 'n' Roll* [Cambridge: Harvard University Press, 1995]). Indeed, the book opens with a critique of the same "negative association of femininity and popular culture" (5) that I've been tracing, even making use of the very same essay by Huyssen. Regardless of the rhetorical maneuver of the *Village Voice* article to set up a foil to what Reynolds champions, the text nevertheless attests to "the tenacity," as Petro puts it, "of hierarchical gender oppositions both in our culture and our theoretical discussions" (Petro, "Mass Culture," 6).

20. Mavis Bayton, "Women and the Electric Guitar," in *Sexing the Groove: Popular Music and Gender,* ed. Sheila Whiteley (New York: Routledge, 1997), 40. The key text on fandom remains Fred Vermorel and Judy Vermorel, *Starlust: The Secret Life of Fans* (London: Comet, 1985). See also Joli Jenson, "Fandom as Pathology: The Consequences of Characterization" in *The Adoring Audience: Fan Culture and Popular Media,* Lisa A. Lewis, ed. (New York: Routledge, 1992), 9–29, for the ways in which fan cultures are legitimated through gendered descriptions.

21. Of course, the home of our cultural imaginary, as both private refuge and as a "woman's place," also has a history. As Griselda Pollock contends, the long-standing dictate (especially in the West) legislating a dichotomy between public and private and its attendant assigning of sexual difference intensified in the nineteenth century, becoming a constitutive feature of modernity: "As both ideal and social structure, the mapping of the separation of the spheres for women and men on to the division of public and private was powerfully operative in the construction of a specifically bourgeois way of life" (Pollock, "Modernity and the Spaces of Femininity," in *Vision and Difference: Femininity, Feminism and Histories of Art* (London: Routledge, 1988), 68.

22. This displacement of "family" musicians was anticipated by the player piano, but the phonograph accelerated empirically the passing of the "piano girl." See Holly Kruse, "Early Audio Technology and Domestic Space," *Stanford Humanities Review* 3, no. 2 (1993): 1–4; Judith Tick, "Passed Away Is the Piano Girl: Changes in American Musical Life, 1870–1900," in *Women Making Music: The Western Art Tradition,* ed. Jane Bowers and Judith Tick (Urbana: University of Illinois Press, 1986); and Richard

Leppert, *The Sight of Sound: Music, Representation, and the History of the Body* (Berkeley and Los Angeles: University of California Press, 1993).

In the pre-World War I period of early phonography, the Edison firm sought to distinguish its cylinder format from the competing gramophonic disc by emphasizing the cylinder's capacity to be recorded at home. Unlike the disc, which as something of a pure commodity offered only a playback mode, the cylinder's double function as both playback and recording device allowed it to be marketed as the lone phonograph for "record parties"—a new form of family entertainment oriented around mediated listening: "There is more real fun and pleasure to be derived from an evening spent in making homemade Records than in a dozen recitals" (*Edison Phonograph Monthly* 8, no. 10 [October 1910]: 9). While home recording largely went the way of the cylinder for a better part of the century, the development of tape technology following World War II eventually brought about a new era of amateur recording in the home. And with the advent of four-track tape decks in the 1970s, home recording began to be treated as a low-budget alternative to professional recording studio work. On the marketing of recent home recording technology, see Steve Jones, *Rock Formation: Music, Technology, and Mass Communication* (Newbury Park, Calif.: Sage Publications, 1992).

23. "What does a defiantly anti-corporate rock band do when it starts getting too much attention? In Pavement's case, they recoil." So begins a *Rolling Stone* review (for our purposes confirming as well a sense of how production values become coded as corporate or alternative) that ends sounding betrayed, if not a tad resentful: "Maybe this album is a radical message to the corporate-rock ogre—or maybe Pavement are simply afraid to succeed" Mark Kemp, review of *Wowee Zowee, Rolling Stone*, April 20, 1995, 70.

24. Ann Powers quoted in J. D. Considine, "The Critics Pick Rock's Most Overrated Albums," *The Buffalo News*, August 3, 1997, F4.

25. Although McClary is primarily dealing with the "high" culture of classical music, my intimation is that a very similar aesthetic judgment governs pop music criticism as well. See Susan McClary, *Feminine Endings: Music, Gender, and Sexuality* (Minneapolis: University of Minnesota Press, 1991), 9–12. See also Claire Detels, "Soft Boundaries and Relatedness: Paradigm for a Postmodern Feminist Musical Aesthetics," *boundary 2*, 19, no. 2 (1992): 184–204; and John Shepherd, "Music and Male Hegemony," in *Music and Society*, ed. Leppert and McClary. In a similar vein, John Rockwell, writing on Laurie Anderson and postminimalist new music more generally, observes that the emergence of more composers who happen to be women since the 1960s issued a challenge to the protracted "romantic ideal" of the artist as "an exaggeratedly masculine one," a well-worn image that "stresses aggression, flamboyance, competitiveness, assertiveness." And it is no accident that what ensued was a concomitant aesthetic challenge to the "older ideal of tension and release building to a climax and the aggressive imposition of the artist's will onto the listener," all of which contributed to "a general feminization of our musical culture" (Rockwell, "Laurie Anderson: Women Composers, Performance Art, and the Perils of Fashion," in *All American Music: Composition in the Late Twentieth Century* [New York: Alfred A. Knopf, 1983], 131–32).

26. Quoted in *Milk* magazine (Milwaukee, Wisc.), no. 6, 1994, 16. Another layer to the humor here, the *impossibility* of Barlow (the "soft" bespectacled male) imitating the iron man Rollins, has carried over to a Sebadoh video, in which Barlow, clearly aware of his public image, performs his own mediated self—running around in pajamas and crying profusely over lost love.

27. Reynolds and Press, *The Sex Revolts*, 99. See also Fred Pfeil, *White Guys: Studies in Postmodern Domination and Difference* (London: Verso, 1995). On rock as a masculinized form of rebellion, see Leerom Medovoi, "Mapping the Rebel Image: Postmodernism and the Masculinist Politics of Rock in the U.S.A." *Cultural Critique* 20 (winter 1991–1992): 153–188.

28. Simon Frith and Angela McRobbie, "Rock and Sexuality," in *On Record*, ed. Firth and Goodwin. See also Frith's "Afterthoughts" from 1985 in the same collection. For evidence of the gendered narrative to rock and roll history, in which the late 1950s and early 1960s are held to be a period of "Emasculated Rock," see Linda Martin and Kerry Segrave, *Anti-Rock: The Opposition to Rock 'n' Roll* (New York: Da Capo Press, 1993).

29. Norma Coates scrutinizes the recent discourse on "women in rock," taking issue with the category as "a strategy of containment, necessary to stabilise and cohere 'masculinity' as constantly reiterated and reinscribed in the rock formation." She also suggests, however, that the title "may be a politically useful term right now, as a way to designate rock as contested ground" (Coates, "(R)Evolution Now? Rock and the Political Potential of Gender," in *Sexing the Groove*, ed. Whiteley, 53, 61. See also Joanne Gottlieb and Gayle Wald, "Smells Like Teen Spirit: Riot Grrrls, Revolution, and Women in Independent Rock," in *Microphone Fiends: Youth Music and Youth Culture*, ed. Andrew Ross and Tricia Rose (New York: Routledge, 1994).

30. Tony Kirschner charts how "hard rock" (basically, heavy metal-ish Seattle grunge) became the "hip-mainstream" (embraced by middle-class, disaffected white youth) in the late 1980s and early 1990s. For the most part ignoring the extent to which this music has structured gendered subject positions, the article proposes that hard rock expressed a cultural dissonance at variance to the Reagan-era values of fundamentalist conservatism (Kirschner, "The Lalalooziation of American Youth," *Popular Music and Society* 18, no. 1 [spring 1994]: 69–89).

31. Peter Burger, *Theory of the Avant-Garde*, trans. Michael Shaw (Minneapolis: University of Minnesota Press, 1984).

32. John Corbett, "Free, Single, and Disengaged: Listening Pleasure and the Popular Object," *October* 54 (fall 1990): 89.

33. Caryl Flinn, *Strains of Utopia: Gender, Nostalgia, and Hollywood Film Music* (Princeton: Princeton University Press, 1992), 7.

34. "All describe digital technology by its absence: the absence of any interference with simply experiencing the music, the absence of that sense of spatial distance one gets from an LP, the absence of surface noise, of rumbles, pops, and scratches. Digital *is* what it isn't" (Gerald Seligman, "The Compact Disc Experience: Concert Hall Sound at Home," *Village Voice*, "Video Vision/Audio Adventures" supplement, October 22, 1985, 71.

35. "Pure Digital Silence" can be heard on the Melvins LP *Pride* (Amphetamine Reptile Records, 1994). David Berman quoted in Terry Dannemiller, "Silver Jews," *Magnet* 14 (December 1994): 12. John Darnielle of the Mountain Goats quoted in Bill Meyer, "Goat Ease," *Puncture* 31 (fall 1994): 23. Bertolt Brecht, "Stage Design for the Epic Theatre," in *Brecht on Theatre*, ed. and trans. John Willett (New York: Hill and Wang, 1964), 233. The discourse of audio fidelity in the digital age was appropriated by Pavement, who titled an early (and recklessly noisy) recording *Perfect Sound Forever*.

36. The noisy ambivalence of Pavement's *Wowee Zowee* (1995) eventually gave way to 1997's *Brighten the Corners*, which did just that. Meanwhile, the Jon Spencer Blues Explosion, who had somewhat cleaned up their previously messy act for 1994's *Orange*, returned to a wildly seditious production for 1996's *Now I Got Worry* (recorded at Easley Studios in Memphis, the home—so to speak—of lo-fi sound). And Royal Trux, after a brief foray into the major label world, is now back on the lo-fi indie label Drag City.

37. As for this postmodern aesthetic often attributed to such digital technologies as the sampler, Andrew Goodwin asks: "Is it in fact an aspect of economic, historical, and technological developments in pop that need to be understood in the context of the continuing dominance of realism, modernism, . . . and romanticism?" (Goodwin, "Sample and Hold," 272). This disjunction between postmodernism and the discourses of *contemporary* music implies, at least in terms of sound and technology, an utter lack of consensus on what is said to constitute the "postmodern condition." At the same time we might consider the willful celebration of hyperreality in some quarters of postmodern theory less uncritically. This contempt for the "real" in the age of the simulacrum sustains what Peter Sloterdijk calls "cynical reason," where "the expectation of being deceived" has given way to an "enlightened false consciousness" and where "deception as an industry" breeds "a hard-boiled cleverness" (Sloterdijk, *Critique of Cynical Reason*, trans. Michael Eldred [Minneapolis: University of Minnesota Press, 1987], 484, 546).

38. Simon Frith, *Performing Rites: On the Value of Popular Music* (Cambridge: Harvard University Press, 1996), 244.

39. On the "fatalistic marginality" of indie rock in general, see Eric Weisbard, "Over and Out: Indie Rock Values in the Age of Alternative Million Sellers," *Village Voice*, "Rock and Roll Quarterly" (summer 1994): 15–19; and Steve Tignor, "Indie Rock: A Dying Breed—Or Just a Dead Issue?" *Puncture* 31 (fall 1994): 13–15.

40. On the ways in which dub "remind[s] the audience they are listening to a recording," see Paul Gilroy, "Steppin' Out of Babylon: Race, Class and Autonomy," in *The Empire Strikes Back: Race and Racism in '70s Britain* (London: Hutchinson, 1982), 300. See also Steve Jones, *Rock Formation*, 169. On the related practice of "working in the red" found in rap production, see Tricia Rose, *Black Noise: Rap Music and Black Culture in Contemporary America* (Hanover, N.H.: Wesleyan University Press, 1994), 74–80.

41. As Thomas Crow maintains: "The avant-garde serves as a kind of research and development arm of the culture industry: it searches out areas of social practice not yet completely available to efficient utilization and makes them discrete and visible" (Crow, "Modernism and Mass Culture in the Visual Arts," in *Pollock and After: The Critical Debate*, ed. Francis Frascina [New York: Harper and Row, 1985] 257). Although speaking to "high" culture practices, Crow's argument also applies to the "low" culture of lo-fi, suggesting as well the extent to which such phenomena manage to straddle what Andreas Huyssen calls "the Great Divide," and which finally assigns something like lo-fi to a now rudimentary diagnostic of the postmodern. I am indebted to Bernard Gendron for bringing Crow's essay to my attention.

42. See Susan Rubin Suleiman, *Subversive Intent: Gender, Politics, and the Avant-Garde* (Cambridge: Harvard University Press, 1990).

43. Fredric Jameson's approach, for example, "demands that we read high and mass culture as objectively related and dialectically interdependent phenomena, as twin and inseparable forms of aesthetic production under late capitalism" (Jameson, "Reification and Utopia in Mass Culture," *Social Text* 1, no. 1 (winter 1979): 133–34.

The United States is no longer the puppeteer of
a world system of images, but is only one node of
a complex transnational construction of imaginary
landscapes. — Arjun Appadurai, *Modernity at Large*

In a certain sense, the history of Mexico, like that
of every Mexican, is a struggle between the forms
and formulas that have been imposed on us and the
explosions with which our individuality arranges
itself. — Octavio Paz, *The Labyrinth of Solitude*

Can anyone tell me which country we are in?
—Guillermo Gómez-Peña, "The New World Border"

JOSH KUN ✳ ROCK'S *RECONQUISTA*

Distrito Federal, Mexico, 1996: It is the eve of Mexican independence day
and Mexico's most idolized rock icon, Saúl Hernández, is standing shyly on
the stage of the Auditorio Nacional, one of Mexico City's largest and most
prestigious performance spaces. A long, elaborate row of freshly lit can-
delabras drip hot wax and bathe Hernández in a warm, gothic glow. Tower-
ing above him are two enormous video screens that deliver his adored
larger-than-life image—the seductive, piercing eyes; the stringy, unkempt
hair; the charming gapped-tooth smile; the tattooed, wiry frame—to the ten
thousand screaming Mexican fans who have paid top peso just to be in the
same room with him (no matter how big it is) and witness the much-
anticipated public debut of his new band, Jaguares.

"We are priests," he whispers to his rapt congregation. "These concerts
are our ceremonies." A video cuts between shots of a tribal healing circle
and a mosh pit of slam-dancing *rockeros* and *rockeras*. And in his clinging
bell bottoms, powder-blue tank top, and raggedy velvet sports coat, this
former leader of the now-defunct Caifanes (one of Mexico's biggest and
most commercially successful rock bands) looks every bit the rock and roll
brujo, poised and ready to lead an arena rock ritual.

The slightest smile, the most uninspired between-song *gracias*, and the accidental pluck of a single guitar note produce ecstatic screams that can be heard all the way outside the auditorium where row after row of vendors sell bootleg Jaguares merchandise to desperate ticketless devotees. Inside, the audience knows every word that pours from Hernández's mouth, in spite of the fact that the Jaguares's debut album, *El Equilibrio de los Jaguares* (which goes gold within three weeks of its release), has only been out for five days.[1]

Rock, La Invasión

What on the surface may seem like yet another rock and roll spectacle, yet another performance of major-label stadium marketing, is in reality something much more. After all, this is rock en español, or rock in Spanish, a once-outlawed urban musical youth movement that has been brewing within and below the U.S.-Mexico border since the 1950s. I want to use this rousing independence day performance—which offers the mass cultural *grito* (shout) of rock *mexicano* as a musical echo of Miguel Hidalgo y Costilla's historic 1810 *grito de independencia*—as a way into a much larger discussion of musical postnationality as is heard in rock en español's loosely organized, inter-American cultural formations. Indeed, whether it is Irving Plaza in New York City, the Ranas Bar in Tijuana, or a sports arena in Argentina, the sound of rock en español continues to reverberate across the pop soundscape of the Americas—from Control Machete's Monterrey hip hop *norteño* and Julieta Venegas's Tijuana-to-Mexico City art-pop to Todos Tus Muertos's Buenos Aires rasta-punk and Aterciopelados's kitschy Bogota trip-*foclorico*.

The reverberations have become so intense in the last decade, particularly with young Latinos/as living within and across the policed spaces of the "extended U.S.-Mexico borderlands,"[2] that some within the rock en español world have referred to it as a *reconquista*, or reconquest of English-language "U.S. rock"—a racially and culturally hybrid formation that has itself been the subject of repeated cross-racial conquests and appropriations.[3]

Ruben Guevara (aka Funkhuatl, the unknown neo-Aztec god of funk), a veteran Chicano rock historian and founder of 80s Latino rock label Zyanya Records, and Victor Monroy, the twenty-year-old lead singer of Los Angeles alt-rock band Pastilla, have compared the emergence of Spanish-language rock in the United States and Mexico to the British "invasion" of the U.S. music rock scene in the 1950s (a suggestive semiotic move given further pop-cultural cache by a recent, corporate-sponsored multicity U.S. rock en español concert tour known as "Rockinvasión"). But for Guevara and Monroy, the idea of a Latino musical "invasion" of U.S. rock spaces and terrains operates as a clever double play on the nativist antiimmigrant rhetoric of California's xenophobic Proposition 187 that transforms Californians' fear of a Mexican "alien" invasion of California into a bold musical statement of identity empowerment and territorial and cultural reclamation. Thus, rock's *reconquista* involves both the takeover of U.S. rock vocabularies and stylistic lexicons and an audio-geographical takeover of the national and regional territories signified and represented within the music itself.

This double takeover—a musical conquest that escalates into a symbolic takeover of language, culture, and national space (specifically the U.S. Southwest)—is precisely what motivated Guevara to compile the first rock en español collection to be issued by a U.S. label, a collection he titled *Reconquista! The Latin Rock Invasion*. For Guevara, the emergence of rock en español movements among Latinos in the United States, Mexico, and other parts of Latin America signifies "a reconquest of our respect, our humanity as Latinos. We were here and that was taken away from us. It's like setting the record straight—regaining our sense of heritage, our sense of identity." Pastilla's Monroy, who was born in Mexico City and raised in Pomona on the outskirts of Los Angeles, also embraces the idea of a transcontinental Spanish-language rock invasion, but for Monroy the invasion will take place through the taste strategies and consumer tactics of growing numbers of Mexican and Chicano fans: "We're gonna see an invasion of rock in Spanish, from here down to Mexico," he says. "I can just see it. In every little Mexican baby that is born today will be another rock in Spanish fan."[4]

This particular remapping of rock's geography, "from here down to Mexico," also has important consequences for the ways in which rock, race, and nation most commonly get talked about. Except for a few notable examples, rock discourse has traditionally been deployed within the outmoded racial binary of black and white, with the vast majority of discussions of rock's relationship to race never going far beyond the more familiar and ready-made vocabularies of U.S. blackness and whiteness.[5] Rock en español— which is just one large part of an even larger and more general Latino rock movement with distinct histories across the Americas that reaches its most parodic point in the United States with El Vez, the Mexican Elvis, who can turn Presley's "Viva Las Vegas" into "Viva La Raza" without ruffling his neopachuco pompadour[6]—destabilizes rock's whiteness and rock's blackness. It begs for new grammars and lexicons that understand the importance of the transnational flow of documented and undocumented Latino/a culture to contemporary discussions of inter-American racial formation and Latino/a cultural citizenship.[7]

After all, rock en español (and the Latin ska and Chicano *alternativo* scenes that radiate around its generic perimeter),[8] like most emergent rock movements, operates as a youth culture of sound in which music—its performance, consumption, recording, and distribution—is at the heart of the formation of community and is the soundtrack to the scripting of emergent identities and identifications. As Benedict Anderson has noted only all too briefly, nationally minded communities are not just scripted around axes of the scriptural and the printed, but around the aural, the sonic, the musical, as well—what he names the unisonance of "imagined sound."[9] In the context of the global economy of late capitalism that the recording industry is so centrally a part of, the Latin/o American sound culture of rock en español—an aural imagined community if there ever was one—recharts inter-American geographies by applying a transnational ear to the Americas and listening to them as a hemispheric field of sound ripe for plunder, recycling, transformation, and recontextualization.

Audiotopias en Español

This new listening requires a theorization of a direct link between sonic production, sonic reception, and the subsequent construction and deconstruction of national topographies. It entails hearing music as, in part, a spatial practice. Listening to music for what it tells us about local and global geographies and subsequent contests for cultural ownership highlights the shifting nature of contemporary cultural and subcultural forms across the geopolitical and discursive space of the Americas. Because of music's ability—both before and especially after the age of mechanical reproduction—to move between places and locations, understanding it spatially is one way of tracking its movements, witnessing and listening for its migrations and travels.[10]

I have argued elsewhere that one of the more valuable sites for the articulation of music along spatial trajectories is Michel Foucault's notion of the "heterotopia," which he explains as "a kind of effectively enacted utopia" characterized by the juxtaposition "in a single real place of several spaces, several sites that are themselves incompatible."[11] With Foucault's definition as a provisional guide, I have proposed instead that we consider the notion of "audiotopias": sonic spaces of effective utopian longings where several sites normally deemed incompatible are brought together not only in the space of a particular piece of music itself, but in the production of social space and mapping of geographical space that music makes possible.[12] Audiotopias would operate something like what Mary Louise Pratt has termed "contact zones" in that they provide the lived and imagined terrain by which disparate cultures and geographies historically kept and mapped separately are allowed to interact with each other in relationships whose consequences for cultural identification are never predetermined.[13]

My interest in retuning our ears for what music tells us about the (dis)order of spaces and places under global capitalism follows from a number of recent calls for the spatialization of cultural production. Considering the audiotopias performed and produced by the music of rock en español is one way of situating cultural forms within what Jody Berland calls "capitalist spatiality." Berland has convincingly argued for a reconception of music according to the spaces produced for and occupied by its listeners—their spatial positionality—because "much of the time we are not simply listeners to sound . . . but occupants of spaces for listening who, by being there, help produce definite meaning and effects."[14] Yet, while Berland is correct to stress the contingency of textual production on spatial production, I am more interested in the inverse of her own declaration: that the production of space is likewise contingent on the production of cultural texts and, more specifically, the production of sound. By listening for music's audiotopias, we are able to hear these spaces that music itself makes possible—the spaces that music maps, evokes, and imagines.

Furthermore, audiotopic listening within and across the flows of global capitalist culture is one way of approaching the construct of "the global" not as a closed, predetermined system of hegemony but, as Lawrence Grossberg has suggested in his theorization of "spatial materialism," as an ongoing space of becoming and struggle. As in Grossberg's analysis, the audiotopias of rock en español resist a rigid place/space/local/global split that codes places as local and full of meaning and spaces as global nonsites of passage and emptiness. Instead, the audiotopias allow us to hear "the organization of space and place as a geography of belonging and identification."[15]

But what the music of rock en español allows us to hear is an audio-geographical organization, a musical-spatial terrain of becoming, belonging, and identification. My interest here is how a musical assemblage like rock en español reveals movements and flows across the shifting maps, sonorous landscapes, and "rhythmic planes" of the Americas, exposing a nonhemispheric view of "America" as an egregiously U.S.-centric construct and, in Xavier Albo's words, "an error of historical proportions."[16] Through the musical styles it incorporates and the dispersed audiences across the Americas it both reaches and reflects, the sound cultures and audiotopias of rock en español question the one-to-one equivalencies of music, nation, and culture.[17]

"Antes de Que Nos Olviden" (Before They Forget about Us)

Mexican rock en español represents a transnational musical story that has been four decades in the making.[18] It begins in the early 1960s when the combined effect of Bill Haley and the Comets Mexican tour in 1960 and the wide release of films filled with rock and roll, such as *Blackboard Jungle*, *The Wild One*, and *The Girl Can't Help It* helped to generate Mexico's own home-grown version of teenage rock and roll fever. Clean-cut Mexican rock bands like Los Locos del Ritmo, Los Hooligans, Los Apson, Los Crazy Boys, and Los Rockin' Devils quickly emerged, taking plenty of cues from commercial U.S. and U.K. rock sound and style—wearing thin black ties and short-sleeved white Oxfords, slicking their hair into Elvis-inspired pompadours, and frequently covering songs note for note and giving them thorough, and often excruciatingly literal, Spanish language makeovers. Los Ovnis translated the Rolling Stone's "Mother's Little Helper" into "Pequeña Ayuda de Mama," Los Teen Tops reworked "Long Tall Sally" as "Laguirucha Sally," and Los Locos del Ritmo simply changed the title of "Peter Gunn" to "Pedro Pistolas." Imagine the look on Elvis Presley's and Carl Perkins's faces when they found that Los Teen Tops had turned their "Blue Suede Shoes" into "Zapatos de Ante Azul."[19]

The explosive birth of rock in Mexico in the 1960s was coterminous with the beginnings of socioeconomic modernization in Mexico. According to a model outlined by Néstor García Canclini, five structural changes between the 1950s and the 1970s transformed the Latin American "relationship between cultural modernism and social modernization": increased economic development; continued urban growth; expanded markets for cultural goods; newly introduced communications technologies (such as television); and an increase in radical political movements.[20] These factors are of particular importance decades later for young Latinos/as in the United States, in Mexico, and within the U.S.-Mexico borderlands because they remind us that the bulk of rock en español's formative years—particularly in the 1970s—was spent at odds with an oppressive political apparatus determined to demonize the burgeoning genre and relegate it to the margins of Mexican society. Throughout the 1960s, rock bands such as Antorcha, Peace and Love, Toncho Pilatos, and Dug Dugs slowly became the dissident, rebel voice of urban Mexico City youth and students, and because of their open embrace of U.S. culture and style (they even dared to sing much of their songs in English), rock became a viable cultural threat to the government-sponsored *cultura nacional*.[21]

An event that figures centrally in this history is the brutal 1968 massacre of student protesters by national police at Tlateloco Plaza, an event crucial to the formation of what Octavio Paz named "the international subculture of the young." In "The Other Mexico," Paz positions the Tlateloco massacre as the double of the murders at the 1968 Olympics and argues that this contradictory historical couple is at the center of what he writes of as modern Mexico's paradoxical development. Because Mexican rock was a music based in the lives and everyday social realities of urban youth and students, Tlateloco's "swash of blood" destroyed any possible reconciliation between rock youth and the government and further guaranteed the music's subversive, subcultural status. In the mid-1980s, Banda Bostik recorded their tribute to Tlateloco, "Tlateloco 68," and in 1990 Caifanes reminded younger rock listeners of the event's enduring significance in the now anthemic "Antes de Que Nos Olviden." "Before they forget about us," they sang, "We will make history."[22]

That Tlateloco is a landmark in Mexican rock history is doubly significant because of the plaza's position with Mexican cultural and political history as a site of mixture and intercultural contestation. A vital center of pre-*conquista* cultural life, Tlateloco was the last Aztec outpost to surrender to the Spaniards during the conquest, and it remains a living symbol of what Paz calls "Meso-American dualism." This dualism is the result of a history of *mestizaje,* of political, racial, and cultural contact where Aztec nobles were taught Spanish literature, theology, rhetoric, and philosophy. Since then,

Tlateloco has been home to everything from a military prison to low-rent apartment buildings, and it is now officially known as the "Plaza of Three Cultures" because of the recently excavated Aztec pyramid, the Catholic church, and the skyscraper (the Ministry of Foreign Affairs) that coexist within its bounds. And while Paz calls Tlateloco one of the "three pillars" of Mexico's symbolic *visual* history (along with the Zocalo and Chapultepec Park), the effect of the student massacre of October 2 on both rock en español's youth movement and its stylistic *mestizaje* has taken Tlateloco's significance one step further. Its histories of contact, struggle, and mixture are now part of Mexico's symbolic audio history as well.

Police repression of Mexican youth culture continued at Mexico's answer to Woodstock, the 1971 Avándaro "Rock y Ruedas" festival, which is still looked to as the galvanizing moment in Mexican rock history by young and old *rockeros* alike.[23] Drawing a crowd of an estimated three hundred thousand *jipitecas* (Mexican hippies) and *niños bien* (middle-class kids), Avándaro featured such acts as Bandido, Peace and Love, and Three Souls in My Mind (who later changed their name to El Tri and became Mexican rock's most durable act). A gritty bilingual mix of psychedelic rock, shuffling blues, and churning boogie-woogie, Three Souls in My Mind would often follow their "Tributo a Jimi Hendrix" with songs like B. B. King's "How Blue Can You Get" and Muddy Water's "Mannish Boy" and then offer their own home-grown additions to the rock cannon: "Yo Canto el Blues" (I Sing the Blues), "Que Viva el Rock and Roll" (Long Live Rock and Roll), "Abuso de Autoridad" (Abuse of Authority), and "No le Hagas Caso a Tus Papas" (Don't Obey Your Parents).[24] It was this mix of sounds, styles, and attitudes that took the stage at Avándaro (which El Tri would later recall in their song "Chava de Avándaro" [Avándaro Girl]) a peaceful yet avowedly antinational musical gathering designed, according to a festival organizer, "to achieve a union of young people . . . to prove that modern culture, which is already all over the world, has also arrived here."[25]

After Avándaro, *rockeras* and *rockeros* became Mexico's number one social pariahs and the government ensured that rock en español had a difficult time surviving in the public sphere. According to Saúl Hernández, "the government marginalized all the possibilities of rock to exist. They refused to realize the importance of free expression. Everything changed and rock moved underground."[26] Banned from the public sphere and Televisa—Mexico's state-monitored television monopoly—rock survived where it could: on street corners, in the *hoyos fonquis* ("funky holes"), in abandoned factories, in deserted movie theaters, and on the backs of flatbed trucks.[27] But in the mid-1980s and early 1990s, rock en español, or *rock en tu idioma* as it was being called by industry executives, began to receive increasing record industry attention and it has since become one of the fastest growing and most popular genres in the world of commercial Latin music. Major transnational labels like WEA, Sony, BMG, and EMI have all actively added rock en español bands to their rosters and Mexican rock bands can now be found virtually anywhere, from multinational rock tours and Hollywood film soundtracks to the Montreaux Jazz Festival.

In 1997, Cafe Tacuba's *Avalancha de Exitos* sold a breakthrough 120,000 copies in the United States and became the first rock en español album to land on the CMJ 200, the leading U.S. college "alternative rock" radio chart. Due in part to the domestic commercial success of Cafe Tacuba and Argentina's Los Fabulosos Cadillacs, the Grammy Association added a "Latin Rock" category to their awards in 1998. And with the help of MTV Latin America's audiovisual tentacles spreading across 7.3 million homes in over twenty countries throughout the Americas (broadcasting weekly rock en español shows like *Raisonica*)[28] rock en español has simultaneously become a key musical factor in Latin America's negotiations with modernism and postmodernism and a major, emergent force in global pop music and global pop style. As Rocco, the lead singer of Mexico's Maldita Vecindad told critic Rubén Martínez, "it might be true that rock began in the north. But now it's all ours."[29]

Un Canto Fronterizo (A Song of the Borderlands)

The "ours" at work in rock en español, however, grows increasingly unstable as the flow of rock and roll—once seen as primarily unidirectional, from north to south—now begins to change course as rock recrosses the border, growing in popularity and size with Latinos across the United States. Originally inspired by the styles and sensibilities of U.S. rock culture, Mexican rock en español—in an inverted, circuitous cultural migration—has subsequently moved across and within the trans-*frontera* spaces of the U.S.-Mexico borderlands to influence first-, second-, and even third-generation Chicano/a musicians in California.

Such a two-way transnational flow of popular sound adds contemporary weight to 70s rock icon Jaime Lopez's claim that rock en español is *un canto fronterizo* (a song of the borderlands), an insightful recasting of rock en español's origins and futures. For Lopez (who remains best known for his dialogic, slang-drenched anthem of urban rock subcultural style, "Chilanga Banda"), "more than talking about an urban song [*un canto urbano*], we should talk about a borderlands song [*un canto fronterizo*], because that's what our song is like, you do it Chiapas, Yucatan, Mexico City, Nogales, Matamoros, or Tijuana. . . . We're border people [*fronterizos*], not urban people [*urbanos*] . . . we're between the cement and the plains, those are our contradictions."[30] Lopez reveals a musically mapped Mexico that resembles García Canclini's characterization of Mexico as a "transborder region," characterized by the repeated crossings of information, populations, and goods.[31] The Tijuana ska/punk band Tijuana N O echoes Lopez's comments in its own musicalization of border culture, "La Esquina del Mundo" (The corner of the world) when they sing of the border as "the last street of Latin America / the line that marks us from outside / the boundary between pueblo and stone."[32]

Lopez even describes Mexico City, the city from which he drew so much inspiration for his own brand of rock en español in the 1970s and 1980s, as *una ciudad fronteriza* (a border city) full of music from outside of its boundaries that emerges from different coordinates and cartographies. Mexican music critic David Cortes has also written of the sound of 70s bands like Bandido, Peace and Love, and Three Souls in My Mind as being characterized by "that limbo that is *la frontera*: taking the best from the United States in terms of technique and making the best use of Mexico as a creative territory."[33]

Rock's *canto fronterizo* is perhaps now heard the loudest in bars and clubs in U.S. cities with large Latino populations—"independent micro-republics" like New York, Los Angeles, San Jose, and Chicago[34]—that feature regular rock en español nights with live music provided by both local Latino bands as well as by some of Latin America's top touring rock acts. Indeed, throughout the 1990s, rock en español generated its own "exilic media system" in the United States, including multiact Latin alternative tours (Guateque, Watcha, Revolución); the publication of Spanish-language rock magazines like *Pub, Retila,* and the scene's monthly high-gloss bible *La Banda Elastíca* (which boasts a circulation of over twenty thousand); weekly city-specific papers like Los Angeles's *Al Borde!;* an increased radio presence on college,

264   Josh Kun

Internet, public, and commercial stations (including the groundbreaking 1999 debut of *The Red Zone* on Los Angeles's English-language alt-rock station Y107); rock-friendly independent cable shows like Los Angeles's *Illegal Interns;* and perhaps most significantly, the rise of independent rock en español labels like New York's Grita!, Los Angeles's KoolArrow and Bring Your Love, and San Francisco's Aztlán Records, which turns the Aztec-derived Chicano homeland of the U.S. Southwest into a record label homeland for rock en español groups from across the United States (such as Oakland's Orixa and Los Angeles's Pastilla).[35]

In recent years, as the amount of Latin American rock en español distributed and sold in the United States has increased, more and more bands in the U.S.-Mexico borderlands—from Houston's Los Skarnales and New York's King Chango to Los Angeles's Viva Malpache, Voz de Mano, and Satelite—have found rock en español to be an effective sounding board for the interconnected fates of Chicanos/as and *mexicanos/as.* By serving as a traveling, musical bridge between dispersed populations living within the borderlands, rock en español creates a floating, migrating musical audiotopia that maps new borderland regions with coordinates like Mexico City/ Los Angeles and Mexico City/Berkeley.

Rock thus becomes one of the many "mysterious underground railroads" that U.S.-Mexico performance artist and essayist Guillermo Gómez-Peña hears connecting the transnational performance coordinates of the "new world border," where hybridity is the dominant culture—an audio circuit of exchange and communication between dispersed listeners and the shifting national geographies they inhabit. The music of rock en español provides the soundtrack to many of Gómez-Peña's "prophecies, poemas, & loqueras" for the end of the century and is frequently the sonorous landscape that territorializes the drifting, utopian "Fourth World" cartographies of his new world border.[36]

In his vision of a "borderless future," Gómez-Peña sees "grunge rockeros on the edge of a cliff / all passing through Califas / enroute to other selves / & other geographies." The performance piece *The New World Border* imagines a hit TV show called Pura Bi-Cultura which broadcasts across the borders of the Americas and features "fusion rock bands that used to be underground now play[ing] their punkarachi, discolmeca, and rap-guanco at NAFTA functions." The first scene of *The Last Migration: A Spanglish Opera (in progress)* finds Gómez-Peña "training to face the end of the century" by jumping rope while listening to Mexican rock band Cuca. Gómez-Peña so frequently returns to the music of rock en español precisely because of the inter-American sonic mappings it offers, what he describes as its "brave acceptance of our transborderized and denationalized condition."[37]

While Gómez-Peña's use of rock en español to give musical voice to a "borderless future" is undoubtedly a playful, utopian, and performative one that often threatens to empty the border of its site-specific political realities,[38] the music has, at the very least, been a key point of cultural contact—a sort of musical hyperspace—between Latin/o communities on both sides of the border. Indeed, two recent Chicano films, Miguel Arteta's *Star Maps* and Jim Mendiola's *Pretty Vacant*, both employ rock en español as a music of connection between the United States and Mexico, a music that in a sense carries the border with it.

For his debut film about a creatively dysfunctional first-generation Chicano family living in contemporary Los Angeles, *Star Maps* (which begins with the main character returning to L.A. on a bus from Mexico where he had been living with his grandmother), Arteta tellingly did not choose a soundtrack rooted in Chicano rock, pop, and oldies, as for example Gregory Nava did for his 1995 East L.A. Chicano miniepic *Mi Familia*. Arteta instead filled the *Star Maps* soundtrack with rock en español bands from the United States and Latin America and hired Chicana singer-songwriter Lysa Flores and rock en español's most seasoned and well-known producer, Gustavo Santaolalla—who has produced critical, commercial, and Grammy-winning successes for bands like Cafe Tacuba and Julieta Venegas—to be the album's supervisors (Flores, who costars in *Star Maps*, also contributes her "Beg, Borrow, & Steal" to the soundtrack). What the soundtrack to *Star Maps* ends up suggesting is that the music of contemporary Chicano identity is an increasingly transnational formation, both *de aqui* and *de alla*, both de Los Angeles and de Mexico City, both de bilingual hip hop and de urban folk/rock.

Rock en español also makes an appearance at the end of Jim Mendiola's 1996 film *Pretty Vacant*, which chronicles a week in the life of Molly Vasquez, a second-generation Chicana filmmaker, 'zine publisher, and drummer for the all-girl punk band Aztlan A Go Go. When she's not documenting the secret relationship between British punk legends the Sex Pistols and *conjunto* accordion legend Steve Jordan, Molly—whose motto is "Soy punk rocker, y qué?"—tries but fails to avoid her family's annual trip to Mexico.

Throughout most of the film, the soundtrack Mendiola strategically employs is a smart mix of U.S. and U.K. punk (Ramones, Sex Pistols) and rock (Television, Patti Smith, Pretenders) with Tex-Mex *conjunto* (Steve Jordan, Freddy Fender), but when Molly returns from Mexico we hear instead "El Aparato" (The Aparatus), a song by Mexico City rock en español band Cafe Tacuba.

With Cafe Tacuba's electro-acoustic pre-*hispano* rock playing in the background, the film's frame of reference shifts from San Antonio to Mexico City, and Molly tells how she "hooked up with some rockeros at El Chopo" and "turned them on to the new L7 and they gave me some tapes by Cafe Tacuba and Santa Sabina." Joining El Chopo's weekly rock and roll swap-meet of underground trading and pirate cassette transactions, Molly becomes a Chicana participant in its transnational exchange of sounds and goods. After she returns to the United States, the English-language girl-punk of L7 becomes one more sound for Mexican bands to recycle and "re-fry" and Cafe Tacuba and Santa Sabina (led by goth priestess Rita Guerrero) become the perfect soundtrack for Chicana life in San Antonio. *Pretty Vacant*'s Latina feminist take on borderlands rock culture offers a refreshing break from rock en español's predominantly masculine public profile. Although *rockeras* and *chavas banda* (female rock fans) have always constituted a large and important part of Mexican rock's audience since the 1960s, the number of women rock performers—except for well-known figures such as Andrea Echeverri, Julieta Venegas, Alejandra Guzmán, Cecilia Bastida, and Rita Guerrero—has taken significantly longer to grow.[39]

The transnational connections and musical bridges that *Pretty Vacant* and *Star Maps* comment on were already at work in 1989 on "Mojado," a song by Mexico City's Maldita Vecindad y Los Hijos del Quinto Patio. "Mojado" tells the story of a Mexican national who leaves home to cross the border as an undocumented *mojado* to secure work in the United States. He leaves Mexico believing "the other side is the solution," and ends up suffocating to death in a truck along the border. The song is dedicated to "the Mexican workers that illegally cross the border into the United States who they call *mojados* . . . [and] to all those who have been forced to separate themselves from their customs, loved ones, roots, and everyday realities."[40] The fatal border crossing that "Mojado" documents gives literal voice to one of the thousands of so-called silent deaths that have occurred in the process of crossing the U.S.-Mexico border at designated border checkpoints. In the past four years alone—the very period that has seen the rise of such close-the-border campaigns as "Hold the Line" in Texas and "Operation Gatekeeper" and "Light Up the Border" in California—over eleven hundred men, women, and children have died from automobile accidents, drowning, exhaustion, and dehydration while trying to find a way into the United States to locate work and reunite with family.[41]

On the band's 1993 concert tour (which stretched throughout Mexico, the United States, and Europe), Maldita went so far as to dedicate the song to "all those *hermanos* dispersed all over the world and especially for the Chicanos," using the experience of crossing the border as a means of building musical connections between *mexicanos* and Chicanos.[42] Similarly, when Mexican rock veterans El Tri played a sold-out show at Los Angeles's Hollywood Palladium in 1991, they insisted that even "more than a rock concert," the show was "a testimony to our people, to our fans, to our brothers" living in what they jokingly called "the sister republic of hamburgers, hot dogs, and hot cakes." In the liner notes to the recording of the concert, *En Vivo!!! Y a Todo Calor en El Hollywood Palladium*, the band's lead singer and songwriter, Alex Lora, writes that he hoped the concert let the audience forget their frustrations "and above all, that we make you feel at home, that you are in Mexico, and that proudly, we can say that we are brothers and that we are Mexicans."[43] In narrating both the experience of transborder crossings and migrations and drawing audiotopic connections and linkages between Chicanos/as and *chilangos/as*—and actually trying to use music to turn the Hollywood Palladium into a satellite province of Mexico—both El Tri and Maldita insert the spatial stories of music into what Roger Rouse has outlined in another context as a two-way "transnational migrant circuit" of population, media, and information flow between California and Mexico.[44]

Of course, all of this activity went flagrantly unnoticed by MTV when the U.S. division of the international network devoted five minutes to a microtour of rock en español on an episode of its *Indie Outing* program in 1997. Beside the fact that none of the bands mentioned in the hurried spot were indie (all were signed to major Latin American labels) and that a few were even assigned incorrect home countries (Mexico's Control Machete somehow ended up in Uruguay), what the show missed was that rock en español can no longer be talked about as a strictly Latin American phenomenon. By avoiding mention of the numerous U.S. scenes that the music has gone on to influence, MTV was able to maintain the same exoticizing discourse about rock that was applied to mambo in the 1950s, while simultaneously suggesting that Latino rock simply does not exist in the United States. The show's refusal to confront the role of Latinos in the production of U.S. rock culture is only one of the many ways that rock's "latin tinge" continues to be ignored.[45]

Guacarock and Roll

The one thing that can be said for MTV's reductive and uninformed sideswipe of rock en español is that it at least portrayed the genre as an original and self-sufficient movement. This has not always been the case. From the very start, rock en español has been haunted by a recurring question: is it an imitation of U.S. musical style and language or does it constitute its own sound? Is it, to borrow Paz's phrase, "exhibiting a wound," or is it instead the very sound of that wound's creative suturing? Critics in both the United States and Latin America have long chosen to approach rock en español as being purely the derivative and imitative musical residue of U.S. cultural imperialism and domination. Of course, such reductive and myopic accusations of "cultural monopolization" and "cultural syncronization"—by which the supposedly unidirectional flow of First World cultural products homogenizes or "synchronizes" the diversity of the world's cultures into a single, global, consumer-driven monoculture—have been debated and contested on multiple levels, and, I believe, they remain as unsatisfactory approaches to the myriad spheres of influence that constitute and inform all forms of popular production generated within twentieth-century global capitalism.[46]

For example, take Roger Wallis and Krister Malm's influential study of the impact of the transnational recording industry on "small countries." Although the authors go a long way toward painting a musical picture more complex than "the cultural imperialism thesis" allows, they still maintain that the flood of U.S. and British pop and rock music that entered the world's markets in the 1950s and 1960s produced nothing but "imitations"—that is, groups of artists who tended to "copy" artists like the Beatles, Elvis, and Chubby Checker. Indeed, it is precisely acts of "imitation" and "copy" that, they argue, characterize the pre-1970 period in all of the countries they surveyed (which did not include Mexico).[47] While Wallis and Malm are right to make a distinction between the more singular "national" pop styles that developed in each country during the 1970s and 1980s, their willingness to uncritically accept the notions of musical copy and imitation as processes void of original signification needs to be problematized. Holding on to the binary of original and copy reaffirms a colonialist, unilateral West-centered logic of center and periphery—what Chilean critic Nelly Richard has termed "the pact signed between modernity and centrality"[48]—by which the periphery is condemned to reproduce and copy the center and all of the meanings, discourses, and languages that it reigns over.

It remains a commonly held assumption that Mexican rock bands in the 1950s and 1960s were doing nothing more than emulating bands popular in the United States and England (an assumption which, among other things, ignores the fact that the "models" of U.S. and U.K. rock and roll were already themselves copies of African/American jump blues and southern "hillbilly" music). While some Mexican bands did very little to resist such a perception, I want to be careful not to swiftly write off "copy" and "imitation" as aesthetic strategies that do not generate significant national and cultural difference. Many early Mexican bands may have "covered" U.S. songs but I would argue that they did so *with a difference,* changing the meaning of the original lyrics, altering the composition of the sound, and ultimately significantly transforming the way the songs are heard and recognized.

"Hang on Sloopy" is certainly not the same song as Los Freddys's version "Hang on Lupe," and when the question "Who Put the Bomp" is posed as "Quién Pusó el Bomp" (as it was by Los Teen Tops) the set of answers is entirely different. Musical "copies" like these do not aim to wholly reproduce the original but to *re-fry* them, cooking up songs that taste less like cover versions and more like what the 80s band Nopalica preferred to call their songs, "refried nopals." They deploy musical versions of what Frances Aparicio has explored in a literary context as "sub-versive signifiers." In her discussion of U.S. Latino writers Alurista and Helena Maria Viramontes, Aparicio notes that "what on the surface appears to be a praxis that signals cultural assimilation may be defined also as a subversive act: that of writing the self using the tools of the Master, and in the process, infusing those signifiers with the cultural meanings, values, and ideologies of the subaltern sector."[49] Nelly Richard has similarly argued that in the context of Latin American cultural production, we need to understand the copy as "the plagiarizing rite . . . a signifying exercise of cultural transvestism" that subverts the hierarchy of the center as the sole source of meaning by seizing control of its discourses, signs, and symbols.[50]

Listen, for example, to the early 60s album by Agua Prieta's Los Apson, the tellingly titled *Por Eso Estamos Como Estamos!* (Therefore we are who we are).[51] On the album's cover, the band is pictured wearing standard late 50s teen rock attire, only instead of posing in the urban settings typically synonymous with 50s and 60s U.S. and U.K. rock, the band is standing alongside a winding railroad track that cuts through a rural landscape. The music on the album is no less revisionary; the majority of the album's songs are covers of U.S. rock and R&B hits, however most of them are actually listed as being coauthored by the songs' original writers *and* members of Los Apson. The band rightfully credit themselves for rewriting "Wooly Bully" as "Becho Becho," "Game of Love" as "Despierta Nena," and "Midnight Special" as "La Media Noche," and the songs most certainly do not remain the same. The songs on *Por Eso Estamos Como Estamos!*, then, offer a good example of musical reauthorship at work in the early days of Mexican rock, as they become "copies" of originals that instead of simply reproducing the originals opt to completely create them anew. These proto rock en español compositions were already blurring the line between original and translation and between model and copy, thus delegitimizing the very cultural supremacy of the center by altering the established relationship between center and periphery. When "Apple Pie" is rebuilt and reshaped as "El Tren," the periphery is no longer obedient to and dependent on the original. The copy has become its own original.

The debate between musical originality and imitation in Mexico continued well into the 1970s, with a particularly influential early response to rock en español made by leading Mexican Left cultural critic Carlos Monsiváis. He devoted a chapter of his 1977 *Amor Perdido* to a critique of rock en español's first wave, known as *la onda,* which he periodized between 1966 and 1972. Monsiváis characterized the infatuation of bands of that period with U.S. psychedelic rock and drug culture as suffering from "norteamericanización cultural." For Monsiváis, bands of antinational *jipitecas* taking stylistic and ideological inspiration from 60s U.S. countercultural movements (instead of from *boleros* and *rancheras*) were too easily heard as audible products of acculturation and as colonial copies of alleged First World musical originals. He described the Avándaro rock festival as being both "an autonomous and original response" and "a colonial fact, not because a rock festival belongs exclusively to North American culture, but because of its basic claim to unproblematically duplicate a foreign experience; that is, once again, putting ourselves at the mercy of servile emulation."[52]

While Monsiváis's critique sustains the tension between duplication and originality inherent within any cultural exchange, his preference for hearing rock en español as "servile emulation" ignores the ways rock en español deprograms the very codes it supposedly obeys. It leaves no room for the "tactics" and "strategies" of listening consumers—"the ways in which the weak make use of the strong"—that Michel de Certeau has put at the center of his discussion of mass cultural reception. In looking at the various ways consumers use products imposed on them by the dominant order, Certeau gives the example of the Latin American indigenous populations who transformed colonial Spanish laws and rituals into their own sets of cultural practices. They subverted them not by rejecting them, but by using them against the will of their creators.[53]

Similarly, then, rock en español, while responding to the model/copy of U.S. and British rock sound and style, also manages to deprogram rock's most time-tested musical codes, thereby confusing the binary logic of center/periphery and local/global that so much of contemporary cultural theory continues to rely on. It marks a radical break with outmoded center/periphery models of unilateral cultural influence and exchange. As Iain Chambers has so eloquently argued, "Anglo-American rock" may operate as a hegemonic force, but that by no means forbids the creation of "conditions for an international sound network that subsequently encouraged a proliferation of margins and emergence of other voices. In the wake of these developments, surprising trajectories can emerge on the musical map, resulting in stories of unexpected influences and strange combinations."[54]

I have argued elsewhere that one way to track these "surprising trajectories" and "strange combinations" is by considering two different Latin/o American processes of cultural translation, exchange, and creation: the Cuban concept of transculturation (as outlined by sociologist Fernando Ortiz) and the Mexican identity category and vernacular strategy of appropriation—*naco*.[55] Unlike "acculturation," transculturation is meant to convey a process of cultural contact and mixture that does not result in cultural loss, but one that produces new cultural forms. As "the process of transition from one culture to another," transculturation yields offspring that, as Ortiz writes in his classic study of tobacco and sugar in Cuba, *Contrapunteo Cubano*, "has something of both parents but always different from each of them."[56]

I want to emphasize the importance of transculturation to discussions of inter-American rock formations because of the way in which Ortiz uses it to call attention to national cultures as contradictory, shifting, and transitory terrains. He writes:

> There was no more important human factor in the evolution of Cuba than these continuous, radical, contrasting geographic transmigrations, economic and social, of the first settlers, this perennial transitory nature of their objectives, and their unstable life in the land where they were living, in perpetual disharmony with the society from which they drew their living. Men, economies, cultures, ambitions were all foreigners here, provisional, changing, "birds of passage" over the country, at its cost, against its wishes, and without its approval.[57]

A devoted scholar of Cuban music and folklore, Ortiz was well aware of transculturation's usefulness to musical analysis; in a 1952 essay he made an explicit connection between transculturation and Cuban music. After all, Ortiz developed transculturation as a means of accounting for Cuban history as the result of a specifically musical relationship—the contrapuntal relationship between the notes and melodies of Africa (tobacco) and the notes and melodies of Europe (sugar). Just as he had tracked the movement of tobacco between different cultural hands and into disparate national spaces, Ortiz tracked the movement of Afro-Cuban dance music from the lower classes to the European royal courts and referred to it as "musical transculturation."[58] As much of a cultural object as tobacco or sugar, music enables its own form of transculturation by moving between different performers, listeners, and audiences, all of whom are potentially located in disparate national, racial, economic, and cultural settings.[59]

The same spirit of cultural contact and transformation across transnational geographies is at work within the cultural practices of the Mexican *naco*. A term conventionally used to derogatorily refer to Mexico's impoverished indigenous population, naco has been traditionally deployed as an insult against Mexico's most economically marginalized and disenfranchised communities, "the lowest of the low." According to Monsiváis, the naco is "alienated, manipulated, economically devastated . . . without education or manners, ugly and insolent, graceless and unnatural . . . confirmation of the inferiority of a lesser country."[60]

But in contemporary Mexican society, naco and all of its class and racial connotations has often been recuperated in some circles as a mode of cultural self-fashioning, a set of aesthetic practices of self-enactment that through collage, recycling, and mockery subvert dominant cultural forms from below, from the depths of the lowest of *los de abajo*. That is, in the world of Mexican popular culture, the emphasis is as much on who the naco is as what the naco does; or even more generally, how cultural objects can be "nacofied" or "nacoized." My use of naco as one means of listening to rock en español follows from critic and performance artist Yareli Arizmendi, who reads the music and performance of "heavy-Mex" pioneer Sergio Arau through a naco lens. She argues that naco entails the bottom-up rewriting and resounding of Western cultural forms through the celebration of Mexican traditional, vernacular, and "low-brow" popular culture. Naco—the Toltec definition of which is "with or of two hearts"—signals "the insertion of elements clearly associated with traditional Mexican culture in spaces regarded and respected as Western [American]," which is precisely what is at work in Arau's music and performance. Arizmendi demonstrates how, in a flagrantly performative naco move, Arau appropriates U.S. rock form and style only to recycle and transform it using traditional Mexican cultural tools, creating a brand of rock performance he calls "guacarock"—Mexican guacamole mixed with U.S. rock.[61]

In the way that nacoization or nacofication uses the "limits" of poor economic conditions to recycle and transfigure dominant cultural forms (using techniques such as irony, parody, camp, and satire) and in the way it enables dispossessed subjects to fashion and perform a self by critiquing dominant culture, it bears much in common with similar subaltern strategies at work in other cultural and national contexts across the Americas, including African American signifying, Cuban *choteo*, Puerto Rican *vacilón*, and perhaps most relevant to my discussion here, Chicano *rasquachismo*.[62] The end result may be best summed up by the subtitle of one of the early albums of Three Souls in My Mind: "100% Rock n Roll Destilado de Rhythm & Blues Hecho en Mexico."

While Arizmendi has used naco to decode and unpack Arau's more recent work as a performance artist and musician (try his 1994 album of "100% heavy-Mex" music, *Mi Frida Sufrida*), the relationship between naco and rock en español might best be approached through the work of his first band, Botellita de Jerez, with whom Arau exerted the greatest stylistic influence on the aesthetic blueprint of Mexican rock to come. Following in the wake of many bands in the 1970s that chose to sing in English, Botellita was one of the first Mexican bands to make it culturally and socially acceptable to sing in Spanish. Together they opened one of Mexico City's first legitimate rock en español clubs, which they playfully named Rockotitlan—"where the Aztecs heard rock." Another 80s band, Nopalica, followed the Botellita tradition of giving rock an Aztec makeover by announcing that their album *Refried Nopals*, which contained the song "Taj Nopal," was broadcast from "Nezahualrock City," a reference to the impoverished, hardcore Neza barrio in Mexico City.

Botellita's self-titled debut introduced the musical hybrid of guacarock, mixing conventional rock styles with references to Mexican popular culture on songs like "Heavy Metro" and, most famously, "Charrock and Roll," which sounds like a traditional Mexican dance song that accidentally ended up on a Chuck Berry playlist, parodying the popular Mexican icon of rural masculinity, *el charro*, by giving him new rock and roll theme music.[63] Botellita's music performs the inverse of the dialogic border aesthetics of *frontera* poet Gina Valdés, who gives us, instead of guacarock or rock *con aguacate*, "English con salsa"; that is, "English refrito, English con sal y limón. . . . English lighted by Oaxacan dawns, English spilled with mezcal from Juchitan, English with a red cactus blooming in its heart."[64] Botellita's charrock and roll aesthetic (or, if you will, "rock refrito" or "salsa con English") of mixing the traditional with the contemporary, the rural with the urban, the American with the Mexican, and the *charro* with the *rockero* is further illustrated on the album's back cover where all three band members pose in tight, studded charro pants and wear charro boot spurs on the back of their tennis shoes.

According to the band's bassist, Armando Vega Gil, "in a certain sense, what we wanted was to recuperate images of lo mexicano, but in combination with other things. What happened with guacarock was the mixture of the avocado with rock and roll, the mixture of Jose Alfredo Jimenez and Jimi Hendrix, of Lola Beltran and Janis Joplin."[65] Taking their cues from Mexican bands of the 1970s and early 1980s such as Three Souls in My Mind, the rock-*indigeno* of Toncho Pilatos, and the rock-*mariachi* of Nahuatl, Botellita put musical and cultural hybridity at the center of their style and sound. Fittingly, they were also the first Mexican band to publicly claim allegiance to the 1940s culture-hopping *pachuco* performances of Mexican comic Tin Tan, who mixed African American street style and *pachuco caló* and "walked, talked, and loved as if he carried a sinfonola brimming over with boogiewoogies and boleros in his head."[66] In a reference to Mexico City's version of the pachuco—the *tarzan*—Botellita thought of themselves as "part pachucos, part tarzanes." Or as Gil once explained it, "we were singing in Spanish not because we wanted to sound like Tin Tan, but because we want to be like Tin Tan."[67]

Hearing America Sing: Cafe Tacuba's Re

The most obvious heir to the guacarock aesthetic is Cafe Tacuba, a group of former graphic design students from the Satelite district outside of Mexico City. On their 1997 album *Avalancha de Exitos*, they even cover Botellita's "Alarmala de Tos," the acclaimed video for which was directed by Arau himself. Cafe Tacuba's music, which claims influences that range from the U.S. techno-industrialism of Nine Inch Nails to the melancholic and melodramatic *ranchera* eroticism of Mexico's Chavela Vargas, mixes traditional acoustic-based musics from across the Americas with rock, avant-garde, classical, and electronica styles solidified abroad. More than any other band currently working in the commercial rock en español scene, Cafe Tacuba— which has performed with a Mexican upright *tololoche* instead of an electric bass, recorded a duet with the Kronos Quartet, and joined Beck on a Spanish version of his "Jackass" for a 2000 Cinco de Mayo celebration—gives us the sound of what Gómez-Peña has argued is the definition of contemporary Mexican identity: "A syncretic blend of Amerindian and European cultures, of pre-industrial traditions and imported technology—immersed in the past but always welcoming the new, the other, the foreign, no matter how dangerous it is."[68]

Although Tacuba has released a significant amount of new work in the past few years—most notably their landmark, Grammy-winning 1999 double album *Reves/Yo Soy* (Reverse/I am) and *Avalancha de Exitos* (Avalanche of Hits), a collection of cover versions of songs from across Latin America that includes their *son juasteco* detropicalization of Juan Luis Guerra's Dominican *bachata* hit "Ojala Que Llueva Café" (I Hope It Rains Coffee)—I will limit my comments to their first major experiment with inter-American musical *mestizaje*—their 1995 album *Re*.[69] Covering a relentlessly eclectic musical ground that spans the entire hemisphere, *Re* travels across a disparate set of audio-spatial coordinates, from Mexican *huapango, ranchera, banda, norteño,* and *mariachi* and U.S. speed metal to Beatle-esque Britpop,

Tex-Mex polka and *conjunto,* New York disco, Jamaican ska, Cuban and Puerto Rican salsa, and California techno-*banda.* In short, they offer the Americas as a shifting map of overlapping sounds, aptly illustrating Gilles Deleuze and Félix Guattari's notion that "music uses anything and sweeps everything away."[70]

According to the band's lead singer (who changes his name almost as fast as the band changes styles), the cultural and identificatory scope of Cafe Tacuba's music reflects the multiple audiotopic spaces of Mexico City: "Where we live in Mexico City, you hear every type of music. You go to a restaurant and they're playing one type of music. You ride public transportation and the conductor is listening to another type. All of this is attacking your mind at all times. So we try to represent this moment in which we live as well as the multicultural society and mestizo country we live in."[71]

Blending as many styles, national terrains, and racial legacies as their music does, Cafe Tacuba makes music that draws its own audiotopic maps, a feverishly migratory music full of traveling spatial stories that question the national ownership of cultural expression. They beg the very same question of cultural belonging that Michel de Certeau has put at the center of his inquiry into the contradictory and crisscrossed spaces of the frontier: "To whom does it belong?" The songs on *Re* operate as heterotopic spaces of musical emergence built on a series of cultural and geographical interactions, exchanges, and encounters. Heard within de Certeau's framework, their music represents "a transgression of the limit, a disobedience of the law of the place, it represents a departure, an attack on a state, the ambition of a conquering power, or the fight of an exile; in any case, the betrayal of an order."[72]

Music operates here in a double movement between local place and transnational space, acting as a sonic *metaphorai*—vehicles of mass musical transit that move between and map places along spatial trajectories.[73] In short, in the way that their music shuttles across disparate inter-American territories and sonorous landscapes, Cafe Tacuba's music gives us the very sound of what García Canclini has described as Latin American modernity's "multitemporal heterogeneity," in that it sonically challenges "the assumption that cultural identity is based on a patrimony, and that this patrimony is based on the occupation of a territory and by collections of works and monuments."[74]

The nationally transgressive and culturally delinquent border-conscious and border-crossing music of Cafe Tacuba must also be theorized and understood within a larger process of Latin America's (re)construction of hegemony in the context of transnational capitalism and the theoretical and universalizing dominance of postmodern discourse.[75] Cafe Tacuba's music evidences how such codes as local and regional music traditions can be recycled and reformed as they become cultural commodities in national and international marketplaces intended for consumption on both sides of the border.

Nowhere is this more evident than on the song "El Aparato," where the sounds of tradition, of the paramodern, meet the sounds of the machine, the sounds of (post)modern technology.[76] The song begins with the acoustic strumming of a *jarana* guitar (typically associated with the *huapango huasteco* musical tradition of Mexico's Atlantic coast), then is slowly surrounded by acoustic bass, acoustic guitar, hand claps, and synthesizers programmed to simulate the sound of indigenous flutes. By the song's end, a chorus of Amerindian vocal chants is overlaid with a line of keyboard patterns (that sound borrowed from an early 1980s video game soundtrack) and the digitized tapping of a Morse code signal. In such a temporally shifting musical web of old and new, where pre-*hispano* ritual singing collides with Morse codes sequenced through digital synthesizers, traditional soundings are neither silenced nor overemphasized, but reconfigured and reimagined in new relationships and new settings. In the context of the three conventional hypotheses of mass and folk cultural collision, Cafe Tacuba's music represents neither the conflict model (whereby mass culture erases folk culture) nor the evolutionary model (whereby the folk disappears during modernization), but rather the additive model, in which folk culture exists alongside mass culture, calling into question the very line that once pretended to keep them apart.[77]

Cafe Tacuba's specific "additive" mix of historical and technological registers is well in line with the aesthetic strategy that García Canclini terms "cultural reconversion." According to Canclini's model, cultural capital is "reconverted" when it is placed in new settings, relationships, and circuits of exchange and imbued with new systems of meaning and interpretation.[78] A key part of cultural reconversion is the broadening of the market to include folkloric goods within commercial sectors, demonstrating that modernization and traditional culture are not mutually exclusive. As the musical reconversion of a song like "El Aparato" shows, modernization does not require the erasure of preindustrial or paramodern cultural formations, but requires instead their very transformation.

Like all of Cafe Tacuba's style-crossing and genre-dissolving music, "El Aparato" represents just one more example of how the practices commonly affiliated with European and U.S. postmodernism (pastiche, quotation, juxtaposition, parody, recycling) are practices that have long been at work within the cultural syncretism and historical juxtapositions of Latin American culture. Gómez-Peña calls it "vernacular postmodernism" and points to the organic, "involuntary" collision of styles, epochs, cultures, and sensibilities found in Cafe Tacuba's hometown of Mexico City, where pre-Colombian ruins stand beside neoclassical Spanish architecture; Indian markets are just down the block from high-tech nightclubs; and Mexican folk music, European classical music, and rock (in both Spanish and English) bump up against each other on the city's radiowaves. Cafe Tacuba's code-switching juxtapositions of rock and mariachi, cumbia and punk, and banda and disco are akin to the TV screen altars, tennis shoe-wearing Aztec *conchero* dancers, and Tijuana velvet paintings that by coupling with the Virgin of Guadelupe with Madonna, Martin Luther King and Cuahatemoc Cardenas, create "a social dialogue" about the relationship between the United States and Mexico.[79]

By employing these vernacular "esthetics of resistance," Cafe Tacuba's music has much in common with the "cannibalist" movement of Brazilian modernists in the 1920s and the filmic *tropicalismo* movement of the 1960s, both of which advocated an "anthropophagic" devouring of foreign cultural products in order to create, through acts of "artistic jujitsu," new "counterutopian" products of their own.[80] Cafe Tacuba's musical cannibalism is particularly reminiscent of that of 60s *tropicalista* architects Caetano Veloso and Gilberto Gil, who, like Mexican rock bands in the 1960s, were greatly influenced by North American countercultural movements and their musical counterparts. Veloso and Gil took cultural anthropophagy to its musical extreme by merging the industrial with the folkloric, the Beatles with Bahia, and the local traditions of carnaval with North American psychedelic rock until, to paraphrase the classic tropicalista manifesto "Chiclete com Banana," Uncle Sam was beating on a frying pan in a Brazilian jam session.[81]

Cafe Tacuba, of course, is not the only rock en español band whose musical cannibalism incorporates traditional Mexican forms into modern rock idioms. As early as 1988, Caifanes landed rock en español's first major hit with "La Negra Tomasa" a rock-meets-cumbia update of a Cuban standard; later, they included mariachi horns and strings into their hit "La Celula Que Explota" (The Cell That Explodes) on their 1991 song "Mare," Maldita Vecindad combined rock with the oral, proto-rap Yucatan storytelling tradition of *bomba*, a form of traditional Yucatan oral practice/storytelling/rhyming, and their 1996 album *Baile de Mascaras* (Dance of Masks)—which featured traditional Mexican masks on its cover—contained a variety of Mexican *foclorico* rhythms and indigenous singing. On Tijuana NO's tribute to the Zapatista revolution of Chiapas, "Transgresores de la Ley" (Transgressors of the Law) the band's percussionist Mahuiztecatl "Teca" Garcia—who is trained in pre-*hispano* instruments—uses conch shells, pre-Columbian flutes, and Andean rhythms as a prelude to a blistering punk declaration of peasant rebellion. Cuca (in collaboration with U.S. punk band Youth Brigade) gives a traditional, acoustic Mexican *son* an electric, heavy metal bath on the 1997 remake of their 1992 hit "El Son del Dolor" (The Son of Pain).[82] And most recently, the nor-tec collective of Tijuana and Ensenada combine techno, house, and ambient beat textures with digital samples of old *banda* and *norteño* albums.

All of this musical reconversion comes together nicely in Cafe Tacuba's music, when in the space of one song an electronic drum machine provides the synthesized beat for a lilting mariachi melody; Amerindian chants compete with the beeps and bleeps of communications technologies; cumbias erupt into disco infernos; and sweaty ska workouts transform into an accordion-driven conjunto. "Instead of the death of traditional cultural forms," argues García Canclini, "we now discover that tradition is in transition, and articulated to modern processes."[83] Cafe Tacuba's music celebrates the sociocultural hybridity of contemporary Latin America, its multi-temporality and multispatiality, and its mix of the pre-conquista with the post-conquista, the folkloric with transnational media and communications networks.

Like so much of rock en español, because Cafe Tacuba's music is simultaneously national and transnational, simultaneously "local" and "global" it becomes an effective site for witnessing the failure of monocultural, monoracial, and monologic national paradigms to understand emergent cultural expression throughout the musical landscapes of the U.S.-Mexico borderlands. Ultimately, it allows us to witness the unique power of popular music to overflow out of the national boundaries that pretend to contain it and, perhaps most of all, forces us to continue to find new ways of hearing the Americas sing.

Notes

A small portion of this essay appeared as "The Aural Border," *Theatre Journal* 52, no. 1 (March/April 2000). Other portions were developed in two articles for the *San Francisco Bay Guardian* as "Viva los Rockeros!: A New Generation of Latinos Has Seen the Future of Rock and Roll—and It's in Spanish," August 9–15, 1995; and "Independence Day: Saúl Hernández and his Jaguares Galvanize Mexico's Rockeros," November 27–December 3, 1996. Special thanks to my friend and editor Tom Tompkins for giving me the column inches to start thinking about this music in public, to Lafitte Benitez for opening industry doors, and to Ruben Guevara and Pacho Paredes for being my educators on both sides of the border. Thanks are also due to José David Saldívar, José Muñoz, George Yúdice, George Lipsitz, and Gayle Wald for their helpful comments on this essay's various drafts, which were presented under multiple guises at the December 1996 meeting of the Modern Language Association in Washington D.C.; the April 1997 "Representing Rock" conference at Duke University; and the May 1997 "Dischord" conference at the University of California, Los Angeles.

1. Jaguares, *El Equilibrio de los Jaguares* (BMG Mexico, 1996).
2. For a detailed exploration of the borderlands as an extended cartography of belonging, see José David Saldívar, *Border Matters: Mapping American Cultural Studies* (Berkeley and Los Angeles: University of California Press, 1997).
3. Indeed, by referring to "U.S. rock" as a whole I am not trying to elide the multiple cross-racial histories at work in rock as a formation; see George Lipsitz, *Rainbow at Midnight: Labor and Culture in the 40s* (Urbana: University of Illinois Press, 1994). And yet while I realize that "U.S. rock" remains a clunky generalization, from the standpoint of Mexican rock culture in general and the Mexican pop marketplace specifically, the term's currency among Mexican bands and music critics makes it useful to my analysis here.
4. Guevara and Monroy in an unpublished interview with the author, 1997. See *Reconquista!: The Latin Rock Invasion* (Rhino/Zyanya, 1997); and Pastilla, *Pastilla* (Aztlan Records, 1996).
5. While most studies of rock's racial histories continue to revolve around the conventional black and white binary, there have been a number of influential and pathbreaking studies on Latino rock that have begun to carve out new discursive spaces within rock scholarship, all of which inspire and deeply inform my comments here. For Latino rock within the United States, see John Storm Roberts, *The Latin Tinge: The*

Impact of Latin American Music on the United States (Tivoli, NY: Original Music, 1985); Steven Loza, *Barrio Rhythm: Mexican American Music in Los Angeles* (Urbana: University of Illinois Press, 1993); George Lipsitz, *Time Passages: Collective Memory and American Popular Culture* (Minneapolis: University of Minnesota Press, 1990); George Lipsitz, *Dangerous Crossroads: Popular Music, Postmodernism, and the Poetics of Place* (New York: Verso, 1994); Curtis Marez, "Brown: The Politics of Working-Class Chicano Style," *Social Text* 48 (fall 1996): 109–132; Dave Marsh, *Fortunate Son: The Best of Dave Marsh* (New York: Random House, 1985); and especially Ruben Guevara, "The View from the 6th Street Bridge: The History of Chicano Rock," in *The First Rock & Roll Confidential*, ed. Dave Marsh and Lee Ballinger (New York: Pantheon Books, 1985). For rock in Latin America, see Pablo Vila, "Rock Nacional and Dictatorship in Argentina," in *Rockin' The Boat: Mass Music and Mass Movements*, ed. Reebee Garofalo (Boston: South End Press, 1992); Thelma G. Duran and Fernando Barrios, eds., *El Grito del Rock Mexicano: Hablan Los Roqueros* (Mexico City: Ediciones Milenio, 1995); Rubén Martínez, *The Other Side: Fault Lines, Guerrilla Saints, and the True Heart of Rock 'n' Roll* (New York: Verso, 1992); and Ed Morales, "Rock Is Dead and Living in Mexico: The Resurrection of La Nueva Onda," *Village Voice: Rock & Roll Quarterly* (winter 1993).

6. El Vez, "Viva La Raza," *G.I. Ay, Ay! Blues* (Big Pop Ltd, 1996).

7. For a lengthy analysis of the different meanings and uses of "Latino cultural citizenship," see William V. Flores and Rina Benmayor, eds., *Latino Cultural Citizenship: Claiming Space, Identity, and Rights* (Boston: Beacon, 1997).

8. For a Latin ska primer, see the *Puro Eskañol* compilation (Aztlan, 1997); and for Chicano *alternativo*, see *Barrios Artistas, Vol. 1* (Mexnut Enterprises, 1997) and *Sociedad = Suciedad* (BYO, 1998).

9. Benedict Anderson, *Imagined Communities* (London: Verso, 1983), 145.

10. I explore the spatial trajectories of music in greater detail in my "Against Easy Listening: Transnational Soundings and Audiotopic Soundings," in *Everynight Life: Dance, Music, and Culture in Latin/o America*, ed. Celeste Fraser Delgado and José Esteban Muñoz (Durham: Duke University Press, 1997).

11. Michel Foucault, "Of Other Spaces," *diacritics* 16.1 (spring 1986): 24–25.

12. Kun, "Against Easy Listening." My definition of audiotopia is admittedly very much a definition-in-progress, and I have yet to fully realize the scope of its implications and meanings. I offer it as a starting point for further discussion and analysis and use it here more along the lines of what James Clifford has called a "translation term," a word "of apparently general application used for comparison in a strategic and contingent way" (cited in Mark Slobin, *Subcultural Sounds: Micromusics of the West* [Hanover, N.H.: Wesleyan University Press, 1993], 12).

13. Mary Louise Pratt, *Imperial Eyes* (New York: Routledge, 1992), 4, 6.

14. Jody Berland, "Angels Dancing: Cultural Technologies and the Production of Space," in *Cultural Studies,* ed. Lawrence Grossberg, Cary Nelson, and Paula Treichler (New York: Routledge, 1992), 39.

15. Lawrence Grossberg, "The Space of Culture, the Power of Space," in *The Post-Colonial Question: Common Skies, Divided Horizons,* ed. Iain Chambers and Lidia Curt (New York: Routledge, 1996), 175.

16. Xavier Albo, "Our Identity Starting from Pluralism in the Base," *boundary 2* 20.3 no. 3 (fall 1993): 18, special issue: "The Postmodernism Debate in Latin America."

17. In linking sound to geography and, more specifically, rock en español to the transnational geographies of the Americas, I am influenced by Gilles Deleuze and Félix Guattari's notion of the musical refrain as a "territorial assemblage." They claim that music assembles, delineates, and marks territories and that "the territorial assemblage continually passes into other assemblages." In their view, territory is a "sonorous landscape" that is not a closed, self-contained entity existing in a singular location, but rather "a place of passage," movement, and flow that "already unleashes something that will surpass it" (Deleuze and Guattari, *A Thousand Plateaus: Capitalism and Schizophrenia,* trans. Brian Massumi [Minneapolis: University of Minnesota Press, 1987], 322–25). For an application of their theories to the "rhythmic planes" and "rhythmical areas" of the Americas, specifically the Caribbean, see Antonio Benítez-Rojo, *The Repeating Island* (Durham: Duke University Press, 1992), 72–79.

18. The history of rock en español in Mexico has yet to be extensively chronicled and my aim in this essay is not to offer a complete historical survey of the genre. For available microhistories of the contemporary scene, see Martínez, *The Other Side;* and Duran and Barrios, *El Grito del Rock Mexicano.* On the early years of Mexican rock, see Eric Zolov, *Refried Elvis: The Rise of the Mexican Counterculture* (Berkeley and Los Angeles: University of California Press, 1999).

19. While it is less readily available than contemporary rock en español, early Mexican rock is becoming easier to find in the United States. See, for example, Los Teen Tops, *20 de Coleccion* (Sony Discos 1996); and Los Apson, *Llegaron Los Apson* (Eco, 1976). Part of a recent resurgence of interest in Mexican *lucha libre* B-movies and wrestler superheroes like Blue Demon and El Santo are two new expansive collections of 60s Mexican rock, *Mexican Rock and Roll Rumble and Psych-Out South of the Border* (Numero Uno, 1997); and *Blue Demon's Mexican Rock and Roll Favorites* (Numero Uno, 1997).

20. Nestór García Canclini, *Hybrid Cultures: Strategies for Entering and Leaving Modernity* (Minneapolis: University of Minnesota Press, 1995), 55.

21. For a complete history of this period, see Zolov, *Refried Elvis.*

22. Octavio Paz, *The Labyrinth of Solitude, and Other Writings* (New York: Grove Press, 1985), 222, 231. See also Banda Bostik, "Tlateloco 68" on *Lo Machin Del . . . Rock*

Hecho en Mexico, Vol. 3 (Discos y Cintas Denver, 1994); and Caifanes, "Antes De Que Nos Olviden" on *El Diablito* (BMG Ariola, 1990).

23. For the continuing relevance of Avándaro to young *rockeros*, see Octavio Hernandez Cruz, "A 25 Años del Festival de Rock y Ruedas en Avándaro," *La Banda Elástica*, October–November 1996, 4.

24. See Three Souls in My Mind, *Three Souls in My Mind* (Discos y Cintas Denver), *Recluso Oriente en Vivo!* (Discos y Cintas Denver), and Three Souls Boogie, *Adicto al Rock 'N' Roll* (Discos y Cintas Denver).

25. Carlos Monsiváis, *Amor Perdido* (Mexico City: Biblioteca Era, 1977), 248.

26. Josh Kun, "Independence Day: Saul Hernandez and his Jaguares Galvanize Mexico's Rockeros," *San Francisco Bay Guardian*, November 27–December 3, 1996, 41.

27. For more on the history and uses of *hoyos fonquis*, see Carlos Monsiváis, "Dancing: The Funky Dive," in *Mexican Postcards* (London: Verso, 1997).

28. Robert Hanke has recently written of MTV Latino (since renamed MTV Latin America) as "a 'Latin' audiovisual space of juxtaposition, tranculturization, and hybridization." He notes that of all MTV international affiliates, the Miami-based MTV Latin America is the only one centered in the United States (Hanke, "Yo Quiero Mi MTV!: Making Music Television for Latin America," in *Mapping the Beat: Popular Music and Contemporary Theory*, ed. Thomas Swiss, John Sloop, and Andrew Herman, ([Malden, MA: Blackwell Publishers, 1997], 220). See also John Lannert, "MTV Latin America Headquarters in Mexico and Argentina Cater to All Tastes in Español," *Billboard*, September 13, 1997; and Leila Cobo-Hanlon, "Heating Up the MTV Latino Connection," *Los Angeles Times*, November 22, 1994, FII.

29. Martínez, *The Other Side*, 149.

30. Duran and Barrios, "Jamie Lopez: Coherencia Es Lo Que Pido a Estas Alturas," in *El Grito del Rock Mexicano*, ed. Duran and Barrios, 34.

31. García Canclini, "Museos, Aeropuertos, y Ventas de Garage (La Identitidad ante el Tratado de Libre Comercio)," lecture presented at the "Borders/Diasporas" conference, University of California, Santa Cruz, April 1992. For a treatment of the border as a "transfrontier metropolis," see Saldívar, *Border Matters;* and Lawrence Herzog, *Where North Meets South: Cities, Space, and Politics on the U.S.-Mexico Border* (Austin: Center Mexican American Studies, University of Texas, 1990).

32. Tijuana NO, "La Esquina del Mundo," *Transgresores de la Ley* (RCA, 1994).

33. David Cortes, "El Rock Mexicano no Está Muerto," in *El Grito del Rock Mexicano*, ed. Duran and Barrios, 72.

34. Guillermo Gómez-Peña, *The New World Border* (San Francisco: City Lights, 1996), 30.

35. See Hamid Naficy, *The Making of Exile Cultures: Iranian Television in Los Angeles* (Minneapolis: University of Minnesota Press, 1993). Mexican news services and television programming are also readily available in the United States, including the creation of CineLatino, a twenty-four-hour cable service featuring uncut Spanish language films from around the world that additionally will sponsor the production of fifty-two new cable films each year. CineLatino is currently being offered in California, Arizona, Nevada, New Mexico, Texas, Florida, and Puerto Rico (Shauna Snow, "The Morning Report: 'Se Habla Español,'" *Los Angeles Times,* December 2, 1994, F1). There is also the case of Televideo, a videotaping service in Northern California that tapes personal messages from Mexican nationals working and living in the United States and sends them to their families in Mexico.

36. Gómez-Peña, *The New World Border,* 6.

37. Ibid., 2, 37, 171.

38. For a critique of Gómez-Peña's treatment of the border, see Claire F. Fox, "Mass Media, Site Specificity, and the U.S.-Mexico Border," in *The Ethnic Eye: Latino Media Arts,* ed. Chon A. Noriega and Ana M. Lopez (Minneapolis: University of Minnesota Press, 1996); and Claire F. Fox, "The Portable Border: Site-Specificity, Art, and the U.S.-Mexico Frontier," *Social Text* 41 (winter 1994): 61–83.

39. This is, however, less the case in the Chicano *alternativo* scene that Flores is part of, which includes women-led bands such as Frequency, Chicle Atomico, Ollin, Quetzal, Marbles, and Announcing Predictions.

40. Maldita Vecindad y los Hijos del Quinto Patio, "Mojado," Gira Pata de Perro (BMG, 1993).

41. Sam Howe Verhover, "Silent Deaths Climbing Steadily as Migrants Cross Mexico Border," *New York Times,* August 24, 1997. Much of the most recent data on border deaths comes from a detailed study done between 1993 and 1996 by Karl Eschbach, Jacqueline Hagan, and Nestor Rodriguez through the University of Houston's Center for Immigration Research. Their findings were gathered into an unpublished working draft in May 1997 titled "Death at the Border."

42. Maldita Vecindad y los Hijos del Quinto Patio, *Maldita Vecindad y los Hijos del Quinto Patio* (BMG Ariola, 1989). The live version is *Gira Pata Del Perro* (BMG Ariola, 1993).

43. El Tri, *En Vivo!!! Y a Todo Calor en el Hollywood Palladium* (WEA Latina, 1991).

44. Roger Rouse, "Mexican Migration and the Social Space of Postmodernism," *Diaspora* 1, no. 1 (spring 1991): 8–23. In his compelling study of families circulating between the border zones of Aguililla, Mexico, and Redwood City, California, Rouse documents what he sees as the creation of "an alternative cartography of social space."

45. Unfortunately, the attention of U.S. MTV to Latin rock continues to be scant and uninformed.

46. Literature surrounding the so-called cultural imperialism thesis is abundant. For example, see Deanna Campbell Robinson, Elizabeth B. Buck, and Marlene Cuthbert, eds., *Music at the Margins: Popular Music and Global Cultural Diversity* (London: Sage, 1991); Timothy D. Taylor, *Global Pop: World Music, World Markets* (New York: Routledge, 1997); George Lipsitz, *Dangerous Crossroads;* Reebee Garofalo, "Introduction" and "Understanding Mega-Events," in *Rockin' the Boat,* ed. Garafalo; and Andrew Goodwin and Joe Gore, "World Beat and the Cultural Imperialism Debate," in *Sounding Off: Music As Subversion / Resistance / Revolution,* ed. Ron Sakolsky and Fred Wei-Han Ho (New York: Autonomedia, 1995).

47. Roger Wallis and Krister Malm, *Big Sounds from Small Peoples: The Music Industry in Small Countries* (New York: Pendragon, 1984), 269–303.

48. Nelly Richard, "The Cultural Periphery and Postmodern Decentering: Latin America's Reconversion of Borders," in *Rethinking Borders,* ed. John C. Welchman (Minneapolis: University of Minnesota Press, 1996), 73.

49. See Frances R. Aparicio, "On Sub-Versive Signifiers: Tropicalizing Language in the United States," in *Tropicalizations: Transcultural Representations of Latinidad,* ed. Frances R. Aparicio (Hanover, N.H.: University Press of New England, 1997), 202.

50. Nelly Richard, "Cultural Peripheries: Latin America and Postmodernist De-Centering," *boundary 2* 20, no. 3 (fall 1993): 158, special issue: "The Postmodernism Debate in Latin America."

51. Los Apson, *Por eso estamos como estamos* (Eco, catalog no. 388).

52. Monsiváis, *Amor Perdido.*

53. Michel de Certeau, *The Practice of Everyday Life* (Berkeley and Los Angeles: University of California Press, 1984), xvii. For a similar critique based on the literary strategies of Peruvian writer José María Arguedas, see Anibal Quijano, "Modernity, Identity, and Utopia in Latin America," *boundary 2* 20, no. 3 (fall 1993): 152–53, special issue: "The Postmodernism Debate in Latin America."

54. Iain Chambers, *Migrancy, Culture, Identity* (New York: Routledge, 1994), 77.

55. Kun, "Against Easy Listening."

56. Fernando Ortiz, *Cuban Counterpoint: Tobacco and Sugar,* trans. Harriet de Onís (Durham: Duke University Press, 1995), 103. Originally published as *Contrapunteo Cubano del Tobaco y el Azúcar* (Havana: J. Montero, 1940).

57. Ibid., 101.

58. Fernando Ortiz, "La Transculturacion Blanca de Los Tambores Negros," *Archivos Venezolanos de Folklore I,* 2 (1952): 235–65. See also Vernon Boggs, "Musical Transculturation: From Afro-Cuban to Afro-Cubanization," *Popular Music and Society* 15, no. 4 (winter 1991): 76.

59. In their study of international pop music culture, Wallis and Malm also propose transculturation as a musical process, yet they curiously do so with no reference to Ortiz. They propose transculturation as the fourth pattern of musical interaction between "big countries" and "small countries," which typically came about in 1970 when transnational corporations began to make their presence felt on the world market. While they imbue transculturation with qualities well in line with Oritz's formulation—it produces music out of a two-way pattern of exchange—Wallis and Malm can only conceive of transculturation as an effect of transnational capitalism and equate it with what they call "transnationalized culture." As the music I discuss makes clear, transculturation may indeed happen within global capitalism. But as Ortiz's work effectively demonstrates, its definition is certainly not contingent on global capitalism, and as a complex intercultural and historical process it goes far beyond a market-produced transnationalized culture.

60. Monsiváis, *Mexican Postcards*, 52–53.

61. Yareli Arizmendi, "What Ever Happened to the Sleepy Mexican? One Way to Be a Contemporary Mexican in a Changing World Order," *TDR* 38 (spring 1994): 107.

62. On *rasquachismo*, see Tomas Ybarra-Frausto, "Rasquachismo: A Chicano Sensibility," in *Chicano Art: Resistance and Affirmation, 1965–1985*, Richard Griswald del Casillo, a catalog for an exhibit at Teresa McKenna, and Yvonne Yorbro-Bejarano (Tucson: University of Arizona Press, 1993). On signifying, see Henry Louis Gates Jr., *The Signifying Monkey: A Theory of African-American Literary Criticism* (New York: Oxford University Press, 1988). On *choteo*, see José Esteban Muñoz, "Choteo/Camp Style Politics: Carmelita Tropicana's Performance of Self-Enactment," in *Women & Performance: A Journal of Feminist Theory*, 7.2–8.1, issue 14–15, special issue: "New Hybrid Identities: Performing Race, Gender, Nation, Sexuality." On *vacilón*, see Juan Flores and George Yúdice, "Living Borders/Buscando America: Languages of Latino Self-Formation," in *Divided Borders: Essays on Puerto Rican Identity*, ed. Juan Flores (Houston: Arte Publico Press, 1993).

63. Botellita de Jerez, *Botellita de Jerez* (Polygram Discos, 1987).

64. Gina Valdés, "English con Salsa," in *Cool Salsa: Bilingual Poems on Growing Up Latino in the United States*, ed. Lori M. Carson (New York: Fawcett Juniper, 1995), 4–5.

65. Duran and Barrios, "Botellita de Jerez: Rock Con Aguacate," in *El Grito del Rock Mexicano*, ed. Duran and Barrios, 14.

66. Monsiváis, *Mexican Postcards*, 106.

67. Duran and Barrios, "Botellita de Jerez" 14.

68. Guillermo Gómez-Peña, *Warrior for Gringostroika* (Minnesota: Graywolf Press, 1993), 18.

69. Cafe Tacuba, *Re* (WEA, 1995).

70. Deleuze and Guattari, *A Thousand Plateaus*, 349.

71. Josh Kun, "Viva Los Rockeros! A New Generation of Latinos Has Seen the Future of Rock and Roll—and It's in Spanish," *San Francisco Bay Guardian*, August 9–15, 1995, 128.

72. de Certeau, *The Practice of Everyday Life,* 127–29.

73. Ibid.

74. Nestor García Canclini, "Cultural Reconversion," in *On Edge: The Crisis of Contemporary Latin American Culture,* ed. George Yúdice, Jean Franco, and Juan Flores (Minneapolis: University of Minnesota Press, 1992), 32.

75. See George Yúdice, "Postmodernity and Transnational Capital in Latin America," in *On Edge,* ed. Yúdice et al.

76. I use the term "paramodern" following Ella Shohat and Robert Stam's lead in *Unthinking Eurocentrism: Multiculturalism and the Media* (New York: Routledge, 1994), because the term "premodern" leaves the problematic conception of modernity as telos intact.

77. See Robinson, Buck, and Cuthbert, *Music at the Margins,* 106.

78. Nestor García Canclini, "Cultural Reconversion," in *On Edge: The Crisis of Contemporary Latin American Culture,* ed. George Yúdice, Jean Franco, and Juan Flores (Minneapolis: University of Minnesota Press, 1992).

79. Guillermo Gómez-Peña and Coco Fusco, "Bilingualism, Biculturalism, and Borders," in *English Is Broken Here: Notes on Cultural Fusion in the Americas,* ed. Coco Fusco (New York: The New Press, 1995), 154–55; and Gómez-Peña, *Warrior for Gringostroika,* 18.

80. Shohat and Stam, *Unthinking Eurocentrism,* 302–10. See also Celeste Olalquiaga, *Megalopolis: Contemporary Cultural Sensibilities* (Minneapolis: University of Minnesota Press, 1992); and Robert Stam, *Subversive Pleasures: Bakhtin, Cultural Criticism, and Film* (Baltimore: Johns Hopkins University Press, 1989).

81. For an excellent investigation of *tropicalismo,* particularly its overlaps with rock en español's development in Mexico, see Christopher Dunn's wonderful interview with Veloso, "The Tropicalista Rebellion: A Conversation with Caetano Veloso," *Transition: An International Review* 6, no. 2 (1996).

82. See Caifanes, *Caifanes* (BMG, 1993); Maldita Vecindad y Los Hijos del Quinto Patio, *El Circo* (BMG, 1991) and *Baile de Mascaras* (BMG, 1996); Tijuana NO, *Transgresores de la Ley* (BMG, 1994); and Cuca and Youth Brigade, "El Son del Dolor" on *Silencio = Muerte: Red, Hot, & Latin* (HOLA, 1997). For more on nor-tec, visit www.milrecords.com; and see Josh Kun, "New Tijuana Moods: Re-Inventing the Border with Nor-Tec and Julieta Venegas," *LA Weekly,* September 29, 2000.

83. García Canclini, "Cultural Reconversion," 31.

DESIRES / AFFECTS

About once each semester I have an encounter with one of my students that is awkward in a way that somehow seems different from the more common, even *reassuringly* awkward, student-teacher encounters that take place when the lecture is over. If the "reassuringly awkward" encounters are relatively frequent, promising that things haven't gotten any cozier than they need to be, these other encounters have a dimension that sets them apart; hesitant, a bit clumsy in manner, the students who initiate them speak with an embarrassed formality, as if their tongue were on loan. Perhaps because I've come to recognize the symptoms, it's never long before I understand the scene before me.

If with a degree of certainty I believed that my past as a member of the 80s rock band the Del Fuegos could no longer be arrived at with clues from the local cut-out bin, the students in these awkward encounters change all that with a question that gives the moment's embarrassed beginnings a partial explanation: "Did you ever play in a band?" And I say *partial* explanation because I better understand their embarrassment when, almost invariably, a second question arrives: "What's with that fur coat?" And that's the query that seems to reassign the "awkward" aspect of our encounter, leaving me, the teacher, at what feels a momentary disadvantage, as if I'd been caught at something for which the appropriate lie can't immediately be found and the truth—"I was a great fan of Brian Jones and, as such, often found myself shopping for clothes in the teen girls' section of the store, where lace shirts and fur coats can be found in the appropriate styles and sizes"—seems a bit cumbersome.

My relationship with this fur coat, which, in two respects, no longer *fits* me (a coat worn for the photo shoot that produced the cover shot of my former band's third album), is here the specific concern that will lead to some more general questions and observations regarding tendencies within cultural studies that impact on popular music studies. In speaking with a student who has dug up that album (although certainly not always to find that they "dig" it) and who wonders at the odd disparity between my past and my present incarnations—it's this shift, it seems initially, that brings on the mutual embarrassments, as if my former self had been *walked in on,* and the student, in a reciprocal action, was caught catching me—I feel a terrific need to explain, almost *subdue,* something in that image of me with hair past my shoulders, wearing a white fur coat. But my efforts at such control usually result in a confused dissertation that merely circles, spilling quantities of somewhat random anecdotes, never arriving, obsessive; almost an enactment of that same drive to narrate one's past that made the ancient mariner a bit overbearing on his audience. My response, in short, is not so much cool as curiously desperate and, as such, *out of place.*[1]

What interests me here is this feeling that something is happening in the album-jacket image that requires an immediate explanation from me. That my response is to feel "out of place" is not surprising; the contrast between the former vocation and that of the present is striking, but this reaction is not altogether as simple as a moment of conflicting identities. Whatever the nature of the disruption, the scene I find myself wanting to *restabilize* through explanation is a pedagogic one. Something about the fur coat photograph makes that student-teacher encounter awkward for me. In the end, I have to question if the students wondering about this image ever really did feel embarrassed or, instead, if I actually saw their questions coming from a distance and projected my own discomfort onto them. Given the agitation behind my efforts to explain the image, an agitation I've gone so far as to characterize as a curious desperation, whose discomfort did I recognize initially? And what is the nature of this discomfort? What is behind this fur coat image that disrupts the pedagogic scene?

Popular Music Culture and the Image Experience

In analyzing the manifold experiences that mark one's personal engagement with popular music culture, I often find myself interested more in image experiences than in music experiences. This is not to suggest that the two registers aren't finally bound in a complex weave. By way of example, I know the Rolling Stones's material well, but when I recall for myself the impact they had on me I often return to experiences not with music but with pictures. For instance, the 1974 tour returns to me in photographs from an issue of *Life* magazine: I see Mick Jagger's lace-up pants. When these images first arrived on the doorstep my response was unequivocal: "*That* is what I want to be." If at the elementary-school level (which I was at the time) the most common coming-of-age narratives suggested that stepping into father's shoes made sense for a boy, I knew that I'd rather get into Mick Jagger's pants (a point I phrase thus in order to emphasize the slippage between identification as wanting-to-be and identification as wanting-to-have, a matter taken up later in the essay). I spent no small amount of time studying these photographs, dreaming a transformation in front of the mirror, against all odds modeling my image on his. I am confident in believing that I'm not alone in my practices. The importance and intensity of such scenes, I think, has to do with the fact that they are so terrifically banal, that in experiencing popular music many court the exceptional and exceed the "norm" in the mundane.[2] One main reason the experience of popular music *is* exceptional, I think, has to do with the degree to which it is an experience so often accompanied by daydreaming, by fantasy, by excursions, or by detours like the one I describe above.

If we agree that fantasy is indeed a central component of the popular music experience, then it follows that the study of popular music will profit from some study of fantasy as it relates to that experience. And, indeed, fantasy has been a recurring issue. In an essay on dance, Angela McRobbie offers one example of how fantasy has entered the frame of cultural studies, which, in turn, has had an enormous impact on popular music studies and its related areas: "As a purveyor of fantasy, dance has also addressed areas of absolute privacy and personal intimacy, especially important for women and girls. And there is I think a case which can be made for forms of fantasy, daydreaming, and 'abandon' to be interpreted as part of a strategy of resistance or opposition; that is, as marking out one of those areas which cannot be totally colonised."[3] While there is a lot going on in this passage, what interests me here is the manner in which fantasy is regarded as an area of "absolute privacy," an area which "cannot be totally colonized." Rather than understanding fantasy as something that, quite commonly, has been *constructed* or *represented* as an area of "absolute privacy," McRobbie's account suggests that fantasy simply *is* a matter of "absolute privacy." There are, I believe, reasons for this.

Cultural studies has been both celebrated and castigated for its capacity to demarcate, stubbornly at times, areas of resistance. Indeed, in its various efforts to complicate one-dimensional representations of the popular culture audience as passive consumers, cultural studies has come to be identified with such key terms as resistance and empowerment. The passive audience often becomes a surprisingly canny, creative audience that makes meanings with popular cultural artifacts; artifacts that, it seems, function like palimpsests on which oppositional messages can be written.[4] Consistent with this cultural studies interest in resistance, areas that "cannot be totally colonized" become areas of crucial importance. Thus, if fantasy is commonly represented as a "private" area that stands beyond the reach of "colonizing" powers, within cultural studies one sometimes locates efforts to *preserve* rather than critically dismantle such unsatisfactory representations of fantasy. McRobbie's account exemplifies this.

While recognizing that the turn of cultural studies toward issues of resistance and empowerment has done much to complicate crude pictures of popular culture and the experiences of its heterogeneous audiences, my interest here is in looking at some of the negative consequences attached to this otherwise productive development. This is to say, I attend to some of these negative consequences recognizing that a scholarly interest in resistance, the effects of which I scrutinize, has produced the very work that informs, even allows, my present investigation. Nonetheless, McRobbie's description of the "private" realm of fantasy embodies one of the "negative consequences" to which I refer and on which I will focus. Jacqueline Rose's *States of Fantasy* argues that insistence on the autonomy or partial autonomy of fantasy life will lead to a mistaken conception of how power (in her example, state power) is concretized.[5] I believe that a critical approach to popular music culture is similarly weakened when fantasy is not accepted as both central to the experience of popular music *and* profoundly social in ways that leave no room to understanding it as "private."

It is my argument that the social/public dimension of fantasy in popular music culture might be better addressed if the identifications that take place between fans and performers, central to the fantasy life of the fan, are investigated with an eye toward the possibility that such identifications enact complicated mergers across social lines and between social bodies. Among the various celebrations of resistance and empowerment that emphasize the fan's autonomy or mastery—sometimes by arguing fantasy to be "private," sometimes by arguing that fans do not fantasize about *being* the performers with whom they identify—there is a tendency to disallow the complexity of the networks of fan identifications complexities. Henry Jenkins offers an example of the manner in which a focus on empowerment sometimes results in an emphasis on the sovereign powers of the fan: "Fans actively assert their mastery over the mass-produced texts which provided the raw materials for their own cultural productions and the basis for their social interactions."[6] Problems emerge when the possibility of resistance is made out to be one and the same with the possibility of *mastery*. In the case of popular music studies—and, I think, particularly of the music culture scholarship indebted to cultural studies—a fan's identification with a performer, frequently involving something closer to subordination than to mastery, is often denied any substantial critical investigation.[7] Dick Hebdige's distinction between subordination and resistance offers a classic example of the tendency that, I believe, hinders a proper investigation of identification: " 'Humble objects' can be magically appropriated; stolen by subordinate groups and made to carry 'secret' meanings: meanings which express, in code, a form of resistance to the order which guarantees their continued subordination."[8]

In relation to my identifications with rock heroes, I have a particular interest in questioning whether these identifications might mask desires that I cannot examine *unless* identification and its curious subordinations are allowed into the critical frame. More particularly, a study of fan identifications might in fact encourage a more thoroughgoing investigation of the homosocial dimension of popular music culture and the fan experience (again, wanting to be a hero and wanting to get into a hero's pants are perhaps related). Popular music culture is the site of sexual play that is continually surprising in its complexities; there is nothing new in saying this, of course. But there are trends in popular music studies that suggest we need to keep saying it, to ourselves and to others.

Finally, I'm arguing that there's something queer going on in the experience of rock music, and I'd extend this to popular music in general, that contributes enormously to its social significance. Further, I'm isolating an important connection between this "something queer" in popular music culture and the image relations, played out primarily as identifications, that underpin the fan experience. I began this essay by introducing a classroom scene in which a student—this is how I understood the scene in hindsight, at least—witnesses me acting out an identification (having a relationship with Brian Jones; trying, in some sense, to be him). In failing to grasp the complexities of identification, I ultimately failed to understand the nature of my embarrassment, which, importantly, I tried to "subdue" through explanation, through an outpouring of words. Later I will argue that this outpouring of words is in fact a common reaction to such an "embarrassment."

In many respects, this essay is an effort to analyze the album jacket encounter and derive from it some general points.[9] I work out from the assumption that subjectivity is something like a *process*, intimately bound with, even structured on, identification. If in cultural studies one often encounters the residual effects of an emphasis on the "mastery" of the fan, among these effects is a recurring picture of the fan as one who is, for lack of a better word, *whole*. Against this I argue that a subjectivity founded on identification is a messy affair; that it is not clean and not a matter to be discussed with recourse to the language of "mastery." The fan must be considered a complex character.

While scholars often claim fan status for themselves, and fan culture is dealt with regularly in cultural studies, the fan, amidst the flurry, seems too often to lie there quite still and quite flat. The intersubjective relationships on which fan identity hinges, often mediated by and through images, remains largely unexplored. Perhaps in part because of this failure to explore subjectivity as intersubjectivity, the fan scene often appears to be surprisingly free of the antagonisms of forbidden desires and aggressivity—that is, *cleansed*.[10] An important opposition, not terribly new, often structures this cleansed representation: the *fan*, healthy, stands apart from the *fanatic*. In *Sound Effects*, Simon Frith betrays a reliance on this opposition: "Some people are deviant not in the way they value music but in the way they consume it. They are fanatics, and their life revolves around an idol to the extent of imitation, sexual pursuit, a compulsive flaunting of their idolatry."[11] Importantly, this fanatic is presented as prone to "imitation," a deviant *consumer*, though not of music but images or "idols." I will take Frith's comments as a kind of backdrop here for my discussion of identification.

Popular Music Studies: Iconophobia,
or, Understanding the Fear of Identification

Although it is through the figure of the fan that I believe my relation to the album cover in question needs to be explained—the person I see in that fur coat is a fan constructing a sense of self through a rather obvious identification *with* and imitation *of* his rock heroes—I believe this fan/fanatic opposition must be cast aside if I am to make any progress in understanding such fan identifications. Put simply, identification involves the very act of imitation that Frith associates with the fanatic. Following his model, identification is itself pathologized through the mobilization of the fan/fanatic opposition: the fan is in possession of himself or herself while the fanatic loses himself or herself in an identification. The language of "mastery" looms up again in this distinction between the fan and the fanatic—and this despite the paradoxical fact that for Frith identification is a concept central to the experience of pop music. In another essay, he argues thus: "The pleasure that pop music produces is a pleasure of identification—with the music we like, with the performers of that music, with the other people who like it."[12] However, and this is more to my point, his model of identification is quickly qualified: "People do not idolize singers because they wish to be them but because these singers seem able, somehow, to make available their own feelings—it is as if we get to know ourselves via the music."[13] And further: "At a heavy metal concert you can certainly see the audience absorbed in the music; yet for all the air-guitar playing they are not fantasizing being up on stage."[14]

I believe Frith's remarks are lasting symptoms of the privileged place cultural studies gives to resistance and audience/fan canniness. His notion of identification is in tension with one more plainly grounded in psychoanalytic thought, which, following Freud, involves a "wanting to be," an imitation *of* that with which one identifies. In order to make sense of what might seem a curious denial on Frith's part, one might understand his approach as involving an effort to protect the fan as an actor, as an agent *in possession* of himself or herself. Again, this is a protection of a certain "mastery" on the part of the consumer. The fanatic, whom I've referred to as a "deviant consumer," is as a consumer one who possesses, but who in a sense makes the wrong market choices, has the wrong possessions, and is finally possessed by others, by idols (there are, of course, echoes of Marx in this, particularly as the fetish/"idol" leads to a kind of alienation). Frith's effort to protect the music fan's integrity/identity takes the form of a refusal to contemplate the degree to which the fan's identity might hinge on identifications, imitative in nature, such as that with the performer. Again, this refusal seems bound, in part, to an effort to protect the advances made, for example, in British cultural studies—in particular those that have challenged the idea of the mass consumer as a kind of "dupe."

In relation to this last point, I find myself in sympathy with Frith's gesture. But, at the same time, losses accrue with this understanding of the fan experience, an understanding that finally implies that a shared ground exists between the fan who (almost heroically) refused wanting "to be" the performer and the creative consumer who "writes" against the grain of the mass cultural artifact, who is not "duped." As long as these two models of consumer practice are attributed to the *empowered* consumer, the consumer *in possession* of himself or herself, then the fan/fanatic opposition will be perpetuated. And such an opposition certainly results in failures to engage critically with the complex interrelationships that *are* the identifications central to the experience of popular music. Considering that there might be cases in which already marginalized subjects might find the *possibility* of agency in identification, this negative coding of identification might very well hinder studies of empowerment, might even have marginalizing effects.

Tending to the complexities of fan identifications is one of the most important ways in which movements across formations, particularly between fans and performers, might be theoretically elaborated. Identification cannot simply be seen as central to the experience of popular music, it must also be seen as having no *intrinsic* connection to either empowerment or disempowerment, offering instead the possibility of both. In fact, as a kind of interpretive frame, the empowerment/disempowerment model sometimes seems to leave little room for ambivalence. The cultural studies discussion of empowerment and resistance is too often a one-dimensional discourse that obscures the presence of its "other"—that is, subordination. But given the fact that ambivalence marks the fan experience, making it never simply a matter of empowerment or disempowerment, one-sided representations of that experience are forever shot through with that which they attempt to conceal.[15] The fact of subordination leaks through the idealism of the fan-as-textual-poacher narrative. Rather than deny such subordination its possibilities must be minded; it must be studied rather than simply revealed in the form of a leakage.

I believe it worth restating the case, albeit in a slightly different fashion. Perhaps, for Frith and others, a model of identification indebted to psycho-analytic thinking sometimes gives identification too important a place in relation to subject formation, particularly because it implies that the individual subject is constituted from *without,* is the product of his or her identifications with "others." In *The Ego and the Id,* Freud suggests that identifications have a "great share in the form taken by the ego," that they in fact determine the character of the ego.[16] Accepting that subject formation actually *requires* identification's mimetic relation to others, one might say that subjecthood itself involves what for Frith is already a deviant form of consumption; constructing a sense of self thus becomes fanaticism as Frith describes it. I am not out to suggest that Frith is exceptional in putting forward the fan/fanatic opposition that I have isolated in his work. The self/other distinction that Frith's fanatic fails to uphold in his/her imitative idol worship (where Frith's *fan* does not fail) is present in much work within cultural studies, particularly that influenced by subcultural studies. In accounts that describe the artifacts of mass culture losing their power once the "mastery" of the "creative consumer" holds sway, one sees powerful images of self-contained, self-possessed subjects.[17] In a curious turn, these images become something like yet another representation of the unique and coherent self, a self, again, in possession *of* itself, a self altogether different from that constituted by the mimetic processes of identification, which is to say, different from the self constituted in and through an introjection of the other.[18]

Although we can be sympathetic with the effort to protect the agency of the consumer, we have to question what is at stake in this portrayal of identification, to see what is lost when identification becomes a model of *dis*empowerment. How, I ask, might the consequences of the fan/fanatic opposition be understood? A cursory elaboration of identification as Freud presents it marks one place to begin. Using his work, we can recast identification as that which is not a thing of fanaticism but a process required for subject formation, for group formation, and certainly a process central to the fan experience.

Freud and His Fans

In *Group Psychology and the Analysis of the Ego,* Freud provides a model of identification that is useful in relation to the argument being made here. It is a model that might allow *and* encourage an elaboration of the complexities inherent in the two primary fan relationships, that which Freud refers to as the relationship "between a performer and a delighted listener,"[19] and that *between* group members, produced through a mutual identification. Regarding the latter, Freud has this to say:

> Think of the troop of women and girls, all of them in love in an enthusiastically sentimental way, who crowd round a singer or pianist after his performance. It would certainly be easy for each of them to be jealous of the rest; but, in the face of their numbers and the consequent impossibility of their reaching the aim of their love, they renounce it, and, instead of pulling out one another's hair, they act united as a group, do homage to the hero of the occasion with their common actions, and would probably be glad to have a share of *his* flowing locks. Originally rivals, they have succeeded in identifying themselves with one another by means of a similar love for the same object.[20]

What might immediately strike one in this example of group identification, in which rivals come to identify with one another and jealousies are replaced by group feeling (apart, perhaps, from the fact of Freud's gender assignments), is that a renunciation of "the aim of their love" precedes that identification between group members that fosters group coherence. Importantly, the passage suggests that this renunciation is not the renunciation of a love object but of the *aim* of the love for that object. The initial love becomes something like an aim-inhibited love, an approximation of a love that can't be satisfied directly. What is unclear, however, is the relationship between the individual group member and the love object after the fact of aim inhibition; the love for the object continues—clearly, as Freud argues, it allows that identification between group members required for group coherence—but it is, in some way, redirected. Paradoxically, it is redirected but still arrives at the same object, is renounced but kept alive. What then allows this?

In my reading of this passage, this paradox might be explained by positing an earlier identification, one preceding that between group members, an identification that both encourages the identification between group members and, at the same time, allows a continuance of the love for the object. This first identification would be with the performer, the one with whom love cannot be fulfilled. As Lacan suggests, "What one cannot keep outside, one always keeps an image of inside. Identification with the object of love is as simple as that."[21] The renunciation that Freud describes might thus be understood as involving an identification of this order: bringing an image of the performer, whom "one cannot keep outside" as love object, inside. In this way, what I am suggesting is that the two primary fan relationships— between fan and performer and between fans—are intimately bound, the one preceding the other in a sequence of identifications. In part, what the fans love in one another is the performer that each keeps inside through the mechanisms of identification. Although diffused, desire is thus sustained through the identification between fans.

Lacan's statement regarding identification with a love object is in many respects indebted to Freud's essay "Mourning and Melancholia," in which identification functions as a means with which to manage losses, as a way of bringing the unattainable/lost object into the ego and, in a sense, allowing its preservation.[22] This can be understood as a process through which the ego deforms itself, assumes the shape of the lost object so as to counterbalance the loss of that object, becoming, through a psychic function mimetic in nature, the unavailable love object for the id. Identification, which Freud claims may be the "sole condition under which the id can give up its objects,"[23] thus manages such losses and, perhaps more important for my argument, those renunciations that are required for the formation and sustained coherence of groups. In this reading, group formation is made possible only through identification. Thus, rather than see fan groups as different in character from fanatics, who, as Frith suggests, are imitative, it might be that the very thing binding these fan groups is what Frith describes as a "fanaticism."

Diana Fuss makes a point that further describes the social function of identification: "Identification is the mechanism Freud summons to keep desire from overflowing its socially sanctioned borders."[24] Understood this way, beneath an identification might lurk an illicit desire. A thing of ambivalence, identification is thus connected both to the policing of illicit desires *and* their sustenance. Building out from Freud's example above, a desire for the performer that is not inhibited in its aim is a threat to the group and, as such, is illicit. Thus one might say that, contrary to Frith, for Freud the fanatic is more probably the one who *fails* to identify "appropriately" at the moment when an illicit desire is felt, a desire that might otherwise be made "socially acceptable" through its transformation into an identification. Following this, it is in understanding the two stages of group identifications that one might better understand, for instance, how an illicit homosexual desire becomes a homosocial bond, socially acceptable *and,* following Freud, required for group formation (a pattern of identifications that must, *at least,* be entertained as perhaps central to the fan experience).

Not surprisingly, Freud's example of the libidinal connection between the female fans and the male performer is not supplemented with an example of identification's role in same-sex fan/performer relationships. Nonetheless, Freud provides the tools to consider and analyze such relations.[25] However, I must again acknowledge that the analysis his tools allows (in particular, of the homosocial/homosexual circuit) faces an impossible blockade in Frith's fan/fanatic opposition that pathologizes identification. One can begin to understand that just such an opposition might be carrying (even if inadvertently) a socially inscribed, homophobically charged denial. In some sense, when Frith insists that the audience members do not want to be or to have (either sexually or as possession) the performer (except in the case of fanatics), this, if one is to accept Freud's scene as credible, is an inadvertent *enactment* of the law that polices desires rather than a critical understanding of fan relations and their possible vicissitudes; it shuts down any thought of the illicit as perhaps being a stop along the way to the "normal." Frith thus contributes to the cleansing effect of which I've spoken. Rather than discussing the manner in which illicit desire, albeit in an aim-inhibited (and thus *preserved*) form, is central to group coherence, Frith closes down the possibility of such a discussion. This finally disallows an investigation of group formation as involving both the inhibition of illicit desires and their continuance in a socially acceptable form (which, I would add, is also their continuance in a *haunting* form). What is lost is any conception of the relation between desire and identification, particularly as it opens a space to better understand the homosocial and/or homosexual character of popular music culture. Popular music culture's homosocial dimension might, in fact, partially explain the nature of fan groups and the pleasures provided by a participation in them.

Reading the Fan Male

In a recent look through an old box of my band's press clippings, fan letters, radio reports, and other items, I read a piece of fan mail that reminded me of the curious nature of the intimacy that can arise between the fan and the performer. The letter, written in one hand but signed with the names of two college students, both members of a fraternity at a large Boston university, was pretty usual fare. They voiced their approval of the band in unequivocal terms, jokingly suggesting that we play their frat house, a suggestion followed by a kind of crescendo of praise that let us know that the joke was not really a joke but an idea that had played on their imaginations with some persistence. But then, as if this crescendo had turned up the heat more than they had planned, the letter then took a quick turn. The collaborators abruptly felt the need to cool the air, it seems, demanding, in a moment that was difficult *not* to acknowledge as what Freud calls a "negation," that they weren't "homos or anything."[26]

This "crescendo of praise" involves an expression of feelings between males—between the letter writers themselves and between the letter writers and the band members—that again suggests that the experience of popular music is acted out across a complex affective network, which, in turn, has a complex sexual dimension.[27] As a same-sex intimacy, this gift of praise clearly brings the letter's authors up against what is felt to be the far edge of the homosocial. One can explain their clear, committed expression of homophobia as a last line of defense before the homosocial and the homosexual lose their distinct border markings, before the two blur into one. This is to say, the homophobic response perhaps arrives when the homosexual nature of the homosocial bond becomes too keenly felt. Of course, such expressions of homophobia, social declarations with very real effects on real people, create a rather massive *sound barrier* (the wall of name-calling) between the homosocial and homosexual, effectively producing a set of border markings that cannot be produced once and for all because they are illusory, but still must be established forever anew by a repeated name-calling, by repeated homophobic declarations. And, of course, it is often at those sites where the homosocial bond is most intense that expressions of homophobia are voiced most vociferously. The sound barrier is the *erection* produced (as reaction) by what might be called an excessive homosociality. Put another way, the high point of the homosocial is, in this case, a gesture of homophobia that masks the fact of desire. Importantly, homosociality involves identifications, a kind of image relations, and is reacted to (with homophobic declarations) by shifting to the register of language.

The homosocial dimension of fan relations needs to be investigated over the din of this sound barrier. The homophobic in popular music culture has been recognized—so, too, must the homosocial. Accepting that a sound barrier is produced in an attempt to assert a sharp difference between the homosocial and the homosexual, one might, as Fuss suggests, first accept that desire and identification are forever caught up in one another. The love preserved as it is inhibited/renounced through identification returns to haunt the scene; the possibility of a strict division between the homosocial and the homosexual, even with the declarations, the noises that create the sound barrier, is impossible.[28]

What I've been referring to here as a homophobic reaction to an intense, threatening homosociality, however, might be understood in another way. As Fuss suggests, contra Freud, same-sex identification may foment homosexual desire rather than transform it into what in *Group Psychology and the Analysis of the Ego* Freud discusses as a kind of non-libidinous libido.[29] Understood this way, the preservation of an illicit desire through identification fails to preserve desire in a *nonlibidinous* form, instead allowing, even spurring on, that illicit desire that has already been legislated against. Highlighting this point might be one way of emphasizing the haunting, the return of a supposedly renounced love object. Further, the homophobic response, that erection of a sound barrier, might be more surely understood as a reaction to the presence of a keenly felt desire that spills over both sides of the homosocial/homosexual line.

Taken all together, homophobia might be understood as a specific strain of the fear of identification with an *other*, or, more generally, a fear of the desire that identification can mask. Identification must continually be forced back to its roots in desire. I will go so far as to suggest that perhaps the tendency to deny identification as a *complex* psychic mechanism, related to the perpetuation/concealment of illicit desires, a tendency absolutely pervasive in popular music culture, cannot but be understood as a reaction to the feeling that something queer is going on in identification. Denying this "something queer" is to deny popular music culture much of its potentially transgressive energy, is to cleanse it.

Pictures of Brian

In returning to the classroom—to the moment when my student asks, "What's with that fur coat you're wearing?"—I now find myself holding a number of strands of argument that together do not lead me to a final reading of the scene. The uneasiness felt as I stood before both the student and the fur coat image, the feeling of being "out of place" that I described in the beginning of this essay, can certainly be understood as an anxiousness around identification/desire. The album cover is a kind of evidence that my identity is itself a matter of imitation, that my identity becomes possible only in what Mikkel Borch-Jacobsen calls a "detour" through the other.[30] The difference between the then, the performer; and the now, the teacher, surely suggests that I can take radically different "detours" in a relatively short period of time. It is a situation that troubles any residual belief in an authentic self lurking beneath the play, leaving me as one in the middle of a costume change. If the student has walked in on my past, what does this say of the present? What detour is *this*? Does this model of identity undercut the authority traditionally assigned the teacher? If pedagogy is itself a scene in which identification takes place, with the instructor functioning as a kind of model for the student, must the instructor, as a kind of ideal, be imagined as a whole, complete being, not a being for whom identity *is*, inescapably, being "out of place"? If the greatest fiction of the self is that the self is not a fiction, does identification, and therefore the pedagogic scene, require this fiction? If my response in the fur jacket episode is to "explain" the image, an explanation that involves both an outpouring of words, a sound barrier, and a defense of my intentions ("I was very consciously playing with identities, being ironic"), then what is being disavowed in this response? This form of explanation is certainly a mode of control. What's to be controlled? How does this defense then relate to the ambivalence of sexuality? On some level, I find myself acting out the very self/other distinction I locate behind much work in subcultural studies: "I knew what I was doing! I am not possessed! Nothing haunts me!" I cover over the fact of subordination, and certainly its psychic complexity, as I attempt to ground the image.

If one posits both that identification is central to the experience of popular music *and* that identification and desire forever bleed into one another (stirring up reaction formations that have a force not worth underestimating), studying the popular music experience in the classroom will also, necessarily, reveal something about the pedagogic scene itself, particularly regarding its libidinal dimension. In reference to his work on affect and rock culture, Larry Grossberg suggests that he has "too often ignored [affect's] link to particular ideological and libidinal codes." He goes on to say, "nevertheless, I will be satisfied if I have told at least part of the story and managed to put some interesting questions on the agenda."[31] Grossberg's suggestion marks an early stage in the counteroffensive to the cleansing tendencies of which I've spoken. A thorough study of affect will clearly involve questions regarding the libidinal character of the various experiences of popular music culture. But dealing with these questions will necessarily shed light onto the classroom scene itself, possibly leaving exposed the threatening circuitry of identification, which, when followed, reveals the fact that identification and desire are separated by a border that can only be maintained through a (homophobic) law that must be *voiced*. My own outpouring of words as I confront the fur coat image is typical of the response that cannot let the identification "speak."

I'm suggesting both that popular music studies must learn from psychoanalysis, perhaps particularly as it has been mobilized in queer theory, and that queer theory is not there for one to use when studying a queer act or a queer audience, rather it is there to understand the experience of popular music in general. The homosocial dimension of popular music culture requires the introduction of queer theory, which extends an analysis of queer desire beyond the borders of gay and lesbian culture. Brought into the classroom, it will bring discomfort, perhaps say more than feels "appropriate," say too much about the pedagogic scene itself. When confronted by a student who walked in on my past, I found myself feeling "out of place," wanting to control something—was it simply that I wanted to control an identity that suddenly seemed less than whole, constituted from without, or was it that my own sexuality, seen in the light of my strong identification with Brian Jones, in the light of the fur jacket that I want to wrap in a coat of words, was beyond the bounds of a heterosexual norm?

In arguing that popular music culture is a particularly rich site at which identifications take place, I'm arguing that this culture is, conversely, the site at which renounced desires are powerful, haunting presences, contributing to what earlier I suggested was the importance and intensity of popular music culture. Through studying identification as it infects the experiences of popular music, the specters of things refused, which sometimes seem to begin their haunting immediately, might be allowed their voice, which, in turn, might bring us closer to the ambivalences that make popular music culture, thankfully, bizarre in all the mundane places.

Notes

1. Of course, such attention has a gratifying component. However, I'm less interested in that because this student-teacher situation is one of *ambivalence,* and one in which the gratifications are more obvious than the anxieties. In speaking of this scene to others, a common response is something to the effect of, "Oh, come on, you love the attention!" And while this is absolutely true, the very moment that finds me investing in such attention is marked by a concomitant feeling that the fur coat image is somehow *haunted* in a way that finally brings discomfort to the scene. What, I want to know, is the nature of this haunting?

2. A great part of what I'm calling rock culture's "importance" comes in, for instance, Little Richard singing "Tutti Frutti" in the late 1950s, or Elvis Presley singing "Jailhouse Rock." When Elvis pushes on the line, "number 47 said to number 3, you're the cutest jailbird I ever did see," he's taking us somewhere popular culture doesn't often lead. And it's a moment that's lost when, in doing a remake of "Jailhouse Rock," John Cougar Mellencamp refused to sing that very line because of its connotations. Is there a hidden connection between Mellencamp's refusal and what I'll go on to call the "cleansing" of popular music culture from within the academy? I believe so. This is a question I return to later in the essay.

3. Angela McRobbie and Mica Nava, eds., *Gender and Generation* (London: Macmillan, 1984), 133.

4. Dick Hebdige's work on subcultures has been important to this particular cultural studies project, as has the work of John Fiske. See Dick Hebdige, *Subculture: The Meaning of Style* (London: Methuen, 1987). For an example of Fiske's project, see his *Understanding Popular Culture* (Boston: Unwin Hyman, 1989). Among the critiques of the tendency I associate here with Fiske and Hebdige, I single out (as have many others)

Mike Budd, Robert M. Entman, and Clay Steinman, "The Affirmative Character of U.S. Cultural Studies," *Critical Studies in Mass Communication* 7 (1990): 169–84.

5. Jacqueline Rose, *States of Fantasy* (Oxford: Clarendon Press, 1996).

6. Henry Jenkins, *Textual Poachers* (New York: Routledge, 1992), 23.

7. Judith Butler suggests that power must be understood as a multifaceted phenomenon: "We are used to thinking of power as what presses on the subject from the outside, as what subordinates, sets underneath, and relegates to a lower order. This is surely a fair description of what power does. But if, following Foucault, we understand power as forming the subject as well, as providing the very conditions of its existence and the trajectory of its desire, then power is not simply what we oppose but also, in a strong sense, what we depend on for our existence and what we harbor and preserve in the beings that we are." Butler goes on to suggest that in *subordination*—and she discusses identification as working along these lines—one might find the very possibility of subject *formation*. Thus resistance, rather than being a matter of "mastery" and *opposed* to subordination, can never be easily separated from it—the conditions of possibility regarding resistance are marked by, at least, a "founding subordination" (Butler, *The Psychic Life of Power* [Stanford: Stanford University Press, 1997], 2–5).

8. Hebdige, *Subculture*, 367.

9. The risk of making my particular experience as a performer that from which general observations regarding fans and identification might be made seemed and seems a risk worth taking. My experiences as a performer and as a fan are more often than not indistinguishable. That the acting out of my interests as a fan is documented, is *public* in a way that is not altogether common to the fan experience is a boon of sorts (I think of the videos, articles, photographs, interviews, and, of course, album jackets). While acknowledging that the fan and the performer are not simply one and the same, I focus on the substantial common ground in part because it tends to be downplayed, and this in a manner that produces a tenuous opposition.

10. For instance, it strikes me that the subject of "sex, drugs, and rock and roll" doesn't get too much critical attention from cultural studies scholars. The sex and the drugs fall out with great regularity. In Robert Walser's *Running with the Devil*, it's hard not to see that in complicating pervasive stereotypes of a misogynistic heavy metal culture, the author pays little attention to an analysis of the misogyny that he *does* find in that culture. His distinction between "nonviolent fantasies of dominance" and "blatant misogyny" is one curious rhetorical cornerstone that finally leads to a rather lopsided, even "happy" account of gender production in heavy metal culture—it's *just kids working out their gender stuff symbolically*. Similarly—and Walser is hardly alone in this—drugs are quickly bracketed off as a subject, because, it seems, the connection between heavy metal and drugs has been overstated in popular representations of metal culture. This cleansing approach to cultural criticism leads to a representation of metal culture that would make a scout leader rest easy. The question that badgers me, however, is whether it's worth simply countering supposed (mis)representations of metal culture put forward by, for instance, the religious Right. Is it finally a countering of these representations or a determination *by* them? What is lost in the process? See Walser, *Running with the Devil: Power, Gender, and Madness in Heavy Metal Music* (Hanover, N.H.: Wesleyan University Press, 1993).

11. Simon Frith, *Sound Effects: Youth, Leisure, and the Politics of Rock 'n' Roll* (New York: Pantheon, 1981), 224.

12. Simon Frith, "Towards an Aesthetic of Popular Music," in *Music and Society: The Politics of Composition, Performance, and Reception,* ed. Richard Leppert and Susan McClary (New York: Cambridge University Press, 1987), 140.

13. Ibid., 142.

14. Ibid., 140.

15. For more on ambivalence in relation to cultural signifying practices, see Homi K. Bhabha, *The Location of Culture* (New York: Routledge, 1994).

16. Sigmund Freud, *The Ego and the Id,* trans. Joan Riviere (New York: W. W. Norton, 1960), 18.

17. Again, without meaning to underestimate the ways in which this work has actually allowed many questions regarding fan practices to emerge, the model of a creative appropriation/consumption that it has fostered tends to obscure the fan in the fanfare; the celebration of the consumer who is not a dupe ultimately discourages a more probing analysis of the manner in which the consumer/fan (and I would extend this to *subject in general*) is "not his own man." Henry Jenkins's essay "Television Fans, Poachers, Nomads" is a fine example of such fanfare. And while critiques of this approach have themselves become commonplace, I believe that now attention must be given to enumerating some of the critical approaches that have suffered as an unnecessarily crude model of empowerment that has been valorized even by those critical of the "populist" approach that Jenkins exemplifies. See Jenkins, "Television Fans, Poachers, Nomads," in *The Subcultures Reader,* ed. Ken Gelder and Sarah Thornton (New York: Routledge, 1997).

18. It sometimes seems that the real fear badgering cultural studies is not the incorporating giant, ready to steal products back from the margins of culture so as to turn a profit; the real fear is perhaps the incorporating *consumer,* the consumer who does not *resist,* the consumer who is ultimately incorporating the products of mass culture into an identity that does not and cannot preexist such incorporations. To understand identity formation as such a process of incorporation *seems* to threaten the integrity of the fan/consumer. The need to claim that the music fan identifies with the performer but does not want to *be* the performer is one form taken by the obsessive protection of this integrity.

19. Sigmund Freud, *Group Psychology and the Analysis of the Ego,* trans. James Strachey (New York: W. W. Norton, 1959), 91.

20. Ibid., 66–67.

21. Jacques Lacan, *Four Fundamental Concepts,* trans. Alan Sheridan (New York: W. W. Norton, 1978), 243.

22. Philip Reiff, ed., *General Psychological Theory* (New York: Macmillan, 1963), 164–79.

23. Freud, *The Ego and the Id,* 19.

24. Diana Fuss, *Identification Papers* (New York: Routledge, 1995), 45.

25. When speaking of the relation between a group of females and their common ideal, Freud tends to spend more time addressing desire, *wanting to have,* than when he deals with the relation between a group of males and their common ideal, at which point identification overrides desire and is described as "typically masculine," which is further distinguished from what Freud calls a "feminine attitude." In accounting for the omission of male-male *fan* relationships in Freud's model (and also because space determines the scope of my argument), I have knowingly made my own glaring omissions, particularly regarding female fans and performers (Freud, *Group Psychology,* 46).

26. If an identification with a performer might be understood as an identification with an ideal ego, in Lacanian terms an *imaginary identification,* the abrupt swing acted out here suggests that a *symbolic identification* with the ego ideal takes over, manifesting itself as judgment, a superegoic imperative that overshoots itself slightly: "We are not homos! We are not anything!" However, I do not want to schematize the scene thus. Such a move disallows an investigation of the manner in which the two identifications—imaginary and symbolic—can be working at one and the same time, producing that ambivalence to which I've referred.

27. Larry Grossberg's work on "affective communities" marks what I believe is a first important step in countering the cleansing that popular music culture has undergone through the good intentions of critics responding to the one-dimensional representations of popular music culture by conservative Right mouthpieces. I write a more in-depth account of this dilemma in *Reading Rock & Roll,* ed. Kevin J. H. Dettmar and William Richey (New York: Columbia University Press, 1999).

28. We could take this a step further and argue that, in a sense, we need to plug our ears to study the image relations central to identification.

29. Freud, *Group Psychology.*

30. Mikkel Borch-Jacobsen, *The Freudian Subject* (Stanford: Stanford University Press, 1988).

31. Lawrence Grossberg, *We Gotta Get Out of This Place: Popular Conservativism and Postmodern Culture* (New York: Routledge, 1992), 29.

ROGER BEEBE ✳ MOURNING BECOMES...?
KURT COBAIN, TUPAC SHAKUR, AND THE "WANING OF AFFECT"

The "postmodern condition" has frequently been couched as a problem for—and by—Left/Marxian critical theorists. In these accounts, the changes in temporality and affect associated with postmodernism are portrayed as being anathema to older modes of political engagement premised on an affective relation to history.[1] The transformation of time under the postmodern cultural logic is typically characterized by a severing of ties to a "deep" or "genuine" historical tradition (i.e., the "waning of historicity") and a consequent "schizophrenic" immersion in the present. This temporal transformation carries with it a number of repercussions for the transformation of affect—and, consequently, of the subject—collectively referred to, in Fredric Jameson's formulation, as the "waning of affect."[2]

In this essay I explore this transformation of affect and temporality, specifically the relatively recent changes in the nature of mourning in both its affective and temporal dimensions. I first trace the contours of a more or less typically postmodern transformation, seen here in the musico-affective legacy of fallen rock idol Kurt Cobain, before looking at a second cultural phenomenon, the (dis)similar legacy of slain rapper Tupac Shakur. This second set of affective structures suggests a moment for which postmodern theory presents an insufficient analysis and which consequently demands a further theorization of the contemporary state of time and affect (and of the political significance of those transformations).

I will look first at the reception of the death of Kurt Cobain, and will tease out a (heretofore largely ignored) interpretation that plays out the interrelated temporal and affective structures of postmodernism ("the waning of affect"). Rather than contenting myself with this simple postmodern understanding of the state of effect, I then turn my attention to the posthumous legacy of Tupac Shakur, whose death seems to bespeak a very different set of affective and temporal structures. These structures, which vie for hegemony in contemporary culture with the postmodern ones elaborated in the Kurt Cobain section, may ultimately provide a glimpse of the future of mourning beyond the now familiar postmodern moment.

The Secret Death of Kurt Cobain

Kurt Cobain was a pioneer of the Seattle-based grunge scene and sound, and as such was hailed by many as "the savior of rock." In 1991, the legendary "year that punk broke," he and his band Nirvana were at the forefront of the so-called alternative rock revolution. Nirvana's song "Smells Like Teen Spirit" was on its way to becoming the theme song of a generation.[3] But on April 8, 1994, Kurt Cobain blew his brains out with a shotgun.

The violence of this truncated narrative begins to set up the standard account of the "meaning" of Kurt Cobain's death as well as its purported affective import for a generation. I want to elaborate this standard interpretation before suggesting that there exists another important set of meanings and affects around Cobain's suicide that has generally been neglected. The final pages of the epilogue to Elizabeth Wurtzel's *Prozac Nation* provide a typical example of this interpretation, which may be of special interest because her book has also been taken as deeply symptomatic of the (sad) state of generation X. As one of the endorsements on the back cover proclaims, "if you've been wondering why Kurt Cobain meant what he did—what it feels like to be young, gifted, and black of spirit—this book is the CD, tape, video, and literary answer all in one."[4] Wurtzel's musings on Cobain begin with a handy summary of the general media response to his death: "On April 8, 1994, as I was completing this book, Kurt Cobain shot himself in the head and was found dead in his Seattle home. His suicide was quickly

reduced by much of the media into an example of a more general generational malaise gone completely amok, and references were made to 'the
bullet that shot through a generation.' . . . Cobain's suicide, despite the
extremely private nature of his decision or compulsion to blow his brains
out, quickly came to be seen as greatly symbolic."[5] Despite her claim that the
media coverage was somehow reductive (primarily in that they did not give
voice to the full personal anguish of Cobain's private act), she later confirms
the general interpretation proffered by these media sources: "I understand
why people might see Kurt Cobain's death as symbolic. Because, after all,
they would be perfectly correct to see his life and the music he created in that
short time as utterly symbolic. Nirvana's popularity either inaugurated or
coincided with some definite and striking cultural moments."[6] Thus, despite her protestations, Wurtzel does ultimately understand Cobain's suicide to be symptomatic of the depressive culture of generation X.

This interpretation of the import of Cobain's suicide, which continues to
enjoy an almost absolute media hegemony years after his death, is not the
only possible one—nor, I would argue, does it necessarily represent the
dominant experience of a generation. While I do not want to deny the reality
of the suffering that finds form in such widely circulated testaments, I
believe that a second set of meanings and affects has been overlooked largely
due to the prevalence of this interpretation in the media (often as voiced by
highly articulate writers such as Wurtzel, Greil Marcus, etc.).[7] The voices of
these articulate mourners have come to stand in for (and efface) the experience of those who continue unproblematically and without sadness to listen
to Nirvana's music and to watch the band's videos—a body of work that now
includes a number of posthumous albums and videos.[8] It is this last experience to which I will attempt to give voice in exploring another set of meanings and affects around Kurt Cobain's suicide, and to which I will attempt to
dovetail with an understanding of a certain (postmodern) cultural logic that
is reflected in a specific music cultural apparatus.

Mourning, Melancholia, and Beyond

While the binary division between the hegemonic reaction to Cobain's suicide and this other, unvoiced experience may seem immediately to fit the
Freudian binary of mourning and melancholia, I would argue that the new
music cultural apparatus (with its new affective and temporal structures)

precludes such a reading. Although perpetuation of Cobain's life seems superficially like melancholia in that it denies his death rather than (properly) symbolizes it, I would argue that the recourse to pathologies of the ego is foreclosed by the postmodern transformation of the subject (the loss of "deep subjectivity," etc.) and the coincident affective shift that I gesture to above. We can see this transformation in more immediate cultural relief in the difference between Oliver Stone's obsession with the Kennedy assassination in *JFK* and that same historical event as presented in Richard Linklater's *Slacker*. Whereas *JFK* functions as an elaborate working through of the deep generational trauma that the Kennedy assassination represents for Stone, *Slacker*'s Kennedy-obsessive is interested in it as a simple play of elusive surfaces. Indeed, while Tania Modleski has suggested that "Oliver Stone . . . might be seen as an example of the inconsolable melancholiac,"[9] Linklater's postmodern conspiracy theorist defies such a categorization and even troubles the use of the Freudian schema. Therefore, instead of relying on a psychoanalytic model, I will explore how the significance of Cobain's death ultimately lies in the specific functioning of the new music cultural *dispositif* (in which the televisual apparatus plays a prominent role) and in the more general cultural apparatus of (advanced) postmodernism.[10]

Dying on Television

After Cobain's suicide, MTV (and the new music cultural apparatus of which it is a key component) quickly became a life-support system whereby Kurt (or his musical output and persona) lives on while he (that is, his body) pushes up daisies. Immediately after his death, MTV and other networks aired more or less elaborate commemorations of his short life that conformed to the general ritual of mourning the fallen hero. While these memorials were almost by definition based on mourning and sad affects, a longer-lasting legacy that effectively effaces Cobain's death and perpetuates his life as before arose after the memorials passed into the dustbin of cultural ephemera. This longer legacy is partially manifested in the string of posthumous record releases by Nirvana, probably capped off by *From the Muddy Banks of the Wishikah* (although there are rumors of another forthcoming album). More importantly, his sustained life finds form in MTV's continued airing of the predeath videos and release of a series of new Nirvana videos (primarily from MTV's *Unplugged* footage.[11] The music industry also had the good fortune of immediately finding (or creating) various replicas of Kurt Cobain to produce more grunge songs, some of them uncannily like Nirvana songs: chief among these replicas are Daniel Johns, the Aussie wunderkind frontman of Silverchair, who just happens to be Cobain's spitting image (although with the voice of Eddie Vedder of Pearl Jam); and Gavin Rossdale of Bush, whose voice is sometimes a dead ringer for Cobain's (although Rossdale looks more like Eddie Vedder, really).[12] Thus MTV and the music industry were able to prolong Kurt's presence by continually providing a series of "new" musical and televisual documents of him (and his near clones) doing his thing.[13]

Why should the simple issuance of further documents of Kurt Cobain's likeness and voice act as a life-support system rather than a commemoration of his life and music? After all, a similar quantity of posthumously released (or rereleased) documents exists for previous fallen icons like Jimi Hendrix that presumably do not function in a similar fashion. As I have already suggested, the historical and cultural context of Cobain's death seems to necessitate that the reaction to his death be different from those fallen icons of the 1960s (Hendrix, Jim Morrison, Janis Joplin, etc.). Put more simply, these are different times with their own (postmodern) cultural apparatus. An especially telling site for investigating this shift—one often privileged in the discourse of postmodernism—is television. While the prevalent visual documents of Hendrix are cinematic (*Woodstock, Monterey Pop*), Kurt Cobain's legacy is predominantly televisual (perhaps even more than musical).[14] Consequently, I will explore Cobain's continued televisual presence as symptomatic of the greater shifts in the cultural logic.[15]

The difference may also be understood schematically (at least at the outset) as the difference between modernism and postmodernism. Fredric Jameson's suggestion at the start of his "Postmodernism" essay that "the Beatles and the [Rolling] Stones now [stand] as the high-modernist moment of that more rapidly evolving tradition [of rock music]" (versus the postmodern forms of punk and new wave) makes clear the connection between these (seeming) generational differences and the greater aesthetic and cultural logics in popular music.[16] This difference is largely manifested in the questions of authenticity and expression that translate into different kinds of affective investments in the performers. As Larry Grossberg has claimed, "rock's special place [in postwar American youth culture] was enabled by its articulation to an ideology of authenticity."[17] Whereas this modernist impulse promoted a belief in an authenticity rooted in the "deep truths" of musical expression, the postmodern has disarticulated affect from such an authenticating discourse of depth or truth. It instead replaces that logic with what Grossberg terms an "authentic inauthenticity" that revels in a kind of surface play: "To appropriate, enjoy, or invest in a particular style, image, or set of images no longer necessarily implies that such investments make a significant (even affective) difference. Instead, we celebrate the affective ambiguity of images, images which are 'well developed in their shallowness, fascinating in their emptiness.' . . . In the end, only the affective commitment, however temporary or superficial, matters. Authentic inauthenticity, as a popular sensibility, is a specific logic which cannot locate differences outside the fact of its own temporary investment."[18] Thus the affect of postmodern music culture no longer has the same rooting in the expressive truths of modernism (or in any external discourse), but rather becomes its own end in the investment in (a Deleuzian postsubjective) affect itself.

The very images that have defined generational relationships to rock music and culture offer a more concrete glimpse into these divergent logics (and also into the role of television in the postmodern). Our cultural imaginaries are cluttered with images of rock fans of the past mourning their fallen heroes by smoking a joint while listening to Jimi Hendrix or Jim Morrison or Janis Joplin, lying on their backs in their candlelit rooms trading half-articulate nostalgic grunts or more articulate drug-induced rants.[19] The image of our cultural memory of Kurt Cobain (which, admittedly, won't be clear for decades) seems already to be quite different: as the generational clichés associated with grunge/slackers/the 1990s emerge, it appears that the "mourning" for Cobain will be represented as an image of a group of friends on their thrift-store couch across from an illumined cathode-ray tube (in a room lit by a halogen torchère) momentarily breaking off conversation and cranking up the volume (as much as their TV can handle) when the video for "Smells Like Teen Spirit" comes on.

With the shift in medium comes a different context of reception, a different apparatus or *dispositif,* and an altogether different governing logic. I do not want to suggest that somehow we once had a pure, untainted access to the unmediated presence of the rock performer (Hendrix) whereas now we have a mediation that prevents or abolishes the need for mourning (Cobain); on the contrary, what we see is something more like the effectivity of the illusion in the modernist moment and the evacuation of that illusion in the postmodern. Further, the shift in predominant apparatus—from radio and film to television—is surely not indifferent. It has been a theoretical commonplace at least since John Ellis's landmark ruminations on television in *Visible Fictions* that television functions both as a perpetual present ("presentness")[20] and as a full "presence," which has elsewhere been related to television's reliance on the ideology of "liveness"[21] (whether or not the programming is actually live). Unlike cinema which (à la *Screen* theory) is premised on a fundamental lack or "absent presence" that sets in motion the operations of desire, voyeurism, and so forth, television offers an "attainable" present image with a marked "equality" and "intimacy."[22] While both cinema and the 60s/70s rock formation could support the more traditional nostalgic/melancholic affects of a project like Oliver Stone's *The Doors*, the possibility of mobilizing these affects around the televisual image and legacy of Kurt Cobain seems to have already been foreclosed.[23] The way this translation from radio and cinema to TV has altered our new relations to our fallen hero points to a radical shift in the rock formation.

Rock (as suggested by the overwhelming and necessary reliance in popular music studies of the notion of the "rock formation") is no longer simply a question of pure musicality (as if it ever were);[24] rock music comes to us more than ever before with images attached. In fact, the model of MTV spectatorship—distracted attention to the TV image with the sound turned down, punctuated by moments of louder sound and fuller attention for exceptional events (e.g., a Nirvana video for gen-Xers, Limp Bizkit for gen-Yers, a GWAR video for Beavis and Butthead)—signals the continued underrepresentation of the visual in critical accounts of the contemporary rock (cultural) formation. Primary among the images that presently come along with or come to stand in for the music are the televisual images of the performers. Although it has been well documented by Andrew Goodwin and others that in the evolution of MTV there has been a move away from the simple performance video to a more narrative form, even in these latest video forms, shots of the performers remain obligatory, whether as performers alongside the "narrative" or as participants in it.[25] Nirvana videos have been no exception to the rule as the band members have either been the central focus of the video (e.g., "In Bloom," "Lithium," the *Unplugged* videos) or have been key elements in the narrative, the video space, or the allegorical mishmash (e.g., "Smells Like Teen Spirit," "Heart-Shaped Box," "Come as You Are"). In every Nirvana video the televisual (full, present, live, living) image of Kurt Cobain is consistently offered as a major element. For some Nirvana fans it is entirely possible that nothing is missing after Cobain's death: the televisual images offer not a substitute for his absent "real" self, but rather the full symbolic presence that was all they ever had or cared about in the first place since the positing of a deep subjectivity is no longer crucial to the production of the rock affect.[26] This is the second, unvoiced experience that is eclipsed by the standard explanations of the significance of Cobain's suicide.

Contrast this interpretation of the significance of Nirvana with that offered in Wurtzel's epilogue. She reads the success of Nirvana as the triumph of depression: "A peak moment in depression culture arrived with the tremendous success of Nirvana, whose hit single 'Smells Like Teen Spirit' was a call to apathy. This song was so delighted with its passivity that its central demand was, 'Here we are now, entertain us.'"[27] This standard interpretation of the depressive significance of Nirvana's music is ultimately premised on a number of major methodological problems. First, Wurtzel posits the lyrics as the ultimate location of the meaning of a song, completely effacing the aural (i.e., the affective resonance of the driving beats, distorted guitars, and screamed vocals), which seems to compel the listener to action rather than to apathy. As Grossberg nicely sums up this methodological error: "It is difficult to maintain that the lyrics of rock are its most salient element . . . its lyrics are often innocuous, ambiguous or unintelligible."[28] This problem is compounded by a second one, which is alluded to in Grossberg's comments: the assignment of a fixed meaning to a fragmentary and elusive set of lyrics that sometimes even degenerates into nonsense (e.g., the lyrics that follow the line that Wurtzel quotes are "a mulatto, an albino, a mosquito, my libido, yeah," which are difficult to interpret as "a call to apathy" or anything else, for that matter). The best popular rejoinder to Wurtzel is offered by "Smells Like Nirvana," the "Weird Al" Yankovic parody of "Smells Like Teen Spirit," which is essentially one long joke about the unintelligibility of the lyrics.[29] The problems for fixing one interpretation created by these polysemous (if not nonsensical) lyrics are further compounded by the introduction of the possibility of some form of postmodern irony. For example, the line Wurtzel interprets as a call to apathy ("here we are now, entertain us") could just as easily be seen to be an ironic punk jab at consumerist mentality spoken through an assumed voice rather than a motto with which we are meant (or asked) to identify. Furthermore, by not looking at the video for that song—

which has become one of the privileged sites for the continuation of its legacy (with its enshrinement on MTV), especially given its decrease in radio airplay—she ignores a large part of its (re)presentation. Music video has often been critiqued for fixing a certain set of images to a song, but Wurtzel chooses to ignore these images entirely. In fact, if she were to look at them she would find that the video presents a mock pep rally where seemingly "good boys and girls" are indeed driven into a frenzy of punk activity (moshing) as the song builds to its chaotic conclusion, a far cry from the call to apathy she imagines. The methodological blindnesses of Wurtzel's interpretation—typical of much of the discourse of mourning for Cobain—participate in the erasure of the other interpretation and other experience of his death (a second set of meanings suggested by the very polysemy of Nirvana's anthem). If we accept that the music and the video carry a large part of the continued affective import of "Smells Like Teen Spirit" and of Nirvana/Cobain's legacy, then we must also recognize this second set of affects and meanings involved in the less-publicized enjoyment of that legacy, which is not dependent on a relation of either melancholy or mourning.

Spin magazine's 1990s decade wrap-up cover is one of the rare instances in the popular media where we can see this alternative experience laid bare.[30] On its cover *Spin* has arrayed what the editors considered to be the four most influential performers of the 1990s—Beck, Trent Reznor, Lauryn Hill, and Kurt Cobain—in a composite photo that is made to resemble a yearbook picture (i.e., all four images facing the same direction, placed in rows as if standing on tiered risers). Every attempt is made to make these figures appear to be part of the same photographic moment (although a close examination reveals a notable difference in grain in each of the images), and all four of them are smiling.[31] This presentation clearly offers Cobain not as a fallen hero but as a fully accessible entity available for our appreciation and consumption. Such moments as these have been rare in the mainstream representation of Cobain, but may well become less so as the wave of mourning among the voices of an older generational logic ends and the postmodern/gen-X sensibility assumes a greater role in future representations.

This second set of reactions (or lack thereof) to Cobain's suicide is premised at a fundamental level on a quick forgetting of his death. I use "forgetting" (and not "disavowal") here pointedly because I want to stress again that the (music) televisual apparatus and the new *dispositif* of popular music culture assume a new model of spectatorship/fandom that no longer relies on the participation of a Freudian (or even a fragmented Lacanian) psyche. Typically it would seem appropriate to summon some sort of psychoanalytic model to explain the apparent lack of grief at the passing of our ego ideal. Again, melancholia seems to be the obvious Freudian diagnosis and every video serves for us as a necessarily repeated counter to the fact of Cobain's death and as an aid in disavowing the fact. However, this psychoanalytic model, while perhaps (once) appropriate for the cinematic apparatus, becomes suspect when applied to television spectatorship. The apparatus of contemporary television is such that with Kurt Cobain's "real" death (i.e., his bodily death) there is nothing to lament for a large number of his fans because his presence only mattered to them as a symbolic (and largely) televisual surface that continues to be offered regularly on MTV.

This structure can be usefully explained as a postmodern or postpsychic twist on the Lacanian/Žižekian notion of the space between two deaths. Žižek explains this notion with reference to the two deaths of Wile E. Coyote, who first runs off some precipice (the "real" death) but remains momentarily suspended in the air until he "symbolizes" his death by looking down and noticing that he is a long way from terra firma (the second death).[32] In a more concrete example, the "real" death of the body requires a second, symbolic death, which it finds in the funerary rites—the idea being that the first death (and its troubling disruption) is only finally resolved with its symbolization. The postpsychic twist is that Kurt Cobain's death, while "real," does not prove disruptive (to some stable or momentarily stable ego) and hence need not be symbolized. For those who experienced him through this new music cultural apparatus, his real death can be a matter of almost total indifference (without any pathological residuum) because his televisual presence is all that ever mattered in the first place. The second death never comes because the specific mediation of his form of presence does not demand that type of referentiality (i.e., to the actual [perpetually lacking] historical person named Kurt Cobain). Thus, postmodern (and televisual) mediation, with the form of presence and the affective connection it implies, offers a second interpretation of Cobain's suicide that has been largely effaced by the widely circulated narratives of mourning. For those who experience Cobain's legacy in this other manner, his "death" may end up being nothing more than a slow obsolescence as the fans grow tired of his finite posthumous repertoire (perhaps complaining to one another that they wish he would move on to something new).[33]

Tupac Shakur and Televisual Mourning

While I have hinted that the reception of Kurt Cobain's death is not the whole picture, I have heretofore generally done so only in relief against a residual cultural logic (of modernism or the 60s/70s "classic" rock formation). However, we need not only look backward to the fallen icons of yesteryear (Hendrix, Morrison, Joplin) or to performers whose reception was conditioned by that older logic (Jerry Garcia) to see in relief the (non)reaction to Cobain's death. One could just as easily look to Cobain's hip hop contemporaries (most notably the fallen rappers Tupac Shakur and the Notorious B.I.G.) for a very different mobilization of affect surrounding the death of an idol. This comparative study serves as a good reminder of the insufficiency of using television, the contemporary rock formation, or postmodernism as a *total* explanation for the current state of affect at the same time that it highlights the need to continue to flesh out the entire music cultural apparatus (not just the *rock* formation). As other cultural forms vie for hegemony with the prevailing (white, middle-class, suburban) forms of postmodern rock, we must make our theorization of affect sensitive to the different affective structures of these nonrock and non (or differently?) postmodern forms. We can most clearly see this in the differences between the representations of Cobain and Shakur in their posthumous videos.[34]

As I discussed briefly above, a majority of Nirvana's posthumous output consists of footage recorded as part of MTV's *Unplugged* series, which presents popular musicians playing (generally) unamplified instruments. Better than a half dozen videos were released by MTV from this footage (including "Pennyroyal Tea," "All Apologies," and "Dumb" from *In Utero;* "Polly" from *Nevermind;* and covers of David Bowie ["The Man Who Sold the World"], Leadbelly ["Where Did You Sleep Last Night? (in the Pines)"], and the Meat Puppets ["Plateau" and "Lake of Fire"]). While the number of videos they released from this footage was unusual, their presentation was entirely conventional: the videos simply played as any other video taken from any other *Unplugged* show, with no gesture of tribute or mourning. (Rarely, if ever, was such a gesture even included in the accompanying veejay patter.) The videos simply came on with a hard cut, presented the credit information (performer's name, song title, etc.) in the lower-left corner of the screen, and then, with no intervening to-do, repeated that sequence in reverse order at the end of the clip. In the video footage itself, Cobain occasionally smiled, said some brief words to introduce the songs, sipped some water, smoked a cigarette, and so forth, but mostly the footage is simple, conventional multicamera performance material. In all aspects, this footage was packaged as and could readily be consumed as a "live" performance.

This picture contrasts drastically with the posthumous presentation of Tupac Shakur. Shakur was a (so-called) gangsta rapper and sometime actor (in films such as *Poetic Justice, Above the Rim,* and *Gridlock'd*). He had been involved in one of the more notorious East Coast/West Coast rap feuds, squaring off with the Notorious B.I.G. both in interviews and in his music after he was shot in New York City (Shakur claimed that B.I.G. had a hand in the shooting). On September 16, 1996, Shakur was killed, possibly as an outgrowth of this rivalry, when an unknown assailant opened fire on his car in Las Vegas after a boxing match. (B.I.G. was later gunned down, in what many claim was a retaliatory strike.) Their deaths were instrumental in the (at least temporary) lessening of East Coast/West Coast rivalries in the hip hop community and in the wane of gangsta rap.

Two of Shakur's posthumous videos that received considerable play on both BET (Black Entertainment Television) and on MTV employed profoundly different representational strategies than the Cobain *Unplugged* output. The first video for the song "I Ain't Mad at Cha" (released shortly after Tupac's death) had (with its opening sequence in which Shakur gets gunned down and dies) an uncanny resonance that was frequently commented on in the media; but its production prior to his death makes it ultimately a less-telling document of the presentation and reception of his legacy than does the long-awaited follow-up video, "Changes."[35]

The video for "Changes," which accompanies the single from Shakur's *Greatest Hits* album and which ranked twenty-first on MTV's 1999 *Total Request Live* year-end countdown, is composed of a series of clips and still photographs taken from Shakur's other videos and his films, and from the media coverage of his career. The most salient feature of this video is the inscription of these images in a square in the middle of the screen, with a black frame surrounding the image. Aside from the obvious significance of the constant visible presence of this black frame in the video (as a representation of mourning—a black band around the arm of the video), it also serves to alter the functioning of the televisual apparatus. If, as it has been generally theorized (again going back to John Ellis's *Visible Fictions*), one of the key factors facilitating the ideological "liveness" of television is its seeming framelessness, then this second frame in the "Changes" video undermines this liveness by finally making the televisual frame (and thus the finite boundaries of the image) part of our perception of it as an object. Since we are then unable (or, at least, less able) to assume the liveness of the image, we consequently transfer this perception onto Shakur as the bounded object of our televisual gaze. In other words, the finitude of the object allows the clip to present Shakur as a nonlive entity and thus a potential cause of mourning.

This overarching formal device that provides an enabling condition for mourning is furthered by the use of more-localized devices. Among these devices is the use of a number of black-and-white images of Shakur (summoning an aura of pastness); of childhood photos of Shakur (creating an overall feeling of nostalgia by affording a look at a "past past" [his prehistory] and contextualizing the later footage as part of a completed life history); of footage and stills that predominantly depict a serious or contemplative Shakur; of images of Shakur turning away from the camera and walking out of sight (for example, around a corner, into the shadows) especially toward the end of the video (offering a gesture of closure and loss as Shakur leaves us); and, perhaps most notably, of photographic stills. Roland Barthes in *Camera Lucida* suggests a necessary connection between photography and death: "For Death must be somewhere in a society; if it is no longer (or less intensely) in religion, it must be elsewhere; perhaps in this image which produces Death while trying to preserve life. . . . *Life/Death:* the paradigm is reduced to a simple click, the one separating the initial pose from the final print."[36] This morbid failure of the photographic image to preserve the moment it purportedly saves is, surely, part of the haunting power of the still as used in the "Changes" clip. While many of the stills in the video are indeed slightly animated (usually scrolling slowly and gracefully across the frame), their stillness in the context of that most hyperactive of forms, the music video, a form that has become synonymous with fast cutting and extreme motion, is still striking. Barthes also usefully differentiates between cinema and the still photograph in *Camera Lucida:* "The filmic world is sustained by the presumption that, as Husserl says, 'the experience will constantly continue to flow by in the same constitutive style'; but the Photo-graph breaks the 'constitutive style' (this is its astonishment); it is *without future* (this is its pathos, its melancholy); in it, no protensity, whereas the cinema is protensive, hence in no way melancholic (what is it then?—It is, then, simply 'normal,' like life)."[37] It is this lack of a future that links the photographic still with the sad affects (mourning/nostalgia/melancholy).

Although Barthes generally links the still most directly to melancholia—"when [the photograph] is painful, nothing in it can transform grief into mourning"[38]—I would argue that the video constructs a structure of mourn-ing around the stills, most notably through the closure afforded by both the musical structure of the song and by the structural closure of the video (e.g., as noted above, the images of Shakur receding into the distance). The use of stills in a time-based medium thus has three major transformative effects on the basic schema outlined by Barthes. First, because of the bounded dura-tion of the still's presence, the photograph is given a kind of closure that is not offered by the photograph outside of this context (hence the passage from melancholy to mourning). Second, and this reinforces the first, the overall rhythms of the piece and its temporal structure may also function to contain the photograph or to narrativize it sufficiently to disarm it of its melancholy force. And third, the time-based presentation of the photograph may in fact *increase* its pathos by calling even greater attention to the finitude of the still as opposed to the stream of becoming of the cinematic (con)text. The video plays with this discrepancy between the still and its time-based presentation when it echoes the *locus classicus* of the cinematic still, Chris Marker's *La Jetée*. The clip employs a series of dissolves to transition from a shot of Shakur standing before a white background looking down to one of him looking at the camera in front of the same background and then back to the first image; the pathos of the still is only heightened by its final inability to come fully back to life.[39] Thus the photographic image in the "Changes" clip works powerfully alongside the previously mentioned structures, giving aesthetic form (symbolization) to the profound feelings of loss, thereby enabling the process of mourning.[40]

Of course, it would be a mistake not to mention the way the soundtrack supports (and perhaps largely produces) this visual apparatus of mourning. "Changes" is based on Bruce Hornsby and the Range's "The Way It Is" and retains that song's structure, melody, harmony, and even, by and large, its instrumentation. Most prominent though is the melodic hook played on the piano between verses. The use of the piano immediately summons an air of nostalgic pastness in almost all hip hop music (as an "old" musical technology contextualized in the digital urban soundscapes) and this song is certainly no exception. The two-measure piano hook consists of three ascending gestures within an overall descending melodic contour.[41] Yet, despite its consistency in terms of phrase length and formal placement in the song, this hook does not convey a sense of certainty or security. For while it is always two measures long, the syncopation of the first measure counters the prevailing tendency toward four clearly delineated beats per measure. Moreover, the two-measure phrase also represents a shortening of the four-measure phrases of the verse, thereby increasing tension. Melodically, this tension is further heightened by the ascending gestures of the hook, the first two of which are notably angular, contrasting with the lyrical, conjunct movement of the verse. But it is not until the hook ends and the verse returns that the syntactical meaning of the hook becomes apparent. For the hook leads directly into the verse, a move reflected harmonically by a shift from major to relative minor. Thus the overriding feeling is that any comforting sense of security conveyed by the major chords of the hook is thoroughly overturned by the verse that must follow.

As noted above, Shakur's single "Changes" largely attempts to recreate the air of the Bruce Hornsby song. However, the differences between the two are telling. Musically, Hornsby's song ends with a fade out of the hook, which allows him to conclude the piece in a major key. In "Changes" on the contrary, this major resolution is deliberately subverted as Shakur opts for a close in the chorus of male voices singing the refrain after which Shakur adds in a spoken voice: "Some things will never change." While a close would normally offer a moment of great musical stability or security, Shakur's vocal close is less a cadence than a convergence onto a single tone; not a gesture that induces a sense of reassuring finitude. On the contrary, the close here—bolstered by the ominous tone of Shakur's final utterance—creates a sense of foreclosure rather than the comforting resolution normally offered by such an ending, thus further undermining the normal musical syntax of this close. Thus musically "Changes" creates a structure of troubling pastness allied with the other structures of mourning we see throughout the clip.

Lyrically Shakur's song also diverges minimally but significantly from "The Way It Is." In the Bruce Hornsby song, the chorus is "That's just the way it is / Some things will never change / That's just the way it is / But don't you believe them." Here the first three lines are presented as the indirect discourse of a never-located "them," who suggest that things can never change. However, the narratorial voice of the song takes over to warn "but don't you believe them." Thus the Hornsby song is an injunction not to accept things the way they are because things *can* be changed. "Changes," on the other hand, inverts this message through a few small deviations from the original. Its chorus, which is sung by a small group of black male alto voices, is "That's just the way it is / Things will never be the same / That's just the way it is / Oh, yeah." Here, obviously, two major changes have been effected. First, what was indirect discourse has become a direct statement presented essentially as a truth ("that's just the way it is") through the replacement of the fourth line with a simple gesture of concession. Second, in the second line of the chorus, there is a shift from a sense of disempowering inertia ("some things will never change") to one of irrevocability ("things will never be the same"). Taken together, these things point to the truth or reality of the way things are and the loss of a bygone era. While taken separately the first portion might just be another tale of the disempowerment felt by contemporary urban youth, when in combination with the suggestion that there was another era when things were otherwise, it begins to suggest, as one might expect at this point, the irreversible loss of Shakur, the fallen idol.

Shakur's own original lyrics in his raps function to further this interpretation. While Shakur clearly conceived and recorded these raps before his death, attenuating their original pertinence to his own death, the decision to release the song as the single from his *Greatest Hits* album, especially given the kind of tribute video that accompanies it, makes it another important site for reading Shakur's legacy. In fact, the attempt to reinterpret and re-present this predeath material as both presage and tribute actually amplifies my point, because the producers of these posthumous texts are reworking the sometimes resistant material of Shakur's extant work to accommodate the perceived public need for such a tribute. For example, in the central media collage section, Tupac's lyrics that frame that collage are "We gotta make a change" and "To survive." The choice to mask the remaining rhymes—which list a series of items that need to be changed in contemporary society—is surely a decision made to reinflect the song posthumously to point more powerfully to the loss of Shakur.

The final verse of the song is especially significant in its construction of a memorial text for the slain rapper. There Shakur raps, "And I never get to lay back / Cuz I always gotta worry 'bout the payback / Some buck that I roughed up way back / Comin' back after all these years / That's the way it is." Although this verse is probably a reference to his earlier nonfatal shooting and to the general fallout from his self-proclaimed "thug life,"[42] the circulation of this song as his final testament and, indeed, this verse as his final words gives it an air of foreboding and tragic destiny. These lyrics also may partially be seen as an attempt to insist, as many have, that toward the end of his life Shakur had renounced his thug life, thus inserting a note of redemption and a further note of tragedy (i.e., "just when he had renounced his evil ways . . ."). Also here we see another attempt to rework the extant material to make this video a fitting memorial: the penultimate line of Shakur's final rap—"Rat-a-tat-tat-tat-tat" (the sound of gunfire from that "buck from way back" as he seeks revenge on Shakur)—has been excised from the video version of the song, lest it disrupt with its shocking interjection the structure of mourning.

All of the tragedy of this reconstructed final verse is then brought home after one final repetition of the chorus in which Shakur and his backup singers break it down in his final spoken words in the song, "Some things'll never change." Presented in the context of everything else (musical, lyrical, and visual) that we've experienced throughout the video, it becomes nearly impossible to understand this line as anything other than Shakur's final words telling us that he's gone and he'll never come back—"Some things will never change." Again this reinforces the cathartic structure of mourning by essentially instructing us, after the sadness of the look back at Shakur's life, that we must move on because our grief cannot change the fact of his death.

This video is hardly alone as a testament to the existence of structures of mourning in hip hop culture. The Lox's "We'll Always Love Big Poppa" was a fairly big crossover hit in which the performers pay their final respects to the Notorious B.I.G. Even more notable, however, is Sean "Puffy" Combs's tribute (single and video) to the Notorious B.I.G., "I'll Be Missing You," which samples the sad melodic line from the Police's "Every Breath You Take." This single consistently ranked among the top of the various all-time hip hop video countdowns on both MTV and BET for years after B.I.G.'s death. Dozens of other such tribute videos for both B.I.G. and Shakur, with structures that are explicitly designed to encourage mourning, have circulated since their deaths, bespeaking the general currency of mourning in the hip hop structure of feeling, against the more orthodox postmodern affect surrounding the death of Cobain.

Mediated Mourning

The point of my analysis is not simply to show the persistence of an older form of mourning in hip hop culture. If I desired only to point to a residual form of affect, the interpretation of Cobain's life that I sought to counter at the beginning of this section of the essay would have been sufficient. On the contrary, what I hope to do is to elaborate the difference of the structure of mourning surrounding Shakur from both that of the residual modernist form and the second postmodern form that I elaborated at length earlier in the sections on Cobain. We can most clearly see this third set of affects in the one sequence of the "Changes" video that does not make use of the black frame within the frame.

This sequence takes place about halfway through the video, just after the start of a verse that begins "You gotta make a change." The music drops into the background and is masked by an audio collage of television reporting that narrates (albeit somewhat disjointedly and occasionally unintelligibly) Shakur's final days and the time immediately after his shooting.[43] As this sequence begins, the frame is entirely filled by a series of short shots of television news footage of Shakur. To emphasize the televisuality of the clips, the image appears to have been reshot off of a monitor or resized from the original image so that the pixels of the image are visible, an effect that is used throughout the video to mark certain mass-mediated images. In this section, as the audio collage unfurls, the camera appears to slowly pull back from this initial image (through a video simulation of camera dolly or zoom out), eventually revealing another media collage—this time visual rather than auditory—wherein Shakur's face is composed of hundreds of tiny frames of the mass media images of Shakur that we encounter throughout the clip.

Clearly this exception to the use of the framed image works to further the same goals: namely, the framing of the media and the presentation of Shakur as a fallen idol. However—and this is where the difference from Cobain's posthumous presentation becomes most theoretically interesting—

rather than presenting "the real" Shakur as the antithesis of the mediated celebrity (as one tends to see with the rockist discourse around that older era of musical heroes), Shakur is portrayed as the composite of his media representations. This observation is crucial in that it suggests that the structure of mourning in hip hop culture is not simply allied with the older structure of feeling of this residual cultural logic, but rather that it represents a third alternative that is able to reconcile mass mediation and mourning. Within the confines of the postmodern understanding of the waning of affect, the kind of surface play associated with postmodern mass media should be anathema to the kind of deep affective investment required for mourning.

This third alternative (mediated mourning) and its association with hip hop culture diverges from the more typically postmodern waning of affect that we saw in the case of Kurt Cobain's rock legacy. As hip hop culture increasingly vies for hegemony in the cultural marketplace, the problems created by ignoring this other model can only become progressively more severe. We must then look at this structure of mediated mourning not simply as a marginal reminder of the necessity of tempering the totalizing impulse of postmodern theory; on the contrary we must understand it as an increasingly central aspect of the cultural dominant that must be accounted for in any theorization of contemporary culture and the cultural dominant.

The final image of the video significantly reprises the metatelevisual impulse of the rest of the video. That image, a slow-motion extreme close up of Shakur's eye, presented with the now-familiar televisual pixels, is our final farewell to Shakur. Thus, rather than the final image being some kind of candid shot that appears to give us unmediated access to the private individual (as we might have expected with that older trinity of Hendrix, Morrison, and Joplin, whose reception was so fully invested in the modernist conceptions of expression and authenticity), our final image of Tupac Shakur insists yet again on his meaning to us as a televisually mediated entity. Interestingly, however, this metadiscourse doesn't result in the erasure of pathos as it generally has done in postmodern culture, but actually is made to increase the pathos we feel toward this media celebrity—it seems to point to a kind of contemporary deep affect created by the very act of mediation. Until we start to understand such seemingly paradoxical affective reconciliations, our analyses of contemporary culture will remain flawed and partial at best. And without an understanding of the emergent logic of hip hop culture as a supplement to the dominant postmodern rock culture, our analyses can only be diagnostic, rooted in a past moment, rather than prognostic, and thereby offering new avenues for engagement.

Notes

1. Lawrence Grossberg, *We Gotta Get Out of this Place: Popular Conservatism and Postmodern Culture* (New York: Routledge, 1992; and Fredric Jameson, *Postmodernism, or, The Cultural Logic of Late Capitalism* (Durham: Duke University Press, 1991).

2. It should be noted here that the "affect" referred to in Jameson's phrase is specifically that type of affection or feeling associated with an older notion of "deep" subjectivity. This is not (as in Deleuze's use of the term or in Lyotard's notion of "intensities") the broader—and more proximately postmodern—notion of affect as a desubjectified bodily stimulation or arousal.

3. An indication of the overwhelming importance of "Smells Like Teen Spirit" for a generation of youth is provided by its (temporary) assumption of the number one position on MTV's frequent iterations of the all-time best videos. In taking on this position, it displaced Michael Jackson's "Thriller," which had been the perennial number one because of its role as a historical landmark in the music video form.

4. Elizabeth Wurtzel, *Prozac Nation: A Memoir* (New York: Riverhead Books, 1994). The endorsement on the back cover is attributed to "Daphne Merkin, author of *Enchantment.*" The Merkin quote is telling with reference to one of the key factors that led to the erasure of alternative reactions to Kurt Cobain's death: namely, the age of the commentators (and their allegiance to a residual cultural order). Merkin, who was born in 1954, shows her hand by suggesting that she, as an outsider to present youth culture, needs someone like Wurtzel, a purported insider, to explain the significance of Kurt Cobain to her (and to her generation). This distortion occurs less explicitly (but just as powerfully) when middle-aged writers such as Anthony DeCurtis and Greil Marcus, who derive their music-critic apparatuses from a 60s or 70s rock formation, are allowed to give voice to "our" grief about Cobain's passing on the pages of *Rolling Stone*.

5. Ibid., 347.

6. Ibid., 350.

7. Marcus concisely advances the same depressive thesis as Wurtzel (albeit with his signature prose stylings) in the *Rolling Stone* 1990s wrap-up issue. See Greil Marcus, "Artist of the Decade: Kurt Cobain," *Rolling Stone*, no. 812, May 13, 1999, 46–50.

8. Part of the reason that this other experience has been so readily effaced is the very lack of trauma central to it; while trauma has often served to spark the creative process (sublimation as art), without it there is obviously nothing that requires expression or representation.

9. Tania Modleski, "Real Women and a Lost War" in *The New American Cinema*, ed. Jon Lewis (Durham: Duke University Press, 1998), 142. Modleski is specifically referring to Stone's obsession with Vietnam, but her comments apply equally well to his other generational obsessions (music, politics).

10. The term *dispositif*, for which "apparatus" is the standard but insufficient English translation, refers not simply to the technological apparatus of the reception (in French, *appareil*) but rather to the entire arrangement of social, psychic, economic, ideological, and mechanical circumstances that come into play in the consumption of an aesthetic object. Although I am taking MTV as exemplary of this new apparatus of popular music, a number of corresponding changes partake of this apparatus, including deregulation of radio ownership, the consolidation of ownership in the recording industry, the steady disappearance of smaller venues (rock clubs) for the presentation of live rock music, and so forth. For more on the nature of these related transformations, see, among many others, Grossberg, *We Gotta Get Out of This Place*, esp. 131–242; and Will Straw, "Popular Music and Postmodernism in the 1980s," in *Sound and Vision: The Music Video Reader*, ed. Simon Frith, Andrew Goodwin, and Lawrence Grossberg (London: Routledge, 1993).

11. The *Unplugged* footage served well in perpetuating the string of posthumous releases because it included, in addition to the acoustic versions of familiar Nirvana songs, a handful of covers of the Meat Puppets, David Bowie, and Leadbelly that could be presented as "new" Nirvana songs.

12. Rossdale actually said in an interview on MTV's *120 Minutes* in 1994 that the main influence on Bush was Nirvana, which bespeaks the directness of the lineage from the fallen hero to the next wave of alternative posterboys.

13. A slightly more extreme erasure (although one that is also somewhat less emblematic of the generational zeitgeist) took place surrounding the death of Bradley Nowell, guitarist and singer of Sublime, who died from a drug overdose before the band's self-titled hit CD was even released. His death was almost entirely effaced as Sublime rose to fame on MTV and radio during summer 1997 with their feel-good single "What I Got." Had someone wanted to look to the music for a deep and ominous presage of Nowell's death, the occasion was certainly there—"What I Got" contains the lyrics "Life is too short so enjoy the one you got, cuz you might get run over or you might get shot." Other than the occasional tribute in rear-guard, rockist publications such as *Spin* and *Rolling Stone*, few seemed to notice the suggestiveness of these lyrics.

14. Hendrix's televisual image (suggestively) only began to enjoy a wide circulation in the second half of the 1990s, primarily thanks to the use of his appearance on *The Dick Cavett Show* on a TV commercial.

15. Note that while TV is the primary locus for the playing out of certain aspects of the current social formation, televisuality should not be taken as being determinate of that formation but instead merely manifests it or gives it form.

16. Jameson, *Postmodernism*, 1.

17. Grossberg, *We Gotta Get Out of This Place*, 205. Although I cite only short passages of Grossberg's book, all of chapter 8, "Rock, Postmodernity, and Authenticity," is germane to this discussion and is a significant site of further elaboration on these shifts between the modern and postmodern popular music apparatuses.

18. Ibid., 225–26.

19. While the repetition of these historical clichés are too many to number, *Forrest Gump* contains some of the more circulated iterations of these images.

20. The "presentness" of TV is an interesting nexus in the context of this investigation because it provides a link between postmodern discourse and recent academic descriptions of the medium (where each aids in defining the other in what at times approaches tautology): TV (or postmodernism) is characterized as a perpetual urgent "liveness," a schizophrenic immersion in the present with no noticeable past or future.

21. Cf. Jane Feuer, "The Concept of Liveness: Ontology as Ideology," in *Regarding Television*, ed. E. Ann Kaplan (Los Angeles: University Publications of America, 1983).

22. John Ellis, *Visible Fictions: Cinema, Television, Video* (London: Routledge & Kegan Paul, 1982), 131.

23. The 1998 documentary *Kurt and Courtney* appears to give preliminary confirmation of this hypothesis because the primary interest in the film has (thus far) been scandal, not nostalgia. Additionally, *Hype!* (1996), the definitive documentary on grunge music and culture, is more invested in elaborating the media mechanics of the explosion of a local movement than it is in exploring nostalgic longing for an earlier time of purity.

24. Andrew Goodwin, in his landmark study of MTV, *Dancing in the Distraction Factory* (Minneapolis: University of Minnesota Press, 1997), argues that positing a moment prior to the contamination of pure musicality by the visual "is based on the . . . assumption that the emphasis on imagery is a new development in pop. This is a difficult view to sustain in light of what we know of pop history. Pop has always stressed the visual as a necessary part of its apparatus—in performance, on record covers, in magazine and press photographs, and in advertising." Although I certainly agree with this corrective gesture, clearly the advent of music television heralds a substantial extension and transformation of the relation between the visual and the musical.

25. "Narrative" seems like a particularly poor choice of words for describing many of the forms of video that emerged during the waning of the performance-based video. For example, one of the most widely influential forms in the mid to late 1990s was the inscrutably allegorical/surrealist form first seen in the video of R.E.M.'s "Losing My Religion."

26. The historical context of which this transformation is a part can be further sensed in the similar shifts in film studies where scholars have recently noted the production affect by means other than identification. Tom Gunning's work on the cinema of attractions has generally been cast as the founding text of that related discursive shift.

27. Wurtzel, *Prozac Nation,* 348.

28. Grossberg, *We Gotta Get Out of This Place,* 10. This refusal of lyrics as the site of meaning is not unique to Grossberg, of course. Wurtzel might have learned the same lesson three decades ago from the epigraph to Richard Meltzer's *The Aesthetics of Rock:* there Meltzer meticulously transcribes every "Papa-ooma-mow-mow" of "Surfer Bird" by the Trashmen as a baldfaced demonstration of the utter nonutility of the typical literary tools for the analysis of popular music (Meltzer, *The Aesthetics of Rock* [New York: Da Capo Press, 1987]).

29. Yankovic's antianthem begins thus:

> [chorus]
> What is this song all about?
> Can't figure any lyrics out.
> How do the words to it go?
> I wish you'd tell me I don't know.

> [refrain]
> Now I'm mumblin'
> and I'm screamin'
> and I don't know
> what I'm singin'.
> Crank the volume.
> Ears are bleedin'.
> I still don't know.
> what I'm singin'.
> We're so loud and
> incoherent.
> We're Nirvana.
> Bug your parents.

The rest of Yankovic's lyrics play out this joke in endless permutations. It's hard to imagine a more resounding critique of Wurtzel's depressive interpretation than that offered by these lyrics. "Weird Al" Yankovic Off the Deep End (BMG 1992).

30. *Spin* 15, no. 9 (September 1999).

31. Trent Reznor of the moody gothic group Nine Inch Nails is not quite smiling, although he is uncharacteristically well behaved, as if posing for a yearbook picture. And there is the (again uncharacteristic) hint of a smile.

32. Slavoj Žižek, The Sublime Object of Ideology (London and New York: Verso, 1989), 133–34.

33. Indeed, this obsolescence has already largely taken place as alternative has quickly receded into the annals of rock history, slowly entering rotation on "classic rock" radio.

34. We could easily see this also in the difference between any number of elements at any number of sites—for example, in the difference between the ongoing public mourning of the Notorious B.I.G. by the Family versus the erasure of Kurt Cobain's death by Dave Grohl (as he becomes frontman for the Nirvanaesque Foo Fighters) or in the difference between the use of footage of Bradley Nowell of Sublime and of B.I.G. in posthumous videos featuring their performances. The Cobain/Shakur pairing seems to offer both the most dramatic and the most symptomatic of these sites of inscription of this differentiation.

35. A long dispute between Shakur's mother and his record labels over the rights to his recordings delayed the release of this video for about two years.

36. Roland Barthes, *Camera Lucida* (New York: Noonday Press, 1981), 92.

37. Ibid., 89–90.

38. Ibid., 90.

39. Marker's film differs from the "Changes" video in that its own thematics seem more invested in the photograph as the representation of the Barthesian morbid melancholic obsession of its protagonist, ultimately leading to his death, whereas the video seeks to provide that proper symbolization of Shakur's death that, for the audience, should allow for the more healthy experience of mourning.

40. In this context, the hip hop injunction to "keep it real" takes on an interesting Lacanian/Žižekian resonance. Understanding this mantra as a counter to the derealization of death in postmodern rock culture, the "real" referred to is that traumatic kernel that it has, at least purportedly, been cast aside with the "death" of the Freudian subject.

41. My deepest gratitude to Anthony John and Janice Horvath for their help with the transcription of this song as well as other suggestions that serve as the basis for this section of the essay.

42. "Thug Life" was famously tattooed across Shakur's stomach.

43. The fragments in the audio collage run as follows: "Rap star and actor Tupac Shakur" / "Tupac Shakur was riding in his black BMW" / "The 25 year-old rapper had long been" / "Shakur is also charged with" / "hundreds on the streets outside a Nation of Islam school to pay their respects to the slain rapper" / "Not Guilty."

JASON MIDDLETON ✳ D.C. PUNK
AND THE PRODUCTION OF AUTHENTICITY

"Everybody's talking about their hometown scenes" *(Fugazi, "Song #1")*

In the wake of 1991, "the year punk broke" with the overwhelming success of Nirvana's *Nevermind,* the notions of the "alternative" or "underground" in rock music have become increasingly slippery. The rise of the "modern rock" radio format, the high chart positions and heavy MTV rotation of previously obscure and commercially unviable bands, and the "best alternative performance" category at the Grammys are all trends within the general dissolution of an easy distinction between alternative and mainstream. With this dissolution have come the inevitable debates about authenticity versus commercialism. Tim Yohannon, of hardline punk 'zine *Maximumrocknroll,* for example, published in an early 1990s issue on major labels a three-point litmus test for distinguishing "true punk" from "corporate alternative," stressing the need to avoid all and any collusion with government or corporate sponsors and to maintain a class consciousness in all punk practices.[1]

Granted, punk style in England in the 1970s was turned into top dollar runway fashion almost immediately; the phenomenon of "incorporation" was readily recognized by Dick Hebdige and others from the Birmingham

School.[2] Moreover, it could be argued that the Sex Pistols were fabricated by Malcom McLaren with profit as the primary motivation, and the imbrication of early British punk with commodification is apparent when one considers the important role McLaren's and Vivien Westwood's punk fashion shop "Sex" played as a locus of the scene.[3] Developing forms of resistance to commercialism and commodification has been, however, a crucial uniting principle of the various punk scenes that have emerged since the Sex Pistols's brief moment of glory. This principle has received a greater challenge since 1991 as the process of incorporation accelerates so rapidly that it sometimes seems to anticipate and precede the development of new subcultural formations.

In a period in which punk and other underground forms of cultural production became increasingly marketable, the notion of authenticity becomes simultaneously valuable to claim and elusive to define. Major-label signers like Jawbox, Butthole Surfers, and L7 are denounced with vehemence in the pages of punk 'zines, and even Kurt Cobain maintained the right to call Pearl Jam fake just after his own band's commercial explosion. The question of authenticity has been especially relevant to academic analyses of subcultures since the work in the late 1970s by Dick Hebdige, John Clarke, and others in the Birmingham School.[4] In his 1979 study *Subculture*, Hebdige argued that subcultures provide an imaginary resolution to real contradictions in the lived experience of British working-class youth. This theory, which Hebdige uses to analyze the various new youth subcultures in postwar Britain, would seem to provide a formula for authenticity: subcultures are authentic to the degree to which their practices (stylistic, musical, etc.) are homologous with the primary concerns and self-image of the group as rooted in the lived experience of their class position.

But Hebdige actually complicates this seemingly reductive formula. For one thing, he acknowledges that the stylistic practices are formed in response not only to the perceived weaknesses of the parent culture but are also based on the appropriation of styles and affects from other cultures. For example, the skinhead image not only was a sort of hyperbolic affirmation of the image of the "model worker," designed to assert a sense of working-class pride and masculine toughness that the skinheads found waning in the parent culture, it also drew heavily on the style and affect of the West Indian "rude boy," finding in this figure a model of the sort of identity they wanted to affirm.[5] This racial dialectic complicates the "imaginary resolution" formula insofar as "lived experience" is no longer understood to be simply based in the class position inherited by the youth from the parent culture, but is affected by other factors such as immigration and the new racial composition of working-class neighborhoods. Moreover, subcultural participants are acknowledged as having more agency in this process because they are not simply *reacting* to the contradictions passed down to them by the parent culture but are actively picking and choosing from among available cultural materials in the formation of the imaginary solution.

This brings us to the second and more profound problematization that Hebdige makes of his own formula. In the section "Sources of Style," Hebdige acknowledges that following from the media's incorporation of subcultural styles, subcultural members begin to constitute their styles/identities through the appropriation and use of the very media representations of their groups. When subcultural identity begins to be fashioned in this way, when subcultural styles are available to all classes and age groups through the media, the Birmingham frameworks, which rely on a stable notion of working-class experience and identity as the root of subcultural stylistic practices, begin to unravel.

It is this process of unraveling that has accelerated more and more rapidly in the twenty years since Hebdige's landmark study. The advent of cable television, especially MTV in 1981, and its continued expansion to households across the United States and abroad throughout the 1980s, contributed to the greater availability of forms of music and style that previously would have been limited to people in the urban centers in which underground music scenes were taking place. The formation in the United States in the 1980s of subcultural groups like mods, punks, and skinheads modeled after their British predecessors cannot be regarded as stemming first and foremost from the problems and contradictions of life in particular sectors of the population. This is not to say that there is no correspondence at all between subcultural practices and other aspects of lived experience, but simply that these newer U.S.-based subcultures, with many of their rituals derived from media representations of subcultures, share a far less coherent set of experiences than the working-class kids of Hebdige's postwar England.

To examine American youth cultures of the 1980s, I think it is necessary to make a shift from Hebdige's mode of analysis, a shift he himself seems to suggest with his discussion of subcultures forming their styles in response to media representations of subcultures. In recent years, many theorists working within the British cultural studies tradition have suggested new ways of interpreting the practices of subcultural groups. Many have focused on the imbrication of subcultures with commodification and marketing, including Sarah Thornton in her analyses of rave and club cultures in contemporary England. Adapting Bourdieu's concepts of "distinction" and "cultural capital," Thornton has argued that subcultures need to be understood as "taste cultures" in which specialized forms of knowledge and commodity consumption create social hierarchies.[6] Angela McRobbie has commented on the particular forms of "entrepreneurship" prevalent among subcultures. Drawing on McRobbie, David Muggleton has argued, conflating subcultural theorists with participants under the label "post-subculturalists," "all post-subculturalists are aware . . . that there are no rules, that there is no authenticity, no reason for ideological commitment, [that it is] merely a stylistic game to be played."[7]

But the problem with these various revisionary theories of Hebdige and the other initial formulations of the Birmingham School is that they shift the focus too far onto habits of consumption and ignore the many forms of *productivity* still so important within subcultures. By "productivity" I do not simply mean, as McRobbie describes, the creation and selling of products (although this is a significant part of subcultural practice, and I will discuss it at length in a later section of this essay). Rather, I refer as well to the production of affects, actions, and politics. These various forms of productivity often are linked by a shared set of values among the subculture that its participants identify as criteria of authenticity. Thus, rather than looking for a homology between subcultural practices and some authentic form of class-based experience, as we would do if we retained Hebdige's original formulations (or throw out the notion of authenticity altogether as Muggleton suggests), it is more useful to examine how a group attempts to construct common bases of experience, identity, and authenticity *through* subcultural practices. This process, which involves a constellation of linked practices, is what I term "the production of authenticity."

The first part of my project in this essay is to explore these possibilities of subcultural practice by examining a significant U.S. subculture of the 1980s, the Washington, D.C. punk scene. By looking back on the practices, musical and otherwise, that comprised the 80s D.C. punk scene, I examine the complications and contradictions inherent in a project of forming what

Larry Grossberg has termed an "affective alliance"; that is, "an organisation of concrete material practices and events, cultural forms and social experience which both opens up and structures the space of our affective investments in the world."[8] I examine two important aspects of the production of authenticity: first, developing affinities with marginalized groups in a society, or disarticulating oneself from a dominant subject position; and, second, the attempt to develop modes of articulating subcultural practices with the commodity form in ways that soften the distinction between producer and consumer and provide a space of relative autonomy from the demands of the market. Finally, I explore conflicts and communication breakdowns between different members of the D.C. punk scene, especially after 1991, and question how rapidly increasing penetration of previously subterranean cultural practices by the mass media and corporate interests disrupts the processes of the production of authenticity. This reconsideration should help us understand some of the stakes in the post-1991 debates about punk and authenticity.

In my discussion of the D.C. punk scene I focus in particular on Fugazi, the band that since its inception in 1987 has become something of a figurehead for the scene. Fugazi's refusal to sign to a major label, their maintenance of price restrictions on their shows and albums, and their eschewal of most forms of promotion, including videos, have endowed them with an aura of authenticity that in the popular discourse on rock has taken on a greater significance since 1991. Fugazi has come to be regarded by many as the standard bearer for punk rock ethics in a time of crisis.

"I Wanted a Language of My Own" *(Fugazi, "Burning")*

In his 1979 essay "Reification and Utopia in Mass Culture" Fredric Jameson describes the dissolution by capitalism of the fabric of social groups, and the ensuing difficulty of aesthetic production to have its source in any form of collective lived experience. The fissure of aesthetic expression into modernism and mass culture brings with it the assurance that neither can be an authentically political form of art. Jameson posits, however, "the collective experience of marginal pockets of the social life of the world system" as still enabling the production of art that is an authentic, and political, expression of this experience. These authentic expressions are possible "only to the degree of which these forms of collective life and collective solidarity have not yet been fully penetrated by the market and by the commodity system."[9] Jameson's positing of marginality as the last possible condition for authenticity in aesthetic production is both an enabling and highly complicated avenue for an examination of rock music. The way that "British working-class rock" follows "black literature and blues" in Jameson's list of forms of authentic cultural production reminds us of the problematic relationship between a predominantly white musical form and its often repressed sources in black music. Dick Hebdige's analysis of subcultures, as mentioned above, makes clear the imbrication of the mostly white subcultures he analyzes with the music, styles, and structures of feeling of black youth. This is not simply a matter of musical influence, as, for example, punk drawing on reggae and dub, but of the very grounds of experience as dialectically constituted in relation to the Other. These symbolic appropriations, or elective affinities, like the skinheads' adaptation of rude boy styles, are fraught with tension and ambiguity over the very questions of authenticity, belonging, and group interest.[10]

An analysis of American punk is aided by David James's observation in reference to 80s Southern California punk culture: "[It] has structurally more in common with hippies and other essentially middle class counter-cultures than with early British punk—that is, it is a 'diffuse counter-cultural milieu,' rather than a 'tight sub-culture.' "[11] In addition to the media, factors such as the economic mobility of the U.S. population in the regions where punk subcultures developed determine this difference. The formation of a subculture in the United States in the 1980s would seem to depend on the access of youth in an particular area to certain forms of knowledge about previous subcultural formations, particularly British ones.[12] Nonetheless, I think it is crucial to recognize that Jameson's two criteria for authentic cultural production—social marginality and forms of experience that stand in a different relation to the commodity form from those of the dominant culture—are standards according to which American punk developed its forms of production and to which these forms have been judged. These are standards that punk has needed to *produce* rather than, as in the Birmingham model, being givens of working-class lived experience that punk can *express*.

The first of these standards is punk's production of social marginality. The bands and audiences of American punk, or hardcore (as distinct from the art-school punk of 1970s New York), in its early incarnations in Southern California and Washington, D.C. were primarily middle-class males, who, it might seem, could not be construed as socially marginal by any criteria other than the construction of youth in general as a marginalized group. Punks have often adopted a strategy of self-marginalization, living in squats and scrounging for money and food. This is not to say that many punks living in such conditions did so entirely out of choice; many were homeless kids from troubled backgrounds who turned to punk for community and support. Nor do I mean in any sense to disparage what I describe as self-marginalization in the case of choosing to live in a squat for a while despite having a comfortable home to return to. Such practices could be very instructive about the different strata of a society and forms of daily life that might otherwise only be accessible through media representations. Nonetheless, the lyrics and affects of performance of early Southern California punk bands like Fear and the Circle Jerks, as well as the subcultural practices in this scene, were often about giving form to collective experiences of middle-class disaffection and boredom, experiences that acquired a certain legitimation through self-marginalization.[13] The punk scene in D.C., by contrast, involved ideals of transforming such disaffection into more productive and political forms of collective practices, and it is these practices that I will now address.

D.C. punk had its origins in the late 1970s with bands like the Slickee Boys, Over Kill, White Boy, and the extremely influential Bad Brains. Bad Brains was initially formed in 1978 by four African Americans from the poor neighborhoods of southeast D.C.—Gary Miller, Daryl Jenifer, Earl Hudson, and Earl's brother Paul, who later took the nickname H. R. Bad Brains evolved from a jazz-fusion outfit into a punk band under the influence of British punk records by the Damned, the Sex Pistols, and the Clash. Bad Brains transgressed the racial boundary that had maintained punk as a white musical form in both Britain and the United States and revived a D.C. punk scene that by 1979 had begun to falter, especially in the wake of the shutdown of Georgetown's student radio station, WGTB, by the school's administration. Bad Brains would prove extremely influential on young punks from D.C.'s private schools, such as Georgetown Day School and Sidwell Friends, as well as public schools like Wilson High. Among the young punks who attended Bad Brains's early shows were Ian MacKaye and Jeff Nelson, who would soon form the seminal D.C. punk band Minor Threat. Inspired by the frenzied, powerful music of the Bad Brains as well as the realization, after attending free punk shows held in the band's basement, that playing in a band could require no more than the will to do it, MacKaye and Nelson formed their first band, the Slinkees, which was soon followed in 1980 by the Teen Idles. At this point, a new wave of teenage punk bands began forming in D.C., including the Untouchables, State of Alert, and Government Issue. Often described derisively by older members of the D.C. music scene as "teenypunks" or "Georgetown punks," these groups were accused of trying to revive musical and sartorial styles that some considered to have no organic relation to their existence as mostly middle-class (and upper-middle-class) kids. Punk, it was argued, had its true moment among the working-class kids of London in 1977, and as Crass had declared in a song released in 1979, "punk is dead."[14]

By 1984–85, several factors—including the less-than-amicable breakup of Minor Threat, the breakup of other popular bands like Faith and Insurrection, and tensions in the punk rock community nationwide over ideological positions propounded by members of the Bad Brains—led to internal strife and a dissolution of some of the collective energy that characterized the early 1980s in D.C. D.C. punk had a political side from the outset, with Ian MacKaye and others engaged in struggles with club owners over admitting underage kids to shows, for example. Out of these struggles, resolved through the innovation of drawing large Xs on the hands of underage kids, coupled with Minor Threat's songs "Straight Edge" and "Out of Step," emerged the "straight-edge" movement. Straight-edge, often written as sXe, involved claiming the Xs that signified exclusion and reinscribing their meaning such that they signified an affirmation of the choice to abstain from drugs and alcohol. MacKaye's lyrics to the songs above described his abstention from drugs, alcohol, and sex, and the subsequent increase in his intelligence and pleasure in living that came from this abstinence. But while MacKaye intended the songs as personal statements rather than as doctrines meant for others to follow, many kids quickly adapted the lyrics as a dogmatic set of rules. Straight-edge thus became a somewhat puritan and self-righteous "movement," which led to separatism within the community.

In response to the growing problem of separatism, members of the scene came together in 1985 in the formation of new bands and a new ethos, which was spontaneously dubbed "revolution summer." The period deemed revolution summer marked a sort of second rebirth for the D.C. punk scene (after the first rebirth sparked by Bad Brains and comprised of the teenypunk bands), and included the formation of bands such as Embrace, Rites of

Spring, Beefeater, and Lunchmeat. In August 1985, Ian MacKaye (then of Embrace), Tomas Squip of Beefeater, Mark Sullivan of Kingface, and other members of the scene were interviewed for the punk 'zine *Flipside* at Dischord house, the home of Ian MacKaye and Jeff Nelson's independent record label. In this interview they describe the challenges they faced in trying to develop a new ethos within D.C. punk. They were contending not only with the way straight-edge had become a dogmatic and potentially divisive movement, but also with the anti-straight-edge development known as "bent-edge"—that is, the celebration, basically, of getting wasted and partying in connection with punk rock music. Squip describes the alienation of the participants in revolution summer from what he described as an overinvestment in fashion, the affects of anger, and the drugs, alcohol, and partying prevailing both in D.C. and in other punk scenes. Their response, he said, was not to impose new norms, not to "fix" the punk scene, but to open up a new subdivision in it. This subdivision focused on articulating punk to different practices, musical and otherwise, that could lead to new forms of experience and feeling. Vegetarianism and abstention from drugs and alcohol could be one form of this. Squip and the others repeatedly emphasize, however, that these practices are not rules, and that the important thing is an ethic of personal responsibility and awareness of the repercussions of one's personal practices on broader social issues. The subdivision also had to do with opening up practices narrowly associated with punk rock—playing music, going to shows, buying records—to alliances with other sorts of practices and people. A primary example of this was the "punk percussion protests," in which large crowds of punks would converge in public spaces in D.C. to create an incredible racket in support of causes, such as was done outside the South African embassy for the anti-Apartheid cause that was then being protested by Trans-Africa and other groups.

Involvement in politics, MacKaye and Squip emphasize, must stem from the same personal impulses that drive the creation of punk rock music as well as personal choices such as vegetarianism. The music of revolution summer reflected this ethos. The lyrics of earlier D.C. punk often embodies the "snotty" punk attitude—railing against authority figures from the government to parents to clubowners, or railing against other kids whose attitudes and activities (drug use, religion) contradicted one's own. The music itself generally conformed to the short, fast, and loud aesthetic. In 1985, however, bands like Rites of Spring began playing a different sort of punk rock that later would be dubbed "emo-core" or just "emo" (despite the disavowal of these terms by many bands regarded as originators of the form) for its openly emotional and introspective qualities. Emo songs were relatively long and melodic, and the lyrics were about baring one's soul and taking stock of what was found there. Early performances by Rites of Spring often left both band and audience literally in tears. The increase in affect and intensity at such shows, produced, in the philosophy of revolution summer, a collective energy that could be channeled into other activities such as involvement in political demonstrations and in volunteer organizations. Mark Andersen, a college student from rural Montana who had recently moved to D.C., took inspiration from punk rock for his work in political organizing. He made a significant contribution to forging links between punk music and other community concerns by founding a D.C. branch of the organization Positive Force. Positive Force was a network of affinity groups in cities such as Las Vegas, San Francisco, and Los Angeles that, among other activities, worked with local music scenes to organize benefit shows for community causes like free health clinics and rape crisis centers.[15] With the energy of the new bands of revolution summer and the political links forged by Positive Force, punk rock became a means not simply for self-marginalization, but for opening up new realms of collective experiential possibilities.

"You Are Not What You Own" *(Fugazi, "Merchandise")*

Angela McRobbie has pointed out that accounts of subcultural practices in the work of the Birmingham School in the 1970s often avoided addressing the actual modes of production, consumption, and profit necessary to the maintenance of a subcultural community, the activities she terms "subcultural entrepreneurship."[16] Addressing these forms of entrepreneurship, McRobbie points out, would be threatening for many theorists who looked to subcultures as authentic expressions of working-class experience and as modes of resistance to the interests of capital. In these models the only ways in which capital could enter the picture was from the outside with the purposes of incorporating and profiting from the subculture. This is, McRobbie points out, a romantic and in some ways counterproductive perspective because it is often in the entrepreneurial activities within a subculture—producing and selling records, designing art for records or flyers for shows, organizing shows, designing and selling clothes, and so on—that many participants in subcultures develop skills for careers in creative areas such as art and fashion, which are not necessarily made accessible or encouraged in their schools. McRobbie's valuable intervention in subcultural theory allows an avenue for examining another side of the production of authenticity in the D.C. punk scene: forms of entrepreneurship wherein profit is sought more as a means of maintaining the community and its practices than as a means of making anyone rich.

In 1981, Ian MacKaye, then seventeen years old, cofounded with Jeff Nelson the Dischord record label in order to release a record by their band the Teen Idles. Dischord was based on a number of principles that it managed to maintain, including complete creative control for the bands, price caps lower than standard prices for its products, little or no involvement in promotional or merchandising activities, and active participation in community politics. Dischord, like other small local labels, provided support and a "home" for local bands who might not otherwise have been able to release their records. Fugazi, MacKaye's later group, continued to put their own records out on Dischord, despite being actively courted by most major labels, especially after 1991.

Fugazi eschewed the "souvenir" commodities associated with rock concerts, like the always absurdly overpriced band t-shirt, stickers, and so forth. The shows provided a space for acts of exchange, but the audience was not positioned as a buyer of merchandise. Instead, the audience members exchanged 'zines, tapes, bootleg t-shirts, and the like: their own products for those of their peers.[17] These products were as often traded or given away as sold. I would describe such activities not as an effort to break out of capitalism, but simply to develop a space of relative autonomy within it. Within this space, the exchange of 'zines or other self-produced materials softens the distinction between producer and consumer, enabling a new set of affects to be produced through the act of exchange. This, along with the softening of the distinction between performer and audience through proximity and participation, encourages an ongoing exploration of new experiential possibilities and subjective positions. Ideally, the audience will not feel sated after a show, but agitated to go out and start their own band or 'zine or some other form of collective and productive activity.

"To Surge and Refine, to Rage and Define Ourselves"
(Fugazi, "Bulldog Front")

The reconfiguration of the performer/audience relation has always been an important part of punk rock shows and punk rock communities generally.[18] The organizational principles behind many punk shows, especially in the D.C. scene, marked them as quite distinct from the average rock performance in a bar or small club. From the earliest "teenypunk" shows in which the bands themselves were too young to perform in the clubs and bars that traditionally served as musical venues, D.C. punk always involved a search for alternative spaces in which music could be played and heard. Shows were held in spaces such as the health food restaurant Food for Thought, and Positive Force sponsored shows at community centers and church basements. Fugazi in particular consistently maintained certain principles that set their shows apart from other rock shows at clubs. Whether a Positive Force show or a club date, admission was always limited to five dollars. Any show Fugazi played is open to all ages. These nonexclusionary principles brought with them conditions for participation in the event; the shows involved a consensus on what sort of behavior is appropriate. The dissolution of the boundaries between performer and audience and among the members of the audience themselves increased the participatory nature of the event, linking pleasure with responsibility. Dancing aggressively, for example, also meant being prepared to help people up off the floor and to discourage stage diving and anything else endangering anyone.

The audience's physical proximity to the band and to each other created a sort of provisional consensus, a collective assumption of different speaking positions. This was literally manifested when audience members were given the microphone to sing the lyrics themselves. Mic sharing was a feature at Bon Jovi or U2 concerts as well, but an audience member had much more access to the mic and the space of the stage in general in a small crowd than in a crowd of ten thousand. The songs of Fugazi inscribe the collective experience of the shows into the very lyrics of the songs, many of which are sung with a collective rather than an individual voice, implicating the audience into a position of responsibility for the contradictions, such as political apathy, that this collectively assumed voice expresses. Another way in which Fugazi's lyrics manifest a contradiction in the subjective positions of themselves and their audience and attempt to rearticulate these positions is when the speaker is a marginalized person. In "Give Me the Cure," it is someone dying from AIDS; in "Glue Man," a junkie; in "Repeater," a convicted drug dealer; and in one of their most well-known songs, "Suggestion," a woman subject to sexual harassment and rape. Like all their songs, "Suggestion" is not an unproblematic assumption of a different subject position. The song starts out from a woman's perspective, with the lyrics describing frustration and anger at sexual harassment: "Why can't I walk down a street free of suggestion? / Is my body my only trait in the eyes of men?" Halfway through the song, the voice shifts to the perspective of an observer of an incident of sexual harassment, describing the scene and concluding with the lines "We blame her for being there" followed by the screamed-out "But we are all guilty." The song thus fragments any attempt at recreating a single subject position, and instead represents multiple, shifting points of identity/identification.

At shows, this song often drew some of the most intense collective participation from the crowd, revealing many of the contradictions and problematics inherent to the attempt to forge a collective identification with a marginalized position. Although Fugazi often invited women onto the stage to sing the song, an invitation that was accepted to very powerful effect, the song was also criticized by women who found it presumptuous for men to assume this speaking position. From my own experiences at Fugazi shows, as well as from watching videos and talking to people about other shows, I found the audience participation in all the songs, "Suggestion" included, to be overwhelmingly male. What does it mean for a band comprised of white males, and their audience, largely white and male, to temporarily speak from these positions?

To prevent this question, and other questions raised by the identity politics of Fugazi, from slipping into binaristic categories of thought—that is, that men singing the words to "Suggestion" is either liberatory or oppressive—it is useful to turn to the theories of identity developed by Gilles Deleuze and Félix Guattari in *A Thousand Plateaus*. Deleuze and Guattari make a break with psychoanalytic models of identity rooted in the theories of Freud and Lacan, models of the subject as *subject to* such determining factors as the Oedipal triangle or the linguistic signifier, a subject whose desire is premised on an unfillable lack. Drawing from a number of philosophical and literary works, including the philosophies of Nietzsche and Spinoza, Deleuze and Guattari forge a concept of a subject free from this "sickness of interiority," from desire-as-lack, a subject as a continual work-in-process, whose desire originates with itself and is directed outward rather than originating with a lost object outside itself.

Deleuze and Guattari offer two related concepts that are a part of the model of the subject-as-process: "minoritarian usages" and "minoritarian becomings."[19] A minoritarian usage of language would not just involve forging a *separate* form of language from the dominant one, but rather would involve using dominant forms in new and oppositional ways that rearticulate their meaning. All minoritarian usages are also "becomings," because the old, dominant form is transformed. There are many kinds of becomings; the notion of "becoming-woman" is particularly relevant to Fugazi's song "Suggestion" and the politics of its performance. "Becoming-woman" does not mean becoming like a woman; it does not have some notion of "woman" as its endpoint, but is rather, as Michael Hardt puts it, "a deviation or flight from the standard of Man that creates an alternative, a passage."[20] These flights, or becomings, are only possible toward a minoritarian position, the site of creativity and productivity. Overall, they can be said to be about rearticulating the majoritarian subject position of the white male.

This is a precarious project to undertake. There is certainly the danger that, rather than provoking successful becomings and creative participation in activities related to the contradictions and problems the songs express, the performances could provide an experience of catharsis, a feeling of resolution through the aesthetic form of the songs, making the show more a container than a distributor of energy. This is a danger recognized by Deleuze and Guattari in their description of how "lines of flight" away from majoritarian positions can sometimes be destructive and other times creative and productive. The crucial point, perhaps, is that the identity politics of Fugazi's performances of "Suggestion" and other such songs cannot be understood as *inherently* good or bad, liberating or oppressive, but must be considered in terms of their effects on a broader network of practices. Participation in the shows is meant to encourage a breaking down and rendering fluid of the subject positions of both performers and audience, which would then lead to the forging of new collective grounds of experience. Thus, what I term the "production of authenticity" might be better termed the "production of effectivity," indicating that the standard for judging these practices should be not how real something is but how well it works. Certainly the D.C. punks, who were from the start scorned as inauthentic imitations of their British predecessors, might be happy to throw out the term "authenticity" altogether.

"Conflicting Histories Tear Us Apart" *(Fugazi, "Provisional")*

In a 1991 interview, Ian MacKaye expressed his frustration with what he perceived as his audience's persistent enactment of rituals that to him no longer bore any organic relation to the motivations of the music and its performance. Slamdancing and stage diving, for MacKaye, were part of a rupture that D.C. punk made at its inception with the prevalent musical forms and practices popular in America: "In 1980, I was 18 years old. We danced aggressively, we jumped off stages, whatever. We did this totally in concert with the music and in response to 10 years of the bump and hustle and all that kind of dancing. We were doing something new and something that we thought was fresh. If I was 18 years old in 1991, the last fucking dance I'd be doing is one that's been going on for the past twelve years! I don't take this hand-me-down shit. The past is not nearly as important as the present."[21] The ideals MacKaye expresses here and has consistently voiced elsewhere demonstrate an explicit concern with change, innovation, and contemporary relevance. But these ideals of aesthetic production have often come into conflict with the practices of consumption by Fugazi's audience, leading to certain antagonisms. The conflicts between band and audience over the issue of slamdancing and stage diving are a significant manifestation of these antagonisms. Many people, including the band, regard these activities as pointless, dangerous, and also exclusionary toward women's participation in the shows. Others, particularly some of the band's younger fans, regard them as fun, energizing, and real expressions of their enthusiasm about the music. Some fans have expressed resentment at what they perceive as the band's self-righteousness about these issues, as well as a feeling that MacKaye is trying to exclude them from enjoying rituals he himself once enjoyed and had a hand in developing. Conflicts like these between bands and audience and among the audience also function to point up the band's very real position of authority at the event of the show; they have the privilege of demanding certain modes of behavior from the audience. This situation complicates many of the collective and egalitarian ideals expressed by members of the punk community. It also challenges the

D.C. Punk and the Production of Authenticity   349

ethic expressed by MacKaye, Squip, and others in the revolution summer era that no one in the community wanted to put forth a doctrine for anyone else to follow, that personal responsibility was valued over any kind of group rules. This sort of ethos relies on a trust in a collective community "spirit" that will not be violated, but such a spirit is always threatened as the ideals within a scene spread to a wider and more geographically diffuse group of people. Punk communities everywhere faced this set of conflicts increasingly after 1991, with crowds at shows often much larger and less aware of the protocols that accompany particular scenes and bands. This diffusion of the ideals of a scene always carries with it the increased difficulty of claiming, as Squip did in *Flipside* about revolution summer, that a set of ideals is "just this understood thing." Instead it becomes something that must be asserted, perhaps with the weight of authority.

Ian MacKaye and other prominent figures in the D.C. punk scene tried to encourage a form of ethics based on active participation in a variety of activities. Political demonstrations, the production and circulation of 'zines, vegetarianism, and other choices and actions were associated with the scene, yet none was put forth as part of a doctrine. It was not a subculture in which particular styles and practices signified inclusion, but was intended rather as a range of creative practices held together by affective alliances.[22] The authenticity that MacKaye and others sought, then, was in the newness and creativity of practices and in the smooth space within which the alliances could form and reform, rather than in any rigid standards of behavior or appearance.[23] The problem with a scene thus constituted is its immanent drive to territorialize, to privilege certain practices and styles over others and to draw boundaries of inclusion and exclusion. Another problem is with the universalizing tendency of the ethical framework itself. The different practices are supposed to remain heterogeneous, but the very criteria of originality and participation that link them clearly excludes other practices with their own pleasures. It is problems like these that in conclusion I will consider here.

In Deleuze and Guattari, deterritorialization—the disruption of traditions and boundaries—is always followed by reterritorialization, the redrawing of new boundaries. The aesthetic politics of Fugazi and other D.C. bands, based on deterritorializing musical practices and identities, is often reterritorialized by the audiences. An example of this process is the straight-edge movement discussed above. Despite MacKaye's constant protests that the song was not intended as a doctrine for anyone else to follow, straight-edge continued to develop into a broad movement and genre of punk rock. Songs MacKaye wrote in the effort of dissolving boundaries, in this case the boundary that kept abstention out of the realm of acceptable practices in the world of rock and roll, turned into a movement that redrew boundaries to exclude from its domain of punk anyone who did not conform to its rules. Mac-Kaye's frustration with kids stage diving at Fugazi shows also marks an increasing disparity, based partly in age difference, between the band's logic of aesthetic production and its audience's logics of consumption. By dancing in this way these kids were simulating a style of dancing, signifying rebellion, that had been available to them through TV and movies since they were children because of the ongoing incorporation of punk subcultures by the media. The kind of immediacy of experience that MacKaye hoped for was not available to them. In keeping with Jameson's notion of "nostalgia for the present" as a salient feature of postmodernism, these kids experienced the present by mobilizing and recombining various stereotyped images of the past. Another perspective might be Žižek's appropriation of Pascal's formula for religious faith, "kneel and you will believe":[24] they simulated the notions of the dance as if to feel the affect that in MacKaye's view preceded and gave rise to these forms of dancing as its spontaneous expression. In Deleuze and Guattari, however, reterritorialization is not necessarily a bad thing because it produces further deterritorializations. The question, then, is where things go from here and what do these deterritorializations entail?

I have proposed in this essay the model of "the production of authenticity" for understanding subcultural practices associated with the D.C. punk scene in the 1980s. This model marks an attempt to adapt Hebdige's mode of analyzing subcultures to a contemporary situation in which, due to the ever-increasing penetration of social life by the media and the commodity market, we can no longer look to an authentic ground of lived experience as the root of subcultural practices and must look instead to the effects of the practices themselves. But even the sort of practices that I describe under the rubric of the production of authenticity have come under fire since Nirvana appeared on MTV in their video "Smells Like Teen Spirit." In an interview I conducted in December 1997, Mark Andersen of Positive Force explained his views on the effects on the D.C. punk scene of *Nevermind* and the rush since 1991 to market punk rock. Describing "Teen Spirit," Andersen stated that "it is the axis upon which history shifts—it's like it's capturing the promise while it is destroying it. . . . What it led to was a dramatic transformation of the punk rock community, in ways that were extremely destructive . . . even as they carried the seed for some profound transformations." Andersen talked about how in the D.C. scene it was now much harder to get people outside the clubs to attend Positive Force benefit shows, and how he sensed a waning in people's interest in putting on their own shows. The scene, he said, is much more focused on the clubs now, where the bottom line is profit, and "there is no venue for wack stuff . . . a nurturing space which could be the home for a new scene." This new consumerist mentality, Andersen suggests, was reflected at the last show Fugazi had played in D.C. at that point, at the 9:30 Club in 1996. This show seemed to mark a shift, he explained, from crowd surfing and stage diving—the "wrong" kind of participation—to total passivity on the part of the crowd—no participation.[25] The performer/audience split that D.C. punk bands worked to deterritorialize was here rigidly reterritorialized.

But what about the "seed for a profound transformation" that Andersen spoke of? The notion that breaking into the mainstream could involve a significant transformation of that mainstream, such that radical ideas could reach a far broader audience than ever before, seems to have fizzled. The millions of sales of Chumbawamba's "Tubthumper," for example, do not seem to have translated into discussions of socialist politics on MTV or radio. Rather, what we are seeing is one of the most intensive moments ever of the Hebdigean process of incorporation of subcultural practices. The moment of punk's spotlight with the popularity of bands like Green Day and Rancid seems to have passed, but hip hop, techno, and drum and bass now comprise the soundtrack to television advertisements for everything from soda to luxury cars. Dyed hair, piercings, hip hop and rave fashions, and other subcultural signifiers are domesticated through characters in sitcoms and Hollywood films. At the same time, countless young punk bands continue to produce music on an underground level, despite such intrusions as major label scouts who would never have been there ten years ago. Much of the reaction to these intrusions has been hostility and an attempt to close the folds of punk from within so as to keep it from being corrupted from without—as in the ostracism of major-label signers such as Green Day, who returned to their old haunt Gilman St., a punk club in Berkeley, to find graffiti reading "Fuck Green Day for bringing MTV to our scene." Of course this ostracism is more systematic than simply writing graffiti; the reaction to major-label signers is, as sheri gumption puts it in *Maximumrocknroll*, "we simply refuse to support them because of their actions. We don't buy their records, we don't go to their shows, and 'zines don't take their ads."[26] These defensive measures indicate the profound challenges punk subcultures faced in the 1990s, and this defensiveness is of course a reterritorialization that may cause stagnation in the practices of punk rock. It may be that punk itself will soon be an exhausted form, a possibility acknowledged by Mark Andersen, or it may transform itself in the face of current pressures and in the context of a whole new youth cultural formation wherein the dominance of hip hop, techno, drum and bass, and rock/rap hybrids have rendered the old concept of "rock and roll," definable loosely as white boys with guitars, largely moot. It remains to be seen whether or not punk can, in the words of Fugazi, "rearrange and see it through."

Notes

For their valuable help with this essay, I would like to acknowledge the following people: Lawrence Grossberg provided valuable comments on an early draft. Roger Beebe and Deborah Broderson read drafts and helped me formulate my ideas. Finally, Mark Andersen of Positive Force was kind enough to share with me in an interview his prolific knowledge of the history of D.C. punk as well as his comprehensive insider's account of this history in his manuscript "Dance of Days: A History of the D.C. Punk Underground, 1976–1993."

1. Mark Andersen, "Dance of Days: A History of the D.C. Punk Underground, 1976–1993," unpublished manuscript cited with permission of the author, chap. 14, p. 16. The increased marketability since 1991 of the previously subterranean has affected other areas of cultural production as well, such as the 'zine world. Major publishing houses have recently seen fit to finance books by 'zine editors, such as Lisa Carver of *Rollerderby's Dancing Queen* (New York: Henry Holt, 1996), Carla Sinclair of *boing boing's Net Chick*, and Chip Rowe's "greatest hits" collection *The Book of Zines* (New York: Henry Holt, 1996).

2. In Dick Hebdige's *Subculture: The Meaning of Style* (London: Routledge, 1979), for example, incorporation is defined as taking two forms: the conversion of subcultural signs into mass-produced objects (the commodity form), and the redefinition of deviant behavior by dominant groups (the ideological form).

3. Jon Savage provides a rich and incisive history and analysis of the Sex Pistols and early punk rock in his book *England's Dreaming*. The disjuncture between some of the romantic, revolutionary ideals many have conferred on the band and on McLaren's initial goals are apparent in statements like the following: "You knew all the girls were going to love him [Johnny Rotten]. I thought they could be the Bay City Rollers: that was in my head, I was so out of it. To think he would be the alternative to the Bay City Rollers: dour and tough and the real thing. A genuine teenage group. For me, that was anarchy in the record business, . . . that was the best selling point" (Savage, *England's Dreaming: Anarchy, Sex Pistols, Punk Rock, and Beyond* [New York: St. Martin's, 1991], 122).

4. Stuart Hall and Tony Jefferson, eds., *Resistance through Rituals: Youth Cultures in Post-War Britain* (London: Hutchinson, 1976); and Hebdige, *Subculture*.

5. Hebdige, *Subculture*, 57–59.

6. Sarah Thornton, "Moral Panic, the Media, and British Rave Culture," in *Microphone Fiends: Youth Music and Youth Culture*, ed. Andrew Ross and Tricia Rose (New York: Routledge, 1995); and Thornton, "The Social Logic of Subcultural Capital," in *The Subcultures Reader*, ed. Ken Gelder and Sarah Thornton (New York: Routledge, 1997).

7. Angela McRobbie, "Second-Hand Dresses and the Role of the Ragmarket," in McRobbie, *Postmodernism and Popular Culture* (London: Routledge, 1994); and David Muggleton, "The Post-Subculturalist," in *The Clubcultures Reader*, ed. Steve Redhead (Oxford: Blackwell, 1997), 198.

8. Lawrence Grossberg, "Another Boring Day in Paradise: Rock and Roll and the Empowerment of Everyday Life," in *The Subcultures Reader*, ed. Gelder and Thornton, 477–94.

9. Fredric Jameson, "Reification and Utopia in Mass Culture," in *Signatures of the Visible* (New York: Routledge, 1990), 23–24.

10. Such ambiguity, and the imbrication of envy with affinity, is apparent in the famous song "White Riot" by the Clash, a middle-class band with working-class identifications, whose music drew liberally on the sounds of reggae, declaring "I want a riot of my own."

11. David James, *Power Misses: Essays across (Un)Popular Culture* (London: Verso, 1996), 198.

12. This is not to say that youth culture or subcultures evolved solely in postwar Britain. Indeed, it could be argued that punk rock itself originated not in England with the Sex Pistols and the Clash but rather in New York in the early 1970s, with bands like the Ramones, Blondie, and the Patti Smith group. These bands, and many of the bands that followed them in the New York punk scene of the 1970s, such as Talking Heads and Television, arose from a strikingly different cultural context from that which Hebdige describes surrounding the early British punk bands. Rather than being comprised of often uneducated, working-class kids, the New York scene was comprised largely of middle-class, college-educated art school kids. It is, however, the more straightforward punk rock of the British bands, rather than the more experimental sounds of the New York based groups, that proved most influential on young American punks at the inception of the L.A. and D.C. scenes in the early 1980s.

13. The lyrics of Southern California punk were also often replete with misogyny and homophobia. For a discussion of the androcentrism and misogyny of some Southern California 80s punk as well as feminist responses and punk rock practices, see Joanne Gottlieb and Gayle Wald, "Smells Like Teen Spirit: Riot Grrrls, Revolution, and Women in Independent Rock," in *Microphone Fiends*, ed. Ross and Rose.

14. I am indebted for the preceding portion of my discussion to Andersen's "Dance of the Days."

15. Ibid., chap. 7, p. 32; chap. 11, p. 36.

16. McRobbie, "Second-Hand Dresses," 143.

17. A popular bootleg shirt reading "this is not a Fugazi shirt" represents the contradictory nature of a commodity produced in opposition to the standard commodity form of the rock t-shirt. The band expressed a certain disregard for the t-shirt bootleggers, but also noted that the bootleggers could be doing much more destructive things. 'Zines, on the other hand, represent a crucial component of the punk community and are exemplary of the DIY (do-it-yourself) ethic. These independent publications—written, illustrated, assembled, and distributed often by a single person or a small collective—have provided a forum for the expression of ideas free from the imperatives of advertising (they generally are available free or at a very low price). Jen Anger, in the October 1997 issue of *Maximumrocknroll*, gave this eloquent description of the DIY ethic: "All of us punk kids *make* things and *create* things and don't really realize how important that is. You are making something happen. You are creating something, and a ripple of events extends out from it." Some 'zines from the D.C. scene have included the early *Descenes; Off-Center*, the Positive Force 'zine; Sharon Cheslow's *Interrobang*, which provided a forum for the Nation of Ulysses; and the original Riot Grrrl 'zine, *Riot Grrrl*. For an extensive academic discussion of 'zines, see Stephen Duncome, *Notes from Underground* (London: Verso, 1997); for listings and reviews of all the 'zines under the sun, see the magazine *Factsheet Five;* for compilations of 'zine writings, see Rowe's *The Book of Zines* or Seth Friedman's *The Factsheet Five Zine Reader* (New York: Three Rivers Press, 1997).

18. In his *Dissonant Identities*, Barry Shank offers a valuable discussion of the complex interactions of physicality—aggression, rhythm, sexuality—and the visual and aural signifiers of musical performance in the context of a punk rock show. As Shank writes: "[The] physical interaction among musical signs and individual bodies establishes the conditions that allow for the allusive combinatorial associations of cultural signifiers of identity and community. Within this fluid stream of potential meanings, the audience and the musicians together participate in a nonverbal dialogue about the significance of the music and the construction of their selves" (Shank, *Dissonant Identities: The Rock 'N' Roll Scene in Austin, Texas* [Hanover, N.H.: Wesleyan University Press, 1994], 125).

19. Gilles Deleuze and Félix Guattari, *A Thousand Plateaus: Capitalism and Schizophrenia*, trans. Brian Massumi (Minneapolis: University of Minnesota Press, 1987), esp. 105–6.

20. Michael Hardt, Deleuze and Guattari seminar lecture, Duke University, November 24, 1996.

21. *Pulse!*, October 1991, 87–90.

22. This could be compared to what Guattari has termed a "molecular revolution," a nonhierarchical network of productive activities without a central organizing principle or telos.

23. In the first song Fugazi wrote together, perhaps acknowledging their imminent role as D.C. "supergroup" and as representatives of the scene, they dismiss the notion of a unified "scene" and any attempts to fashion an identity through such terms. Simply titled "Song #1," it includes lyrics like "Fighting for a haircut? / then grow your hair / crying for the music? / I doubt you really care / looking for an answer? / you can find it anywhere."

24. Slavoj Žižek, *The Sublime Object of Ideology* (London: Verso, 1989), 38–39.

25. Mark Andersen, unpublished interview, 1997.

26. *Maximumrocknroll*, October 1997.

Would I write a book, or

Should I take to the stage?

—Pet Shop Boys,

"Left to My Own Devices"

Look to the Queen!

—William Shakespeare, *Hamlet*

IAN BALFOUR ✳ QUEEN THEORY: NOTES ON THE PET SHOP BOYS

No doubt my use of the word "theory" in the title of this essay is a bit disingenuous, even if it is hard to know these days exactly what "theory" means. In a 1994 essay Jacques Derrida noted how the function of the word "theory" in the past few decades bore little relation to its prior use in Western thought.[1] The word seems to have been much abused, overextended to no end, as if virtually any thought or idea had a claim to being "theory." To "theorize" has become a veritable synonym for to "think." For starters, we might want to question why we now tend so readily to divide things into gay and lesbian criticism, on the one hand, and queer "theory," on the other. Not that there might not be some real affinity between the queer and the theoretical. Both are a little harder to pin down than most discourses: their characters are at once more shadowy and more resonant—proper, perhaps, to the realm of allegory—of something that always points to something else.

"Theory" is that kind of discourse that operates at a certain level of generality, if not necessarily universality. But if we entertain the possibility of that generality being rendered either directly (explicitly) or indirectly (implicitly), then theory could always lurk, implicitly, in a seemingly innocuous pop song or maybe even a single word. Some such implicit faith animated a good many of the speculations of Walter Benjamin, who in his *Moscow Diary* and elsewhere thought of facts as already of the order of theory. The idea that one finds one's theories ready-made, almost as if all one has to do is come along and register what was already there, is, of course, a seductive notion for any analyst or critic.

But how exactly does theory exist in or as the work of art? If Hegel is right (and he often is), the work of art is in crucial respects always on the way to philosophy: it is philosophy or theory not (and not yet) in the form of theory. And so it is, for example, that Sophocles's *Antigone* can be read in Hegel's *Phenomenology of Spirit* as the implicit embodiment of a properly philosophical dialectic. Another way of understanding this situation is to say that the work of art is an implicit version of a philosophical or theoretical discourse still to be made explicit. For Hegel, in his *Aesthetics* and indeed throughout his entire canon, art is of the order of truth. Adorno, in his turn, and in his *Aesthetic Theory*, is fond of invoking the Hegelian formulation of art as the "unfolding of truth," even as he would like to disentangle that notion from Hegel's claim that art participates in what the latter calls absolute knowledge or spirit. It all turns on how things are folded or unfolded, to take up the metaphor of the "pli" or fold buried in the words implicit and explicit.[2]

All of this might seem a little much to bring to bear on some of the pop songs performed by the Pet Shop Boys. Aren't we told so often by the critics of the study of popular culture that there's hardly any "there" there, that pop pales in comparison to culture proper—that is, "high culture"? If academic discourse is bad enough already—baroque in its stylings, abstract in its formulations—how much worse would it be when applied to an object beneath its dignity that offers too little material for what Adorno might call "reflection"? In recent years, numerous strong arguments and case studies have been marshalled in an effort to counter this tendency.[3] Still, one cannot quite assume that it may help to think about the Pet Shop Boys as and with theory: the proof can only be in the reading, whether my own or that of others.[4]

For what it's worth, the distinction between low art and high, or between popular and "unpopular" culture, is not especially pertinent or tenable in the work of the Pet Shop Boys. Sure it's pop, sure the music can be formulaic; and it is undeniable that the Pet Shop Boys cultivate a certain superficiality, which they promote in opposition to what they think of as the pomposity of much rock music—exemplified most nefariously, in their eyes, by U2. This pretentiousness that they oppose is exacerbated if it is combined with acting as spokespersons for various ethical or political causes, however unimpeachable. But as much as U2 aims at being profound and ends up being superficial, the Pet Shop Boys do something opposite, in classic Oscar Wilde fashion. Not that the Pet Shop Boys are not capable of putting on airs in their almost inimitable way. The last few records especially are riddled with allusions to Shostakovitch and to scenes out of Harold Pinter. Yet these exist side-by-side with invocations to pure pop songs like "Tainted Love" and any number of staples of disco culture. Moreover, the Pet Shop Boys, in their modes of production, also move between the worlds of "high" and "low." How many pop groups have the stage design and choreography for a tour done by opera directors and producers? Or have videos done by premiere "art" filmmakers like Derek Jarman? So the Pet Shop Boys, in more ways than one, ooze cultures of various supposedly incompatible sorts. Rather notoriously, the Pet Shop Boys are an inordinately cerebral band, on and off the stage. But the palpably intellectual character of their lyrics is not the only place to locate the quasitheoretical character of their work.

A lot depends on what is implicit and what is explicit in and out of the works in question. Certainly that is the case in one of the most prominent critiques of the Pet Shop Boys, which comes in the opening chapter of John Gill's *Queer Noises*.[5] There, in one of the relatively few full-blown studies of gay and queer pop and not-so-pop music (classical, jazz, and more), one can read a scathing attack on the Pet Shop Boys for not being utterly "out" starting from the moment in 1986 of the reception of their first album, *Please*. At the time, Gill was working as a critic for London's *Time Out*, where he gave the album a rave review. However, apparently he "fell afoul" of the band for having commented that the album has a strong gay subtext. The band was reported to be "climbing the walls" about the review, even though in Gill's account any number of his gay friends, and some heterosexuals to boot, were picking up on that same subtext. For some reason, the Pet Shop Boys were able and willing to write a subtext but not a text proper—not a text that simply said exactly what it meant.

So much depends on this text being "sub," Because in the end John Gill can't abide the text simply remaining "sub." Ideally, for Gill, a text should be explicit or be accompanied by one that is. The animating spirit of Gill's informative but contentious study is the desire for gay and lesbian people to be out and adamantly so. In Gill's book, where the subject is queer music, all three epigraphs—by Holly Near, Armistead Maupin, and D. A. Miller—

underscore the political and moral stakes in being out, and all of them concur that to participate in the closeting of oneself or others is to collude in a homophobic agenda. To be out, for Gill, is a categorical imperative. Clearly what is at issue here is not music per se, not notes and sounds, but the positioning of music and all that attends it in culture at large. Music is not just music. The desire to be out oneself and to have others be the same is eminently understandable, given the long, massive, and systematic oppression of gays and lesbians by the heterosexual and heterosexist powers that be and that were. But the matter of outing oneself and others is a vexed one, always inscribed in complex and overdetermined histories.[6] Gill's charge against the Pet Shop Boys was leveled in 1986 when AIDS was still a relatively new phenomenon in the public sphere. Indeed, there was in those days a wholly new demonization of gay men especially, who all of a sudden were perceived as a threat to the population at large in ways that even the most die-hard homophobes could not previously have imagined. One could certainly argue that the new threat to gay communities made it all the more imperative to come out and fight the new fight. But it is not clear that to come out or to out oneself was, even and especially then, quite the categorical imperative that Gill wanted it to be.

D. A. Miller's epigraph for Gill's book comes from Miller's *Bringing Out Roland Barthes*. The point of departure for Miller's enterprise comes from his reading Barthes's book on Japan, *Empire of Signs*. There Miller found, although only after he had belatedly come to "know himself" as gay, a reference to a map of what Miller then recognized as a gay quarter of Tokyo, and yet Barthes had not exactly "flagged" this gay quarter as such. Miller describes the trace of this gay presence in Barthes's text as "discreet but discernible."[7] This is arguably the perfect situation for a critic, gay or otherwise, who wants to "bring out" anything in a text. For if the matter at hand were not discernible, then there would not necessarily even be anything to bring out. And were it not discreet, then the critic would be reduced simply to belaboring the obvious. So a text like Barthes's on Japan, subtly but not blatantly gay, is exactly the right kind of vehicle for the critic.

This "bringing out" is not a simple gesture in and for Miller's work, but the corresponding problematic in Gill's volume is clumsier and more dubious in aesthetic and political terms. For one thing, Gill doesn't seem to take account of the fact that the Pet Shop Boys's medium is precisely the aesthetic, where the force of the implicit is rather different than in other discourses. Gill wants the Pet Shop Boys to be explicit. But can one really imagine—or would one really want—a gay or queer version of Helen Reddy's screaming "I Am Woman" in the immortal song by that name? Percy Shelley, whose daring and radical politics were fairly unimpeachable, argues that poetry, unlike most other discourses, had to follow a path of indirection, had to avoid, for example, didacticism and moralism in order for it to succeed as poetry; indeed, for it even to qualify as art in the first place. Something similar holds, I would argue, for the status of the explicit in the Pet Shop Boys. To be as explicit in their art as Gill seems to want them to be (inside and outside of their art) would undermine its very status as art. To say nothing of giving the critic less to do.

What further infuriates Gill is that after their first refusal to say that they were out, somehow it became common knowledge that the Pet Shop Boys were gay and in some sense "out." After a certain point, this knowledge was, as Gill says, aping what he imagines were the Pet Shop Boys's sentiments: "old hat, a nontopic, stale news." And so it may be all rather beside the point for Gill, myself, or any other critic to come along and point out the suggestive nature of the band's songs, such as "Music for Boys," "My Funny Uncle," and "Bet She's Not Your Girlfriend." Nor would it help to point to the several poignant narratives of coming into one's own homosexuality, as in "Can You Forgive Her?" At most, one might be enlightening the odd dull-witted or tone-deaf heterosexual—hardly a lofty goal for criticism. In such work perhaps one always risks belaboring the obvious, as I may well do here.

Nonetheless, Gill wanted and wants the Pet Shop Boys to be explicit. And about what, in all of this, is it that one should be explicit? Sex, of course, or sexuality, strangely in keeping with which those discourses (of censorship, mainly) that think of "explicit language" as essentially sexual. Gill's diatribe—which concedes that he, like George Orwell commenting on Salvador Dali, "loves" the work of the Pet Shop Boys even as he "loathes" the artists— culminates in the charge that the Pet Shop Boys refuse to make "a simple statement about their sexuality."[8]

For one thing, it is not clear that sexuality is usually or essentially simple, such that one can make simple statements about it. But even if it were the case that one could make a simple statement about sexuality—rather than a complex statement about something simple, or a complex statement about something complex—the Pet Shop Boys have given every indication of refusing to make such simple statements. Indeed, they often positively thrive on a certain ambiguity, or at least a nontransparency, and not just in the realm of sexuality.

I have suggested elsewhere that one of the most characteristic structures in the work of the Pet Shop Boys is the ellipsis: grammatical, figural, and musical.[9] This laconic figure is probably most legible in the titles that announce each of their records, all of them consisting only of a single word. Their collected titles read, in chronological order: *Please, Actually, Introspective, Disco, Behaviour, Alternative, Very,* and *Bilingual.* The very simplicity of these titles, these single words, is one mark of their complexity. *Alternative,* for example, is a word more or less permanently alternative even to itself, but perhaps signals, among other things, that the Pet Shop Boys provide an alternative to what is so often called "alternative" music. Or it could even mean something like "queer," or at least "not straight," alluding to the discourses of those right-wing pundits and their followers who think of gay and lesbian existence as an "alternative lifestyle," as if one simply chooses that life somewhat as one chooses what clothes to wear.[10] A recent Pet Shop Boys song, "Metamorphosis" on the *Bilingual* album, features a retrospective moment from an individual who started out expecting to be heterosexual like a lot of other people. He explains, "What I wanted to be was a family man," only to find that "nature had some alternative plans."[11] *Bilingual,* released in 1996, names itself as speaking at least two different languages, two tongues. ("I'm single, bilingual" runs the refrain of the title track, with the word "bilingual" slightly mispronounced so as to rhyme with single.) And so the single is double, one tongue is at least two, in the vernacular of the Pet Shop Boys.

The lapidary title *Very* all but asks us to complete somehow the phrase "very. . . ." Very what? Very good?, very pop?, very gay?, very . . . very? The very simplicity of the word is excessive. None of these titles constitutes a simple statement, about sexuality or anything else. Indeed, what looks like a statement may turn out to be something of a question.

The one time the Pet Shop Boys contemplated a title of more than one word, it was for their greatest hits record; before they settled on *Discography*—a single word, obviously—the two atypical title candidates were *As It Were* and *The Importance of Being Pet Shop Boys.* The first working title marks the omnipresence of the figural and fictional dimension in the work of the Pet Shop Boys, the perpetual putting of everything, potentially, into quotation marks—but not literally. (Walter Benjamin described this technique in his legendary, montage-like work on the Paris Arcades as a practice of "quoting without quotation marks.")

The second discarded title nods to Oscar Wilde, a figure from another Gay Nineties era, the very model of wit, strategic ambiguity, and a certain queerness. In particular, the allusion to *The Importance of Being Earnest* can serve to recall how one and the same work can be, as it were, bilingual. I am thinking of how on the one hand, for example, Wilde's most famous play conforms perfectly in its structure to the dominant model of Western comedy that issues in heterosexual union: there are no less than three marriages in the offing in the closing moments of the play. But if one attends to what is said about marriage from the opening scene, one finds that the meaning of that time-honored institution is all but undermined and evacuated. Lady Bracknell (whose role is often played by a man) remarks that Lady Harbury, who has just suffered the loss of her husband, "looks quite twenty years younger." Wilde even conspires to insinuate, via the character of Chasuble (whose name means a sacred vestment) that the church is in some ways opposed to marriage and all the christening of children that goes with it. Wilde's masterpiece teaches us that a text can be bilingual, hetero, and queer at the same time.

This is certainly true of numerous videos of the Pet Shop Boys, including ones directed by Derek Jarman, surely one of the mostly resolutely gay filmmakers there ever was—if there ever was one. In Jarman's version of "Rent," for example—a song that seems to refer primarily to "rent boys" and that once included so pointed an allusion to Elton John that it subsequently had to be removed—the relationship dominating the visual and narrative space is a heterosexual one. One almost has to work to find a gay subtext in the piece, unless camp is of itself necessarily and essentially gay, which is a hard argument to sustain. Or consider the video of "Domino Dancing," where we watch the machinations of a young woman and two young men, both of whom apparently rival for her affections, as they jockey for position. Yet the heterosexual model, so to speak, is undermined when we often are treated to seeing the two strapping young men stripped to the waist. The video closes with a scene, repeatedly cut and replayed, of the two men seemingly "fighting" with each other over the young woman—but in doing so they are pictured clutching each other as they fall to the sandy beach and the surf, caught in each other's arms, a little like Burt Lancaster and Deborah Kerr in the famous beach scene in *From Here to Eternity*. None of this, neither in Wilde nor in the Pet Shop Boys, adds up to a simple statement about sexuality nor a statement that sexuality is simple. But let us abandon the perhaps too simple critique of Gill's notion of simplicity and no longer defer the announced topic of "queen theory."

*

The bad pun of my title derives from "Dreaming of the Queen," a notable song from the Pet Shop Boys's 1994 album *Very*. The song is not quite what you'd expect, even for a dream; the scenario is as follows: the speaker—in the voice of Neil Tennant—dreams of the Queen-with-a-capital-Q, the Queen of England, that is. The Queen and Lady Di are improbably visiting the speaker and his partner for tea. The initial note is one of distance, marked by the odd, not to say queer, ungrammaticality of the phrase "you and her and Lady Di" where it should read "you and she and I," placing the Queen in something other than a subject position—an object position, actually. But this note is soon followed by a certain rapprochement. The Queen says:

> I'm aghast,
> Love never seems to last,
> However hard you try.
> And Di replied:

> That there were no lovers left alive
> No one has survived.
> So there were no more lovers left alive
> And that's why love has died.

What happens in this exchange between the Queen, the woman-who-would-be-queen, and the men who may be queens? The lamentable dissolution of love and marriage in the royal family is strangely generalized, and in such a way as to voice a sentiment more proper to another community of queens and/or queers: a response to the seemingly unique predicament of love in the age of AIDS. It is of course not quite true to say that there are no more lovers left alive, but, as hyperbole, the claim has a certain undeniable force and poignancy.

It is the aptly named Lady "Di" who is the vehicle for voicing what it now means to "die"—such is the punning logic of the dream. (And the whole song appears to rely on the old Elizabethan, but not only Elizabethan, pun on the verb "to die," meaning, in addition to its most common sense, to have an orgasm; and as such a figure that unites love and death inextricably.) The Queen, the Princess, and the others are what the Pet Shop Boys elsewhere, in a song of that name on *Bilingual,* term "the survivors"—the survivors of the love that has not survived.

The crossover in the song between the "old Queen," the Princess, and the men who may be queens could well lead us to question what exactly a queen is. (I leave the vexed topic of "princess theory" for others to take up.) So what *is* a queen? The compact edition of the Oxford English Dictionary, normally so reliable, is strangely unhelpful on this score, giving us among its fifteen definitions almost only the notion of a female monarch, with no trace of that other sense of queen. The unabridged version of the *OED* is more to the point, offering as its twelfth definition the sense of "a male homosexual, especially the 'effeminate' partner in a relationship." If we turn to Webster, we make out a little better, but only to find a definition of a queen as "a flamboyantly campy" man. Notice that the queen is not just flamboyant, not just campy, but is flamboyantly campy, as if to be queen one had to be, as it were, doubly a queen, a queen to the second power.[12] We have known that at least since medieval times the king has had two bodies, but now we know that the queen too seems to have at least two to herself—or himself. The derogatory, or initially derogatory, sense of queen as an effeminate man seems to be tied to the closely related word "quean," a term of derision and abuse in middle English, reserved for women and especially for harlots or hussies. But even as late as Byron's *Don Juan* we can still find a reference to someone characterized as a "queen of queans."

In terms a little more familiar, the queen is, in Lee Edelman's phrase, "a certain type of gay man," a type more or less inextricably linked to the theatrical.[13] A good deal of recent thinking on queer topics has turned on notions of theatricality, performance, and performativity.[14] The first phase of this work seemed to revel in the emancipatory and even subversive potential of theatricality, of cross-gendering or gender blurring, only to give way to a second phase that pulled back from or even recanted that earlier position, at least on the score of theatricality. Judith Butler, for one, had to insist, explicitly, that one doesn't take gender or even "queerdom" on and off as one does an item of clothing.[15]

Some recent queer theory downplays the importance of the theatrical by shifting to a more neutral and linguistic sense of performativity and citationality (often indebted to the officially antitheatrical J. L. Austin, the brains behind speech-act theory). This is a timely and salutary development because, as Julie Carlson has forcefully demonstrated in her essay on the queer dimensions of Romantic culture, the theatrical metaphor enlisted by queer theory is not always what it is cracked up to be.[16] Far from being the clear marker of subversive and progressive gender trouble, theatricality comes beset with a whole range of epistemological and even ontological questions that do not necessarily translate into the transformational performance of identity and nonidentity sometimes dreamed of by queer theorists. For one thing, there is a permanent possibility of a discrepancy between what we tend to think of as "external" and "internal"—inside and out. Seeing is not, reliably, believing. It is in the nature of signs, as Hegel says in so few words in his *Aesthetics,* to be, in principle, ambiguous. Can we always be sure what an earring means, or the gesture of a hand, a bit of leather, or the timbre of a falsetto? And if not, then how do we know how closely those external signs correspond to a (corresponding) interior? But if queer theorists need to pause before invoking the theatrical, it may be that queen theorists just can't do without it—leaving all pathos of the theatrical aside, if that is possible. For isn't "queendom" that which can be adopted or not, not once and for all as if it were a matter of being, but rather precisely "staged," now and then. Couldn't anyone be, as it were, queen for a day, a year, a decade or two?

The history of the Queen-with-a-capital-Q moves from a distant period, when the theory of divine right conferred a substantial authority on her person, down to our own time when the Queen is largely a figure, a figurehead with only the trappings of royalty.[17] As it happens, the first Queen Elizabeth, as Marjorie Garber records in her *Vested Interests,* presided over certain sumptuary laws which, while in general regulating dress codes along class lines (thus keeping people in their sartorial place), nonetheless left a space for "theatre people" to exceed the normal dress codes and, famously, to cross-dress.[18] Perhaps the most familiar instance is the notorious matter of Shakespeare's boy actors. A kind of gender vertigo could arise when one of the boys was called on to play the role of a woman who was pretending to be a man, when in fact the actor, as everyone knew, was a boy in the first place.[19] (The situation is not unlike the dizzying cross-gender and same-sex identifications and desires chartered in Blur's 1994 song "Girls & Boys," the extended version of which was produced by the Pet Shop Boys. Its refrain runs: "Boys who do girls who do girls like their boys.") In any event, by opening up the possibilities for a certain kind of cross-dressing, the Queen was in effect saying, "Let there be queens."

But if "queen" as distinct from "queer" seems to suggest a certain type of gay man, a man more theatrical than not, the sense of the former term cannot be delimited very easily. One good example of the slippery continuum of terms for gay men that features a powerful mobilization of such words is Simon Gray's stage play from the early 1970s, *Butley*, which subsequently was filmed by the American Film Theater. In this densely articulate drama about two male English professors who had had a long affair, although one was married at the time, the words "queer," "queen," "fruit," "pansy," "poof," and more are used in multiple configurations that make the words all virtually interchangeable. The diction suggests that here the queen, a certain type of gay man, is not all that certain, after all. Or perhaps we should say, not simply certain. For what makes theatricality possible is also what makes the absence of something like theatricality impossible; namely, the permanent possibility of a discrepancy between inside and outside—something that Brecht understood and exploited to great effect in his "theater," forcing everyone to rethink what theater was and could be.[20]

In "Dreaming of the Queen" the rapprochement between the two pairs—the Queen and Lady Di, the singer and his partner—is not quite sustained. We learn that at a certain moment Diana dries her eyes and "looked surprised" for, as the speaker says "I was in the nude / The old Queen disapproved." So in the end the Queen and possible queens go their separate ways, but not without bringing together the two terms, Queen and "queen" (unspoken), in a queer proximity. And it is not so clear that in this context one can limit the resonance of the phrase "the old Queen" just to the elderly Elizabeth of contemporary England.[21]

In bringing to a close this sketchy consideration of some aspects of the Pet Shop Boys's *oeuvre*, I want to turn to their version of "Go West," a virtual emblem of their later work. The song covers—and recovers—the anthem of that name recorded by the Village People, a "flamboyantly campy" pop group if ever there were one. The Village People are probably best known for another anthem, "Y.M.C.A.," which wryly advocates staying at "the Y" to enjoy all the pleasures of an all-boy enclave ("You can get yourself clean!" "You can have a good time"). It's some kind of irony that "Y.M.C.A." has become a ubiquitous song at (mainly hetero) sports events all over North America, chanted by people, most of whom have little or no idea of what they are singing but who enjoy framing facsimiles of the letters Y, M, C, A with their outstretched arms. Another bilingual song. But is it implicit or explicit?

The Pet Shop Boys's aural and video versions of the Village People's "Go West" song reconfigure the decidedly 70s song—post-Stonewall—to feature a large collection of background vocalists who resemble nothing more nor less than A Gay Men's Chorus, a social formation that postdates the heyday of the Village People. So the song echoes its model, even as it marks its distance from the ur-version. In the original, "Go West" most likely referred, for a gay New York group, to going west to San Francisco ("sun in winter-time!"), a haven then and now for gay culture.[22] But in the 90s version by the Pet Shop Boys the song's not-so-sub text invokes the collapse of the Soviet Union. And so the slogan "Go West" here means, a little ironically, that what is now Russia should "go west and western."[23] A statue of Lenin is even enlisted so that he can, even from beyond the grave, point the direction to the West. (This is marxist revisionism with a vengeance.)

In the video of "Go West" the most striking feature is the buff, athletic body of the twenty- or thirty-something men, set against the odd spectacle of the Pet Shop Boys in vaguely space-age suits with cone-headed hats that could look like dunce caps, if the Pet Shop Boys could be confused with dunces.[24] These male figures, dominating almost the entire video, are supplemented by a revamped Statue of Liberty come to life in the figure of a black diva. The statue, as we know, wears a crown, which makes her look rather like a queen, even though we know that in America there is no monarchy and hence no such thing as a queen. The future of this queen who is not a queen is open ended, as are so many things in the Pet Shop Boys's work. Even this straightest of pop songs, in musical terms, closes with a dominant seventh, that is to say, in a pointed departure from the norm that dictates a return to the tonic we have come to know and expect.

In this reading of the Pet Shop Boys, which in accepting in part the framework provided by John Gill has risked reducing their work to "queer" art, I have only been able to intimate the complexity or even undecidability of the queen, to suggest how it embodies and demands a certain "theory," even if that theory of the "certain type of gay man" entails a good deal of uncertainty. But let us risk a slogan that hints at what I take to be an implicit message of the Pet Shop Boys: "The Queen is (more or less) dead, long live the queens!"

Notes

1. Jacques Derrida, "Some Statements and Truisms about Neologisms, Newisms, Postisms, Parasitisms, and Other Small Seismisms," in *The States of "Theory": History, Art, and Critical Discourse*, ed. David Carroll (Stanford: Stanford University Press, 1994), 63–94.

2. Here I am pointing to the etymology of the words implicit and explicit, both of which contain the root pli, or fold. For a full-blown examination of some of the implications of the figure of the fold, see Gilles Deleuze, *Le Pli: Leibniz et le Baroque* (Paris: Editions de Minuit, 1988).

3. For an eloquent and informed discussion of these debates, see Andrew Ross, *No Respect: Intellectuals and Popular Culture* (New York: Routledge, 1989).

4. "Readings" of the Pet Shop Boys take various forms. For a brief, spirited defense of the value of the Pet Shop Boys, see Simon Frith, *Performing Rites: On the Value of Popular Music* (Cambridge: Harvard University Press, 1996), 6–9.

5. John Gill, *Queer Noise: Male and Female Homosexuality in Twentieth-Century Music* (Minneapolis: University of Minnesota Press, 1995).

6. It is one of the many signal achievements of Eve Kosofsky Sedgwick's *Epistemology of the Closet* to have demonstrated the virtual impossibility of someone simply being "out" once and for all, at all times, and to everyone.

7. D. A. Miller, *Bringing Out Roland Barthes* (Berkeley and Los Angeles: University of California Press, 1992), 16. The full sentence reads: "Precisely when the discreet but discernible gay specificity of Barthes' text is ignored does this text present the most propitious occasion for rehearsing an antigay doxology."

8. Gill, *Queer Noises*, 9.

9. Ian Balfour, "The Pet Shop Boys Forever" *surfaces* 1, no. 1 (1991): 5–21. In this essay I focus on the structure of the long song, especially as it is made, potentially anyway, virtually infinite with sequencers and digital technology. I relate this to a thematics of things "going on and on," emphasized in various ways in their lyrics. But the flip side, so to speak, of this preoccupation with infinity, is a certain elliptical or laconic rhetoric. Not that this minimalism is simply opposed to the more open-ended structures I identify in the Pet Shop Boys's work. Indeed, they reinforce each other.

10. Not that what to wear is such a simple choice.

11. It would be too much to decide here whether the Pet Shop Boys are expounding their general theory on the origins of sexual orientation. But the phrase "nature had some alternative plans" (which needn't be taken all that seriously) in itself clearly sides with "nature" in the debate over whether nature or culture is the determining factor in sexual orientation.

12. For an incisive analysis of camp (and of the famous essay on camp by Susan Sontag), see Ross, *No Respect*, chap. 5, "The Uses of Camp."

13. See the illuminating study by Lee Edelman, *Homographesis: Essays in Gay Literary and Cultural Theory* (New York: Routledge, 1994), especially the title essay and the final chapter, "Imagining the Homosexual: *Laura* and the Other Face of Gender."

14. See the excellent collection of essays in Andrew Parker and Eve Kosofsky Sedgwick, eds., *Performativity and Performance* (New York: Routledge, 1995).

15. See, for example, Judith Butler's, "Imitation and Gender Insubordination," in *Inside/Out*, ed. Diana Fuss (New York: Routledge, 1991), 13–31; as well as her "Critically Queer," *GLQ: A Journal of Gay and Lesbian Studies* 1, no. 1 (1993): 17–32.

16. See Julie A. Carlson's superb essay "Forever Young: Master Betty and the Queer Stage of Youth in English Romanticism," *South Atlantic Quarterly* 95, no. 3 (summer 1996): 575–602. The essay is suggestive well beyond its circumscribed title.

17. For a brilliant analysis of the topic, see Tom Nairn, *The Enchanted Glass: Britain and Its Monarchy* (London: Pan, 1990).

18. Marjorie Garber, *Vested Interests: Cross-Dressing and Cultural Anxiety* (New York: Routledge, 1992), 26.

19. On this topic, see the excellent account by Stephen Orgel in *Impersonations: The Performance of Gender in Shakespeare's England* (Cambridge: Cambridge University Press, 1996).

20. I am assuming here the stability of a distinction that is not so stable, but on which most Western discourse on theater is based—namely, that between outside and inside.

21. This may be the place to note that there is more than one instance in pop music of the "queen" phenomenon. I am thinking not only of the band famously named Queen, with its prominent frontman, Freddy Mercury (the Pet Shop Boys, no particular fans of Queen, played at the concert commemorating Freddy Mercury's death) but also of the Smiths's song "The Queen Is Dead." Ben Saunders (in correspondence) has suggested the striking affinities between the Smiths's song and the queen scenario in the work of the Pet Shop Boys. The queen, Saunders rightly notes, is "surprisingly in the know" ("Hey I know you / And you cannot sing"). Moreover, according to Saunders, that song "imagines the refusal of ambiguity as a royal fantasy ("Charles, don't you ever crave / To appear on the front of the Daily Mail / Dressed in your mother's bridal veil?"). That the veil unveils is a good emblem of the paradoxes that beset the matter of queening.

22. Unless used for the Village People, to "go west" meant going from the East Village to the West Village.

23. Neil Tennant is not unambiguously in favor of the westernization of Russia. He claimed, in the wake of the Soviet Union's breakup, to want to become a communist: "I love lost causes," he states. (cited in Chris Heath, *The Pet Shop Boys versus America* [London: Viking, 1993], 111).

24. They are the furthest thing from it.

INDEX

Dale, Alan, 141

Dali, Salvador, 361

Damned, the, 341

Dance music, 7, 29, 50–51, 80; Afro-
  Cuban, 273

Darnielle, John. *See* Mountain Goats, the

Daugherty, Michael, 61, 71

Dayou, Luo, 217–28; "Capital," 224–25;
  "Pearl of the East," 222–24

Dean, James, 100, 108 n.53

Deffaa, Chip, 144

Def Leppard, 175

Delaney & Bonnie, 151

Deleuze, Gilles, 316, 330 n.2, 347–48,
  350–51, 369 n.2

Del Fuegos, 3, 291

DeMent, Iris, 162, 178–79

Denver, John, 174

Derek and the Dominos, 151–52; *Layla
  and Other Assorted Love Songs*, 151

Desperately Seeking Susan, 192

Dick Cavett Show, The, 331 n.14

DiFranco, Ani, 210

Disco, 29, 38, 47, 51, 65, 205, 211, 279–
  80, 359

Dixon, Willie: "Little Red Rooster," 148

Dominoes, the, 152

Donna Reed Show, The, 96

Doors, The, 317

Dug Dugs, 261

Dylan, Bob, 12, 17 n.10, 110–12, 115, 162,
  171; "Mr. Tambourine Man," 149

Eagles, the, 176, 181

Earle, Steve, 162, 178, 183, 187 n.34

Echeverri, Andrea, 267

Eclecticism, 47–48, 218

Edmunds, Dave, 168

Ed Sullivan Show, The, 96, 98

808 State, 80

Electronica, 5, 6, 81, 141, 276

Eliot, Ramblin' Jack, 162

Eliot, T. S., 166, 168

Elliot, Missy "Misdemeanor," 5, 213 n.8

El Tri, 268; "Chava de Avándaro," 262

El Vez: "Viva La Raza," 257

Embrace, 342–43

Emerson, Lake, and Palmer, 78

Eminem, 20 n.18

Emo/Emo-core, 344

Empiricism, 42, 55 n.10, 58 n.29

Enigma, 80

Eno, Brian, 80

Eroticism, 276; musical, 83, 95–96,
  99–102

Ertegun, Ahmet, 150

Escovedo, Alejandro, 178

Esquire, 203

Eternal, 217

Evita, 209

Existensialism, 108 n.53

Fabulosos Cadillacs, Los, 263

Faith, 342

Fascism, 230

Fatal Attraction, 105 n.12

Fear, 341

Femininity, 192–95, 205, 208, 216, 239;
  Asian, 202–4, 214 n.26; Chinese,
  219

Feminism, 13, 84, 190 n.93, 193–98,
  201, 204, 208, 212 n.3, 225, 232 n.22;
  Chinese, 223, 225; Latina, 267; Japanese, 226; queer, 208

Feminist theory, 37, 41

Ferry, Bryan, 134

Film, 28, 44, 48, 56 nn.20, 21, 87–89,
  260, 323, 352, 359; Chicano, 266;

Film (cont.)
    critics, 32, 34, 37; soundtracks, 263;
    studies, 40–42, 58 n.31; theory, 40.
    See also Screen theory
Flack, Roberta: "Killing Me Softly with
    His Song," 153
Flaming Lips, the, 233
Flat and Scruggs, 171
Flatt, Lester, 171
Fleetwood Mac, 5
Fletcher, Dusty, 137–38
Flipside, 343, 350
Flores, Lysa, 266; "Beg Borrow and
    Steal," 266
Foghat, 151
Folk Implosion, the, 145
Folk music, 74, 80, 83, 86, 111, 170, 178,
    234; and folk culture, 278
Fontana, D. J., 98–102
Foo Fighters, 9, 334 n.34
Formalism, 77, 85, 89, 91–92, 125
Franklin, Aretha, 12, 111, 114, 116;
    "Think," 117–27; This Girl's in Love
    with You, 125
Freddy Bell and the Bellboys, 100;
    "Hound Dog," 97
Freddys, Los: "Hang on Lupe," 270
Freed, Alan, 143, 168
Frequency, 285 n.39
Freud, Sigmund, 297–304, 310 n.25. See
    also Psychoanalysis: Freudian
Frith, Simon, 1, 3, 54 n.4, 162, 164, 237,
    243, 296–99, 301–2
From Here to Eternity, 363
Frumpies, the, 200
Fugazi, 15, 339, 345–53, 355 n.17; "Give
    Me the Cure," 347; "Glue Man," 347;
    "Repeater," 347; "Song #1," 356 n.23;
    "Suggestion," 347–48

Fugees, The: "Killing Me Softly with His
    Song," 153
Futurism, 247

Garcia, Jerry, 151, 321
Garcia, Mhuiztecatl "Teca." See Tijuana
    NO
Gaye, Marvin, 114; "What's Going On?,"
    137
Gender, 2, 4, 17 n.6, 55 n.9, 91, 103 n.3,
    149, 193–95, 197, 202, 206–9, 229,
    238, 241–43, 246–47, 250 n.19, 300,
    365–66; national, 223; norms, 219–
    21, 226; politics, 235; tourism, 206–7;
    transnational, 13–14, 220–22, 224–
    25
Gibbs, Georgia, 139, 145; "The Hula
    Hoop Song," 154 n.13; "Tra La La,"
    143–44; "Tweedle Dee," 141, 143–44
Gil, Gilberto, 279
Gill, John, 359–61, 364, 368
Gill, Vince, 182
Girl Can't Help It, The, 260
Girl Germs, 199
Glass, Phillip, 71, 81–82
Glen, Darell, 135–36
Godard, Jean-Luc, 87
Gómez-Peña, Guillermo, 265–66, 276,
    279
Goodwin, Andrew, 1, 3
Gordon, Kim. See Sonic Youth
Gordon, Michael, 71
Gordy Jr., Berry, 113
Government Issue, 342
Grand Ole Opry, 171, 174
Gray, Simon, 367
Green Day, 352
Gridlock'd, 322
Grifters, the, 233, 237, 249 n.12

Ndegeocello, Me'Shell, 210

Near, Holly, 359

Nelson, Jeff. *See* Minor Threat

Nelson, Willie, 169, 177, 181

Neoconservatism, 30, 53, 68, 88

Neoliberalism, 30, 44, 53

New Country, 178

New Musicology, 60–63, 70, 75–77, 84–86, 89, 91–95

Newton-John, Olivia, 174

New York Times, 63, 99, 201, 235–36

Nine Inch Nails, 276, 319, 334 n.31; "Closer," 18–19 n.13

Nirvana, 2, 9, 195, 202, 312–22, 331 nn.11, 12; "All Apologies," 321; "Come As You Are," 19 n.13, 317; "Dumb," 321; *From the Muddy Banks of Wishikah,* 314; "Heart-Shaped Box," 317; "In Bloom," 317; *In Utero,* 321; "Lake of Fire," 321; "Lithium," 317; "The Man Who Sold the World," 321; *Nevermind,* 16 n.3, 17 n.10, 335, 351; "Pennyroyal Tea," 321; "Plateau," 321; "Polly," 321; "Smells Like Teen Spirit," 18–19 n.13, 312, 316–19, 330 n.3, 351; "Where Did You Sleep Last Night? (in the Pines)," 321

No Depression, 178–83

No Doubt, 13, 191, 198, 211; "I'm Just a Girl," 191–96, 208

Nopalica, 270; *Refried Nopals,* 275; "Taj Nopal," 275

Notorious B.I.G., 5, 9–10, 78, 321–22, 327, 334 n.34

Nowell, Bradley. *See* Sublime

Oasis: "Don't Go Away," 106 n.21

Objectification, 37

O'Kanes, the, 179

Ollin, 285 n.39

Onasis, Jackie, 71

Once Upon a Time in the West, 81

Ono, Yoko, 203–4, 210

"Open the Door, Richard," 137–38

Option, 81

Orb, the, 83; *Adventures Beyond the Underworld,* 81, 107 n.25

Orbison, Roy, 150–51

Orbital, 81; "Times Becomes," 82; "Moebius," 82

Oregon Symphony, 65–67, 73

Ortiz, Fernando, 272–73, 287 n.59

Orwell, George, 361

Oswald, John: *Plexus,* 73. *See also* Kronos Quartet, the

Over Kill, 341

Ovnis, Los: "Pequeña Ayuda de Mama," 260

Owens, Buck, 133, 171

Page, Patti: "Oh What a Dream," 150

Paget, Debra, 100

Palmer, Robert, 170, 224

Paradinas, Mike. *See* M-ziq

Parker, Junior: "Mystery Train," 145

Parody, 97, 194, 197, 202–6, 257, 274, 279, 318

Parsons, Gram, 178, 181

Parton, Dolly, 177

Pastilla, 256–57

Paterson, Alex. *See* Orb, the

Pavement, 233, 236–43, 251 n.23; *The Arizona Record,* 244; *Wowee Zowee,* 241

Paz, Octavio, 255, 261–62, 269

Peace and Love, 261–64

Pearl Jam, 315, 336; "Jeremy," 18–19 n.13

Penny, Hank, 138

United States, 13, 30, 32, 39, 43–45, 51–52, 64, 68, 110, 134, 171, 175, 191, 196, 202–7, 213 n.8, 240, 255–57, 260–61, 263–71, 274, 279–80, 337, 340–41
Untouchables, the, 342
Utopian discourse, 11, 48–50, 66, 229, 258, 265–66, 339

Valdés, Gina, 275
Valli, June: "Crying in the Chapel," 135–36
Van Halen: "Hot for Teacher," 18–19 n.13
Vanilla Ice, 142
Vargas, Chavela, 276
Vasquez, Molly, 266
Vedder, Eddie. *See* Pearl Jam
Veloso, Caetano, 279
Venegas, Julieta, 256, 266–67
Verdi, Giusseppe, 75–79; *Requiem*, 74
Verve, the, 15 n.3
VH1, 3
Vibe, 215 n.30, 217
Village People, the: "Go West," 368; "Y.M.C.A.," 367
Village Voice, 20 n.18, 239, 250 n.19
Viramontes, Alurista and Helena Maria, 270
Virgil, 166
Viva Malpache, 265
Voz de Mano, 265

Wallflowers, the, 5, 243
Ward, Billy. *See* Dominoes, the
Warhol, Andy, 80
Warrant, 17 n.10
Webber, Andrew Lloyd, 209
Ween, 236; *Pure Guava*, 235
Weezer: "Buddy Holly," 21 n.22

Welch, Lenny: "A Taste of Honey," 149
Welk, Lawrence, 68
Westwood, Vivien, 336
Whiskeytown, 180–81; "Hard Luck Story," 181
White, Barry, 78
White Boy, 341
Whitlock, Bobby, 152
Who, the, 9, 146
Wilco, 177, 181
Wilde, Oscar, 359, 363–64
Wild One, The, 260
Williams, Hank Sr., 165–67, 171, 182; "Long Gone Lonesome Blues," 180
Williams, Raymond, 19 n.13, 28, 40, 45, 166, 243
Willis, Chuck, 149–52, 149, 157 n.30
Wills, Bob, 169–70
Wilson, Brian, 68
Winger, 17 n.10
Wolfe, Julia, 71
Wonder, Stevie, 114
Wray, Link, 150
Wu Tang Clan, 5

X, 177
Xenaxis, Iannis, 71
X-Ray Spex, 192

Yamano, Atsako and Naoko. *See* Shonen Knife
Yankovic, "Weird Al": *Off the Deep End*; 333 n.29; "Smells Like Nirvana," 318
Yanni, 68
Yardbirds, the, 146
Yoakum, Dwight, 143, 171, 176–78; *Under the Covers*, 133–34, 153, 154 n.1

CONTRIBUTORS

Ian Balfour teaches in the English Department and in the Graduate Programme in Social and Political Thought at York University. He is the author of *Northrop Frye* and *The Rhetoric of Romantic Prophecy*. He has been a Fellow of the Society for the Humanities at Cornell and a visiting professor at Williams College, University of California at Santa Barbara, SUNY Buffalo, and Stanford. He has published on Walter Benjamin, Paul de Man, and on topics in popular culture, including on Pee-wee Herman and the Pet Shop Boys, and is a founding editor of the journal/book series *Alphabet City*.

Roger Beebe is Assistant Professor of Film and Media Studies at the University of Florida. He is also an award-winning experimental filmmaker and, when he has the time, plays avant-rock guitar. He is currently coediting (with Jason Middleton) a collection on music video.

Michael Coyle is Associate Professor of English at Colgate University, where he teaches courses on modernist poetry, fiction, and contemporaneous popular song; he also teaches courses on the emergences of jazz, R&B, and rock and roll. His publications include *Ezra Pound, Popular Genres, and the Dis-*

course of Culture; the collection *Ezra Pound and African American Modernism*; numerous journal articles on T. S. Eliot, Raymond Williams, and the shaping of modernist critical principles; and the essay "Modeling Authenticity, Authenticating Commercial Models," written with *Spin* contributor Jon Dolan and published in Kevin J. H. Dettmar's collection *Reading Rock and Roll*.

Robert Fink teaches at the University of California at Los Angeles, where his "History of Electronic Dance Music" course regularly enrolls over five hundred students. He has published articles in *American Music,* the *Journal of the American Musicological Society, Nineteenth-Century Music, Repercussions,* and the online journal *Echo.* His scholarly interests include music, media, advertising, and technology; minimalism; popular culture; ubiquitous musics; postmodernism; and groove-based dance musics from funk to trance. He is currently working on a book manuscript "Repeating Ourselves: Minimal Music as Cultural Practice."

Denise Fulbrook is Visiting Assistant Professor at Duke University. She received in 2001 a Ph.D. in English literature from Duke, where she completed her dissertation "Medusa's Tails and Leonardo's Heads: Fantasies of Female Anal Creation in Nineteenth-Century Theory and Psychoanalytic Literature." She has published journal articles on sexuality, gender, Victorian literature, and disco.

Tony Grajeda received his Ph.D. in Modern Studies/English from the University of Wisconsin–Milwaukee and has taught courses in film, music, cultural studies, and sound theory at su ny Buffalo, St. Lawrence University, West Chester University, and the University of Illinois at Chicago. A former employee of Ani DiFranco's Righteous Babe Records, he is currently Assistant Professor of cultural studies in the Department of English, University of Central Florida, Orlando.

Lawrence Grossberg is Morris Davis Professor of Communication Studies and Cultural Studies at the University of North Carolina at Chapel Hill. He has published widely in the areas of cultural studies and popular music and is coeditor of the journal *Cultural Studies.* He is currently writing a book on the war on children in the United States and the unbecoming of American modernity.

Trent Hill is currently rocking the free world in Seattle, where he is in the Information School at the University of Washington. He is frequently amazed and delighted by the goddamned wonder of it all.

Josh Kun is Assistant Professor of English at the University of California at Riverside. A writer and cultural critic, his work appears regularly in *Spin, LA Weekly,* and *CMJ New Music Monthly.* His weekly arts column, "Frequencies," appears in the *San Francisco Bay Guardian* and the *Boston Phoenix.* From 1999 to 2000, he was the host of Southern California's first commercial latin rock radio show, *The Red Zone* on 107.1 FM in Los Angeles.

Jason Middleton is a Ph.D. candidate in the Literature Program at Duke University, concentrating in film and television studies. His publications include "Buffy as *Femme Fatale*: The Cult Heroine and the Male Fan" (forthcoming in Lisa Parks and Elana Levine, eds., *Red Noise: Buffy the Vampire Slayer in the Post-Network Era*) and "Heroin Use, Gender, and Affect in Rock Subcultures" (*Echo* 1, no. 1). He is a member of the editorial collective of *Polygraph: An International Journal of Culture and Politics* and issue editor of *Polygraph* 11, "Margins of Global Culture."

Lisa Parks is Assistant Professor of Film Studies at the University of California at Santa Barbara, where she is finishing a book entitled "Cultures in Orbit: Satellite Technologies and Visual Media" and coediting the volume "Planet TV: A Global Television Studies Reader." In addition to publishing articles on media technologies and gender representation in several books and journals, Parks has produced activist videos on media globalization for Paper Tiger TV and she serves on the boards of CULTSTUD-L and *Intensities.*

Ben Saunders is Assistant Professor of English at the University of Oregon, specializing in sixteenth and seventeenth-century poetry and drama. His articles have appeared in *Journal X, The Journal of Medieval and Early Modern Studies,* and the *Yale Journal of Criticism.* He likes to play his music loud.

John J. Sheinbaum has taught at Cornell University and the University of Rochester, and he is currently Assistant Professor of Musicology at the Lamont School of Music of the University of Denver. His primary research interests include Western art music of the nineteenth and early twentieth centuries, popular music, and historiography.

Gayle Wald teaches African American literature and cultural studies at George Washington University. She is author of *Crossing the Line: Racial Passing in Twentieth-Century U.S. Literature and Culture,* and she publishes frequently on U.S. youth and music cultures.

R. J. Warren Zanes is finishing his doctorate in the University of Rochester's Program in Visual and Cultural Studies.

Library of Congress Cataloging-in-Publication Data

Rock over the edge : transformations in popular music culture /

edited by Roger Beebe, Denise Fulbrook, and Ben Saunders.

p. cm.   Includes index.

ISBN 0-8223-2900-X (cloth : alk. paper)

ISBN 0-8223-2915-8 (pbk. : alk. paper)

1. Rock music—History and criticism. I. Beebe, Roger.

II. Fulbrook, Denise. III. Saunders, Ben.

MI3534.R6336 2002   781.66—dc21   2001008588